Robert Pollok Kerr

Hymns of the Ages for Public and Social Worship

Robert Pollok Kerr

Hymns of the Ages for Public and Social Worship

ISBN/EAN: 9783337089818

Printed in Europe, USA, Canada, Australia, Japan

Cover: Foto ©Lupo / pixelio.de

More available books at **www.hansebooks.com**

FOR

𝔓ublic and Social 𝔚orship

SELECTED AND ARRANGED

BY

ROBERT P. KERR, D. D.

NEW YORK
ANSON D. F. RANDOLPH & COMPANY
1891

PREFACE.

IN the classification of hymns according to subjects in a book of hymns and tunes, perfect accuracy is unattainable without frequently repeating the same tune, and thereby increasing the size and cost of the collection. The object which the *Editor* has had in view has been to prepare a book containing all the *good* hymns and tunes suitable for congregational praise, at the same time to keep down the number of pieces to a moderate limit, and to have the price so low that in churches where it is used, every worshipper may have a book.

In the preparation of the "*Hymns of the Ages,*" the Editor has expended a vast amount of time and labor, and has attempted to gather the best hymns and tunes both of Europe and America. The cost of copyrights has been very great. He wishes to return thanks to those composers who have kindly allowed him to use their pieces *gratis*; and to a large number of European composers whose addresses it has been impossible to secure. He is under lasting obligation to the accomplished musician Prof. N. Bowditch Clapp, for his revision of the musical part of the work; and, for their help in the selection of hymns and tunes, to Rev. M. D. Hoge, D. D., Rev. W. A. Campbell, D. D., Rev. T. D. Witherspoon, D. D., Rev. W. S. Lacy D. D., and Rev. J. P. Smith D. D. These distinguished divines have afforded invaluable assistance by giving the benefit of their experience and taste in the preparation of the work.

A large chorus choir, trained to sing rapidly, and with spirit, is the best inspiration for congregational singing. After the introduction of a new book, there should also be meetings held on some evening during the week for congregational practice that the people may learn new tunes.

The book "*Hymns of the Ages*" is dedicated to the great cause of congregational singing, with the hope that in this important part of public worship it may be owned of God, and that the use of it may redound to the glory of His name.

ROBERT P. KERR.

INTRODUCTION.

THE ever growing interest of the religious public in hymnology is evident from the number of new collections which are issued—each compiler attempting to improve on the work of his predecessor. These attempts are successful just as a better classification of subjects is secured, a more skilful adaptation of the tunes to the words to be sung, and when hymns of real merit, because rich in evangelical truth and clothed in poetic diction, are substituted for those which are wanting in either of these essential elements.

It is a cause for congratulation when these ends are attained, inasmuch as the service of song constitutes such a delightful and edifying department of religious worship.

In the public services of the church, preaching, prayer and praise are the chief parts. In preaching the pastor pleads with men for God; in prayer he pleads with God for men; but in praise, pastor and people are one in offering their united adoration, as when, in psalms and hymns and spiritual songs, they make melody with heart and voice to the Lord.

Hymns which give fit expression to the common experience of the truly regenerate souls of all lands and centuries, though composed by men holding different views of church government and adhering to different forms of worship, yet furnish a happy illustration of the real unity of the church of God.

Such hymns are also the conservators of evangelical truth, and keep alive loyalty to the faith delivered to the saints in churches which are tempted to heretical departures from orthodoxy. Even when the sermon contains error, it is a safeguard to the people when they sing hymns breathing the sweetness of a pure gospel.

The use of a good hymn book is not limited to the great congregation nor to the family altar. It furnishes one of the best manuals for private devotion, expressing, as it does, every emotion of the Christian heart,—

INTRODUCTION.

penitence, faith, hope, joy and holy aspiration, and adapted also to all the vicissitudes of Christian life, whether the cup overflowing with blessings calls for thanksgiving, or whether the bitter cup of bereavement constrains the soul to seek the grace which sustains and sanctifies.

The "HYMNS OF THE AGES," as the author entitles them, is the result of long and patient labor. They have been chosen from what would make a whole library of such compositions, ancient and modern; and equal research and consideration has been given to the choice of the tunes to which the hymns are set.

Many of these are comparatively new, and their introduction gives variety and freshness to the collection, but they have not displaced the old hymns and tunes which have become endeared by sacred associations and tender memories.

There is a class of brave old tunes, fit companions for hymns of lofty cheer, which have come down to us from the heroic days of suffering and glory through which our fathers passed, and which, so far from growing wearisome by repetition, become more precious as time wears on.

But whether the hymns and tunes be new or old, the chief care has been to select such as are suitable for congregational singing and intrinsically worthy of a place in the regards of devout worshippers.

Dr. Kerr, after devoting many months of conscientious labor to this work, has submitted it to the criticism and revision of eminent musicians and of others who have made hymnology a special study. He has availed himself of all the suggestions received from these sources, and now commits his completed work to the Christian public; and I, who have been for so many years in sympathy and co-operation with him in his labors of love, am sure that he desires no greater recompense than that of being instrumental in making any contribution to the reverential and pure worship of Him who is worthy to receive everlasting adoration and praise.

MOSES D. HOGE.

ORDER OF ARRANGEMENT.

	HYMNS.
HYMNS OF PRAISE . . .	1 — 23
HYMNS OF DEVOTION . .	24 — 199
BELIEVERS' COMFORT . . .	200 — 210
MISCELLANEOUS AND OCCASIONAL . .	211 — 220
PRAYER FOR THOSE AT SEA . .	221 — 224
OPENING AND CLOSING HYMNS .	225 — 303
THE SCRIPTURES . . .	304 — 312
THE HOLY SPIRIT . .	313 — 329
CHRISTIAN ACTIVITY . .	330 — 342
THE ADVENT	343 — 359
THE PASSION	360 — 377
PRAISE TO THE RISEN LORD .	378 — 419
LOVE TO CHRIST . . .	420 — 472
INVITATIONS	473 — 500
COMMUNION HYMNS . .	501 — 525
THE CHURCH	526 — 532
MISSIONS	533 — 554
YOUTH	555 — 557
THE DEATH OF A CHILD .	558 — 559
THE JUDGMENT . . .	560 — 568
HEAVENLY ANTICIPATIONS . .	569 — 583
TIME AND ETERNITY . .	584 — 627
DEATH OF A CHRISTIAN . .	628 — 644
CHANTS	645 — 655
DOXOLOGIES	656 — 682

HYMNS OF THE AGES.

OLD HUNDRED. L. M. GUILLAUME FRANC, 1545. Genevan Psalter, 1554.

1. All peo-ple that on earth do dwell, Sing to the Lord with cheer-ful voice; Him serve with mirth, His praise forth tell, Come ye be-fore Him and re-joice.

1
Psalm 100.

1 All people that on earth do dwell,
Sing to the Lord with cheerful voice;
Him serve with mirth, His praise forth tell,
Come ye before Him and rejoice.

2 Know that the Lord is God indeed;
Without our aid He did us make;
We are His flock, He doth us feed,
And for His sheep He doth us take.

3 Oh, enter then His gates with praise,
Approach with joy His courts unto;
Praise, laud, and bless His name always,
For it is seemly so to do.

4 For why? the Lord our God is good,
His mercy is forever sure;
His truth at all times firmly stood,
And shall from age to age endure.
Rev. William Kethe, 1561.

2
Doxology.

Praise God from whom all blessings flow;
Praise Him, all creatures here below;
Praise Him above, ye heavenly host;
Praise Father, Son, and Holy Ghost.
Bishop Thomas Ken (1637—1711), 1697.

3
Psalm. 100.

1 Before Jehovah's awful throne,
Ye nations bow with sacred joy;
Know that the Lord is God alone;
He can create and He destroy.

2 His sovereign power, without our aid,
Made us of clay, and formed us men;
And when, like wand'ring sheep, we strayed,
He brought us to His fold again.

3 We are His people, we His care,
Our souls and all our mortal frame;
What lasting honors shall we rear,
Almighty Maker, to Thy name?

4 We'll crowd Thy gates with thankful songs,
High as the heavens our voices raise;
And earth, with her ten thousand tongues,
Shall fill Thy courts with sounding praise.

5 Wide as the world is Thy command,
Vast as eternity Thy love;
Firm as a rock Thy truth must stand,
When rolling years shall cease to move.
Rev. Isaac Watts (1674—1748).
Rev. John Wesley (1703—1791).

HYMNS OF PRAISE.

A SAFE STRONGHOLD. P. M. MARTIN LUTHER (1483—1546), 1529.

4 "*Ein feste Burg ist unser Gott.*"

1 A safe stronghold our God is still,
  A trusty shield and weapon;
He'll help us clear from all the ill
  That hath us now o'ertaken.
    The ancient Prince of hell
    Hath risen with purpose fell;
    Strong mail of craft and power
    He weareth in this hour,
  On earth is not his fellow.

2 With force of arms we nothing can;
  Full soon were we down-ridden;
But for us fights the proper Man,
  Whom God himself hath bidden.
    Ask ye who is this same?
    Christ Jesus is His name,
    The Lord Sabaoth's Son,
    He and no other one,
  Shall conquer in the battle.

3 And were this world all devils o'er,
  And watching to devour us,
We lay it not to heart so sore,
  Not they can overpower us.
    And let the Prince of ill
    Look grim as e'er he will,
    He harms us not a whit:
    For why? His doom is writ,
  One little word shall slay him.

4 That word, for all their craft and force,
  One moment will not linger,
But, spite of hell, shall have its course,
  'T is written by His finger.
    And though they take our life,
    Goods, honor, children, wife,
    Yet is their profit small;
    These things shall vanish all,
  The Kingdom ours remaineth.

Martin Luther (1483—1546).
Tr. by Thomas Carlyle (1795—1881).

HYMNS OF PRAISE.

MIDDLETON. 8s & 7s, D.   ENGLISH.

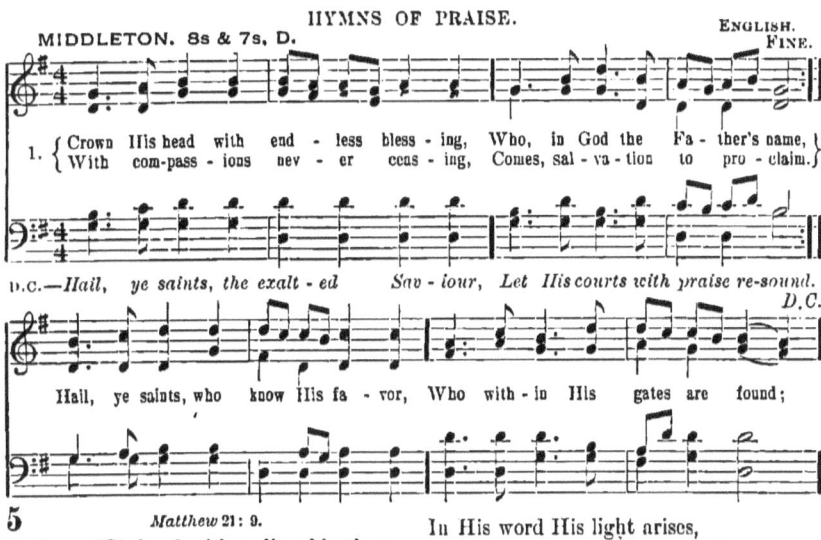

5   *Matthew 21: 9.*

1 Crown His head with endless blessing,
   Who, in God the Father's name,
With compassions never ceasing,
   Comes, salvation to proclaim.
Hail, ye saints, who know His favor,
   Who within His gates are found;
Hail, ye saints, the exalted Saviour,
   Let His courts with praise resound.

2 Lo, Jehovah we adore Thee ;
   Thee our Saviour ! Thee our God !
From His throne His beams of glory
   Shine through all the world abroad.

In His word His light arises,
   Brightest beams of truth and grace;
Bind, oh, bind your sacrifices,
   In His courts your offerings place.

3 Jesus, Thee our Saviour hailing,
   Thee our God in praise we own;
Highest honors, never failing,
   Rise eternal round Thy throne;
Now, ye saints, His power confessing,
   In your grateful strains adore;
For His mercy never ceasing,
   Flows, and flows for evermore.
             Rev. W. M. Goode, 1811.

SHAWMUT. S. M.   LOWELL MASON (1792—1872).

6   *Psalm 48.*

1 Far as Thy name is known
   The world declares Thy praise;
Thy saints, O Lord, before Thy throne
   Their songs of honor raise.

2 With joy Thy people stand
   On Zion's chosen hill,
Proclaim the wonders of Thy hand,
   And counsels of Thy will.

3 Let strangers walk around
   The city where we dwell,
Compass and view the holy ground,
   And mark the building well.

4 The God we worship now
   Will guide us till we die;
Will be our God while here below,
   And ours above the sky.
            Rev. Isaac Watts (1674—1748)

HYMNS OF PRAISE.

CREATION. L. M. D. FRANCIS JOSEPH HAYDN (1732—1809), 1798.

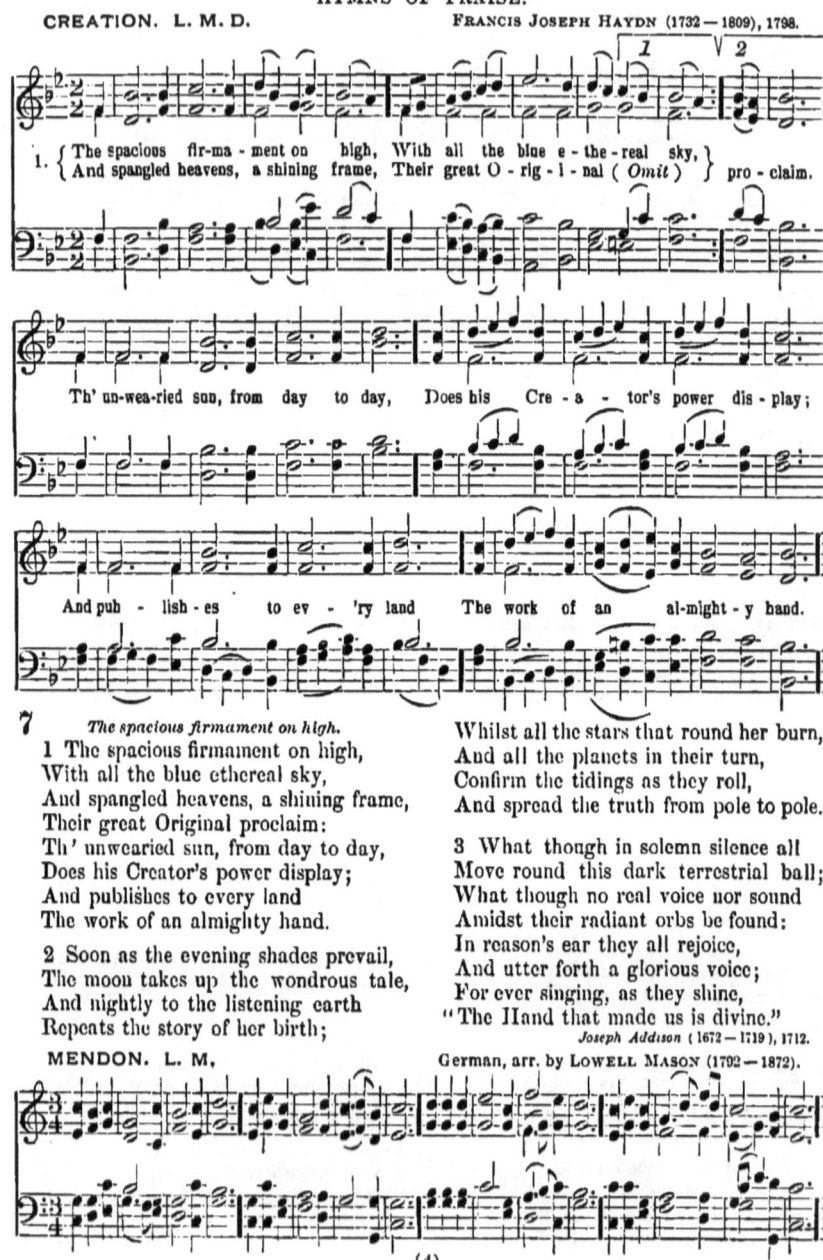

7   *The spacious firmament on high.*

1 The spacious firmament on high,
With all the blue ethereal sky,
And spangled heavens, a shining frame,
Their great Original proclaim:
Th' unwearied sun, from day to day,
Does his Creator's power display;
And publishes to every land
The work of an almighty hand.

2 Soon as the evening shades prevail,
The moon takes up the wondrous tale,
And nightly to the listening earth
Repeats the story of her birth;

Whilst all the stars that round her burn,
And all the planets in their turn,
Confirm the tidings as they roll,
And spread the truth from pole to pole.

3 What though in solemn silence all
Move round this dark terrestrial ball;
What though no real voice nor sound
Amidst their radiant orbs be found:
In reason's ear they all rejoice,
And utter forth a glorious voice;
For ever singing, as they shine,
"The Hand that made us is divine."

Joseph Addison (1672 — 1719), 1712.

MENDON. L. M,   German, arr. by LOWELL MASON (1792—1872).

HYMNS OF PRAISE.

ROTHWELL. L. M.   WILLIAM TANSUR (1699—1770).

8   *Psalm 92.*

1 Sweet is the work, my God, my King,
To praise Thy name, give thanks and sing,
To show Thy love by morning light,
And talk of all Thy truth at night.

2 Sweet is the day of sacred rest;
No mortal care shall seize my breast;
O! may my heart in tune be found,
Like David's harp of solemn sound!

3 My heart shall triumph in my Lord,
And bless His works and bless His word;
Thy works of grace how bright they shine,
How deep Thy counsels! how divine!

4 Then I shall share a glorious part,
When grace hath well refined my heart,
And fresh supplies of joy are shed,
Like holy oil upon my head.

5 Then shall I see, and hear, and know
All I desired or wished below;
And every power find sweet employ,
In that eternal world of joy.
              Rev. Isaac Watts (1674—1748).

9   *Prayer to the Holy Trinity.*

1 Father of all, whose love profound
A ransom for our souls hath found,
Before Thy throne we sinners bend;
To us Thy pardoning love extend.

2 Almighty Son, incarnate Word,
Our Prophet, Priest, Redeemer, Lord,
Before Thy throne we sinners bend;
To us Thy saving grace extend.

3 Eternal Spirit, by whose breath
The soul is raised from sin and death,
Before Thy throne we sinners bend;
To us Thy quickening power extend.

4 Jehovah! Father, Spirit, Son,
Mysterious Godhead, Three in One!
Before Thy throne we sinners bend;
Grace, pardon, life to us extend.
              Anon.

10   *Psalm 84.*

1 Great God, attend while Sion sings
The joy that from Thy presence springs;
To spend one day with Thee on earth
Exceeds a thousand days of mirth.

2 God is our sun, He makes our day;
God is our shield, He guards our way
From all th' assaults of hell and sin,
From foes without and foes within.

3 All needful grace will God bestow,
And crown that grace with glory too;
He gives us all things, and withholds
No real good from upright souls.

4 O God, our King, whose sovereign sway
The glorious hosts of heaven obey,
And devils at Thy presence flee;
Blest is the man that trusts in Thee.
              Rev. Isaac Watts (1674—1748).

HYMNS OF PRAISE.

TICHFIELD. 7s. D.   John Richardson (1816—1879).

1. Ho-ly, ho-ly, ho-ly Lord God of hosts! When heaven and earth, Out of darkness, at Thy word, Is-sued in-to glorious birth, All Thy works before Thee stood, And Thine eye be-held them good, While they sang, with one ac-cord, Ho-ly, ho-ly, ho-ly Lord!

11 *"All Thy works shall praise Thee, O Lord, and Thy saints shall bless Thee."*

1 Holy, holy, holy Lord
   God of hosts! When heaven and earth,
Out of darkness, at Thy word,
   Issued into glorious birth,
All Thy works before Thee stood,
   And Thine eye beheld them good,
While they sang, with one accord,
   Holy, holy, holy Lord!

2 Holy, holy, holy! Thee,
   One Jehovah evermore,
Father, Son, and Spirit we,
   Dust and ashes, would adore:
Lightly by the world esteemed,
   From that world by Thee redeemed,
Sing we here, with glad accord,
   Holy, holy, holy Lord!

3 Holy, holy, holy! All
   Heaven's triumphant choir shall sing,
When the ransomed nations fall
   At the footstool of their King:
Then shall saints and seraphim,

Hearts and voices, swell one hymn,
   Round the throne, with full accord,
Holy, holy, holy Lord!
          Rev. James Montgomery (1771—1854).

12   *Psalm 116.* (Tune, Peniel.)

1 What shall I render to my God
   For all His kindness shown?
My feet shall visit Thine abode,
   My songs address Thy throne.

2 Among the saints that fill Thy house,
   My offerings shall be paid;
There shall my zeal perform the vows
   My soul in anguish made.

3 How much is mercy Thy delight,
   Thou ever blessed God!
How dear Thy servants in Thy sight!
   How precious is their blood!

4 Now I am Thine, forever Thine,
   Nor shall my purpose move;
Thy hand hath loosed my bonds of pain
   And bound me with Thy love.
              Rev. Isaac Watts (1674—1748).

HYMNS OF PRAISE.

PENIEL. C. M.   THOMAS HASTINGS (1784—1872).

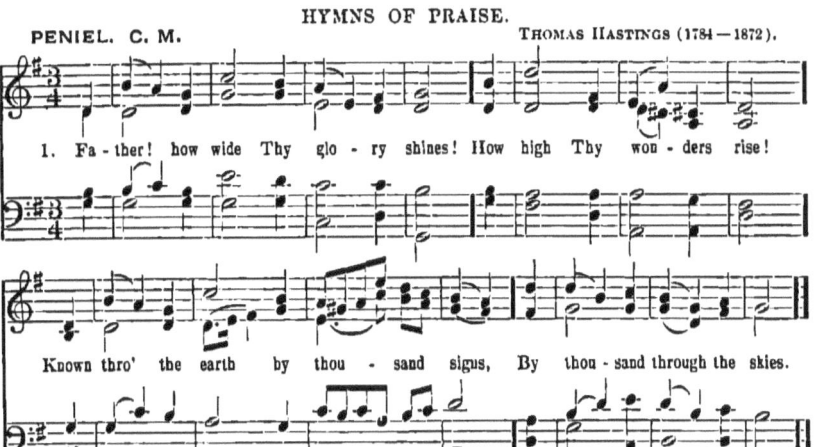

1. Father! how wide Thy glory shines! How high Thy wonders rise! Known thro' the earth by thousand signs, By thousand through the skies.

13   *Nature and Grace.*
1 Father! how wide Thy glory shines!
   How high Thy wonders rise!
Known thro' the earth by thousand signs,
   By thousand through the skies.

2 But, when we view Thy strange design,
   To save rebellious worms,
Where vengeance and compassion join
   In their divinest forms,—

3 Here the whole Deity is known;
   Nor dares a creature guess,
Which of the glories brightest shone,
   The justice, or the grace.

4 Now the full glories of the Lamb
   Adorn the heavenly plains;
Bright seraphs learn Immanuel's name,
   And try their choicest strains.

5 Oh, may I bear some humble part,
   In that immortal song;
Wonder and joy shall tune my heart,
   And love command my tongue.
         Rev. Isaac Watts (1674—1748).

14   *Psalm* 119.
1 Oh, that the Lord would guide my ways
   To keep His statutes still;
Oh, that my God would grant me grace
   To know and do His will.

2 Oh, send Thy Spirit down, to write
   Thy law upon my heart;
Nor let my tongue indulge deceit,
   Nor act the liar's part.

3 From vanity turn off my eyes;
   Let no corrupt design,
Nor covetous desires, arise
   Within this soul of mine.

4 Order my footsteps by Thy word,
   And make my heart sincere;
Let sin have no dominion, Lord!
   But keep my conscience clear.

5 Make me to walk in Thy commands—
   'Tis a delightful road;
Nor let my head, nor heart, or hands,
   Offend against my God.
         Rev. Isaac Watts (1674—1748).

15   *Psalm* 119.
1 Thou art my portion, O my God!
   Soon as I know Thy way,
My heart makes haste to obey Thy word,
   And suffers no delay.

2 I choose the path of heavenly truth,
   And glory in my choice;
Not all the riches of the earth
   Could make me so rejoice.

3 The testimonies of Thy grace
   I set before mine eyes;
Thence I derive my daily strength,
   And there my comfort lies.

4 Now I am thine,—for ever thine;—
   Oh, save Thy servant, Lord!
Thou art my shield, my hiding-place,
   My hope is in Thy word.
         Rev. Isaac Watts (1674—1748).

HYMNS OF PRAISE.

CLAREMONT. H. M.   CARMINA SACRA, 1844.

1. Ye tribes of Adam, join With heav'n, and earth, and seas, And offer notes divine To your Creator's praise; Ye holy throng Of angels bright, In worlds of light Begin the song.

16   *Psalm* 148.

1 Ye tribes of Adam, join
With heaven, and earth, and seas,
And offer notes divine
To your Creator's praise:
Ye holy throng | In worlds of light,
Of angels bright, | Begin the song.

2 The shining worlds above
In glorious order stand;
Or in swift courses move,
By His supreme command:
He spake the word, | From nothing came,
And all their frame | To praise the Lord!

3 Let all the nations fear
The God that rules above;
He brings His people near,
And makes them taste His love:
While earth and sky | His saints shall raise
Attempt His praise, | His honors high.
Rev. Isaac Watts (1674—1748).

PLEYEL'S HYMN. 7s.   IGNACE PLEYEL (1757—1831).

1. Children of the heavenly King, As ye journey, sweetly sing: Sing your Saviour's worthy praise, Glorious in His works and ways.

17   *Isaiah* 35: 8-10.

1 Children of the heavenly King,
As ye journey, sweetly sing;
Sing your Saviour's worthy praise,
Glorious in His works and ways.

2 Ye are traveling home to God
In the way the fathers trod;
They are happy now, and ye
Soon their happiness shall see.

3 Shout, ye little flock, and blest!
Soon you'll enter into rest;
There your seat is now prepared;
There your kingdom and reward.

4 Fear not, brethren; joyful stand
On the borders of your land;
Jesus Christ, your Father's Son,
Bids you undismayed go on.

5 Lord, submissive make us go,
Gladly leaving all below;
Only Thou our Leader be,
And we still will follow Thee.
Rev. John Cennick (1717—1755).

HYMNS OF PRAISE.

HANOVER. 10s, & 11s. SUPPLEMENT TO NEW VERSION OF PSALMS, 1708.

1. Oh! worship the King all-glorious above; Oh! grateful-ly sing His pow'r and His love;

Our Shield and Defender, the Ancient of Days, Pa-vil-ioned in splendor and girded with praise.

18 *The Glorious King.*

1 Oh! worship the King all-glorious above:
Oh! gratefully sing His power and His love;
Our Shield and Defender, the Ancient of Days,
Pavilioned in splendor and girded with praise.

2 We sing of Thy might, we sing of Thy grace,
Whose robe is the light, whose canopy space,
Thy chariots of wrath the thunder-clouds form,
And dark is Thy path on the wings of the storm.

3 Frail children of dust, and feeble as frail,
In Thee we do trust, nor find Thee to fail;
Thy mercies how tender, how firm to the end,
Our Maker, Defender, Redeemer and Friend.

4 O measureless Might, ineffable Love,
While angels delight to hymn Thee above,
Thy ransomed creation, though feeble their lays,
With true adoration shall sing to Thy praise.
Sir Robert Grant, (1785—1838).

NOTTINGHAM. C. M. J. CLARK.

1. Lift up to God the voice of praise, Whose breath our souls inspired; Loud and more loud the anthem raise, With grateful ardor fired.

19 *The Voice of Praise.*

1 Lift up to God the voice of praise,
Whose breath our souls inspired;
Loud and more loud the anthem raise,
With grateful ardor fired.

2 Lift up to God the voice of praise,
Whose goodness, passing thought,
Loads every minute, as it flies,
With benefits unsought.

3 Lift up to God the voice of praise,
From whom salvation flows,
Who sent His Son our souls to save
From everlasting woes.

4 Lift up to God the voice of praise,
For hope's transporting ray,
Which lights, through darkest shades of death,
To realms of endless day.
Rev. Ralph Wardlaw, D. D. (—1853).

HYMNS OF PRAISE.

PROMISE. 8s & 7s, D. HYMNS ANCIENT AND MODERN, 1861.

20 *Through the night of doubt and sorrow.*

1 Through the night of doubt and sorrow
Onward goes the pilgrim band,
Singing songs of expectation,
Marching to the Promised Land.
Clear before us through the darkness
Gleams and burns the guiding light;
Brother clasps the hand of brother,
Stepping fearless through the night.

2 One the strain that lips of thousands
Lift as from the heart of one;
One the conflict, one the peril,
One the march in God begun:
One the gladness of rejoicing
On the far eternal shore,
Where the One Almighty Father
Reigns in love for evermore.

3 Onward, therefore, pilgrim brothers,
Onward with the Cross our aid!
Bear its shame, and fight its battle,
Till we rest beneath its shade.
Soon shall come its great awaking,
Soon the rending of the tomb;
Then the scattering of all shadows,
And the end of toil and gloom.
*Bernhardt Severin Ingemann (1789—1862).
Tr. by Rev. Sabine Baring-Gould (1834—) 1867.*

21 *Praise to God.*

1 Praise to Thee, Thou great Creator,
Praise to Thee from every tongue :
Join, my soul, with every creature,
Join the universal song.
Father, source of all compassion,
Pure, unbounded grace is Thine:
Hail the God of our salvation !
Praise Him for His love divine.

2 For ten thousand blessings given,
For the hope of future joy,
Sound His praise thro' earth and heaven,
Sound Jehovah's praise on high.
Joyfully on earth adore Him,
Till in heaven our song we raise;
There, enraptured, fall before Him,
Lost in wonder, love, and praise.
Rev. John Fawcett (1739—1817).

HYMNS OF PRAISE.

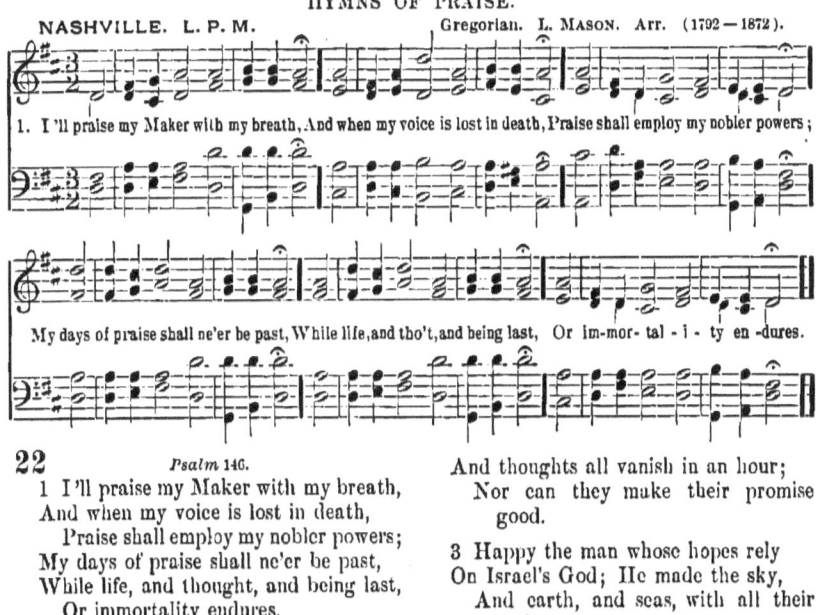

NASHVILLE. L. P. M.   Gregorian. L. MASON. Arr. (1792—1872).

1. I'll praise my Maker with my breath, And when my voice is lost in death, Praise shall employ my nobler powers;

My days of praise shall ne'er be past, While life, and tho't, and being last, Or im-mor-tal-i-ty en-dures.

22   *Psalm 146.*

1 I'll praise my Maker with my breath,
And when my voice is lost in death,
Praise shall employ my nobler powers;
My days of praise shall ne'er be past,
While life, and thought, and being last,
Or immortality endures.

2 Why should I make a man my trust?
Princes must die and turn to dust;
Vain is the help of flesh and blood;
Their breath departs; their pomp and power
And thoughts all vanish in an hour;
Nor can they make their promise good.

3 Happy the man whose hopes rely
On Israel's God; He made the sky,
And earth, and seas, with all their train,
His truth forever stands secure;
He saves th' oppressed, He feeds the poor,
And none shall find His promise vain.
   Rev. Isaac Watts (1674—1748).

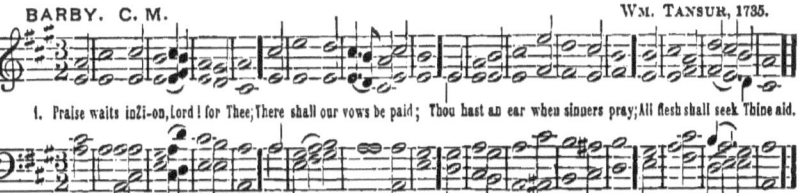

BARBY. C. M.   WM. TANSUR, 1735.

1. Praise waits in Zi-on, Lord! for Thee; There shall our vows be paid; Thou hast an ear when sinners pray; All flesh shall seek Thine aid.

23   *Psalm 65.*

1 Praise waits in Zion, Lord! for Thee;
There shall our vows be paid;
Thou hast an ear when sinners pray;
All flesh shall seek Thine aid.

2 O Lord! our guilt and fears prevail,
But pardoning grace is Thine;
And thou wilt grant us power and skill,
To conquer every sin.

3 Blest are the men, whom Thou wilt choose
To bring them near Thy face;
Give them a dwelling in Thy house,
To feast upon Thy grace.

4 In answering what Thy church requests,
Thy truth and terror shine;
And works of dreadful righteousness
Fulfil Thy kind design.

5 Thus shall the wondering nations see
The Lord is good and just;
The distant isles shall fly to Thee,
And make Thy name their trust.
   Rev. Isaac Watts (1674—1748.)

HYMNS OF DEVOTION.

NICAEA. 11s, 12s & 10s.   Rev. John Bacchus Dykes (1823—1876).

24

Which was, and is, and is to come. Rev. iv: 8.

1 Holy, holy, holy! Lord God Almighty!
Early in the morning our song shall rise to Thee;
Holy, holy, holy! merciful and mighty!
God in Three Persons, Blessèd Trinity!

2 Holy, holy, holy! all the saints adore Thee,
Casting down their golden crowns around the glassy sea;
Cherubim and seraphim falling down before Thee,
Which wert, and art, and evermore shalt be.

3 Holy, holy, holy! though the darkness hide Thee,
Though the eye of sinful man Thy glory may not see,
Only Thou art holy, there is none beside Thee,
Perfect in power, in love, and purity.

4 Holy, holy, holy! Lord God Almighty,
All Thy works shall praise Thy Name, in earth, and sky, and sea;
Holy, holy, holy! Lord God Almighty!
God in Three Persons, Blessèd Trinity!

Bp. Reginald Heber (1783—1826).

(12)

HYMNS OF DEVOTION.

LENOX. H. M.   L. Edson (1748—1820).

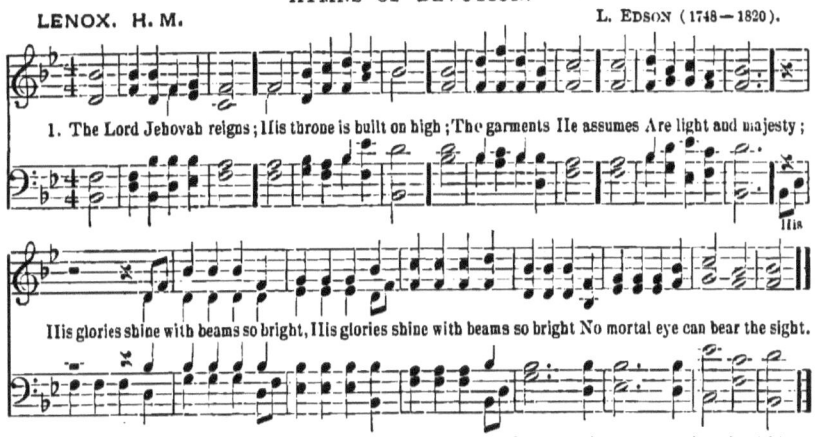

1. The Lord Jehovah reigns; His throne is built on high; The garments He assumes Are light and majesty; His glories shine with beams so bright, His glories shine with beams so bright No mortal eye can bear the sight.

25
Psalm 93.

1 The Lord Jehovah reigns;
  His throne is built on high;
The garments He assumes
  Are light and majesty;
His glories shine with beams so bright
No mortal eye can bear the sight.

2 The thunders of His hand
  Keep the wide world in awe;
His wrath and justice stand
  To guard His holy law;
And where His love resolves to bless,
His truth confirms and seals the grace.

3 And can this mighty King
  Of glory condescend,
And will He write His name,
  My Father and my Friend?
I love His name, I love His word;
Join all my powers, and praise the Lord!
Rev. Isaac Watts (1674—1748.)

26
Rejoice, the Lord is King!

1 Rejoice! the Lord is King;
  Your Lord and King adore:
Mortals, give thanks and sing,
  And triumph evermore!
Lift up your hearts, lift up your voice;
Rejoice aloud, ye saints, rejoice.

2 Jesus, the Saviour, reigns,
  The God of truth and love;
When He had purged our stains,

  He took His seat above:
Lift up your hearts, etc.

3 His kingdom can not fail;
  He rules o'er earth and heaven;
The keys of death and hell
  Are to our Jesus given:
Lift up your hearts, etc.
Rev. Charles Wesley (1708—1788).

27
Year of Jubilee.

1 Blow ye the trumpet, blow,
  The gladly solemn sound,
Let all the nations know,
  To earth's remotest bound,
The year of jubilee is come:
Return, ye ransomed sinners, home.

2 Jesus, our great High Priest,
  Hath full atonement made;
Ye weary spirits, rest;
  Ye mournful souls, be glad:
The year of jubilee, etc.

3 Extol the Lamb of God.
  The all-atoning Lamb;
Redemption in His blood
  Throughout the world proclaim:
The year of jubilee, etc.

4 The gospel trumpet hear,
  The news of heavenly grace;
And, saved from earth, appear
  Before your Saviour's face;
The year of jubilee, etc.
Rev. Chas. Wesley (1708—1788.)

HYMNS OF DEVOTION.

28 *Lost but found.*

1 I was a wandering sheep,
  I did not love the fold;
I did not love my Shepherd's voice,
  I would not be controlled:
I was a wayward child,
  I did not love my home,
I did not love my Father's voice,
  I loved afar to roam.

2 The Shepherd sought His sheep,
  The Father sought His child,
They followed me o'er vale and hill,
  O'er deserts waste and wild:
They found me nigh to death,
  Famished, and faint, and lone;
They bound me with the bands of love;
  They saved the wandering one.

3 Jesus my Shepherd is,
  'T was He that loved my soul,
'T was He that washed me in His blood,
  'T was He that made me whole;
'T was He that sought the lost,
  That found the wandering sheep,
'T was He that brought me to the fold,
  'T is He that still doth keep.

Rev. Horatius Bonar (1808—1890).

29 *Psalm 31.*

1 My spirit on Thy care,
  Blest Saviour, I recline;
Thou wilt not leave me to despair,
  For Thou art love divine.

2 In Thee I place my trust;
  On Thee I calmly rest :
I know Thee good, I know Thee just,
  And count Thy choice the best.

3 What e'er events betide,
  Thy will they all perform;
Safe in Thy breast my head I hide,
  Nor fear the coming storm.

4 Let good or ill befall,
  It must be good for me,—
Secure of having Thee in all,
  Of having all in Thee.

Rev. H. F. Lyte (1793—1847).

HYMNS OF DEVOTION.

BERA. L. M.   J. E. GOULD (1822—1875).

1. O Thou, the con-trite sin-ner's Friend, Who lov-ing, lovest him to the end, On this a-lone my hopes de-pend, That Thou wilt plead for me, for me.

30   *Christ's Intercession.*
1 O Thou, the contrite sinner's Friend,
Who loving, lovest him to the end,
On this alone my hopes depend,
That Thou wilt plead for me. [for me.]

2 When weary in the Christian race,
Far off appears my resting-place,
And, fainting I mistrust Thy grace,
Then, Saviour, plead for me. [for me.]

3 When Satan, by my sins made bold,
Strives from Thy cross to loose my hold,
Then with Thy pitying arms enfold,
And plead, oh, plead for me. [for me.]

4 And when my dying hour draws near,
Darkness with anguish, guilt, and fear,
Then to my fainting sight appear,
Pleading in heaven for me. [for me.]
Miss Charlotte Elliott (1789—1871).

31   *Worship at the Cross.*
1 Oh, the sweet wonders of that cross
Where my Redeemer loved and died:
Its noblest life my spirit draws [side.
From His dear wounds, and bleeding

2 I would forever speak His name
In sounds to mortal ears unknown;
With angels join to praise the Lamb,
And worship at His Father's throne.
Rev. Isaac Watts (1674—1748).

32   *Christ our Teacher.*
1 How sweetly flowed the gospel's sound
From lips of gentleness and grace,
When list'ning thousands gather'd round,
And joy and rev'rence filled the place.

2 From heav'n He came, of heav'n He spoke;
To heav'n He led His followers' way;
Dark clouds of gloomy night He broke,
Unveiling an immortal day.

3 "Come, wanderers, to my Father's home,
Come, all ye weary ones, and rest!"
Yes! sacred Teacher, we will come,
Obey Thee, love Thee, and be blest!
Sir John Bowring (1792—1812).

33   *Sympathy of Christ.*
1 Where high the heavenly temple stands,
The house of God not made with hands,
A great High Priest our nature wears,
The Advocate of saints appears.

2 He, who for men in mercy stood,
And poured on earth His precious blood
Pursues in heaven His plan of grace
The Saviour of the chosen race.

3 Though now ascended up on high,
He bends on earth a brother's eye;
Partaker of the human name,
He knows the frailty of our frame.

4 Our Fellow-Sufferer yet retains
A fellow-feeling of our pains;
And still remembers in the skies,
His tears, and agonies and cries.

5 In every pang that rends the heart,
The Man of sorrows had a part;
He sympathizes in our grief,
And to the sufferer sends relief.
Michael Bruce (1746—1767).

(15)

HYMNS OF DEVOTION,

RATHBUN. 8s & 7s.   I. CONKEY (1815—1867).

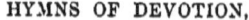

1. Praise the Lord! ye heav'ns adore Him; Praise Him, angels in the height; Sun and moon rejoice before Him; Praise Him, all ye stars of light!

By per. of Oliver Ditson Company, owners of copyright.

34   *Praise the Lord.*

1 Praise the Lord! ye heavens adore Him;
Praise Him, angels in the height;
Sun and moon rejoice before Him;
Praise Him, all ye stars of light!

2 Praise the Lord — for He hath spoken;
Worlds His mighty voice obeyed;
Laws which never can be broken,
For their guidance He hath made.

3 Praise the Lord — for He is glorious;
Never shall His promise fail;
God hath made His saints victorious,
Sin and death shall not prevail.

4 Praise the God of our salvation,
Hosts on high His power proclaim;
Heaven, and earth, and all creation,
Praise and magnify His name!
Anon., 1796.

EVERLASTING REST. 7s. D.   Rev. R. P. KERR. 1891.

1. Lord of earth, Thy forming hand Well this beauteous frame hath planned; Woods that wave and hills that tower, What were all its joys to me? O - cean rolling in its power; Yet a-mid this scene so fair, Should I cease Thy smile to share, Whom have I on earth but Thee?

FINE.   D.S.

Copyright, 1891, by R. P. Kerr.

35   *Whom in heaven or earth but Thee?*

1 Lord of earth, Thy forming hand
Well this beauteous frame hath planned;
Woods that wave and hills that tower,
Ocean rolling in its power;
Yet amid this scene so fair,
Should I cease Thy smile to share,
What were all its joys to me?
Whom have I on earth but Thee?

2 Lord of heaven, beyond our sight
Shines a world of purer light;
Here in love's unclouded reign,
Severed friends shall meet again:
Oh! that world is passing fair;
Yet, if Thou wert absent there,
What were all its joys to me?
Whom have I in heaven but Thee?

3 Lord of earth and heaven, my breast
Seeks in Thee its only rest;
I was lost,— Thy accents mild
Homeward lured Thy wandering child.
Oh! if once Thy smile divine
Ceased upon my soul to shine,
What were earth or heaven to me?
Whom have I in each but Thee?
Sir R. Grant (1785—1838).

HYMNS OF DEVOTION.

ST. HELEN. 10s. WALTER HATELY, 1872.

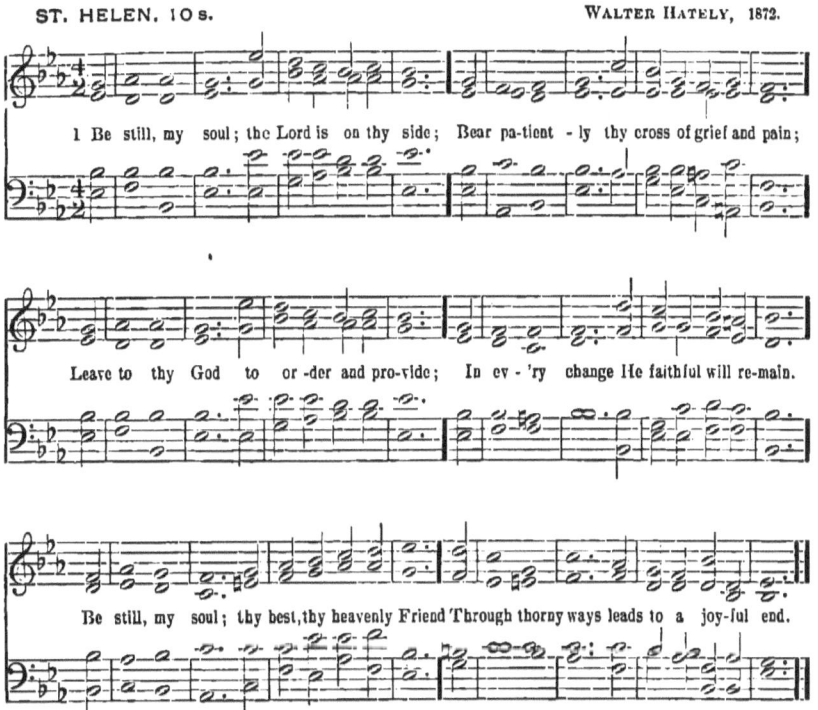

1 Be still, my soul; the Lord is on thy side; Bear pa-tient-ly thy cross of grief and pain; Leave to thy God to or-der and pro-vide; In ev-'ry change He faithful will re-main. Be still, my soul; thy best, thy heavenly Friend Through thorny ways leads to a joy-ful end.

36 *Return unto thy rest, O my soul, for the Lord hath dealt bountifully with thee.*

1 Be still, my soul; the Lord is on thy side;
Bear patiently thy cross of grief and pain,
Leave to thy God to order and provide;
In every change He faithful will remain.
Be still, my soul; thy best, thy heavenly
Friend
Through thorny ways leads to a joyful
end.

2 Be still, my soul; thy God doth undertake
To guide the future as He has the past.
Thy hope, thy confidence, let nothing shake,
All now mysterious shall be bright at last.
Be still, my soul; the waves and winds shall
know
His voice who ruled them while He dwelt
below.

3 Be still, my soul; when dearest friends depart,
And all is darkened in the vale of tears,
Then thou shalt better know His love, His
heart, [fears.
Who comes to soothe thy sorrow and thy
Be still, my soul; thy Saviour can repay
From His own fullness all He takes away.

4 Be still, my soul; the hour is hastening on
When we shall be for ever with the Lord;
When disappointment, grief, and fear are
gone,
Sorrow forgot, love's purest joys restored.
Be still, my soul; when change and tears
are past,
All safe and blessed we shall meet at last.
Hymns from the Land of Luther.

HYMNS OF DEVOTION.

HADDAM. H.M. English Melody. Arr. by L. MASON, (1702—1872).

1. The prom-i-ses I sing, Which sovereign love hath spoke; Nor will the Eternal King His words of grace revoke; They stand se-cure and stead-fast still; Not Zi-on's hill a-bides so sure.

37   *God's Truth.*

1 The promises I sing,
   Which sovereign love hath spoke;
Nor will the Eternal King
   His words of grace revoke;
They stand secure and steadfast still;
Not Zion's hill abides so sure.

2 The mountains melt away,
   When once the Judge appears,
And sun and moon decay,
   That measure mortal years;
But still the same, in radiant lines;
The promise shines through all the flame.

3 Their harmony shall sound
   Through my attentive ears,
When thunders cleave the ground
   And dissipate the spheres;
Midst all the shock of that great scene,
I stand serene, Thy word my rock.
         Rev. Philip Doddridge (1702—1751).

38   *Invoking the presence of Christ.*

1 Come, my Redeemer, come,
   And deign to dwell with me;
Come, and Thy right assume,
   And bid Thy rivals flee:
Come, my Redeemer, quickly come,
And make my heart Thy lasting home.

2 Exert Thy mighty power,
   And banish all my sin;
In this auspicious hour
   Bring all Thy graces in:
Come, my Redeemer, quickly come,
And make my heart Thy lasting home.

3 Rule Thou in every thought
   And passion of my soul,
Till all my powers are brought
   Beneath Thy full control;
Come, my Redeemer, quickly come,
And make my heart Thy lasting home.

4 Then shall my days be Thine,
   And all my heart be love,
And joy and peace be mine,
   Such as are known above:
Come, my Redeemer, quickly come,
And make my heart Thy lasting home.
        Rev. Andrew Reed (1787—1862).

39   *Longing for Christ.*
        Tune, ST. JUDE.

1 My spirit longs for Thee
   Within my troubled breast,
Unworthy though I be
   Of so Divine a Guest.
Of so Divine a guest
   Unworthy though I be,
Yet has my heart no rest
   Unless it come from Thee.

2 Unless it come from Thee,
   In vain I look around;
In all that I can see,
   No rest is to be found.
No rest is to be found
   But in Thy blessèd love:
O let my wish be crowned,
   And send it from above.
        John Byrom (1691—1763).

HYMNS OF DEVOTION.

ST. JUDE. 6s. D. CARL MARIA VON WEBER (1786—1826).

1. My Saviour, as Thou wilt! Oh, may Thy will be mine; In-to Thy hand of love I would my all re-sign. Thro' sorrow or thro' joy. Conduct me as Thine own, And help me still to say, My Lord Thy will be done.

40 *Thy will be done.*

1 My Saviour, as Thou wilt!
  Oh, may Thy will be mine;
Into Thy hand of love
  I would my all resign;
Through sorrow or through joy,
  Conduct me as Thine own,
And help me still to say,
  My Lord, Thy will be done.

2 My Saviour, as Thou wilt:
  If needy here and poor,
Give me Thy people's bread,
  Their portion rich and sure.
The manna of Thy word
  Let my soul feed upon;
And if all else should fail,
  My Lord, Thy will be done.

3 My Saviour, as Thou wilt!
  Though seen through many a tear,
Let not my star of hope
  Grow dim and disappear;
Since Thou on earth has wept,
  And sorrowed oft alone,
If I must weep with Thee,
  My Lord, Thy will be done.

4 My Saviour, as Thou wilt!
  All shall be well for me;
Each changing future scene
  I gladly trust with Thee:

Straight to my home above
  I travel calmly on,
And sing, in life or death,
  My God Thy will be done!
<small>Benjamin Schmolke, Tr. by Jane Borthwick, 1853.</small>

41 *He knoweth the way.*

1 Thy way, not mine, O Lord,
  However dark it be!
Lead me by Thine own hand;
  Choose out my path for me.
I dare not choose my lot:
  I would not, if I might;
Choose Thou for me my God,
  So shall I walk aright.

2 The kingdom that I seek
  Is Thine: so let the way
That leads to it be Thine,
  Else I must surely stray.
Take Thou my cup, and it
  With joy or sorrow fill,
As best to Thee may seem;
  Choose Thou my good and ill.

3 Choose Thou for me my friends,
  My sickness or my health;
Choose Thou my cares for me,
  My poverty or wealth.
Not mine, not mine the choice,
  In things or great or small;
Be Thou my Guide, my Strength,
  My Wisdom and my All.
<small>Rev. H. Bonar (1808—1890).</small>

HYMNS OF DEVOTION.

WHAT A FRIEND WE HAVE IN JESUS. 8s & 7s. D. C. C. CONVERSE (1834—).

By per. C. C. Converse, owner of copyright.

42 *What a friend we have in Jesus.*

1 What a friend we have in Jesus,
 All our sins and griefs to bear;
What a privilege to carry
 Ev'rything to God in prayer!
O what peace we often forfeit,
 O what needless pain we bear,
All because we do not carry
 Ev'rything to God in prayer!

2 Have we trials and temptations?
 Is there trouble any where?
We should never be discouraged,
 Take it to the Lord in prayer.
Can we find a friend so faithful,
 Who will all our sorrows share?
Jesus knows our ev'ry weakness,
 Take it to the Lord in prayer!

3 Are we weak and heavy laden,
 Cumbered with a load of care?—
Precious Saviour, still our refuge,—
 Take it to the Lord in prayer.
Do thy friends despise, forsake thee?
 Take it to the Lord in prayer;
In His arms He'll take and shield thee,
 Thou wilt find a solace there.

Unknown.

43 *God's mercy.*

1 There's a wideness in God's mercy,
 Like the wideness of the sea:
There's a kindness in His justice,
 Which is more than liberty.
There is welcome for the sinner,
 And more graces for the good;
There is mercy with the Saviour;
 There is healing in His blood.

2 There is no place where earth's sorrows
 Are more felt than up in heaven;
There is no place where earth's failings
 Have such kindly judgment given.
There is plentiful redemption
 In the blood that has been shed;
There is joy for all the members
 In the sorrows of the Head.

3 For the love of God is broader
 Than the measure of man's mind;
And the heart of the Eternal
 Is most wonderfully kind.
If our love were but more simple,
 We should take Him at His word;
And our lives would be all sunshine
 In the sweetness of our Lord.

Rev. Frederick William Faber (1814—1863).

(20)

HYMNS OF DEVOTION.

SILVER STREET. S. M. ISAAC SMITH (1735—1800).

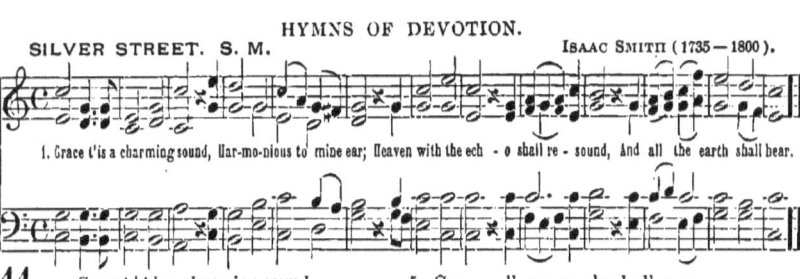

44 *Grace! 't is a charming sound.*
1 Grace! 't is a charming sound,
  Harmonious to mine ear;
  Heaven with the echo shall resound,
  And all the earth shall hear.

2 Grace first contrived the way
  To save rebellious man;
  And all the steps that grace display,
  Which drew the wondrous plan.

3 Grace first inscribed my name
  In God's eternal book;
  'T was grace that gave me to the Lamb,
  Who all my sorrows took.

4 Grace taught my soul to pray,
  And made mine eyes o'erflow;
  'T was grace that kept me to this day,
  And will not let me go.

5 Grace all my work shall crown,
  Through everlasting days;
  It lays in heaven the topmost stone,
  And well deserves the praise.
  Rev. Philip Doddridge (1702—1751).

45 *Psalm 95.*
1 Come, sound His praise abroad,
  And hymns of glory sing;
  Jehovah is the sovereign God,
  The universal King.

2 Come, worship at His throne,
  Come, bow before the Lord;
  We are His works, and not our own;
  He formed us by His word.

3 To-day attend His voice,
  Nor dare provoke His rod!
  Come, like the people of His choice,
  And own your gracious God.
  Rev. Isaac Watts (1674—1748).

GREENWOOD. S. M. J. E. SWEETSER (1825—1873).

46 *Is any merry, let him sing psalms.*
1 Come, we who love the Lord,
  And let our joys be known;
  Join in a song of sweet accord,
  And thus surround the throne.

2 Let those refuse to sing
  Who never knew our God;
  But children of the heavenly King
  May speak their joys abroad.

3 The men of grace have found
  Glory begun below;
  Celestial fruits on earthly ground
  From faith and hope may grow.

4 The hill of Zion yields
  A thousand sacred sweets
  Before we reach the heavenly fields,
  Or walk the golden streets.

5 There shall we see His face,
  And never, never sin;
  There from the rivers of His grace,
  Drink endless pleasures in.

6 Then let our songs abound,
  And every tear be dry;
  We're marching thro' Immanuel's ground
  To fairer worlds on high.
  Rev. Isaac Watts (1674—1748).

HYMNS OF DEVOTION.

NETTLETON. 8s & 7s.   ASAHEL NETTLETON, D.D., (1783—1844).

By permission of Oliver Ditson Company, owners of copyright.

47   *Grateful Recollections.*

1 Come, Thou Fount of every blessing,
  Tune my heart to sing Thy grace;
Streams of mercy never ceasing
  Call for songs of loudest praise.
Teach me some melodious sonnet,
  Sung by flaming tongues above;
Praise the mount — oh, fix me on it,
  Mount of God's unchanging love.

2 Here I raise my Ebenezer,
  Hither by Thy help I'm come;
And I hope, by Thy good pleasure,
  Safely to arrive at home.
Jesus sought me when a stranger,
  Wandering from the fold of God;
He, to rescue me from danger,
  Interposed with precious blood.

3 O! to grace how great a debtor,
  Daily I'm constrained to be;
Let that grace, Lord, like a fetter,
  Bind my wandering heart to Thee.
Prone to wander, Lord, I feel it,
  Prone to leave the God I love;
Here's my heart, Lord, take and seal it,
  Seal it from Thy courts above.
        Rev. R. Robinson (1735 — 1790).

48   *Bought with a Price.*

1 When I view my Saviour bleeding,
  For my sins upon the tree:
O how wondrous, how exceeding
  Great His love appears to me!

Floods of deep distress and anguish,
  To impede His labors, came;
Yet they all could not extinguish
  Love's eternal, burning flame.

2 Sure, such infinite affection
  Lays the highest claims to mine;
All my powers, without exception,
  Should in fervent praises join.
Jesus, fit me for Thy service;
  Form me for Thyself alone;
I am Thy most costly purchase,
  Take possession of Thine own.
        Richard Lee, 1794.

49   *Christ the Desire of all Nations.*

1 Come, Thou long expected Jesus,
  Born to set Thy people free;
From our fears and sins release us,
  Let us find our rest in Thee:
Israel's Strength and Consolation,
  Hope of all the saints Thou art;
Dear Desire of every nation,
  Joy of every longing heart.

2 Born, Thy people to deliver;
  Born a child, and yet a King;
Born to reign in us forever,
  Now Thy precious kingdom bring:
By Thine own eternal Spirit,
  Rule in all our hearts alone;
By Thine all-sufficient merit,
  Raise us to Thy glorious throne.
        Rev. Charles Wesley (1708 — 1788).

HYMNS OF DEVOTION.

50 *How Happy are They.*

1 Oh, how happy are they
Who the Saviour obey,
And have laid up their treasures above;
Oh, what tongue can express
The sweet comfort and peace
Of a soul in its earliest love

2 'T was a heaven below
My Redeemer to know,
And the angels could do nothing more
Than to fall at His feet,
And the story repeat,
And the Lover of sinners adore.

3 Oh, the rapturous height
Of that holy delight,
Which I felt in the life-giving blood!
Of my Saviour possessed,
I was perfectly blest,
As if filled with the fullness of God.

4 Then all the day long,
Was my Jesus my song,
And redemption through faith in His name;
Oh, that all might believe,
And salvation receive,
And their song and their joy be the same.

Rev. Charles Wesley (1708—1788.)
SAMUEL WESLEY, (1766—1837.)

BETHLEHEM. S.M.

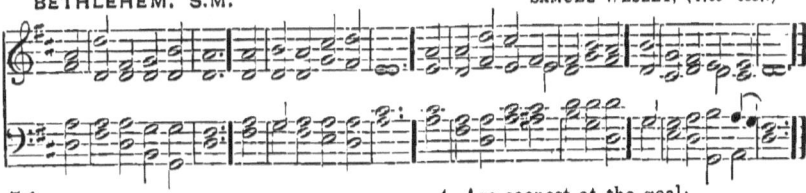

51 *Waiting.*

1 Not soin haste, my heart,
Have faith in God and wait;
Although He linger very long,
He never comes too late.

2 He never comes too late;
He knoweth what is best:
Vex not thyself to-day in vain,
Until He cometh, rest.

3 Until He cometh, rest;
Nor grudge the hours that roll;
The feet that patient wait for God,
Are soonest at the goal.

4 Are soonest at the goal;
That is not gained by speed:
Then hold thee still my anxious heart
For I shall wait His lead.
Anon.

52 *Psalm 133.*

1 Blest are the sons of peace
Whose hearts and hopes are one;
Whose kind designs to serve and please,
Through all their actions run.

2 Thus, on the heavenly hills,
The saints are blest above,
Where joy, like morning dew, distills
And all the air is love.

Rev. Isaac Watts (1674—1748).

HYMNS OF DEVOTION.

DENNIS. S. M.  H. G. NAEGELI (1773—1836.)

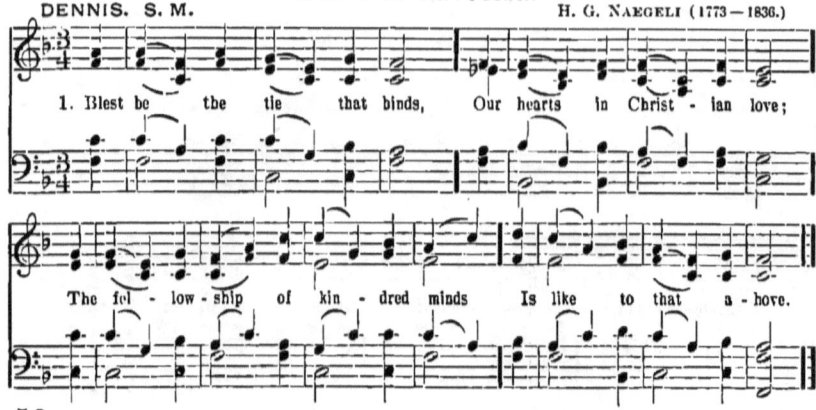

53 *Christian Fellowship.*

1 Blest be the tie that binds
  Our hearts in Christian love;
  The fellowship of kindred minds
  Is like to that above.

2 Before our Father's throne
  We pour our ardent prayers;
  Our fears, our hopes, our aims are one,
  Our comforts and our cares.

3 We share our mutual woes,
  Our mutual burdens bear,
  And often for each other flows
  The sympathizing tear.

4 When we asunder part,
  It gives us inward pain;
  But we shall still be joined in heart,
  And hope to meet again.

5 This glorious hope revives
  Our courage by the way;
  While each in expectation lives,
  And longs to see the day.

6 From sorrow, toil, and pain,
  And sin, we shall be free;
  And perfect love and friendship reign,
  Through all eternity.
  Rev. John Fawcett (1739—1817).

54 *Hiding place.*

1 I have no hiding-place,
  No refuge from the blast,
  But in the arms of Jesus' grace
  Around about me cast.

2 Though I see not His hand,
  I feel its loving power;

And guardian angels near me stand
  In my distressful hour.

3 I dare not look within,
  But heavenward turn my gaze;
  And lest my grief become my sin,
  My tongue breaks out in praise.

4 Though tears mine eyes bedim,
  He dries the tears I shed;
  And in my soul I sing a hymn,
  Content and comforted.
  Thomas. McKellar, Ph. D., 1880.

55 *Behold the Ark of God.*

1 O cease, my wandering soul,
  On restless wing to roam;
  All the wide world, to either pole,
  Has not for thee a home.

2 Behold the Ark of God,
  Behold the open door;
  Hasten to gain that dear abode,
  And rove, my soul, no more.

3 There, safe thou shalt abide,
  There, sweet shall be thy rest,
  And every longing satisfied,
  With full salvation blest.
  Rev. William Augustus Muhlenberg (1796—1877).

56 *Doxology.*

To God the Father, Son,
  And Spirit, One and Three,
Be glory, as it was, is now,
  And shall for ever be.
  Rev. John Wesley (1703—1791).

(24)

HYMNS OF DEVOTION.

HENRY. C. M.   S. B. POND (1792—1871).

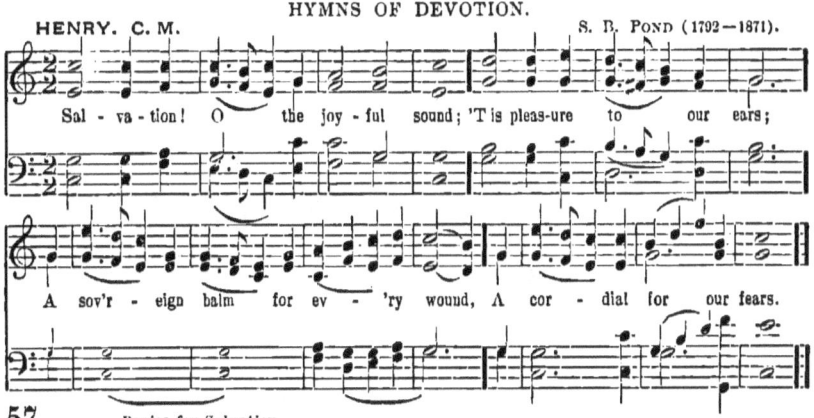

Sal-va-tion! O the joy-ful sound; 'Tis pleas-ure to our ears;

A sov'r-eign balm for ev-'ry wound, A cor-dial for our fears.

57 *Praise for Salvation.*
1 Salvation! O the joyful sound;
   'T is pleasure to our ears;
A sovereign balm for every wound,
   A cordial for our fears.

2 Buried in sorrow and in sin,
   At hell's dark door we lay;
But we arise by grace divine,
   To see a heavenly day.

3 Salvation! let the echo fly
   The spacious earth around;
While all the armies of the sky
   Conspire to raise the sound.
        Rev. Isaac Watts (1674—1748).

58 *Christian Fellowship.*
1 Joined in one Spirit to one Head,
   Where He appoints we go;
And still in Jesus' footsteps tread,
   And show His praise below.

2 Oh! may we ever walk in Him,
   And nothing know beside;
Nothing desire, nothing esteem,
   But Jesus crucified.

3 Closer and closer let us cleave
   To His beloved embrace;
Expect His fullness to receive,
   And grace to add to grace.

4 Partakers of the Saviour's grace,
   The same in mind and heart,
Nor joy, nor grief, nor time, nor place,
Nor life, nor death can part.
        Methodist Hymns.

59 *Power of Faith.*
1 When musing sorrow weeps the past
   And mourns the present pain,

'T is sweet to think of peace at last,
   And feel that death is gain.

2 'T is not that murmuring thoughts arise,
   And dread a Father's will;
'T is not that meek submission flies,
   And would not suffer still.

3 It is that heaven-born faith surveys
   The path that leads to light,
And longs her eagle plumes to raise,
   And lose herself in sight.

4 Oh, let me wing my hallowed flight
   From earth-born woe and care,
And soar above these clouds of night,
   My Saviour's bliss to share.
        Rev. G. T. Noel (1782—1851).

60 *Gratitude for Providential Care.*
1 O Thou, my light, my life, my joy,
   My glory, and my all;
Unsent by Thee, no good can come,
   Nor evil can befall.

2 Such are Thy schemes of providence,
   And methods of Thy grace,
That I may safely trust in Thee,
   Through all the wilderness.

3 'T is Thine outstretched and pow'rful arm
   Upholds me in the way;
And Thy rich bounty well supplies
   The wants of every day.

4 For such compassions, O my God!
   Ten thousand thanks are due;
For such compassions, I esteem
   Ten thousand thanks too few.
        Rev. James Montgomery (1771—1854).

HYMNS OF DEVOTION.

SELF-SURRENDER. P. M.   ANONYMOUS.

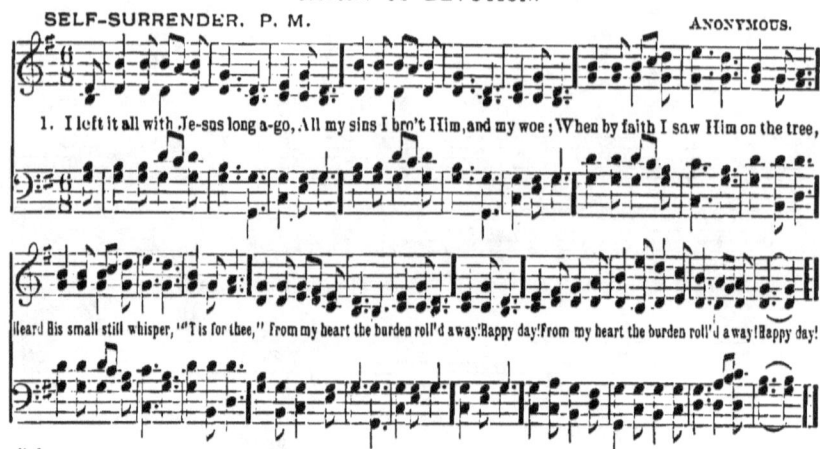

61   *Leaving all with Jesus.*

1 I left it all with Jesus long ago,
All my sins I brought Him, and my woe;
When by faith I saw Him on the tree,
Heard His small, still whisper, "'T is for thee,"
From my heart the burden rolled away!
    Happy day!

2 I leave it all with Jesus, for He knows
How to steal the bitter from life's woes;
How to gild the tear-drop with His smile,
Make the desert-garden bloom awhile;
When my weakness leaneth on His might
    All seems light.

3 I leave it all with Jesus, day by day;
Faith can firmly trust Him, come what may
Hope has dropped her anchor, found her rest
In the calm, sure haven of His breast:
Love esteems it Heaven to abide
    At His side.

4 O leave it all with Jesus, drooping soul!
Tell not half Thy story, but the whole;
Worlds on worlds are hanging on His hand,
Life and death are waiting His command;
Yet His tender bosom makes thee room —
    O come home.
       Miss Ellen H. Willis.

STELLA. L. M. 61.   From CROWN OF JESUS.

1. My hope is built on noth-ing less Than Je-sus' blood and right-eous-ness; I lean on
{ I dare not trust the sweet-est frame, But whol-ly [*Omit.*] . . . . . . }
Je-sus, name. On Christ the sol-id rock I stand; All oth-er ground is sink-ing sand.

HYMNS OF DEVOTION.

VARINA, C. M. D. Arr. by G. F. Root (1820—).

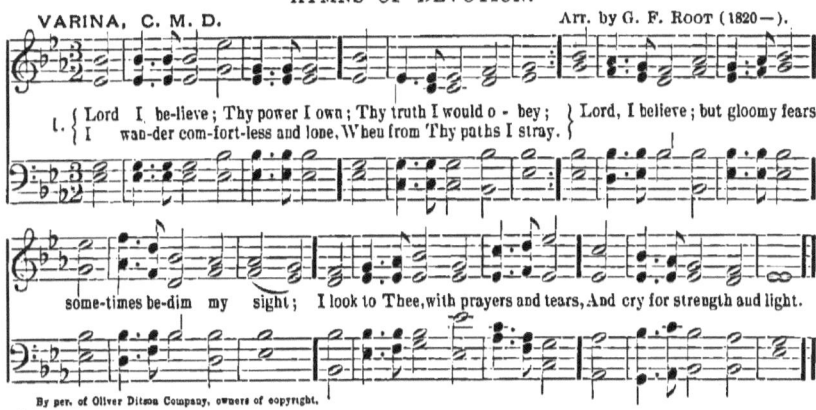

Lord I believe; Thy power I own; Thy truth I would o-bey; Lord, I believe; but gloomy fears
I wander comfortless and lone, When from Thy paths I stray.
some-times be-dim my sight; I look to Thee, with prayers and tears, And cry for strength and light.

By per. of Oliver Ditson Company, owners of copyright.

62 *Faith's Struggle.*

1 Lord, I believe; Thy power I own;
Thy truth I would obey;
I wander comfortless and lone,
When from Thy paths I stray.
Lord, I believe; but gloomy fears,
Sometimes bedim my sight;
I look to Thee, with prayers and tears,
And cry for strength and light.

2 Lord, I believe; yet Thou dost know,
My faith is cold and weak;
Pity my frailty, and bestow
The confidence I seek;
Yes, I believe! and only Thou,
Canst give my doubts relief;
Lord, to Thy truth my spirit bow,
Help Thou, my unbelief.
Rev. J. R. Wreford, 1881.

63 *Humble Reliance.*

1 My God, my Father, blissful name,
Oh, may I call Thee mine?
May I with sweet assurance claim
A portion so divine?
This only can my fears control,
And bid my sorrows fly;
What harm can ever reach my soul
Beneath my Father's eye?

2 Whate'er Thy providence denies,
I calmly would resign,
For Thou art good and just and wise;
Oh, bend my will to Thine.
Whate'er Thy sacred will ordains,
Oh, give me strength to bear;

And let me know my Father reigns,
And trust His tender care.

3 Thy sovereign ways are all unknown
To my weak erring sight;
Yet let my soul adoring own
That all Thy ways are right.
My God, my Father, be Thy name
My solace and my stay;
Oh, wilt Thou seal my humble claim,
And drive my fears away.
Miss Anne Steele (1717—1778).

64 *The Solid Rock.*
Tune, STELLA.

1 My hope is built on nothing less
Than Jesus' blood and righteousness;
I dare not trust the sweetest frame,
But wholly lean on Jesus' name:
On Christ the solid rock, I stand;
All other ground is sinking sand.

2 When darkness seems to vail His face,
I rest on His unchanging grace;
In every high and stormy gale,
My anchor holds within the vail:
On Christ the solid rock I stand;
All other ground is sinking sand.

3 His oath, His covenant, and blood,
Support me in the whelming flood;
When all around my soul gives way:
He then is all my hope and stay:
On Christ the solid rock, I stand;
All other ground is sinking sand.
Rev. Edward Mote, 1865.

(27)

HYMNS OF DEVOTION.

ORTONVILLE. C. M.   Dr. HASTINGS (1784—1872).

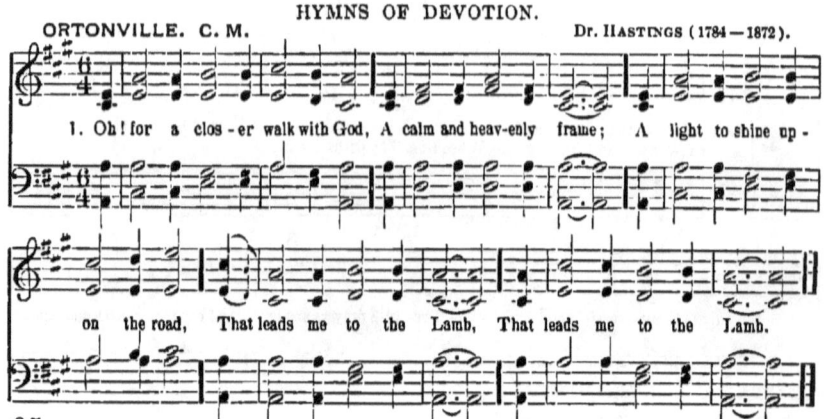

1. Oh! for a clos-er walk with God, A calm and heav-enly frame; A light to shine up-on the road, That leads me to the Lamb, That leads me to the Lamb.

65 *Prayer for the return of the Spirit.*

1 Oh! for a closer walk with God,
   A calm and heavenly frame;
A light to shine upon the road,
   That leads me to the Lamb.

2 Where is the blessedness I knew
   When first I saw the Lord?
Where is the soul refreshing view
   Of Jesus and His word?

3 What peaceful hours I once enjoyed,
   How sweet their memory still!
But they have left an aching void,
   The world can never fill.

4 Return, O Holy Dove, return,
   Sweet messenger of rest!
I hate the sins that made Thee mourn,
   And drove Thee from my breast.

5 The dearest idol I have known,
   Whate'er that idol be,
Help me to tear it from Thy throne,
   And worship only Thee.

6 So shall my walk be close with God,
   Calm and serene my frame:

So purer light shall mark the road,
   That leads me to the Lamb.
                   Wm. Cowper (1731—1800).

66 *In distress pleading with God.*

1 Oh, that I knew the secret place,
   Where I might find my God!
I'd spread my wants before His face,
   And pour my woes abroad.

2 I'd tell Him how my sins arise,
   What sorrows I sustain;
How grace decays, and comfort dies,
   And leaves my heart in pain.

3 He knows what arguments I'd take
   To wrestle with my God;
I'd plead for His own mercy's sake,
   And for my Saviour's blood.

4 My God will pity my complaints,
   And heal my broken bones;
He takes the meaning of His saints,
   The language of their groans.

5 Arise, my soul, from deep distress,
   And banish every fear;
He calls thee to His throne of grace,
   To spread thy sorrows there.
                 Rev. Isaac Watts (1674—1748).

BRADFORD. C. M.   Arr. from GEORGE FREDERICK HANDEL (1685—1759).

1. Oh, that I knew the secret place, Where I might find my God! I'd spread my wants before His face, And pour my woes abroad.

HYMNS OF DEVOTION.

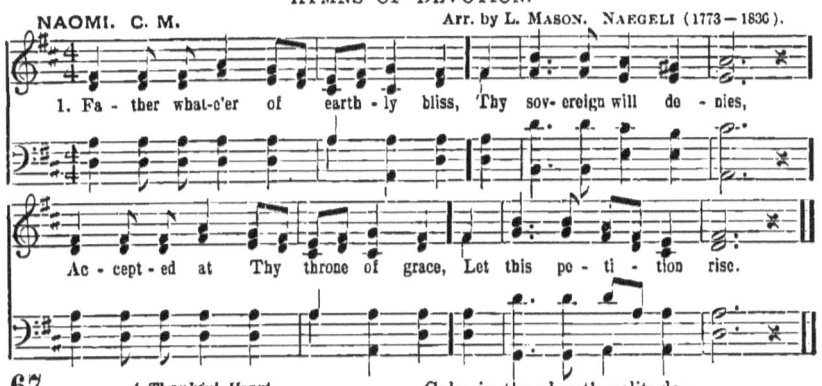

NAOMI. C. M.   Arr. by L. Mason. Naegeli (1773—1836).

1. Father what-e'er of earth-ly bliss, Thy sov-ereign will de - nies,
Ac - cept - ed at Thy throne of grace, Let this pe - ti - tion rise.

67   *A Thankful Heart.*

1 Father, whate'er of earthly bliss,
   Thy sovereign will denies,
Accepted at Thy throne of grace,
   Let this petition rise: —

2 Give me a calm, a thankful heart,
   From every murmur free;
The blessings of Thy grace impart,
   And make me live to Thee.

3 Let the sweet hope that Thou art mine,
   My life and death attend;
Thy presence through my journey shine,
   And crown my journey's end.
         Miss Anne Steele (1717—1778).

68   *Prayer for Increasing Holiness.*

1 O! for a heart to praise my God,
   A heart from sin set free;
A heart that always feels Thy blood,
   So freely shed for me.

2 A heart resigned, submissive, meek,
   My great Redeemer's throne;
Where only Christ is heard to speak;
   Where Jesus reigns alone.

3 A heart in every thought renewed,
   And full of love divine;
Holy, and right, and pure, and good,
   A copy, Lord of Thine.
         Rev. Chas. Wesley (1708—1788).

69   *Calmness from God.*

1 Calm me, my God, and keep me calm;
   Let Thy outstretched wing,
Be like the shade of Elim's palm,
   Beside her desert spring.

2 Yes, keep me calm, though loud and rude
   The sounds my ear that greet;

Calm in the closet's solitude;
   Calm in the busy street.

3 Calm in the hour of buoyant health,
   And in the hour of pain,
Calm in my poverty or wealth,
   And in my loss or gain.

4 Calm in the sufferance of wrong,
   Like Him who bore my shame;
Calm 'mid the threatening, taunting throng,
   Who hate Thy holy name.

5 Calm me, my God, and keep me calm,
   Soft resting on Thy breast;
Soothe me with holy hymn and psalm,
   And bid my spirit rest.
         Rev. Horatius Bonar (1808—1890).

70   *The Debt of Love.*

1 All that I was, my sin, my guilt,
   My death was all my own;
All that I am I owe to Thee,
   My gracious God alone.

2 The darkness of my former state,
   The bondage, all was mine;
The light of life in which I walk,
   The liberty, is Thine.

3 Thy grace first made me feel my sin,
   It taught me to believe;
Then in believing, peace I found,
   And now I live, I live.

4 All that I am, e'en here on earth,
   All that I hope to be,
When Jesus comes, and glory dawns,
   I owe it, Lord, to Thee.
         Rev. Horatius Bonar (1808—1890).

HYMNS OF DEVOTION.

PETERBORO'. C. M. Rev. R. HARRISON (1748—1810).

1. How oft, alas! this wretched heart Has wandered from the Lord! How oft my roving thoughts depart, Forgetful of His word!

71 *Backslider Returning.*
1 How oft, alas! this wretched heart
Has wandered from the Lord!
How oft my roving thoughts depart,
Forgetful of His word!

2 Yet sovereign mercy calls, "Return;"
Dear Lord, and may I come?
My vile ingratitude I mourn;
O! take the wanderer home.

3 And canst Thou, wilt Thou, yet forgive,
And bid my crimes remove?
And shall a pardoned rebel live
To speak Thy wondrous love?

4 Almighty grace, Thy healing power,
How glorious, how divine!
That can to life and bliss restore
So vile a heart as mine.

5 Thy pardoning love, so free, so sweet,
Dear Saviour, I adore;
O! keep me at Thy sacred feet,
And let me rove no more.
Miss Anne Steele (1717—1778).

72 *Longing for Christ.*
1 O could I find, from day to day,
A nearness to my God;
Then should my hours glide sweet away,
And live upon Thy Word.

2 Lord, I desire with Thee to live,
Anew from day to day,
In joys the world can never give,
Nor ever take away.

3 O Jesus, come and rule my heart,
And I'll be wholly Thine;
And never, never more depart,
For Thou art wholly mine.
Benjamin Cleveland, 1790.

73 *Repentance at the Cross.*
1 Alas! and did my Saviour bleed,
And did my Sovereign die?
Would He devote that sacred head
For such a worm as I?

2 Thy body slain, dear Jesus, Thine,
And bathed in its own blood,
While all exposed to wrath divine,
The glorious Sufferer stood.

3 Was it for crimes that I had done,
He groaned upon the tree?
Amazing pity! grace unknown!
And love beyond degree!

4 Well might the sun in darkness hide,
And shut his glories in,
When Christ the great Creator died,
For man, the creature's sin.

5 Thus might I hide my blushing face,
While His dear cross appears;
Dissolve my heart in thankfulness,
And melt my eyes to tears.

6 But drops of grief can ne'er repay
The debt of love I owe:
Here, Lord, I give myself away;
'T is all that I can do.
Rev. Isaac Watts (1674—1748).

HYMNS OF DEVOTION.

ST. JOHN'S. C. M.   A. WILLIAMS' COLLECTION, 1770.

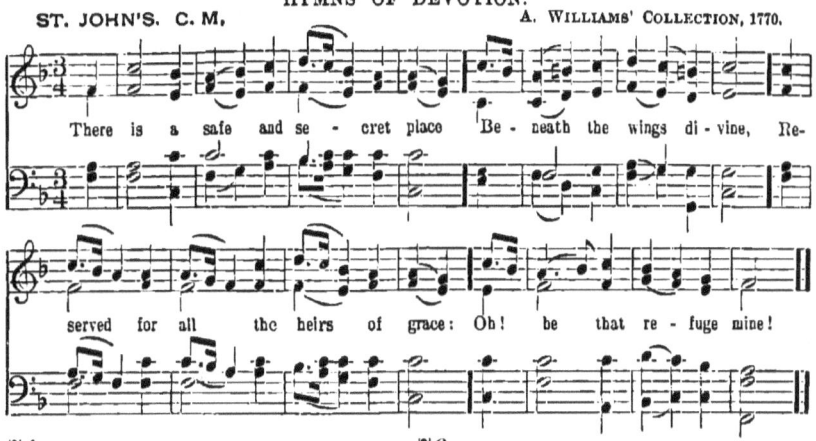

There is a safe and se-cret place Be-neath the wings di-vine, Re-served for all the heirs of grace: Oh! be that re-fuge mine!

74   *Blessedness of the Righteous.*

1 There is a safe and secret place
Beneath the wings divine,
Reserved for all the heirs of grace;
Oh, be that refuge mine!

2 The least and feeblest there may bide
Uninjured and unawed;
While thousands fall on every side,
He rests secure in God.

3 He feeds in pastures large and fair,
Of love and truth divine;
O child of God, O glory's heir,
How rich a lot is thine!

4 A hand almighty to defend,
An ear for every call,
An honored life, a peaceful end,
And heaven to crown it all.
Rev. H. F. Lyte, (1793 — 1847).

75   *Christian Confidence and Gratitude.*

1 How can I sink with such a prop
As my eternal God,
Who bears the earth's huge pillars up,
And spreads the heavens abroad?

2 How can I die while Jesus lives,
Who rose and left the dead?
Pardon and grace my soul receives
From my exalted Head.

3 All that I am, and all I have,
Shall be for ever Thine;
Whate'er my duty bids me give,
My cheerful hands resign.
Rev. Isaac Watts (1674 — 1748).

76   *Impart Thyself to Me.*

1 O Lord, impart Thyself to me,
No other good I need;
When Thou, the Son, shalt make me free
I shall be free indeed.

2 I cannot rest till in Thy blood
I full redemption have;
But Thou, through whom I come to God
Canst to the utmost save.

3 From sin, the guilt, the power, the pain,
Thou wilt redeem my soul:
Lord, I believe, and not in vain;
My faith shall make me whole.

4 I too, with Thee, shall walk in white;
With all Thy saints shall prove
The length, and depth, and breadth, and height
Of everlasting love.
Rev. Charles Wesley. (1708 — 1788).

77   *Suffered for Sin.*

1 Oh, if my soul were formed for woe,
How would I vent my sighs!
Repentance should like rivers flow
From both my streaming eyes.

2 'Twas for my sins my dearest Lord
Hung on the cursed tree,
And groaned away a dying life
For thee, my soul! for thee.

3 Oh, how I hate these lusts of mine
That crucified my Lord;
Those sins that pierced and nailed his flesh
Fast to the fatal wood!
Rev. Isaac Watts (1674 — 1748).

HYMNS OF DEVOTION.

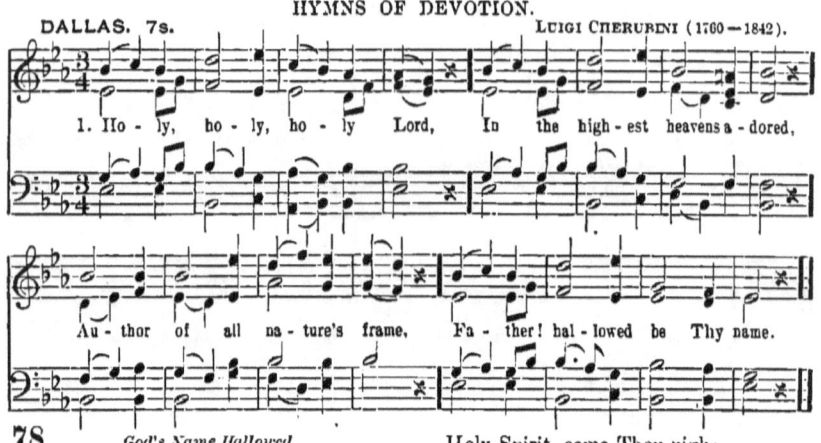

DALLAS. 7s.   LUIGI CHERUBINI (1760—1842).

1. Ho-ly, ho-ly, ho-ly Lord, In the high-est heavens a-dored,
Au-thor of all na-ture's frame, Fa-ther! hal-lowed be Thy name.

78   *God's Name Hallowed.*

1 Holy, holy, holy Lord,
In the highest heavens adored,
Author of all nature's frame,
Father! hallowed be Thy name.

2 Though estranged from Thee in heart,
Doubtless Thou our Father art,
From Thy hand our spirits came;
Father! hallowed be Thy name.

3 Nor by nature's tie alone
Thou art as our Father known;
Nearer now in Christ our claim,
Father! hallowed be Thy name.

4 Born anew, oh, may we feel
Filial love, the Spirit's seal,
Cleansed from guilt, redeemed from shame;
Father! hallowed be Thy name.
          Rev. James Montgomery, (1771—1854).

79   *The Incarnation.*

1 God with us! O glorious name!
Let it shine in endless fame,
God and man in Christ unite;
O mysterious depth and height!

2 God with us! the eternal Son
Took our soul, our flesh, and bone;
Now, ye saints, His grace admire,
Swell the song with holy fire.

3 God with us! O wondrous grace!
Let us see Him face to face;
That we may Immanuel sing,
As we ought, our God and King.
          Miss Sarah Slinn, 1779.

80   *The Trinity.*

1 Holy Father, hear our cry,
Holy Saviour, bend Thine ear,
Holy Spirit, come Thou nigh;
Father, Saviour, Spirit, hear.

2 Father, save us from our sin,
Saviour, we Thy mercy crave,
Gracious Spirit, make us clean;
Father, Son and Spirit, save.

3 Father, let us taste Thy love,
Saviour, fill our souls with peace,
Spirit, come our hearts to move;
Father, Son, and Spirit, bless.

4 Father, Son, and Spirit, Thou
One Jehovah, shed abroad
All Thy grace within us now;
Be our Father and our God.
          Rev. H. Bonar (1808—1890).

81   *The Eternal Shepherd.*

1 To Thy pastures fair and large,
Heavenly Shepherd, lead Thy charge,
And my couch, with tenderest care,
Mid the springing grass prepare.

2 When I faint with summer's heat
Thou shalt guide my weary feet
To the streams that, still and slow,
Through the verdant meadows flow.

3 Safe the dreary vale I tread,
By the shades of death o'erspread,
With Thy rod and staff supplied,
This my guard, and that my guide.

4 Constant to my latest end,
Thou my footsteps shalt attend;
And shalt bid Thy hallowed dome
Yield me an eternal home.
          Rev. James Merrick (1720—1769).

HYMNS OF DEVOTION.

AURELIA. 7s & 6s, D. S. S. WESLEY (1810—1876).

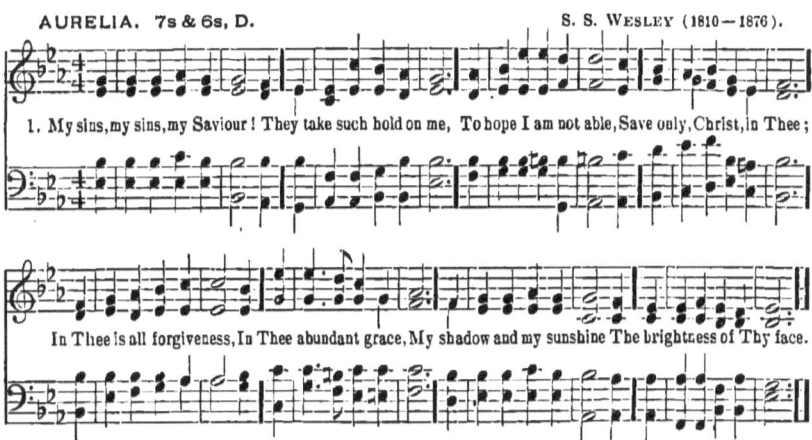

1. My sins, my sins, my Saviour! They take such hold on me, To hope I am not able, Save only, Christ, in Thee; In Thee is all forgiveness, In Thee abundant grace, My shadow and my sunshine The brightness of Thy face.

82   *My Sins, my Saviour.*

1 My sins, my sins, my Saviour!
  They take such hold on me,
To hope I am not able,
  Save only Christ, in Thee;
In Thee is all forgiveness,
  In Thee abundant grace,
My shadow and my sunshine
  The brightness of Thy face.

2 My sins, my sins, my Saviour!
  How sad on Thee they fall!
Seen through Thy gentle patience,
  I tenfold feel them all.
I know they are forgiven,
  But still, their pain to me
Is all the grief and anguish
  They laid, my Lord, on Thee.

3 My sins, my sins, my Saviour!
  Their guilt I never knew
Till, with Thee, in the desert
  I near Thy passion drew;
Till, with Thee, in the garden
  I heard Thy pleading prayer,
And saw the sweat-drops bloody
  That told Thy sorrow there.

4 Therefore my songs, my Saviour,
  E'en in this time of woe,
Shall tell of all Thy goodness
  To suffering man below.
Thy goodness and Thy favor,
  Whose presence from above,

Rejoice those hearts, my Saviour,
  That live in Thee and love.
    Rev. J. B. S. Monsell (1811—1875).

83   *At the Door.*

1 O Jesus, Thou art standing,
  Outside the fast-closed door,
In lowly patience waiting
  To pass the threshold o'er;
We bear the name of Christians,
  His name and sign we bear;
Oh, shame, thrice shame upon us!
  To keep Him standing there.

2 O Jesus, Thou art knocking;
  And lo! that hand is scarred,
And thorns Thy brow encircle,
  And tears Thy face have marred;
Oh, love that passeth knowledge,
  So patiently to wait!
Oh, sin that hath no equal,
  So fast to bar the gate!

3 O Jesus, Thou art pleading
  In accents meek and low,—
"I died for you, my children,
  And will ye treat me so?"
O Lord, with shame and sorrow
  We open now the door;
Dear Saviour, enter, enter,
  And leave us nevermore.
    Bp. W. W. How (1823—).

HYMNS OF DEVOTION.

VOX DILECTI. C. M. D.   Rev. J. B. DYKES (1823—1876).

84   *I heard the voice of Jesus.*

1 I heard the voice of Jesus say,—
  "Come unto Me and rest;
Lay down, thou weary one, lay down
  Thy head upon my breast!"
I came to Jesus as I was,
  Weary, and worn, and sad;
I found in Him a resting-place,
  And He hath made me glad.

2 I heard the voice of Jesus say,—
  "Behold, I freely give
The living water; thirsty one,
  Stoop down, and drink, and live!"

I came to Jesus, and I drank
  Of that life-giving stream;
My thirst was quench'd, my soul revived,
  And now I live in Him.

3 I heard the voice of Jesus say,—
  "I am this dark world's light;
Look unto Me, thy morn shall rise,
  And all thy day be bright!"
I looked to Jesus, and I found
  In Him my Star, my Sun;
And in that light of life I'll walk,
  Till travelling days are done.

    Rev. Horatius Bonar (1808—1890).

ATHENS. C. M. D.   FELICE GIARDINI, (1716—1796).

(34)

HYMNS OF DEVOTION.

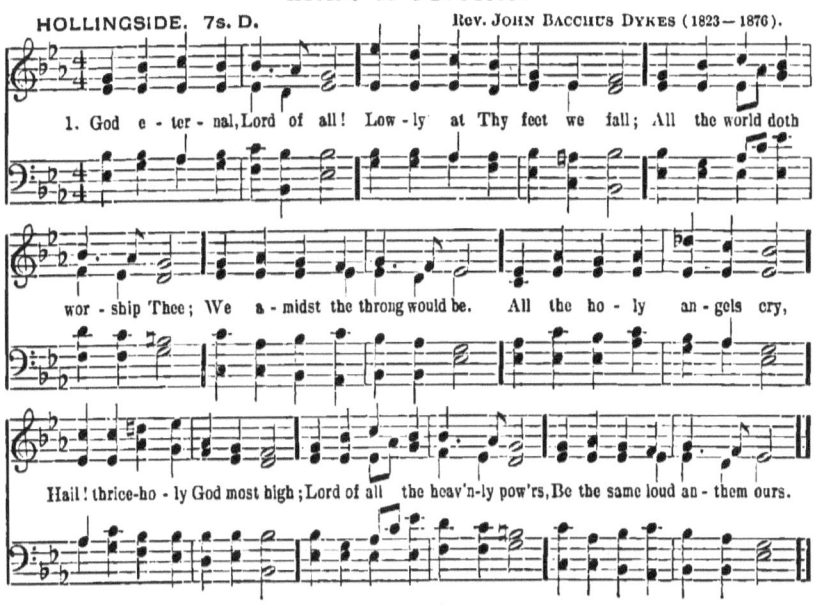

HOLLINGSIDE. 7s. D.   Rev. John Bacchus Dykes (1823—1876).

1. God e-ter-nal, Lord of all! Low-ly at Thy feet we fall; All the world doth wor-ship Thee; We a-midst the throng would be. All the ho-ly an-gels cry, Hail! thrice-ho-ly God most high; Lord of all the heav'n-ly pow'rs, Be the same loud an-them ours.

85   *Te Deum.*

1 God eternal, Lord of all,
Lowly at Thy feet we fall;
All the rest doth worship Thee;
We amidst the throng would be.
All the holy angels cry,
Hail thrice-holy God most high?
Lord of all the heavenly powers,
Be the same loud anthem ours.

2 Glorified apostles raise,
Night and day continual praise;
Hast thou not a mission too
For the children here to do?
With the prophet's goodly line
We in mystic bound combine;
For Thou hast to babes revealed
Things that to the wise were sealed.

3 Martyrs, in a noble host,
Of Thy cross are heard to boast;
Since so bright the crown they wear,
We with them Thy cross would bear.
All Thy church, in heaven and earth,
Jesus hail Thy spotless birth; —
Seated on the judgment-throne,
Number us among Thine own.

Tr., Rev. J. E. Millard, D. D.

86   *Lead Me.*

1 Jesus, merciful and mild,
Lead me as a helpless child;
On no other arm but Thine
Would my weary soul recline;
Thou art ready to forgive,
Thou canst bid the sinner live —
Guide the wanderer day by day,
In the strait and narrow way.

2 Thou canst fit me by Thy grace
For the heavenly dwelling place;
All Thy promises are sure,
Ever shall Thy love endure;
Then what more could I desire,
How to greater bliss aspire?
All I need, in Thee I see,
Thou art all in all to me.

3 Jesus, Saviour all divine,
Hast Thou made me truly Thine?
Hast Thou bought me by Thy blood?
Reconciled my heart to God?
Hearken to my tender prayer,
Let me Thine own image bear;
Let me love Thee more and more,
Till I reach heaven's blissful shore.

Dr. Thos. Hastings (1784—1872).

HYMNS OF DEVOTION.

IONA. L. M.   Rev. R. P. KERR, D. D., 1891.

1. With tearful eyes I look a-round, Life seems a dark and storm-y sea; Yet mid the gloom I hear a sound, A heaven-ly whis-per, "Come to me."

Copyright, 1891, by R. P. Kerr.

87   *Come to Me!*

1 With tearful eyes I look around,
   Life seems a dark and stormy sea;
Yet mid the gloom I hear a sound,
   A heavenly whisper, "Come to Me!"

2 It tells me of a place of rest,
   It tells me where my soul may flee;
Oh, to the weary, faint, opprest,
   How sweet the bidding, "Come to Me"!

3 When the poor heart with anguish learns
   That earthly props resigned must be,
And from each broken cistern turns,
   It hears the accents, "Come to Me!"

4 O voice of mercy, voice of love,
   In conflict, grief and agony,
Support me, cheer me from above,
   And gently whisper, "Come to Me!"

5 I Come; all else must fail and die;
   Earth has no resting-place for me;
To Christ I lift my weeping eye;
   Thou art my hope; I come to Thee.
             Miss Charlotte Elliott (1789—1871).

88   *O Thou, to whose All-searching Sight.*

1 O Thou, to whose all-searching sight,
   The darkness shineth as the light,
Search, prove my heart, it pants for Thee;
   Oh, burst these bonds, and set it free.

2 Wash out its stains, refine its dross;
   Nail my affections to the cross;
Hallow each thought; Let all within
   Be clean, as Thou, my Lord, art clean.

3 If in this darksome wild I stray,
   Be Thou my light, be Thou my way;
No foes, no violence I fear,
   No fraud, while Thou, my God, art near.

4 When rising floods my soul o'erflow;
   When sinks my heart in waves of woe,
Jesus Thy timely aid impart,
   And raise my head, and cheer my heart.

5 Saviour, where'er Thy steps I see,
   Dauntless, untired, I follow Thee;
Oh, let Thy hand support me still,
   And lead me to Thy holy hill.
        Gerhard Tersteegen (1697—1769).
   Tr. by Rev. John Wesley (1703—1791).

89   *Longing for Communion with Christ.*

1 Oh, that I could forever dwell
   With Mary at my Saviour's feet,
And view the form I love so well
   And all His tender words repeat.

2 The world shut out from all my soul,
   And heaven brought in with all its bliss;
Oh, is there aught, from pole to pole,
   One moment to compare with this?

3 This is the hidden life I prize,
   A life of penitential love,
When most my follies I despise,
   And raise the highest thoughts above.

4 Thus would I live till nature fail,
   And all my former sins forsake;
Then rise to God within the vail,
   And of eternal joys partake.
        Rev. Andrew Reed (1787—1862).

HYMNS OF DEVOTION.

THEODORA. 7s. From GEORGE FREDERICK HANDEL (1685 — 1759).

1. Take my life, and let it be Con-se-crat-ed, Lord, to Thee. Take my hands, and let them move At the im-pulse of Thy love.

90   *All for Jesus.*

1 Take my life, and let it be
Consecrated, Lord, to Thee;
Take my hands, and let them move
At the impulse of Thy love.

2 Take my feet, and let them be
Swift and beautiful for Thee;
Take my voice, and let me sing
Always, only, for my King.

3 Take my lips, and let them be
Filled with messages from Thee;
Take my silver and my gold;
Not a mite would I withold.

4 Take my love; my Lord, I pour
At Thy feet its treasure-store;
Take myself, and I will be,
Ever, only, all, for Thee.
Miss F. R. Havergal (1836—1879).

MENDEBRAS. 7s & 6s. GERMAN MELODY. Arr. by LOWELL MASON (1792 — 1872).

1. { Our yet un-finished sto-ry Is tending all to this : } Our plans may be dis-jointed,
   { To God the greatest glo-ry, To us the great-est bliss. }

But we may calm-ly rest; What God has once ap-point-ed, Is bet-ter than our best.

91   *God's Way Best.*

1 Our yet unfinished story
Is tending all to this:
To God the greatest glory,
To us the greatest bliss.
Our plans may be disjointed,
But we may calmly rest;
What God has once appointed
Is better than our best.

2 We cannot see before us,
But our all-seeing Friend
Is always watching o'er us,
And knows the very end;

And when amid our blindness
His disappointments fall,
We trust His loving-kindness
Whose wisdom sends them all.

3 They are the purple fringes
That hide His glorious feet;
They are the fire-wrought hinges
Where truth and mercy meet;
By them the golden portal
Of Providence shall ope,
And lift to praise immortal
The songs of faith and hope.
Miss Frances Ridley Havergal. (1836—1879).

(37)

HYMNS OF DEVOTION.

ENTREATY. 6s, & 5s, D.   E. G. MONK.

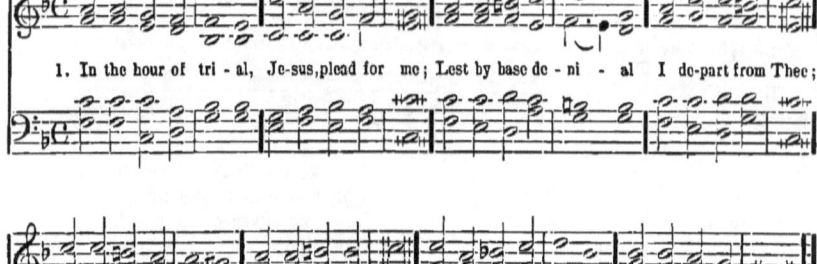

92

In the Hour of Trial.

1 In the hour of trial,
  Jesus, plead for me;
Lest by base denial
  I depart from Thee;
When Thou see'st me waver,
  With a look recall,
    Nor for fear or favor
  Suffer me to fall.

2 With forbidden pleasures
  Would this vain world charm;
Or its sordid treasures
  Spread to work me harm;
Bring to my remembrance
  Sad Gethsemane,
Or, in darker semblance,
  Cross-crown'd Calvary.

3 Should Thy mercy send me
  Sorrow, toil, and woe;
Or should pain attend me
  On my path below;
Grant that I may never
  Fail Thy hand to see;
Grant that I may ever
  Cast my care on Thee.

4 When my last hour cometh,
  Fraught with strife and pain,
When my dust returneth
  To the dust again;
On Thy truth relying,
  Through that mortal strife,
Jesus, take me, dying,
  To eternal life.

Rev. James Montgomery (1771 — 1854).

93

2 *Cor.* xii: 9. (TUNE VIRGO.)

1 Let me but hear my Saviour say,
"Strength shall be equal to thy day;"
Then I rejoice in deep distress,
Leaning on all-sufficient grace.

2 I can do all things — or can bear
All suffering, if my Lord be there;
Sweet pleasures mingle with the pains,
While He my sinking head sustains.

3 I glory in infirmity,
That Christ's own power may rest on me;
When I am weak, then am I strong;
Grace is my shield, and Christ my song.

Rev. Isaac Watts (1674 — 1748).

HYMNS OF DEVOTION.

VIRGO. L. M. JOHN PIETRONI.

94 *I am Thine.*
1 Lord, I am Thine, entirely Thine,
Purchased and saved by blood divine;
With full consent Thine I would be;
And own Thy sovereign right in me.

2 Grant one poor sinner more a place
Among the children of Thy grace;
A wretched sinner, lost to God,
But ransomed by Immanuel's blood.

3 Thine would I live, Thine would I die,
Be Thine through all eternity;
The vow is past beyond repeal;
Now will I set the solemn seal.

4 Here, at that cross where flows the blood
That bought my guilty soul for God,
Thee my new Master now I call,
And consecrate to Thee my all.
Rev. Samuel Davies (1724—1761).

PILOT. 7s. 6l. J. E. GOULD.

95 *Saviour, Pilot Me.*
1 Jesus, Saviour, pilot me
Over life's tempestuous sea;
Unknown waves before me roll,
Hiding rock and treacherous shoal;
Chart and compass come from Thee;
Jesus, Saviour, pilot me.

2 As a mother stills her child,
Thou canst hush the ocean wild;
Boisterous waves obey Thy will,
When Thou sayst to them "Be still!"
Wondrous Sovereign of the sea,
Jesus, Saviour, pilot me.

3 When at last I near the shore,
And the fearful breakers roar
'Twixt me and the peaceful rest,
Then, while leaning on Thy breast,
May I hear Thee say to me,
"Fear not, I will pilot thee!"
Rev. Edward Hopper (1818—).

HYMNS OF DEVOTION.

DUNDEE. C.M.   G. FRANC, Genevan Psalter, 1545.

1. Great God! how in-fi-nite art Thou! What worthless worms are we! Let the whole race of creatures bow, And pay their praise to Thee.

96   *Infinity of God.*

1 Great God! how infinite art Thou!
 What worthless worms are we!
Let the whole race of creatures bow,
 And pay their praise to Thee.

2 Thy throne eternal ages stood,
 Ere seas or stars were made;
Thou art the ever living God,
 Were all the nations dead.

3 Eternity, with all its years,
 Stands present in Thy view;
To Thee, there's nothing old appears;
 Great God, there's nothing new.

4 Our lives through various scenes are drawn,
 And vexed with trifling cares,
While Thine eternal thought moves on
 Thine undisturbed affairs.

5 Great God! how infinite art Thou!
 What worthless worms are we!
Let the whole race of creatures bow,
 And pay their praise to Thee.
                     Rev. Isaac Watts (1674—1748).

97   *The Divine Perfections.*

1 How shall I praise the eternal God,
 That Infinite Unknown?
Who can ascend His high abode,
 Or venture near His throne?

2 Those watchful eyes, that never sleep,
 Survey the world around;
His wisdom is a boundless deep
 Where all our thoughts are drowned.

3 He knows no shadow of a change,
 Nor alters His decrees;
Firm as a rock His truth remains,
 To guard His promises.
                     Rev. Isaac Watts (1674—1748).

98   *God our Help and Security.*

1 O God, our help in ages past,
 Our hope for years to come;
Our shelter from the stormy blast,
 And our eternal home;

2 Before the hills in order stood,
 Or earth received her frame,
From everlasting Thou art God,
 To endless years the same.

3 A thousand ages, in Thy sight,
 Are like the evening gone;
Short as the watch that ends the night,
 Before the rising sun.

4 Time, like an ever-rolling stream,
 Bears all its sons away;
They fly, forgotten, as a dream
 Dies at the opening day.

5 O God, our help in ages past,
 Our hope for years to come,
Be Thou our guard while troubles last,
 And our eternal home.
                     Rev. Isaac Watts (1674—1748).

99   *Mysteries of Providence.*

1 God moves in a mysterious way,
 His wonders to perform;
He plants His footsteps in the sea,
 And rides upon the storm.

2 Deep in unfathomable mines
 Of never failing skill,
He treasures up His bright designs,
 And works His sovereign will.

3 Ye fearful saints, fresh courage take;
 The clouds ye so much dread
Are big with mercy, and shall break
 In blessings on your head.

4 His purposes will ripen fast,
 Unfolding every hour;
The bud may have a bitter taste,
 But sweet will be the flower.
                     Wm. Cowper (1731—1800).

HYMNS OF DEVOTION.

BROCKWAY. C. M.   L. O. EMERSON.

Through all the chang-ing scenes of life, In trou-ble and in joy, The prais-es of my God shall still My heart and tongue em-ploy.

By permission of Oliver Ditson Company, owners of copyright.

100 *Through all the Changing Scenes of Life.*

1 Through all the changing scenes of life,
  In trouble and in joy,
The praises of my God shall still
  My heart and tongue employ.

2 My soul shall make her boast in Him,
  And celebrate His fame;
Come magnify the Lord with me,
  With me exalt His name.

3 The hosts of God encamp around
  The dwellings of the just;
Deliverance He affords to all
  Who on His succour trust.

4 O! make but trial of His love;
  Experience will decide
How blest are they, and only they,
  Who in His truth confide.

5 Fear Him, ye saints; and you will then
  Have nothing else to fear;
Come, make His service your delight;
  He'll make your wants His care.
  Tate and Brady, 1696.

101 *Submission Under Various Ills of Life.*

1 Through all the downward tracts of time,
  God's watchful eye surveys;
O! who so wise to choose our lot,
  And regulate our ways?

2 I cannot doubt His bounteous love,
  Unmeasurably kind;
To His unerring, gracious will,
  Be every wish resigned.

3 Good when He gives, supremely good,
  Nor less, when He denies;
E'en crosses, from His sovereign hand,
  Are blessings in disguise.
  Anon.

102 *At Eve it Shall be Light.*

1 We journey through a vale of tears,
  By many a cloud o'er cast;
And worldly cares and worldly fears
  Go with us to the last.

2 Not to the last: God's word hath said,—
  Could we but read aright,—
Poor pilgrim, lift in hope Thy head,
  At eve it shall be light.

3 When tempest clouds are dark on high,
  His bow of love and peace
Shines sweetly on the vaulted sky,
  A pledge that storms shall cease.

4 Hold on thy way, with hope unchilled,
  By faith and not by sight,
And Thou shalt own His word fulfilled;
  At eve it shall be light.
  Bernard Barton (1784—1849).

103 *The Mercy Seat.*

1 There is a heavenly mercy seat,
  To calm the sinner's fears;
There is a Saviour, at whose feet
  The mourner dries his tears.

2 When friends depart, and hopes are riven,
  And gathering storms I see,
My soul is but the sooner driven,
  Eternal Rock, to Thee.
  Anon.

(41)

HYMNS OF DEVOTION.

GREEN ISLAND. S. M.   Rev. R. P. KERR, 1889.

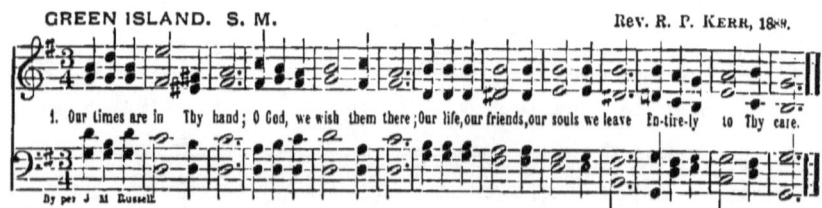

104   *Sovereignty of God.*
1 Our times are in Thy hand;
    O God, we wish them there;
    Our life, our friends, our souls we leave
    Entirely to Thy care.

2 Our times are in Thy hand,
    Whatever they may be,
    Pleasing or painful, dark or bright,
    As best may seem to Thee.

3 Our times are in Thy hand,
    Why should we doubt or fear?
    A father's hand will never cause
    His child a needless tear.

4 Our times are in Thy hand,
    Jesus, the crucified;
    The hand our many sins have pierced
    Is now our guard and guide.
       Rev. H. Bonar (1808—1890).

ADRIAN. S. M.   JOHN EDGAR GOULD (1822—1875).

105   *Value of Present Time.*
1 To-morrow, Lord, is Thine,
    Lodged in Thy sovereign hand;
    And if its sun arise and shine,
    It shines by Thy command.

2 The present moment flies,
    And bears our life away;
    Oh, make Thy servants truly wise,
    That they may live to-day.

3 Since on this winged hour
    Eternity is hung,

Waken by Thy Almighty power
    The aged and the young.

4 One thing demands our care;
    Oh, be it still pursued,
    Lest, slighted once, the season fair
    Should never be renewed.

5 To Jesus, may we fly,
    Swift as the morning light,
    Lest life's young golden beam should die
    In sudden endless night.
       Rev. Philip Doddridge (1702—1751).

HYMNS OF DEVOTION.

OLNEY. S. M.   L. MASON (1792—1872).

1. The Lord my Shep-herd is, I shall be well sup-plied;
Since He is mine, And I am His, What can I want be-side!

106   *Psalm 23.*
1 The Lord my Shepherd is,
   I shall be well supplied;
Since He is mine, and I am His,
   What can I want beside?

2 He leads me to the place
   Where heavenly pasture grows,
Where living waters gently pass,
   And full salvation flows.

3 If e'er I go astray,
   He doth my soul reclaim,
And guides me in His own right way,
   For His most holy name.

4 While He affords His aid,
   I cannot yield to fear;
Tho' I should walk thro' death's dark shade
   My Shepherd's with me there.

5 Amid surrounding foes
   Thou dost my table spread;
My cup with blessings overflows,
   And joy exalts my head.

6 The bounties of Thy love
   Shall crown my following days;
Nor from Thy house will I remove,
   Nor cease to speak Thy praise.
        Rev. Isaac Watts (1674—1748).

107   *The Mourner Comforted.*
1 Your harps, ye trembling saints,
   Down from the willows take;
Loud to the praise of love divine,
   Bid every string awake.

2 Though in a foreign land,
   We are not far from home,
And nearer to our house above,
   We every moment come.

3 His grace will, to the end,
   Stronger and brighter shine;
Nor present things, nor things to come,
   Shall quench the love divine.

4 When we in darkness walk,
   Nor feel the heavenly flame;
Then is the time to trust our God,
   And rest upon His name.

5 Soon shall our doubts and fears
   Subside at His control;
His loving-kindness shall break through
   The midnight of the soul.

6 Blest is the man, O God,
   That stays himself on Thee;
Who waits for Thy salvation, Lord,
   Shall Thy salvation see.
        Rev. A. M. Toplady (1740—1778).

108   *Doxology.*
Give to the Father praise,
   Give glory to the Son,
And to the Spirit of His grace
   Be equal honors done.

HYMNS OF DEVOTION.

PROTECTION. 11s.   **AMERICAN.**

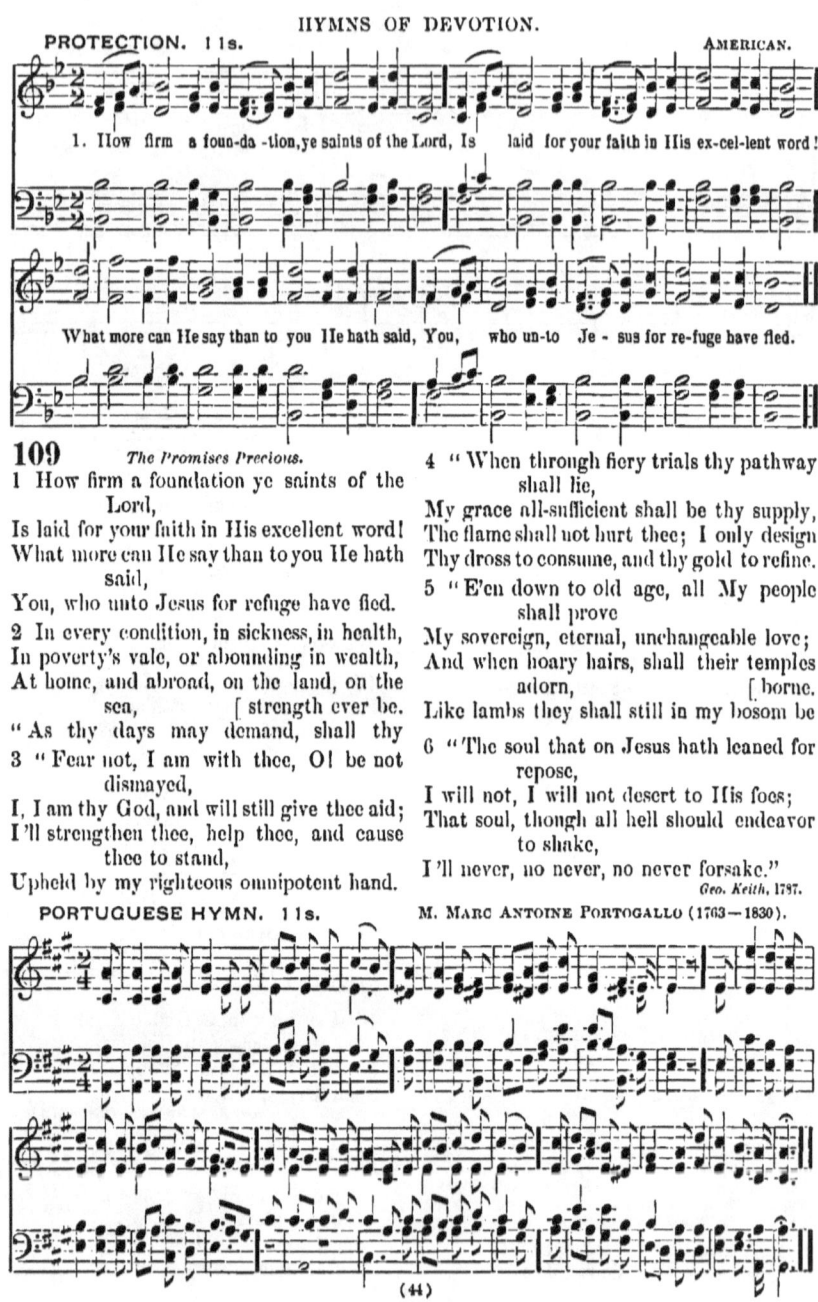

1. How firm a foun-da-tion, ye saints of the Lord, Is laid for your faith in His ex-cel-lent word! What more can He say than to you He hath said, You, who un-to Je-sus for re-fuge have fled.

109   *The Promises Precious.*

1 How firm a foundation ye saints of the Lord,
Is laid for your faith in His excellent word!
What more can He say than to you He hath said,
You, who unto Jesus for refuge have fled.

2 In every condition, in sickness, in health,
In poverty's vale, or abounding in wealth,
At home, and abroad, on the land, on the sea, [strength ever be.
"As thy days may demand, shall thy

3 "Fear not, I am with thee, O! be not dismayed,
I, I am thy God, and will still give thee aid;
I'll strengthen thee, help thee, and cause thee to stand,
Upheld by my righteous omnipotent hand.

4 "When through fiery trials thy pathway shall lie,
My grace all-sufficient shall be thy supply,
The flame shall not hurt thee; I only design
Thy dross to consume, and thy gold to refine.

5 "E'en down to old age, all My people shall prove
My sovereign, eternal, unchangeable love;
And when hoary hairs, shall their temples adorn, [borne.
Like lambs they shall still in my bosom be

6 "The soul that on Jesus hath leaned for repose,
I will not, I will not desert to His foes;
That soul, though all hell should endeavor to shake,
I'll never, no never, no never forsake."
Geo. Keith, 1787.

PORTUGUESE HYMN. 11s.   M. MARC ANTOINE PORTOGALLO (1763—1830).

HYMNS OF DEVOTION.

MERRILL. 7s.   Rev. ROBERT P. KERR, 1891.

1. Sov'r-eign Rul-er of the skies, Ev-er gra-cious ev-er wise, All my times are in Thy hand, All e-vents at Thy com-mand.

Copyright, 1891, by R. P. Kerr.

110   *God's Sovereignty.*
1 Sovereign Ruler of the skies,
Ever gracious, ever wise,
All my times are in Thy hand,
All events at Thy command.

2 Times of sickness, times of health;
Times of penury and wealth;
Times of trial and of grief;
Times of triumph and relief.

3 Times the tempter's power to prove;
Times to taste a Saviour's love;
All must come, and last, and end,
As shall please my heavenly Friend.

4 Thee at all times will I bless;
Having Thee, I all possess;
How can I bereavèd be,
Since I cannot part with Thee.
                         John Ryland, 1777.

111   *Support in Trial.*
1 Oft in danger, oft in woe,
Onward Christians, onward go;
Bear the toil, maintain the strife,
Strengthened with the Bread of Life.

2 Let not sorrow dim your eye,
Soon shall every tear be dry;
Let not fear your course impede,
Great your strength, if great your need.

3 Let your drooping hearts be glad;
March in heavenly armor clad;
Fight, nor think the battle long;
Soon shall victory wake your song.

4 Onward, then, to glory move,
More than conquerors ye shall prove;
Though opposed by many a foe,
Christian soldiers, onward go.
                         H. K. White, (—1806).

112   *Jesus, Jesus, visit me.*
1 Jesus, Jesus, visit me,
How my soul longs after Thee!
When, my best, my dearest Friend,
Shall our separation end?

2 Lord, my longings never cease;
Without Thee I find no peace;
'T is my constant cry to Thee,
Jesus, Jesus, visit me.

3 Come inhabit then my heart,
Purge its sin and heal its smart.
See, I ever cry to Thee,
Jesus, Jesus, visit me.

4 Patiently I wait Thy day;
For this gift alone I pray,
That when death shall visit me,
Thou my Light and Life shall be.
       Angelus, (—1677), Tr. by Rev. R. P. Dunn.

113   *Christ Forever.*
1 Thine forever! God of love,
Hear us from Thy throne above!
Thine forever may we be,
Here and in eternity!

2 Thine for ever! oh, how blest
They who find in Thee their rest!
Saviour, Guardian, Heavenly Friend,
Oh! defend us to the end.

3 Thine for ever! Saviour keep,
These, Thy frail and trembling sheep:
Safe alone beneath Thy care,
Let us all Thy goodness share.

4 Thine for ever! Thou our Guide,
All our wants by Thee supplied,
All our sins by Thee forgiven,
Lead us, Lord, from earth to heaven.
                         Mrs. M. F. Maude, 1848.

HYMNS OF DEVOTION.

GRATITUDE. L. M.   Rev. T. Hastings. Arr. (1784—1872).

1. My God, how end-less is Thy love! Thy gifts are ev-'ry ev'n-ing new;
And morn-ing mer-cies from a-bove, Gen-tly dis-till like ear-ly dew.

114   *Gratitude.*

1 My God, how endless is Thy love!
  Thy gifts are every evening new;
And morning mercies from above,
  Gently distil like early dew.

2 Thou spread'st the curtains of the night,
  Great guardian of my sleeping hours;
Thy sovereign word restores the light,
  And quickens all my drowsy powers.

3 I yield my powers to Thy command;
  To Thee I consecrate my days;
Perpetual blessings from Thine hand
  Demand perpetual songs of praise.
        Rev. Isaac Watts (1674—1748).

115   *Show Pity, Lord.* Psalm 51.

1 Show pity, Lord; O Lord, forgive;
Let a repenting rebel live;

Are not Thy mercies large and free?
May not a sinner trust in Thee?

2 Oh! wash my soul from every sin,
And make my guilty conscience clean;
Here on my heart the burden lies,
And past offences pain mine eyes.

3 My lips with shame my sins confess,
Against Thy law, against Thy grace;
Lord, should Thy judgments grow severe,
I am condemned, but Thou art clear.

4 Yet save a trembling sinner, Lord,
Whose hope, still hovering round Thy word,
Would light on some sweet promise there,
Some sure support against despair.
        Rev. Isaac Watts (1674—1748).

ERNAN. L. M.   Dr. L. Mason (1792—1872).

1. Come, sacred Spirit, from a-bove, And fill the coldest heart with love, Soften to flesh the flinty stone, And let Thy Godlike power be known.

116   *Prayer for Reviving Influences.*

1 Come, sacred Spirit, from above,
And fill the coldest heart with love;
Soften to flesh the flinty stone,
And let Thy Godlike power be known.

2 Speak Thou, and from the haughtiest eyes
Shall floods of pious sorrow rise;
While all their glowing souls are borne,
To seek that grace which now they scorn.

3 O let a holy flock await,
Numerous, around Thy temple gate;
Each pressing on, with zeal, to be
A living sacrifice to Thee.

4 In answer to our fervent cries,
Give us to see Thy church arise;
Or, if that blessing seems too great,
Give us to mourn its low estate.
        Rev. P. Doddridge (1702—1751).

HYMNS OF DEVOTION.

117 *Prayer for Faith.*
1 Oh, for a faith that will not shrink,
  Though pressed by every foe;
  That will not tremble, on the brink
  Of any earthly woe.

2 That will not murmur nor complain,
  Beneath the chastening rod;
  But in the hour of grief or pain,
  Can lean upon its God.

3 A faith that shines more bright and clear,
  When tempests rage without;
  That when in danger knows no fear,
  In darkness feels no doubt:

4 That bears unmoved the world's dread frown,
  Nor heeds its scornful smile;
  That sin's wild ocean cannot drown,
  Nor its soft arts beguile.

5 A faith that keeps the narrow way
  By truth restrained and led,
  And with a pure and heavenly ray,
  Lights up a dying bed.
  Rev. W. H. B. Bathurst (1796—1877).

118 *Thy Will be Done.*
1 How sweet to be allowed to pray
  To God, the Holy One,
  With filial love and truth to say,
  "O God, Thy will be done."

2 Here in these sacred words we find
  A cure for every ill;
  They calm and soothe the troubled mind,
  And bid all care be still.

3 Oh, could my heart thus ever pray,
  Thus imitate thy Son!
  Teach me, O God, with truth to say,
  "Thy will, not mine, be done."
  Social Choir.

119 *Prayer for Resignation.*
1 Thou boundless source of every good,
  Our best desires fulfil;
  Help us adore Thy wondrous grace,
  And mark Thy sovereign will.

2 Teach us, in time of deep distress,
  To own Thy hand, O God;
  And in submissive silence learn
  The lessons of Thy rod.

3 In every changing scene of life,
  Whate'er that scene may be,
  Give us a meek and humble mind,
  A mind at peace with Thee.

4 Then shall we close our eyes in death,
  Free from distracting care,
  For death is life — and labor rest,
  If Thou art with us there.
  Rev. P. Doddridge (1702—1751).

HYMNS OF DEVOTION,
BRATTLE STREET. C.M. D. I. J. PLEYEL (1757—1831), Arr. by N. MITCHELL.

1. Whilst Thee I seek protecting Pow'r, Be my vain wishes stilled;
And may this consecrated hour With better hopes be filled.
Thy love the pow'r of thought bestowed, To Thee my tho'ts would soar; Thy mercy o'er my life has flowed, That mercy I adore.

120 *Goodness of Divine Providence.*

1 Whilst Thee I seek, protecting Power,
Be my vain wishes stilled;
And may this consecrated hour
With better hopes be filled.

2 Thy love the power of thought bestowed
To Thee my thoughts would soar;
Thy mercy o'er my life has flowed;
That mercy I adore.

3 In each event of life, how clear
Thy ruling hand I see;
Each blessing to my soul most dear,
Because conferred by Thee.

4 In every joy that crowns my days,
In every pain I bear,
My heart shall find delight in praise,
Or seek relief in prayer.

5 When gladness wings the favored hour,
Thy love my thoughts shall fill;
Resigned, when storms of sorrow lower,
My soul shall meet Thy will.

6 My lifted eye, without a tear,
The gathering storm shall see,
My steadfast heart shall know no fear;
That heart will rest on Thee.
Miss Helen M. Williams (1762—1827).

121 *Sweet is the Memory.*

1 Sweet is the memory of Thy grace,
My God, my heavenly King,
Let age to age Thy righteousness,
In sounds of glory sing

2 God reigns on high, but ne'er confines
His goodness to the skies;
Through the whole earth, His bounty shines,
And every want supplies.

3 With longing eyes Thy creatures wait
On Thee for daily food;
Thy liberal hand provides their meat,
And fills their mouths with good.

4 How kind are Thy compassions, Lord!
How slow Thine anger moves!
But soon He sends His pardoning word,
To cheer the souls He loves.
Rev. Isaac Watts (1674—1748).

122 *God Calling yet.* (TUNE GERMANY).

1 God calling yet! shall I not hear?
Earth's pleasures shall I still hold dear,
Shall life's swift passing years all fly,
And still my soul in slumber lie?

2 God calling yet! and shall He knock,
And I my heart the closer lock?
He still is waiting to receive,
And shall I dare His spirit grieve?

3 God calling yet! and shall I give
No heed, but still in bondage live?
I wait, but He does not forsake;
He calls me still; my heart, awake!

4 God calling yet! I cannot stay;
My heart I yield without delay;
Vain world, farewell, from Thee I part;
The voice of God hath reached my heart.
*Gerhard Tersteegen (1697—1769).
Tr. by Miss Jane Borthwick, 1854.*

HYMNS OF DEVOTION.

HEBRON. L. M. L. Mason (1792—1872).

1. Thus far the Lord has led me on, Thus far His pow'r prolongs my days, And every evening shall make known Some fresh memorial of His grace.

123 *Evening Hymn.*

1 Thus far the Lord has led me on,
Thus far His power prolongs my days,
And every evening shall make known
Some fresh memorial of His grace.

2 Much of my time has run to waste,
And I, perhaps, am near my home;
But He forgives my follies past;
He gives me strength for days to come.

3 I lay my body down to sleep,
Peace is the pillow for my head;
While well appointed angels keep
Their watchful stations round my bed.

4 Thus when the night of death shall come,
My flesh shall rest beneath the ground,
And wait Thy voice to rouse the tomb,
With sweet salvation in the sound.
Rev. Isaac Watts (1674—1748).

124 *Hope for the Suffering.*

1 Oh, deem not they are blest alone,
Whose lives a peaceful tenor keep;
For God, who pities man, has shown
A blessing for the eyes that weep.

2 The light of smiles shall fill again
The lids that overflow with tears;
And weary hours of woe and pain
Are promises of happier years.

3 There is a day of sunny rest
For every dark and troubled night;

And grief may bide an evening guest,
But joy shall come with early light.

4 Nor let the good man's trust depart,
Though life its common gifts deny;
Though with a pierced and broken heart,
And spurned of men, he goes to die.

5 For God has marked each sorrowing day,
And numbered every secret tear,
And heaven's long age of bliss shall pay
For all His children suffer here.
Wm. Cullen Bryant (1794—1878).

125 *Christian Walking by Faith.*

1 'Tis by the faith of joys to come,
We walk through deserts dark as night;
Till we arrive at heaven our home,
Faith is our guide, and faith our light.

2 The want of sight she well supplies;
She makes the pearly gates appear;
Far into distant worlds she pries,
And brings eternal glories near.

3 Cheerful we tread the desert through,
While faith inspires a heavenly ray,
Though lions roar and tempests blow,
And rocks and dangers fill the way.

4 So Abram, by divine command,
Left his own house to walk with God;
His faith beheld the promised land,
And fired his zeal along the road.
Rev. Isaac Watts (1674—1748).

GERMANY. L. M. Ludwig von Beethoven (1770—1827).

1. 'Tis by the faith of joys to come, We walk through deserts dark as night; Till we ar-rive at heaven our home, Faith is our guide, and faith our light.

HYMNS OF DEVOTION.

WOODSTOCK. C. M.   D. Dutton, 1829.

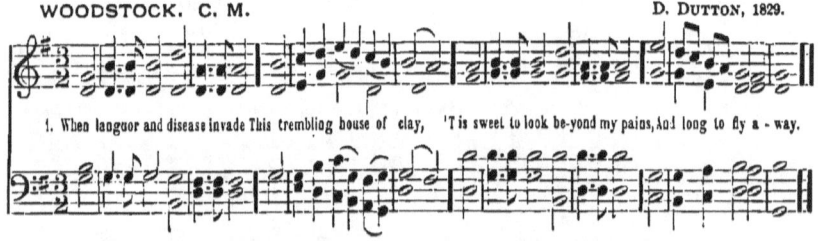

1. When languor and disease invade This trembling house of clay, 'T is sweet to look beyond my pains, And long to fly away.

126   *Consolations in Sickness.*
1 When languor and disease invade
    This trembling house of clay,
'T is sweet to look beyond my pains,
    And long to fly away.
2 Sweet to reflect how grace divine
    My sins on Jesus laid;
Sweet to remember that His blood
    My debt of suffering paid.
3 Sweet on His righteousness to stand,
    Which saves from second death;
Sweet to experience, day by day,
    His Spirit's quickening breath.
4 Sweet in the confidence of faith,
    To trust His firm decrees;
Sweet to lie passive in His hands,
    And know no will but His.
5 If such the sweetness of the streams,
    What must the fountain be,
Where saints and angels draw their bliss
    Immediately from Thee.
                Rev. A. M. Toplady (1740 — 1778).

127   *Prayer for Assurance.*
1 Why should the children of a King
    Go mourning all their days?
Great Comforter, descend and bring
    Some tokens of Thy grace.
2 Dost Thou not dwell in all the saints,
    And seal the heirs of heaven?

When wilt Thou banish my complaints,
    And show my sins forgiven?
3 Assure my conscience of my part
    In the Redeemer's blood;
And bear Thy witness with my heart
    That I am born of God.
4 Thou art the earnest of His love,
    The pledge of joys to come;
And Thy soft wings celestial Dove,
    Will safe convey me home.
                Rev. Isaac Watts (1674 — 1748).

128   *No Tears in Heaven.*
1 What if our bark, o'er life's rough wave,
    By adverse winds be driven—
And howling tempests round us rave—
    There are no tears in heaven.
2 What though affliction be our lot,
    Our hearts with anguish riven,
Still let it never be forgot—
    There are no tears in heaven.
3 Our sweetest joys here vanish all,
    And fade like hues at even;
Our fairest hopes like flowers fall —
    There are no tears in heaven.
4 Thou God, our joy and rest shalt be,
    And sorrow far be driven;
And sin and death forever flee —
    There are no tears in heaven.
                Hunter's Sel. Mel.

WOODLAND. C. M.   N. G. Gould (1781 — 1864).

1. What if our bark o'er life's rough wave, And howling tempests round us rave, There are no tears in heaven.
    By adverse winds be driven, And howling tempests round us rave,

HYMNS OF DEVOTION.

ARLINGTON. C. M.   T. A. ARNE (1710—1778).

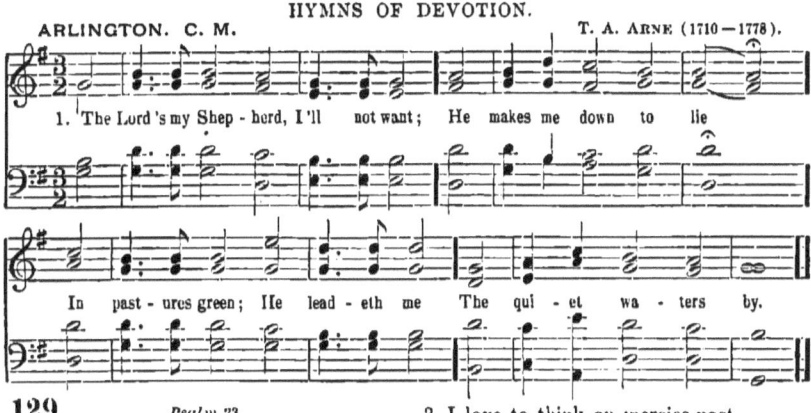

1. The Lord's my Shep-herd, I'll not want; He makes me down to lie
In past-ures green; He lead-eth me The qui-et wa-ters by.

129   *Psalm 23.*

1 The Lord's my Shepherd, I'll not want;
He makes me down to lie
In pastures green; He leadeth me
The quiet waters by.

2 My soul, He doth restore again,
And me to walk doth make
Within the paths of righteousness,
Even for His own name's sake.

3 Yea, though I walk in death's dark vale,
Yet will I fear no ill;
For Thou art with me, and Thy rod
And staff, me comfort still.

4 My table Thou hast furnished
In presence of my foes;
My head Thou dost with oil anoint,
And my cup overflows.

5 Goodness and mercy all my life,
Shall surely follow me;
And in God's house for evermore
My dwelling-place shall be.
    Rev. Francis Rouse (1579—1658).

130   *Evening Prayer.*

1 I love to steal awhile away
From every cumbering care,
And spend the hours of setting day
In humble, grateful prayer.

2 I love in solitude to shed
The penitential tear,
And all His promises to plead,
Where none but God can hear.

3 I love to think on mercies past,
And future good implore,
And all my cares and sorrows cast
On Him whom I adore.

4 I love by faith to take a view
Of brighter scenes in heaven;
The prospect doth my strength renew,
While here by tempests driven.

5 Thus, when life's toilsome day is o'er,
May its departing ray
Be calm as this impressive hour,
And lead to endless day.
    Mrs. Phoebe H. Brown (1783—1861).

131   *Psalm 139.*

1 In all my vast concerns with Thee,
In vain my soul would try
To shun Thy presence, Lord, or flee
The notice of Thine eye.

2 Thy all-surrounding sight surveys
My rising and my rest,
My public walks, my private ways,
And secrets of my breast.

3 My thoughts lie open to the Lord,
Before they're formed within;
And ere my lips pronounce the word,
He knows the sense I mean.

4 O wondrous knowledge, deep and high,
Where can a creature hide;
Within Thy circling arms I lie,
Enclosed on every side.

5 So let thy grace surround me still,
And like a bulwark prove,
To guard my soul from every ill,
Secured by sovereign love.
    Rev. Isaac Watts (1674—1748).

(51)

HYMNS OF DEVOTION.

BETHANY. 6s, 4s. Dr. L. Mason (1792—1872)

1. { Nearer, my God to Thee, Near- er to Thee,
     E'en though it be a cross [Omit.]   That raiseth me! Still all my song shall be, Nearer, my God to Thee,
  D.C. Nearer my God, to Thee, [Omit.]   Nearer to Thee!

132
Genesis 28: 10-22.

1 Nearer, my God, to Thee,
  Nearer to Thee!
E'en though it be a cross
  That raiseth me!
Still all my song shall be,
Nearer, my God, to Thee,
  Nearer to Thee!

2 Though, like a wanderer,
  The sun gone down,
Darkness be over me,
  My rest a stone,
Yet in my dreams I'd be
Nearer, my God, to Thee,
  Nearer to Thee!

3 Then with my waking thoughts
  Bright with Thy praise,
Out of my stony griefs
  Bethel I'll raise;
So by my woes to be
Nearer, my God, to Thee,
  Nearer to Thee.

4 Or, if on joyful wing
  Cleaving the sky,
Sun, moon and stars forgot,
  Upward I fly,
Still all my song shall be,
Nearer, my God, to Thee,
  Nearer to Thee.

Mrs. Sarah Flower Adams (1805—1848).

133
So Shall We be Ever With the Lord.

1 Ever, my Lord, with Thee,
  Ever with Thee!
Through all eternity
  Thy face to see!
I count this heaven, to be
Ever, my Lord, with Thee,
  Ever with Thee.

2 Fair is Jerusalem,
  All of pure gold,
Garnished with many a gem
  Of worth untold:
I only ask, to be
Ever, my Lord, with Thee,
  Ever with Thee.

3 River of Life there flows
  As crystal clear;
The Tree of life there grows
  For healing near;
But this crowns all, to be
Ever, my Lord, with Thee,
  Ever with Thee.

4 No curse is there, no night,
  No grief, no fear;
Thy smile fills heaven with light,
  Dries every tear:
What rapture, there to be
Ever, my Lord, with Thee,
  Ever with Thee

*Abraham Coles, M. D., LL. D. (1813—1891).
From "The Microcosm and other Poems." by per*

GENNESARET. L. M. Rev. Robert P. Kerr, D. D., 1891.

1. O Jesus, Saviour, sweet Desire Of all the saints, those who aspire To find life's pleasure, in Thy love, Till comes the grander life above;

Copyright, 1891, by R. P. Kerr.

HYMNS OF DEVOTION.

MANEPY. 8s. SELAH.

1. In-spir-er and bear-er of prayer, Thou Shep-herd and Guard-ian of Thine, My all to Thy cov-e-nant care I, sleep-ing and wak-ing, re-sign,

134 *Angels Watching Over Us.*

1 Inspirer and hearer of prayer,
Thou Shepherd and Guardian of Thine,
My all to Thy covenant care
I, sleeping and waking, resign.

2 If Thou art my Shield and my Sun,
The night is no darkness to me,
And, fast as my moments roll on,
They bring me but nearer to Thee.

3 Thy ministering spirits descend,
And watch while Thy saints are asleep;
By day and by night they attend,
The heirs of salvation to keep.

4 Bright seraphs, despatched from the
Fly swift to their stations assign'd; [throne,
And angels elect are sent down,
To guard the redeemed of mankind.

5 Thy worship no interval knows;
Their fervor is still on the wing;
And while they protect my repose,
They chant to the praise of my King.

6 I too, at the season ordained,
Their chorus forever shall join,
And love and adore, without end,
Their gracious Creator and mine.
Rev. Augustus Montague Toplady (1740—1778).

135 *Abide Thou with Us.*

1 O Jesus, Saviour, sweet Desire
Of all the saints, those who aspire
To find life's pleasures, in Thy love,
Till comes the grander life above;

2 O Jesus, Saviour, deign to meet
With us around Thy mercy seat;
And with Thy Holy Spirit's power,
To bless us in this favored hour.

3 O Jesus, Saviour, all our hope,
While thro' life's clouded maze we grope,
Be Thou the light within our hearts,
And give the strength that faith imparts.

4 O Jesus, Saviour, grant us grace
To know, and love, and seek Thy face,
To feel all else beside is small,
And Thou alone our all in all.

5 O Jesus, Saviour, come abide
Forever constant at our side,
That we may surer choose the way
That leadeth unto endless day.
Robert Whittet, 1891.

HYMNS OF DEVOTION.

VIGILATE. 7s & 3s. Rev. W. H. MONK, Mus. Doc. (1823–).

136 *Watch and Pray.*

1 "Christian! seek not yet repose,"
  Hear thy loving Saviour say;
Thou art in the midst of foes;
        "Watch and pray."

2 Principalities and powers,
  Mustering their unseen array,
Wait for Thy unguarded hours:
        "Watch and pray."

3 Gird thy heavenly armor on,
  Wear it ever night and day;
Ambush'd lies the evil one;
        "Watch and pray."

4 Hear the victors who o'ercame;
  Still they mark each warrior's way;
All with one sweet voice exclaim,
        "Watch and pray."

5 Hear, above all, hear thy Lord,
  Him thou lovest to obey;
Hide within thy heart His word,
        "Watch and pray."

6 Watch, as if on that alone
  Hung the issue of the day;
Pray that help may be sent down,
        "Watch and pray."
Miss Charlotte Elliott (1789–1871).

ST. SYLVESTER. 8s, 7s. Rev. J. B. DYKES (1823–1876).

HYMNS OF DEVOTION.

ANGEL VOICES. 8s, 5s, 4s & 3s. — Hymns Ancient and Modern.

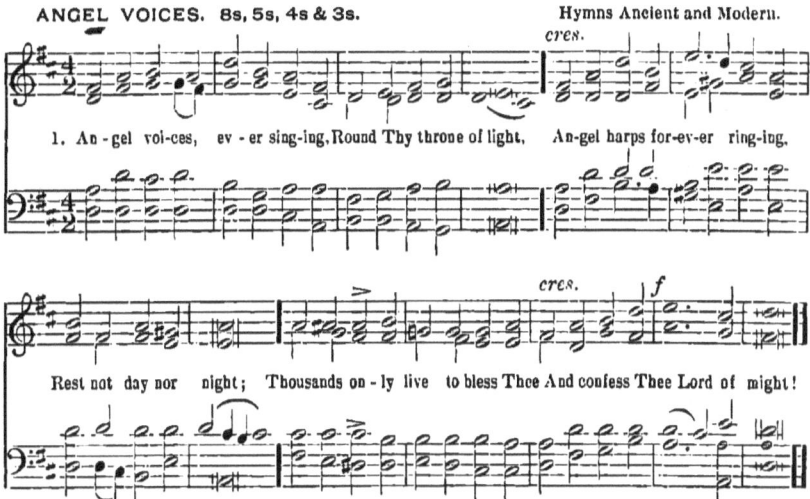

1. Angel voices, ever singing, Round Thy throne of light, Angel harps forever ringing, Rest not day nor night; Thousands only live to bless Thee And confess Thee Lord of might!

137 *Adoration.*

1 Angel voices, ever singing,
  Round Thy throne of light,
Angel harps forever ringing,
  Rest not day nor night;
Thousands only live to bless Thee
And confess Thee
  Lord of might!

2 Thou, who art beyond the farthest
  Mortal eye can scan,—
Can it be that Thou regardest
  Songs of sinful man?
Can we know that Thou art near us,
And wilt hear us?
  Yea, we can.

3 In Thy house, great God, we offer
  Of Thine own to Thee;
And for Thine acceptance proffer,
  All unworthily,
Hearts and minds and hands and voices,
In our choicest
  Psalmody.

4 Honor, glory, might, and merit
  Thine shall ever be.

Father, Son, and Holy Spirit,
  Blessèd Trinity!
Of the best that Thou hast given,
  Earth and Heaven
  Render Thee.

Hymns Ancient and Modern.

138 *Days and Moments.*
Tune, ST. SYLVESTER.

1 Days and moments quickly flying
  Blend the living with the dead:
Soon will you and I be lying
  Each within our narrow bed.

2 Soon our souls to God Who gave them
  Will have sped their rapid flight:
Able now by grace to save them,
  Oh, that while we can we might!

3 Jesus Infinite Redeemer,
  Maker of this mighty frame,
Teach, oh, teach us to remember
  What we are, and whence we came.

4 Whence we came, and whither wending
  Soon we must through darkness go,
To inherit bliss unending,
  Or eternity of woe.

Rev. Edward Caswall (1814—1878).

HYMNS OF DEVOTION.

WILMARTH. L. M. I. B. WOODBURY (1819—1858).

1. O Sun of Righteous-ness di-vine, On us with beams of mer-cy shine; Chase the dark clouds of guilt a-way, And turn our dark-ness in-to day.

139 *Sun of Righteousness.*

1 O Sun of Righteousness divine,
On us with beams of mercy shine;
Chase the dark clouds of guilt away,
And turn our darkness into day.

2 While mourning o'er our guilt and shame,
And asking mercy in Thy name,
Dear Saviour cleanse us with Thy blood,
And be our advocate with God.

3 Sustain when sinking in distress,
And guide us through this wilderness;
Teach our low thoughts from earth to rise,
And lead us onward to the skies.
Anon.

140 *Pleading for Mercy.*

1 With broken heart and contrite sigh,
A trembling sinner, Lord, I cry;
Thy pardoning grace is rich and free:
O God, be merciful to me!

2 I smite upon my troubled breast,
With deep and conscious guilt oppressed;
Christ and His cross my only plea:
O God, be merciful to me!

3 Far off I stand with tearful eyes,
Nor dare uplift them to the skies;
But Thou dost all my anguish see:
O God, be merciful to me!

4 Nor alms, nor deeds that I have done,
Can for a single sin atone;
To Calvary alone I flee:
O God, be merciful to me!

5 And when redeemed from sin and hell,
With all the ransomed throng I dwell,
My raptured song shall ever be,
God has been merciful to me!
Rev. Richard Elvin (1797—).

141 *When Thou Art Converted.*

1 Lord, speak to me, that I may speak
In living echoes of Thy tone;
As Thou hast sought, so let me seek
Thy erring children lost and lone.

2 Oh, lead me, Lord, that I may lead
The wandering and the wavering feet;
Oh, feed me, Lord, that I may feed
Thy hungering ones with manna sweet.

3 Oh, give Thine own sweet rest to me,
That I may speak with soothing power
A word in season, as from Thee,
To weary ones in needful hour.

4 Oh, fill me with Thy fullness, Lord,
Until my very heart o'erflow
In kindling thought and glowing word,
Thy love to tell, Thy praise to show.
Miss Frances Ridley Havergal (1836—1879).

ROCKINGHAM. L. M. Dr. L. MASON (1792—1872).

1. Lord, speak to me, that I may speak In living echoes of Thy tone; As Thou hast sought, so let me seek Thy erring children lost and lone.

HYMNS OF DEVOTION.

LAND OF HOLY LIGHT. 8s, 7s. D.   Rev. ROBERT P. KERR, D. D., 1891.

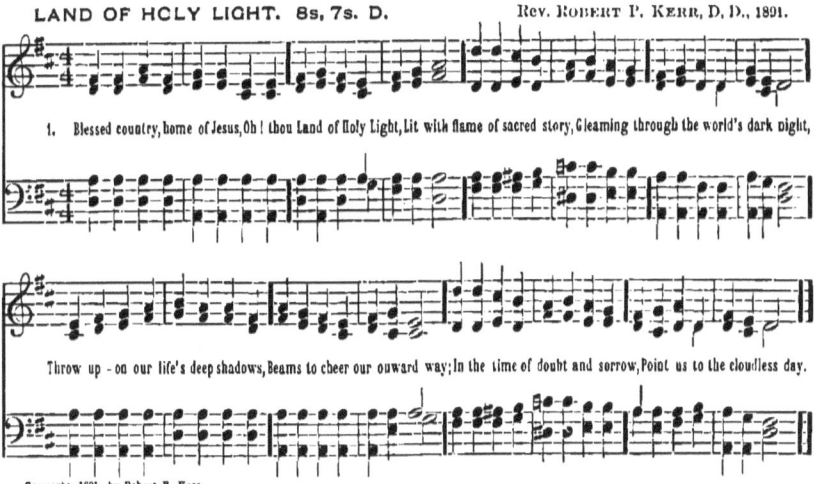

Copyright, 1891, by Robert P. Kerr.

142   *The Land of Holy Light.*

1 Blessed country, home of Jesus,
  Oh! thou Land of Holy Light,
Lit with flame of sacred story,   [night,
  Gleaming through the world's dark
Throw upon our life's deep shadows,
  Beams to cheer our onward way;
In the time of doubt and sorrow,
  Point us to the cloudless day,

2 Show us Him who is the brightness
  Of thy long enduring fame,
Him who gave thy hills the glory
  Of His own immortal name;
Let us see the shining Presence
  Which, in luminous attire,
Phrophets and apostles worshipped
  On the mount of heavenly fire.

3 Land of sacred brook and river,
  Holy hill and solemn sea,
May thy very dust and ruins
  Tell us, while we think of thee,
Wondrous tales of love and blessing,
  That our souls may not repine;
How were healed the sick and sorrowing
  By the lonely Man divine.

4 Show us now in holiest visions,
  Him who wept and prayed and died
In the garden, on the mountain, —
  Show us Christ the crucified;
Lead us to Him in the morning,
  Clad in resurrection might;
Bring us near our glorious Saviour,
  Oh! thou Land of Holy Light.
          Rev. Robert P. Kerr, D. D., 1891.

143 *Worthy the Lamb.*
          (Tune, Rockingham.)

1 What equal honors shall we bring
  To Thee, O Lord our God, the Lamb,
When all the notes that angels sing
  Are far inferior to Thy name?

2 Worthy is He that once was slain, [died,
  The Prince of Peace that groaned and
Worthy to rise and live, and reign,
  At His almighty Father's side.

3 Honor immortal must be paid
  Instead of scandal and of scorn;
While glory shines around His head,
  And a bright crown without a thorn.

4 Blessings forever on the Lamb,
  Who bore the curse for wretched men:
Let angels sound His sacred name,
  And every creature say, Amen!
          Rev. Isaac Watts (1674 — 1748).

(57)

HYMNS OF DEVOTION.

DE FLEURY. 8s, D.　　　　　　　　　　　　　JONATHAN EDSON, 1782.

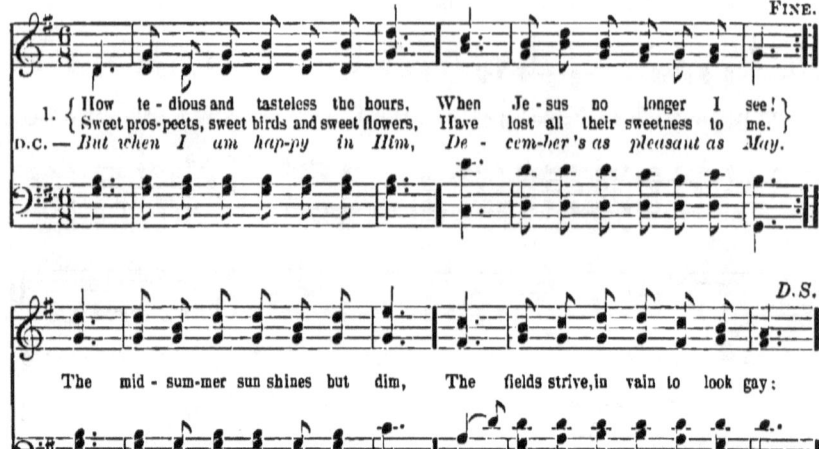

144　*Chief Object of a Believer's Love.*
1 How tedious and tasteless the hours,
　When Jesus no longer I see; [flowers,
Sweet prospects, sweet birds, and sweet
　Have lost all their sweetness to me;
The midsummer sun shines but dim,
　The fields strive in vain to look gay;
But when I am happy in Him,
　December's as pleasant as May.

2 His name yields the richest perfume,
　And sweeter than music His voice;
His presence disperses my gloom,
　And makes all within me rejoice;
I should, were He always thus nigh,
　Have nothing to wish or to fear;
No mortal so happy as I,
　My summer would last all the year.

3 Content with beholding His face,
　My all to His pleasure resigned,
No changes of season or place
　Would make any change in my mind.
While blessed with a sense of His love,
　A palace a toy would appear;
And prisons would palaces prove,
　If Jesus would dwell with me there.

4 Dear Lord, if indeed I am Thine,
　If Thou art my sun and my song,
Say, why do I languish and pine,
　And why are my winters so long?
O! drive these dark clouds from my sky,
　Thy soul-cheering presence restore;
Or take me unto Thee on high,
　Where winter and clouds are no more.
　　　　　Rev. John Newton (1725—1807).

145　*My Gracious Redeemer.*
1 My gracious Redeemer I love;
　His praises aloud I'll proclaim;
And join with the armies above,
　To shout His adorable name.
To gaze on His glories divine
　Shall be my eternal employ;
To see them incessantly shine,
　My boundless, ineffable joy.

2 He freely redeemed with His blood
　My soul from the confines of hell,
To live on the smiles of my God,
　And in His sweet presence to dwell.
To shine with the angels in light,
　With saints and with seraphs to sing,
To view with eternal delight,
　My Jesus, my Saviour, my King!
　　　　　Rev. Benj. Francis (1734—1799).

(58)

HYMNS OF DEVOTION.

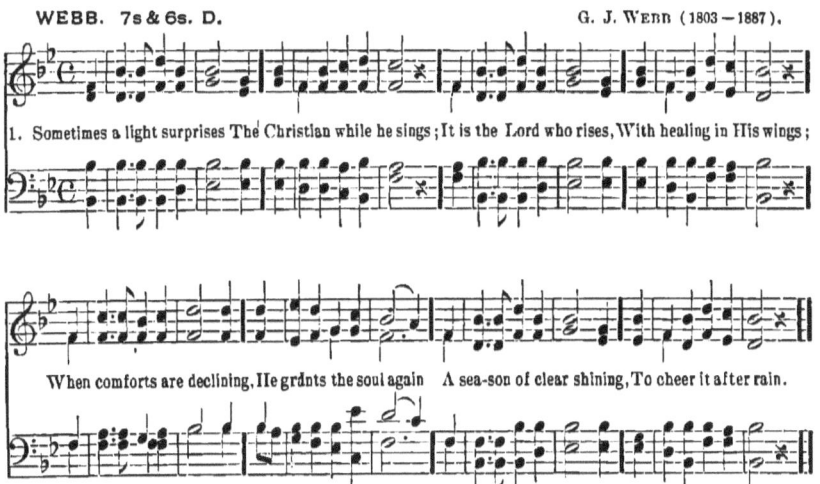

146 *Divine Light.*
1 Sometimes a light surprises
 The Christian while he sings;
 It is the Lord who rises,
 With healing in His wings;
 When comforts are declining,
 He grants the soul again
 A season of clear shining,
 To cheer it after rain.

2 In holy contemplation,
 We sweetly then pursue
 The theme of God's salvation,
 And find it ever new:
 Set free from present sorrow,
 We cheerfully can say,
 Let the unknown to-morrow
 Bring with it what it may.

3 It can bring with it nothing,
 But He will bear us through;
 Who gives the lilies clothing,
 Will clothe His people too:
 Beneath the spreading heavens,
 No creature but is fed;
 And He who feeds the ravens,
 Will give His children bread.

4 Though vine nor fig-tree neither,
 Their wanted fruit should bear,
 Though all the fields should wither,
 Nor flocks nor herds be there;
 Yet God the same abiding,
 His grace shall tune my voice;
 For while in Him confiding,
 I cannot but rejoice.
  Wm. Cowper (1731 – 1800).

147 *God First Chose Me.*
1 'Tis not that I did choose Thee,
 For, Lord, that could not be;
 This heart would still refuse Thee;
 But Thou hast chosen me;
 Thou from the sin that stained me,
 Hast cleansed and set me free,
 Of old Thou hast ordained me,
 That I should live to Thee.

2 'Twas sovereign mercy called me,
 And taught my opening mind;
 The world had else enthralled me,
 To heavenly glories blind;
 My heart owns none before Thee;
 For Thy rich grace I thirst;
 This knowing, if I love Thee,
 Thou must have loved me first.
  Josiah Conder (1789 – 1855).

HYMNS OF DEVOTION.

BOYLSTON. S. M.   Dr. L. Mason (1792—1872).

1. The pit-y of the Lord, To those that fear His name,
Is such as ten-der par-ents feel; He knows our fee-ble frame.

148   *The Lord's Pity.*
1 The pity of the Lord,
   To those that fear His name,
Is such as tender parents feel;
   He knows our feeble frame.

2 He knows we are but dust,
   Scattered with every breath;
His anger like a rising wind,
   Can send us swift to death.

3 Our days are as the grass,
   Or like the morning flower;
If one sharp blast sweep o'er the field
   It withers in an hour.

4 But Thy compassions, Lord,
   To endless years endure;
And children's children ever find
   Thy words of promise sure.
                Rev. Isaac Watts (1674—1748).

149   *Suffering Saviour.*
1 Did Christ o'er sinners weep?
   And shall our cheeks be dry?
Let floods of penitential grief
   Burst forth from every eye.

2 The Son of God in tears
   Angels with wonder see;
Be thou astonished, O my soul,
   He shed those tears for thee.

3 He wept that we might weep;
   Each sin demands a tear;

In heaven alone no sin is found,
   And there's no weeping there.
             Rev. B. Beddome (1717—1795).

150   *Adoption.*
1 Behold what wondrous grace
   The Father has bestowed
On sinners of a mortal race,
   To call them sons of God.

2 A hope so much divine,
   May trials well endure,
May purge our souls from sense and sin,
   As Christ the Lord is pure.

3 If in my Father's love
   I share a filial part,
Send down Thy Spirit like a dove,
   To rest upon my heart.

4 We would no longer lie
   Like slaves beneath the throne;
My faith shall Abba, Father, cry,
   And thou the kindred own.
              Rev. Isaac Watts (1674—1748).

151   *Doxology.*
The Father and the Son
   And Spirit we adore;
We praise, we bless, we worship Thee,
   Both now and evermore!

HYMNS OF DEVOTION.

AVON. C. M. — Hugh Wilson (1764 – 1824).

1. As pants the hart for cooling streams, When heated in the chase; So longs my soul, O God, for Thee, And Thy refreshing grace.

152 *As Pants the Hart.* Ps: 42.

1 As pants the hart for cooling streams,
When heated in the chase;
So longs my soul, O God, for Thee,
And Thy refreshing grace.

2 For Thee, my God, the living God,
My thirsty soul doth pine;
Oh! when shall I behold Thy face,
Thou Majesty divine?

3 Why restless, why cast down, my soul?
Trust God, and He 'll employ
His aid for Thee, and change these sighs
To thankful hymns of joy.

4 Why restless, why cast down, my soul?
Hope still; and Thou shalt sing

153 *Triumph in Christ.* Rev. H. F. Lyte (1793 – 1847).

The praise of Him, who is thy God,
Thy health's eternal spring.

1 In every trouble, sharp and strong,
My soul to Jesus flies;
My anchor-hold is firm in Him,
When swelling billows rise.

2 His comforts bear my spirits up,
I trust a faithful God;
The sure foundation of my hope
Is in a Saviour's blood.

3 Loud hallelujahs sing, my soul,
To Thy Redeemer's name;
In joy, in sorrow, life and death,
His love is still the same.
Coombs.

ST. AGNES. C. M. — Rev. J. B. Dykes (1823 – 1876).

1. Early, my God, without delay, I haste to seek Thy face; My thirst-y spir-it faints a-way, With-out Thy cheer-ing grace.

154 *Psalm 63.*

1 Early, my God, without delay,
I haste to seek Thy face;
My thirsty spirit faints away,
Without Thy cheering grace.

2 I 've seen Thy glory and Thy power
Through all Thy temples shine;
My God, repeat that heavenly hour,
That vision so divine.

3 Not life itself, with all its joys,
Can my best passions move,
Or raise so high my cheerful voice,
As Thy forgiving love.

4 Thus, till my last expiring day,
I 'll bless my God and King;
Thus will I lift my hands to pray,
And tune my lips to sing.
Rev. Isaac Watts (1674 – 1748).

HYMNS OF DEVOTION.

OLIPHANT. 8s, 7s & 4s, 6l.
PIERRE-MARIE-FRANCOIS de SALES BAILLOT (1771—1842).
Arr. by LOWELL MASON (1792—1872).

1. { Guide me, O Thou great Je-ho-vah, Pil-grim through this bar-ren land;
    I am weak, but Thou art might-y;
Hold me with Thy pow'r-ful hand: Bread of heav-en! Bread of heav-en!
Feed me till I want no more, Feed me till I want no more.

155   *Guide Me.*
1 Guide me, O Thou great Jehovah,
   Pilgrim through this barren land;
I am weak, but Thou art mighty;
   Hold me with Thy powerful hand;
Bread of heaven!
   Feed me till I want no more.

2 Open Thou the crystal fountain,
   Whence the healing streams do flow;
Let the fiery, cloudy pillar
   Lead me all my journey through:
Strong deliverer!
   Be Thou still my strength and shield.

3 When I tread the verge of Jordan,
   Bid my anxious fears subside;
Bear me through the swelling current,
   Land me safe on Canaan's side:
Songs of praises
   I will ever give to Thee.
         Rev. Peter Williams (1719—1796).

156   *Saviour, Keep Us.*
1 God of our salvation! hear us;
   Bless, oh, bless us, ere we go;
When we join the world, be near us,
   Lest we cold and careless grow.
Saviour! keep us,
   Keep us safe from every foe.

2 As our steps are drawing nearer,
   To our everlasting home,
May our view of heaven grow clearer,
   Hope more bright of joys to come;
And, when dying,
   May Thy presence cheer the gloom.
         Rev. Thomas Kelly (1769—1855).

157   *Guard Us, Guide Us.*
1 Lead us, heavenly Father, lead us
   O'er the world's tempestuous sea;
Guard us, guide us, keep us, feed us,
   For we have no help but Thee;
Yet possessing every blessing,
   If our God our Father be.

2 Saviour, breathe forgiveness o'er us,
   All our weakness Thou dost know;
Thou didst tread this earth before us,
   Thou didst feel its keenest woe;
Lone and dreary, faint and weary,
   Through the desert Thou didst go.

3 Spirit of our God, descending,
   Fill our hearts with heavenly joy;
Love with every passion blending,
   Pleasure that can never cloy.
Thus provided, pardoned, guided,
   Nothing can our peace destroy.
         James Edmeston (1791—1867).

HYMNS OF DEVOTION.

BAYLEY. 8s & 7s D.   ENGLISH.

158   *Love Divine.*

1 Love divine, all love excelling,—
   Joy of heaven, to earth come down!
Fix in us Thy humble dwelling,
   All Thy faithful mercies crown:
Jesus! Thou art all compassion,
   Pure unbounded love Thou art;
Visit us with Thy salvation,
   Enter every trembling heart.

2 Breathe, oh, breathe Thy loving Spirit
   Into every troubled breast!
Let us all in Thee inherit,
   Let us find Thy promised rest:
Come, Almighty to deliver,
   Let us all Thy life receive!
Speedily return, and never,
   Never more Thy temples leave!

3 Finish then Thy new creation,
   Pure, unspotted may we be;
Let us see our whole salvation
   Perfectly secured by Thee!
Changed from glory into glory,
   Till in heaven we take our place;
Till we cast our crowns before Thee,
   Lost in wonder, love, and praise.
        Rev. Charles Wesley (1708—1788).

159   *Revival.*
        Tune, OLIPHANT.

1 Saviour! visit Thy plantation,
   Grant us, Lord, a gracious rain;
All will come to desolation
   Unless Thou return again:
Lord revive us, Lord revive us,
   All our help must come from Thee.

2 Keep no longer at a distance,
   Shine upon us from on high,
Lest from want of Thine assistance
   Every plant should droop and die.

3 Let our mutual love be fervent,
   Make us prevalent in prayers;
Let each one esteemed Thy servant
   Shun the world's bewitching snares.

4 Break the tempter's fatal power;
   Turn the stony heart to flesh;
And begin from this good hour
   To revive Thy work afresh.
        Rev. John Newton (1725—1807).

160   *Doxology.*

May the grace of Christ our Saviour,
   And the Father's boundless love,
With the Holy Spirit's favor,
   Rest upon us from above.
Thus may we abide in union
   With each other and the Lord,
And possess, in sweet communion,
   Joys which earth cannot afford.

HYMNS OF DEVOTION.

INVITATION. 8s & 7s. Double.　　　　　H. R. PALMER, 1868.

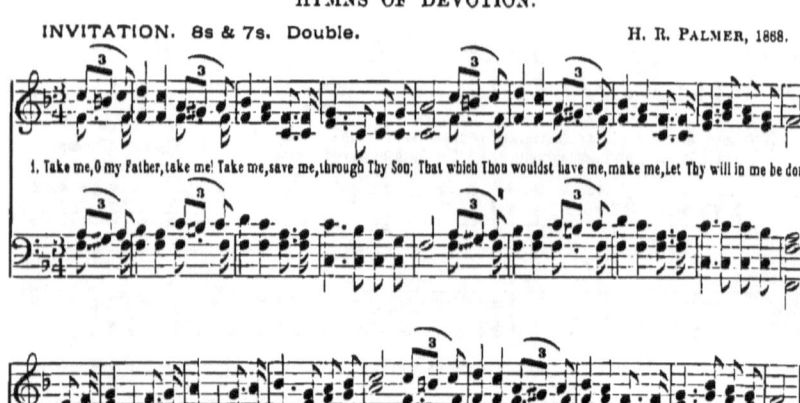

By per. of Oliver Ditson Company, owners of Copyright.

161　　*Going to Christ.*

1 Take me, O my Father, take me!
　Take me, save me, through Thy Son;
That which Thou wouldst have me, make me,
　Let Thy will in me be done.
Long from Thee my footsteps straying,
　Thorny proved the way I trod;
Weary come I now, and praying,
　Take me to Thy love, my God!

2 Fruitless years with grief recalling,
　Humbly I confess my sin;
At Thy feet, O Father, falling,
　To Thy household take me in.
Freely now to Thee I proffer
　This relenting heart of mine;
Freely life and soul I offer —
　Gift unworthy love like Thine.

3 Once the world's Redeemer dying,
　Bare our sins upon the tree;
On that sacrifice relying,
　Now I look in hope to Thee.
Father, take me! all forgiving,
　Fold me to Thy loving breast;
In Thy love for ever living,
　I must be for ever blest!

Rev. Ray Palmer, D. D. (1808—1887).

162　　*Saviour hast Thou fled?*

1 Saviour, hast Thou fled for ever,
　From my tempest-riven breast?
Will Thy gracious Spirit never
　Come and cheer and make me blest?
Long, dear Lord, in silent sorrow,
　I have sighed to taste Thy love;
Hoping on some sweet to-morrow,
　Thou wouldst all my guilt remove.

2 Peace, my soul, the Saviour hears thee,
　He will chase thy fears away;
'T is His gracious presence cheers thee,
　Turning darkness into day.
Precious Saviour, have I found Thee?
　Wilt Thou then my portion be?
Spread Thy sheltering arm around me,
　Let me lean alone on Thee.

3 Through this world, so dark and dreary,
　Be my constant Friend and Guide;
Hungry, thirsty, faint and weary,
　Keep me ever near Thy side.
Blessed be His name for ever,
　For His pardoning grace to me;
Sinners, doubt His promise never,
　Jesus' love is full and free.

Mrs. McCartel.

HYMNS OF DEVOTION.

RUTH. 6s & 5s, D. — ENGLISH. SAMUEL SMITH.

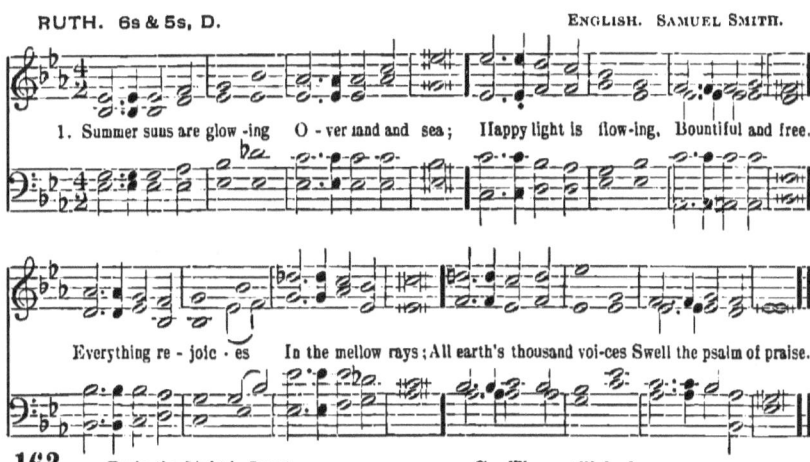

1. Summer suns are glowing
O-ver land and sea;
Happy light is flowing,
Bountiful and free.
Everything rejoices
In the mellow rays;
All earth's thousand voices
Swell the psalm of praise.

163 *Truly the Light is Sweet.*

1 Summer suns are glowing
Over land and sea;
Happy light is flowing,
Bountiful and free.
Everything rejoices
In the mellow rays;
All earth's thousand voices
Swell the psalm of praise.

2 God's free mercy streameth
Over all the world,
And His banner gleameth,
Everywhere unfurled.
Broad and deep and glorious,
As the heaven above,
Shines in might victorious
His eternal love.

3 Lord upon our blindness
Thy pure radiance pour;
For Thy loving-kindness,
Make us love Thee more.
And, when clouds are drifting
Dark across our sky,
Then the veil uplifting,
Father, be Thou nigh.

4 We will never doubt Thee,
Though Thou veil Thy light:
Life is dark without Thee;
Death with Thee is bright.
Light of light! shine o'er us
On our pilgrim way;

Go Thou still before us
To the endless day.
Bp. W. Walsham How (1823—).

164 *The Final Struggle.*
Tune, INVITATION.

1 Tarry with me, oh! my Saviour,
For the day is passing by;
See! the shades of evening gather,
And the night is drawing nigh;
Deeper, deeper grow the shadows,
Paler now the glowing west;
Swift the night of death advances;
Shall it be the night of rest?

2 Lonely seems the vale of shadow;
Sinks my heart with troubled fear;
Give me faith for clearer vision,
Speak Thou, Lord! in words of cheer;
Let me hear Thy voice of mercy,
Calming all these wild alarms;
Let me underneath my weakness,
Feel the everlasting arms.

3 Feeble, trembling, fainting, dying,
Lord! I cast myself on Thee;
Tarry with me through the darkness.
While I sleep, still watch by me.
Tarry with me, oh! my Saviour,
Lay my head upon Thy breast
Till the morning; then awake me —
Morning of eternal rest!
Mrs. Caroline S. Smith (1827—).

(65)

HYMNS OF DEVOTION.

CHIMES. C. M.   Dr. L. Mason (1792—1872).

1. Religion is the chief concern Of mortals here below; May I its great importance learn, Its sovereign virtue know.

165   *Excellence of Religion.*
1 Religion is the chief concern
  Of mortals here below,
May I its great importance learn;
  Its sovereign virtue know.

2 More needful this than glittering
    wealth,
  Or aught the world bestows;
Nor reputation, food nor health
  Can give us such repose.

3 Religion should our thoughts engage,
  Amidst our youthful bloom;
'T will fit us for declining age,
  And for the awful tomb.

4 O! may my heart, by grace renewed,
  Be my Redeemer's throne;
And be my stubborn will subdued,
  His government to own.

5 Let deep repentance, faith, and love,
  Be joined with godly fear;
And all my conversation prove
  My heart to be sincere.
        Rev. John Fawcett (1739—1817).

166   *Christ, the Way, Truth, and Life.*
1 Thou art the way; to Thee alone
  From sin and death we flee;
And he who would the Father seek,
  Must seek Him, Lord, in Thee.

2 Thou art the truth— Thy word alone
  True wisdom can impart;
Thou only canst instruct the mind,
  And purify the heart.

3 Thou art the life,— the rending tomb
  Proclaims Thy conquering arm;
And those who put their trust in Thee,
  Nor death nor hell shall harm.

4 Thou art the way, the truth, the life;
  Grant us to know that way,
That truth to keep, that life to win,
  Which lead to endless day.
        Bishop G. W. Doane (1789—1859).

167   *The Christian Longing for Heaven.*
1 Father, I long, I faint to see
  The place of Thine abode:
I'd leave Thine earthly courts, and flee
  Up to Thy seat, my God.

2 I'd part with all the joys of sense,
  To gaze upon Thy throne:
Pleasure springs fresh for ever thence,
  Unspeakable, unknown.

3 There all the heavenly hosts are seen;
  In shining ranks they move,
And drink immortal vigor in,
  With wonder and with love.

4 The more Thy glories strike my eyes,
  The humbler I shall lie;
Thus while I sink my joys shall rise
  Immeasurably high.
        Rev. Isaac Watts (1674—1748).

168   *Doxology.*
To Father, Son, and Holy Ghost,
  One God whom we adore,
Be glory as it was, is now,
  And shall be evermore.

HYMNS OF DEVOTION.

MESSIAH. 7s, D. Arr. by GEO. KINGSLEY (1811—1884).

1. Brethren, while we sojourn here, Fight we must, but should not fear; Foes we have, But we've a Friend, One that loves us to the end: For-ward, then, with cour-age go; Long we shall not dwell be-low; Soon the joy-ful news will come, "Child your Fa-ther calls — come home!"

By per. of Oliver Ditson Company, owners of Copyright.

169 *Child, your Father Calls.*

1 Brethren, while we sojourn here,
    Fight we must, but should not fear;
Foes we have, but we've a Friend,
    One that loves us to the end:
Forward, then, with courage go;
    Long we shall not dwell below;
Soon the joyful news will come,
    "Child, your Father calls — come home!"

2 In the way a thousand snares
    Lie, to take us unawares;
Satan, with malicious art,
    Watches each unguarded part:
But, from Satan's malice free,
    Saints shall soon victorious be;
Soon the joyful news will come,
    "Child, your Father calls — come home!"

3 But of all the foes we meet,
    None so oft mislead our feet,
None betray us into sin
    Like the foes that dwell within;
Yet let nothing spoil our peace,
    Christ shall also conquer these;
Soon the joyful news will come,
    "Child, your Father calls — come home!"
            Anon.

170 *Thou Art my Rock.*

1 Lord, Thou art my rock of strength,
    And my home is in Thine arms;
Thou wilt send me help at length,
    And I feel no wild alarms;
Sin nor death can pierce the shield
    Thy defence has o'er me thrown,
Up to Thee myself I yield,
    And my sorrows are thine own.

2 When my trials tarry long
    Unto Thee I look and wait;
Knowing none, though keen and strong,
    Can my trust in Thee abate;
And this faith I long have nursed,
    Comes alone, O God from Thee;
Thou my heart didst open first,
    Thou didst set this hope in me.

3 Let Thy mercy's wings be spread
    O'er me, keep me close to Thee;
In the peace Thy love doth shed,
    Let me dwell eternally!
Be my all: in all I do,
    Let me only seek Thy will;
Let my heart to Thee be true
    And thus peaceful calm and still.
Rev. August Hermann Franke (1663—1727).
Tr. by Miss Catherine Winkworth (1821—1878).

HYMNS OF DEVOTION.

LUX BENIGNA. 10s, 4s. 6l.   Rev. J. B. Dykes (1801—1875).

1. Lead, kindly Light! amid the encircling gloom, Lead Thou me on; The night is dark, and I am far from home, Lead Thou me on; Keep Thou my feet; I do not ask to see The distant scene; one step enough for me.

171   *Lead Thou Me on.*

1 Lead, kindly Light! amid the encircling
    Lead Thou me on;   [gloom,
The night is dark, and I am far from home,
    Lead Thou me on;
Keep Thou my feet; I do not ask to see
The distant scene; one step enough for me.

2 I was not ever thus, nor prayed that Thou
    Shouldst lead me on;
I loved to choose and see my path; but now
    Lead Thou me on:

I loved the garish day, and, spite of fears,
Pride ruled my will. Remember not past
    years.

3 So long thy power has blessed me, sure
    Will lead me on   [it still
O'er moor and fen, o'er crag and torrent till
    The night is gone;
And with the morn those angel faces smile
Which I have loved long since, and lost
    awhile.
          Rev. J. H. Newman (1801—1890).

SAVIOUR, COMFORT ME. 7s & 5s.

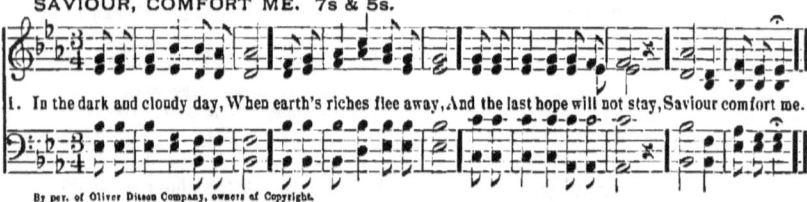

1. In the dark and cloudy day, When earth's riches flee away, And the last hope will not stay, Saviour comfort me.

By per. of Oliver Ditson Company, owners of Copyright.

172   *Saviour, Comfort Me.*

1 In the dark and cloudy day,
When earth's riches flee away,
And the last hope will not stay;
    Saviour, comfort me!

2 When the secret idol's gone,
That my poor heart yearned upon,
Desolate, bereft, alone;
    Saviour, comfort me.

3 Thou, who wast so sorely tried,
In the darkness crucified,

Bid me in Thy love confide;
    Saviour, comfort me!

4 Comfort me; I am cast down;
'Tis my heavenly Father's frown;
I deserve it all, I own;
    Saviour, comfort me!

5 So it shall be good for me,
Much afflicted now to be,
If Thou wilt but tenderly;
    Saviour, comfort me!
          Rev. Geo. Rawson 1876.

HYMNS OF DEVOTION.

MERCY SEAT. L. M.   L. O. EMERSON.

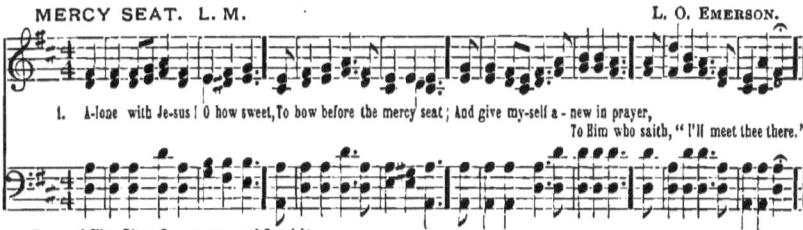

By per. of Oliver Ditson Company, owners of Copyright.

173   *Alone with Jesus.*

1 Alone with Jesus! O how sweet,
To bow before the mercy seat;
And give myself anew in prayer,
To him who saith, "I'll meet thee there."

2 Alone with Jesus! O how blest,
The soul that doth in Jesus rest;
Who knows that He is always near,
And ever waits his saints to hear.

3 Alone with Jesus! O how full,
He sweetly fills the hungry soul;
With heavenly food He will supply
His needy children when they cry.

4 Alone with Jesus every day,
To wait, give thanks, and praise and pray;
I find no spot on earth so sweet,
As that dear place, the mercy seat.
                 M. M. Phinney, A Blind Girl.

FLEMMING. 8s & 6s.   F. F. FLEMMING (1778—1813).

1. O Holy Saviour! Friend unseen, Since on thine arm thou bidd'st me lean, Help me, throughout life's changing scene, By faith to cling to Thee!

By per. Oliver Ditson Company, owners of Copyright.

174   *Clinging to Christ.*

1 O Holy Saviour! Friend unseen,
Since on Thine arm Thou bidd'st me lean,
Help me, throughout life's changing scene,
   By faith to cling to Thee!

2 Without a murmur I dismiss
My former dreams of earthly bliss;
My joy, my recompense be this,
   Each hour to cling to Thee!

3 What though the world deceitful prove,
And earthly friends and hopes remove;
With patient uncomplaining love,
   Still would I cling to Thee.

4 Though oft I seem to tread alone
Life's dreary waste, with thorns o'ergrown,
Thy voice of love, in gentlest tone,
   Still whispers, "Cling to me!"

5 Though faith and hope are often tried,
I ask not, need not, aught beside;
So safe, so calm, so satisfied,
   The soul that clings to Thee!
              Miss Charlotte Elliott (1789—1871).

HYMNS OF DEVOTION.

GREENPORT. C. M. D.   THALBERG.

1. Dear Ref-uge of my wea-ry soul, On Thee, when sor-rows rise, On Thee, when waves of trouble roll, My fainting hope relies.

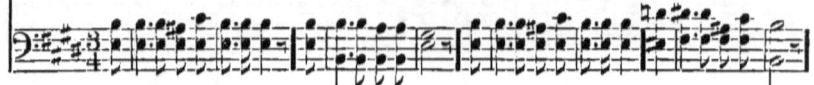

2. To Thee I tell each rising grief, For Thou alone canst heal; Thy word can bring a sweet relief, For ev-'ry pain I feel.

175   *Looking to God in Trouble.*

1 Dear Refuge of my weary soul,
   On Thee when sorrows rise,
On Thee, when waves of trouble roll,
   My fainting hope relies.

2 To Thee I tell each rising grief,
   For Thou alone canst heal;
Thy word can bring a sweet relief,
   For every pain I feel.

3 But O! when gloomy doubts prevail,
   I fear to call Thee mine;
The springs of comfort seem to fail,
   And all my hopes decline.

4 Yet, gracious God, where shall I flee?
   Thou art my only trust;
And still my soul would cleave to Thee,
   Though prostrate in the dust.

5 Hast Thou not bid me seek Thy face?
   And shall I seek in vain?
And can the ear of sovereign grace
   Be deaf when I complain?

6 Thy mercy-seat is open still,
   Here let my soul retreat;
With humble hope attend Thy will,
   And wait beneath Thy feet.
              Miss Annie Steele (1717—1778).

BYEFIELD. C. M.   THOS. HASTINGS (1784—1872).

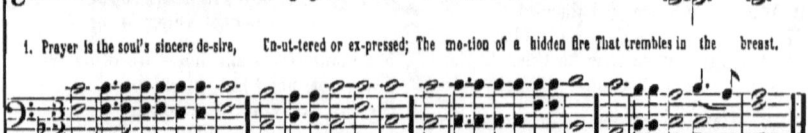

1. Prayer is the soul's sincere de-sire, Un-ut-tered or ex-pressed; The mo-tion of a hidden fire That trembles in the breast.

HYMNS OF DEVOTION.

PARK STREET. L. M.   F. M. A. VENUA, 1788.

1. Fountain of grace, rich, full and free, What need I, that is not in Thee? Full pardon, strength to meet the day, And peace which none can take a-way, And peace which none can take a-way.

176   *My Springs in Thee.*

1 Fountain of grace, rich, full, and free,
What need I, that is not in Thee?
Full pardon, strength to meet the day,
And peace which none can take away.

2 Doth sickness fill my heart with fear,
'Tis sweet to know that Thou art near;
Am I with dread of justice tried,
'Tis sweet to know that Christ hath died.

3 In life, Thy promises of aid
Forbid my heart to be afraid;
In death, peace gently vails my eyes,—
Christ rose and I shall surely rise.
                           James Edmeston (1791—1867).

177 *We Have Access by One Spirit to the Father.*

1 Come, Holy Ghost, and through each heart
    The fulness of Thy glory pour;
Who, with the Son and Father, art
    One Godhead, blest for evermore.

2 So shall our soul and voice conspire
    Thy praise eternal to resound;
So shall Thy love our hearts inspire,
    And kindle every heart around.

3 Father of Mercies, hear our cry;
    Hear us, O sole-begotten Son;
Hear us, O Holy Ghost most high,
    One God, while endless ages run.
                          Tr. Edward Caswall.

178   *Doxology.*

Praise God, from whom all blessings flow;
Praise Him, all creatures here below;
Praise Him above, ye heavenly host;
Praise Father, Son, and Holy Ghost.

179   *Prayer.*
         Tune, BYFIELD.

1 Prayer is the soul's sincere desire,
    Unuttered or expressed;
The motion of a hidden fire
    That trembles in the breast.

2 Prayer is the burden of a sigh;
    The falling of a tear;
The upward glancing of an eye,
    When none but God is near.

3 Prayer is the simplest form of speech
    That infant lips can try;
Prayer, the sublimest strains that reach
    The Majesty on high.

4 Prayer is the contrite sinner's voice
    Returning from his ways,
While angels in their songs rejoice,
    And say — "Behold, he prays."

5 Prayer is the Christian's vital breath,
    The Christian's native air,
His watchword at the gate of death:
    He enters heaven with prayer.
                       Rev. J. Montgomery (1771—1854).

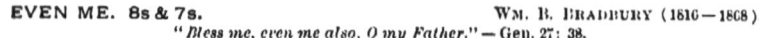

180 *Even Me.*

1 Lord, I hear of showers of blessing
Thou art scattering full and free,
Showers, the thirsty land refreshing:
Let some droppings fall on me.

2 Pass me not, O gracious Father!
Sinful though my heart may be;
Thou might'st leave me, but the rather
Let Thy mercy fall on me.

3 Pass me not, O tender Saviour!
Let me love and cling to Thee;
I am longing for Thy favor;
Whilst Thou 'rt calling, oh, call me.

4 Pass me not, O mighty spirit!
Thou canst make the blind to see;
Witnesser of Jesus' merit,
Speak the word of power to me.

5 Love of God, so pure and changeless;
Blood of Christ so rich and free;
Grace of God, so strong and boundless;—
Magnify them all in me.

6 Pass me not! Thy lost one bringing,
Bind my heart, O Lord, to Thee;
While the streams of life are springing,
Blessing others, oh, bless me.

Mrs. Elizabeth Conder, 1860.

COMMUNION. L. M. *E. Miller, English.*

181 *The Stony Heart.*

1 O for a glance of heavenly day,
To take this stubborn stone away,
And thaw, with beams of love divine,
This heart, this frozen heart of mine.

2 The rocks can rend, the earth can quake,
The seas can roar, the mountains shake;
Of feeling all things show some sign,
But this unfeeling heart of mine.

3 To hear the sorrows Thou hast felt,
Dear Lord an adamant would melt;
But I can read each moving line,
And nothing move this heart of mine.

4 But power divine can do the deed;
And, Lord, that power I greatly need:
Thy Spirit can from dross refine,
And melt and change this heart of mine.

Rev. Joseph Hart (1712—1768).

(72)

HYMNS OF DEVOTION.

MERTON. C. M. — Henry Kemble Oliver (1800—1885).

1. God, my sup-port-er and my hope, My help for-ev-er near,
Thine arm of mer-cy held me up When sink-ing in de-spair.

182 *God Our Portion.* Ps. 73.
1 God, my supporter and my hope,
 My help forever near,
Thine arm of mercy held me up
 When sinking in despair.

2 Thy counsels, Lord, shall guide my feet
 Through this dark wilderness;
Thy hand conduct me near Thy seat,
 To dwell before Thy face.

3 Were I in heaven without my God,
 'T would be no joy to me;
And while this earth is my abode,
 I long for none but Thee.

3 What if the strings of life were broke,
 And flesh and heart should faint?
God is my soul's eternal rock,
 The strength of every saint.

4 But to draw near to Thee, my God,
 Shall be my sweet employ;
My tongue shall sound Thy works abroad
 And tell the world my joy.
 Rev. Isaac Watts (1674—1748).

183 *Value of the Soul.*
1 What is the thing of greatest price,
 The whole creation round;
That which was lost in paradise,
 That which in Christ was found?

2 The soul of man, Jehovah's breath,
 That keeps two worlds at strife;
Hell moves beneath to work its death,
 Heaven stoops to give it life.

3 God to redeem it, did not spare
 His well-beloved Son;
Jesus, to save it, deigned to bear
 The sins of all in one.

4 And is this treasure borne below,
 In earthen vessels frail?
Can none its utmost value know,
 Till flesh and spirit fail?

5 Then let us gather round the cross,
 That knowledge to obtain;
Not by the soul's eternal loss,
 But everlasting gain.
 Rev. J. Montgomery (1771—1854).

184 *Longing for Holiness.*
 Tune, COMMUNION.
1 Oh, that my load of sin were gone!
 Oh, that I could at last submit!
At Jesus feet to lay me down —
 To lay my soul at Jesus' feet.

2 Rest for my soul I long to find:
 Saviour of all, if mine Thou art —
Give me Thy meek, Thy lowly mind,
 And stamp Thine image on my heart.

3 Break off the yoke of inbred sin,
 And fully set my spirit free;
I cannot rest till pure within,
 Till I am wholly lost in Thee.

4 Fain would I learn of Thee, my God;
 Thy light and easy burden prove —
Thy cross all stained with hallowed blood—
 The labor of Thy dying love.
 Rev. Chas. Wesley (1708—1788).

HYMNS OF DEVOTION.

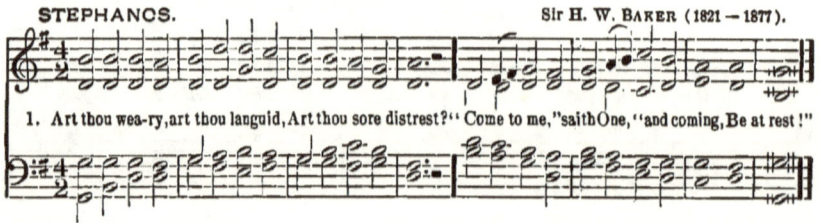

185 *Come Unto Me.*

1 Art thou weary, art thou languid,
 Art thou sore distrest?
"Come to me," saith One, "and coming,
 Be at rest!"

2 Hath He marks to lead me to Him,
 If He be my guide?
"In His feet and hands are wound-prints,
 And His side."

3 Hath He diadem as monarch
 That His brow adorns?
"Yea a crown in very surety,
 But of thorns."

4 If I find Him, if I follow,
 What my future here?

" Many a sorrow, many a labor,
 Many a tear."

5 If I still hold closely to Him,
 What hath He at last?
" Sorrow vanquished, labor ended,
 Jordan past."

6 If I ask Him to receive me,
 Will He say me nay?
" Not till earth and not till Heaven
 Pass away."

7 Finding, following, keeping, struggling,
 Is He sure to bless?
" Saints, apostles, prophets, martyrs,
 Answer, Yes."

Stephen of St. Sabas (725—794).
Tr. by John Mason Neale (1818—1866).

PAX TECUM. G. T. CALDBECK.

186 *Peace, Perfect Peace.*

1 Peace, perfect peace, in this dark world of sin?
 The blood of Jesus whispers peace within.

2 Peace, perfect peace, by thronging duties press'd?
 To do the will of Jesus, this is rest.

3 Peace, perfect peace, with loved ones far away?
 In Jesus keeping we are safe and they.

4 Peace, perfect peace, our future all unknown?
 Jesus we know, and He is on the Throne.

5 Peace, perfect peace, death shadowing us and ours?
 Jesus has vanquish'd death and all its powers.

6 It is enough: earth's struggles soon shall cease,
 And Jesus call us to Heaven's perfect peace.

Bp. Edward H. Bickersteth (1825—).

HYMNS OF DEVOTION.

HENDON. 7s.   Rev. C. MALAN (1787—1864).

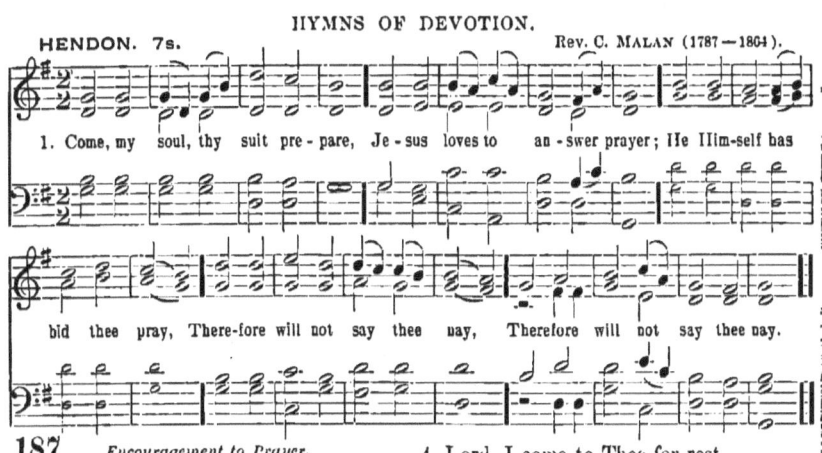

1. Come, my soul, thy suit pre-pare, Je-sus loves to an-swer prayer; He Him-self has bid thee pray, There-fore will not say thee nay, Therefore will not say thee nay.

187   *Encouragement to Prayer.*

1 Come, my soul, thy suit prepare,
Jesus loves to answer prayer;
He Himself has bid thee pray,
Therefore will not say thee nay.

2 Thou art coming to a King,
Large petitions with thee bring;
For His grace and power are such,
None can ever ask too much.

3 With my burden I begin,
Lord, remove this load of sin;
Let Thy blood for sinners spilt,
Set my conscience free from guilt

4 Lord, I come to Thee for rest,
Take possession of my breast;
There Thy blood-bought right maintain,
And without a rival reign.

5 While I am a pilgrim here,
Let Thy love my spirit cheer;
As my Guide, my Guard, my Friend,
Lead me to my journey's end.
                Rev. J. Newton (1725—1807).

188   *Doxology.*

Sing we to our God above
Praise eternal as His love;
Praise Him, all ye heavenly host—
Father, Son and Holy Ghost.

MERRIAL. 6s & 5s.   JOSEPH BARNBY (1838—).

1. Now the day is o-ver, Night is drawing nigh, Shadows of the even-ing Steal across the sky.
                                                        Steal a-cross

189   *The Day is Over.*

1 Now the day is over,
Night is drawing nigh,
Shadows of the evening
Steal across the sky.

2 Jesus, give the weary
Calm and sweet repose;
With Thy tenderest blessing
May our eyelids close.

3 Through the long night-watches,
May Thine angels spread
Their white wings above me,
Watching round my bed.

4 When the morning wakens,
Then may I arise,
Pure and fresh and sinless
In Thy holy eyes.
               Rev. Sabine Baring-Gould (1834—).

HYMNS OF DEVOTION.

GRÖNINGEN. 6s, 8s, & 3s. JOACHIM NEANDER (1640—1680).

190 *Surely the Lord is in This Place.*

1 God reveals His presence:
Let us now adore Him,
And with awe appear before Him.
God is in His temple:
All within keep silence,
Prostrate lie with deepest reverence.
   Him alone
   God we own,
   Him our God and Saviour:
   Praise His name forever.

2 God reveals His presence:
Hear the harps resounding;
See the crowds the throne surrounding;
"Holy, holy, holy!"
Hear the hymn ascending,
Angels, saints, their voices blending.
   Bow Thine ear
   To us here;
   Hearken, O Lord Jesus,
   To our humbler praises.

3 O Thou Fount of blessing,
Purify my spirit;
Trusting only in Thy merit,
Like the holy angels
Who behold Thy glory,
May I ceaselessly adore Thee.
   Let Thy will
   Ever still
   Rule Thy Church terrestrial,
   As the hosts celestial.

4 Jesus, dwell within me;
Whilst on earth I tarry,
Make me Thy blest sanctuary;
Then, on angel pinions,
Waft me to those regions,
Filled with bright seraphic legions.
   May this hope
   Bear me up,
   Till these eyes forever
   Gaze on Thee, my Saviour!

Gerhard of Tersteegen (1606—1769).
Tr. by Wm. Mercer.

HYMNS OF DEVOTION.

VERNON. 7s.   Rev. Wm. S. Lacy. D. D., 1891.

191
Evening Song.

1 Slowly sinks the setting sun,
Now the work of day is done;
Lord, we come a thankful throng,
Raise to Thee our evening song.

2 For Thy tender care bestowed,
For Thy pardoning blood which flow'd;
For Thy love that crowns our days,
Lord, accept our grateful praise.

3 And when sets life's weary sun,
When the toil of earth is done,
To Thy home of peaceful rest,
Lord, receive us, ever blest.

4 For the robe, the palm, the blood,
May we always praise our God,
And with all the ransomed throng,
Swell high heaven's triumphant song.

Rev. Wm. S. Lacy, D.D., 1891.

PLEYEL'S HYMN. 7s.   Ignace Pleyel (1757—1831).

192
Before Sermon.

1 Lord, we come before Thee now,
At Thy feet we humbly bow;
Oh, do not our suit disdain;
Shall we seek Thee, Lord, in vain?

2 Lord, on Thee our souls depend;
In compassion, now descend;
Fill our hearts with Thy rich grace;
Tune our lips to sing Thy praise.

3 In Thine own appointed way,
Now we seek Thee, here we stay;
Lord, we know not how to go,
Till a blessing Thou bestow.

4 Send some message from Thy word,
That may joy and peace afford,
Let Thy Spirit now impart
Full salvation to each heart.

5 Grant that all may seek and find
Thee a God supremely kind;
Heal the sick, the captive free;
Let us all rejoice in Thee.

Rev. Wm. Hammond (—1783).

HYMNS OF DEVOTION.

ST. MARGARET. 8s & 6s. A. L. PEACE, Mus. D.

1. O Love that wilt not let me go, I rest my weary soul in Thee; I give Thee back the life I owe, That in Thine o-cean depths its flow May rich-er, full-er be.

193 *If any man be in Christ; he is a new creature.*

1 O Love that wilt not let me go,
  I rest my weary soul in Thee;
  I give Thee back the life I owe,
  That in Thine ocean depths its flow
    May richer, fuller be.

2 O Light that followest all my way,
  I yield my flickering torch to Thee;
  My heart restores its borrowed ray,
  That in Thy sunshine's glow its day
    May brighter, fairer be.

3 O Joy that seekest me through pain,
  I cannot close my heart to Thee;
  I trace the rainbow through the rain,
  And feel the promise is not vain
    That morn shall tearless be.

4 O Cross that liftest up my head,
  I dare not ask to fly from Thee;
  I lay in dust life's glory dead,
  And from the ground there blossoms red
    Life that shall endless be.
                                  G. Matheson.

HESPERUS. L. M. Rev. Sir HENRY W. BAKER, Mus. Bac. (1821—1877).

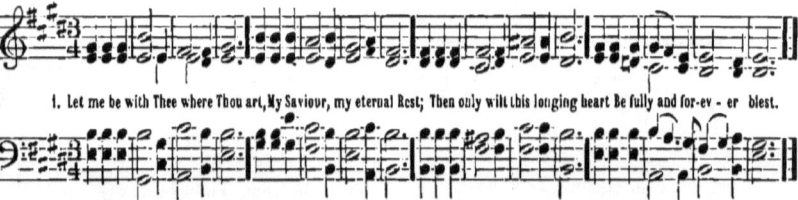

1. Let me be with Thee where Thou art, My Saviour, my eternal Rest; Then only will this longing heart Be fully and for-ev-er blest.

194 *Where I am, there shall also My servant be.*

1 Let me be with Thee where Thou art,
  My Saviour, my eternal Rest;
  Then only will this longing heart
    Be fully and forever blest.

2 Let me be with Thee where Thou art,
  Thy unveiled glory to behold;
  Then only will this wandering heart
    Cease to be treacherous, faithless, cold.

3 Let me be with Thee where Thou art,
  Where spotless saints Thy name adore;
  Then only will this sinful heart
    Be evil and defiled no more.

4 Let me be with Thee where Thou art,
  Where none can die, where none remove;
  There neither life nor death will part
    Me from Thy presence and Thy love.
                          Miss Charlotte Elliott (1789—1871).

HYMNS OF DEVOTION.

CHORAL SONG. C. M.   W. B. CRIDLIN, 1891.

1. Come, let us join with one ac-cord In hymns a-round the throne; This is the day our ris-ing Lord Hath made, and called His own.

195   *There Remaineth a Rest.*
1 Come, let us join with one accord
  In hymns around the throne;
This is the day our rising Lord
  Hath made, and called his own.

2 This is the day that God hath blessed,
  The brightest of the seven,
Type of that everlasting rest
  The saints enjoy in heaven.

3 Then let us in His name sing on,
  And hasten to that day
When our Redeemer shall come down,
  And shadows pass away.

4 Not one, but all our days below,
  Let us in hymns employ;
And in our Lord rejoicing, go
  To His eternal joy.
        Rev. Chas. Wesley (1708—1788).

196   *The Pastoral Office.*
1 Let Sion's watchmen all awake,
  And take the alarm they give;

Now let them from the mouth of God,
  Their solemn charge receive.

2 'T is not a cause of small import,
  The pastor's care demands;
But what might fill an angel's heart,
  And filled a Saviour's hands.

3 They watch for souls, for which the Lord
  Did heavenly bliss forego;
For souls, which must forever live
  In raptures, or in woe.

4 All to the great tribunal haste,
  The account to render there;
And shouldst Thou strictly mark our faults,
  Lord how should we appear?

5 May they that Jesus, whom they preach,
  Their own Redeemer see;
And watch Thou daily o'er their souls,
  That they may watch for Thee.
        Rev. Philip Doddridge (1702—1751).

DOWNS. C. M.   LOWELL MASON (1792—1872).

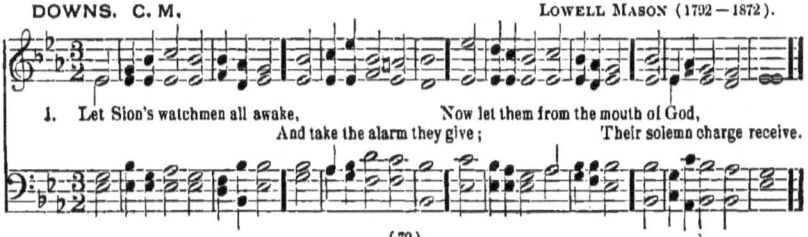

1. Let Sion's watchmen all awake, And take the alarm they give; Now let them from the mouth of God, Their solemn charge receive.

HYMNS OF DEVOTION.

DUKE ST. L. M.   JOHN HATTON, 1790.

1. There is a God who reigns above, Lord of the heaven and earth and seas; I fear His wrath, I ask His love, And with my lips I sing His praise.

197   *Life the Time to Serve God.*
1 There is a God who reigns above,
   Lord of the heaven and earth and seas;
   I fear His wrath, I ask his love,
   And with my lips I sing His praise.

2 There is a law which He has made,
   To teach us all that we must do;
   My soul, be His commands obeyed,
   For they are holy, just and true.

3 There is a gospel rich in grace,
   Whence sinners all their comforts draw;
   Lord, I repent and seek Thy face,
   For I have often broke Thy law.

4 There is an hour when I must die,
   Nor do I know how soon 't will come;
   How many younger much than I, [doom!
   Have passed by death to hear their

5 Let me improve the hours I have,
   Before the day of grace is fled;
   There's no repentance in the grave,
   Nor pardon offered to the dead.
            Rev. Isaac Watts (1674—1748).

198   *Christ Crucified, the Wisdom and Power of God.*
1 Nature with open volume stands,
   To spread her Maker's praise abroad;
   And every labor of His hands
   Shows something worthy of a God.

2 But in the grace that rescued man,
   His brightest form of glory shines;

Here on the cross, 't is fairest drawn
   In precious blood and crimson lines.

3 O! the sweet wonders of that cross,
   Where God the Saviour loved and died;
   Her noblest life my spirit draws   [side.
   From His dear wounds and bleeding

4 I would for ever speak His name,
   In sounds to mortal ears unknown;
   With angels join to praise the Lamb,
   And worship at His Father's throne.
            Rev. Isaac Watts (1674—1748).

199   *Reliance on Christ's Righteousness.*
1 No more, my God, I boast no more
   Of all the duties I have done;
   I quit the hopes I held before;
   To trust the merits of Thy Son.

2 Now for the love I bear His name,
   What was my gain, I count my loss;
   My former pride I call my shame,
   And nail my glory to His cross.

3 Yes! and I must and will esteem
   All things but loss for Jesus' sake;
   O! may my soul be found in Him,
   And of His righteousness partake.

4 The best obedience of my hands
   Dares not appear before Thy throne;
   But faith can answer Thy demands,
   By pleading what my Lord has done.
            Rev. Isaac Watts (1674—1748).

BELIEVERS' COMFORT.

GOSHEN. 11s. GREEK MELODY.

1. { Tho' faint, yet pur-su-ing, we go on our way; }
   { The Lord is our Lead-er, His (Omit) } word is our stay;
   D.C. The Lord is our Ref-uge, and (Omit) whom can we fear.

Though suf-f'ring and sor-row, and tri-al be near,

By per. of Oliver Ditson Company, owners of Copyright.

200 *Faint, yet Pursuing.*

1 Though faint, yet pursuing, we go on our way; [Stay;
The Lord is our Leader, His word is our
Though suffering, and sorrow, and trial be near, [fear?
The Lord is our Refuge, and whom can we

2 He raiseth the fallen, He cheereth the faint; [their complaint;
The weak, and oppressed — He will hear
The way may be weary, and thorny the road, [God.
But how can we falter? — our help is in

3 And to His green pastures our footsteps He leads; [feeds!
His flock in the desert how kindly He
The lambs in His bosom He tenderly bears,
And brings back the wanderers all safe from the snares.

4 Though clouds may surround us, our God is our Light; [our Might;
Though storms rage around us, our God is
So, faint yet pursuing, still onward we come, [our home.
The Lord is our Leader, and heaven is

Rev. J. N. Darby (1800—1882).

201 *Psalm 23.*

1 The Lord is my Shepherd; no want shall I know; [rest;
I feed in green pastures; safe folded I
He leadeth my soul where the still waters flow, [when oppressed.
Restores me when wandering, redeems

2 Through the valley and shadow of death though I stray, [fear;
Since Thou art my Guardian, no evil I
Thy rod shall defend me, Thy staff be my stay; [near.
No harm can befall with my Comforter

3 In the midst of affliction my table is spread: [neth o'er;
With blessings unmeasured my cup run-
With perfume and oil Thou anointest my head; [more?
Oh, what shall I ask of Thy providence

4 Let goodness and mercy, my bountiful God! [above;
Still follow my steps till I meet Thee
I seek, by the path which my forefathers trod, [kingdom of love.
Through the land of their sojourn, Thy

Rev. James Montgomery (1771—1854).

(81)

BELIEVERS' COMFORT.

MUNICH. 7s, 6s, D. Würtemberger Gesangbuch, 1711.
Ascribed to JOHANN HERMANN, 1620.

1. I could not do with-out Thee, O Sav-iour of the lost!
Whose wondrous love redeemed me At such tre-men-dous cost;
Thy righteousness, Thy par-don,
Thy pre-cious blood must be My on-ly hope and com-fort, My glo-ry and my plea.

202 *I Could Not Do Without Thee.*

1 I could not do without Thee,
  O Saviour of the lost!
 Whose wondrous love redeemed me
  At such tremendous cost;
 Thy righteousness, Thy pardon,
  Thy precious blood must be
 My only hope and comfort,
  My glory and my plea.

2 I could not do without Thee,
  I could not stand alone,
 I have no strength or goodness,
  No wisdom of my own;
 But Thou belovéd Saviour,
  Art all in all to me,
 And perfect strength in weakness
  Is theirs who lean on Thee.

3 I could not do without Thee,
  For, O the way is long,
 And I am often weary,
  And sigh replaces song.
 How could I do without Thee?
  I do not know the way;
 Thou knowest and Thou leadest,
  And wilt not let me stray.

4 I could not do without Thee!
  For life is fleeting fast,
 And soon in solemn loneness
  The river must be passed.
 But Thou wilt never leave me,
  And though the waves roll high,
 I know Thou wilt be with me,
  And whisper, "It is I."

Miss Frances Ridley Havergal (1836—1879).

203 *Light in darkness.*
Tune, SBOHR.

1 O Thou who driest the mourner's tear,
  How dark this world would be,
 If, pierced by sins and sorrows here,
  We could not fly to Thee!

2 The friends, who in our sunshine live,
  When winter comes, are flown;
 And he who has but tears to give,
  Must weep those tears alone.

3 But Thou wilt heal that broken heart,
  Which, like the plants that throw
 Their fragrance from the wounded part,
  Breathes sweetness out of woe.

4 When joy no longer soothes or cheers,
  And e'en the hope that threw
 A moment's sparkle o'er our tears,
  Is dimmed and vanished too.

5 Oh, who could bear life's stormy doom,
  Did not Thy wing of love
 Come brightly wafting through the gloom
  Our peace-branch from above?

6 Then sorrow, touched by Thee, grows bright
  With more than rapture's ray;
 As darkness shows us worlds of light,
  We never saw by day.

Thomas Moore (1779—1852).

(82)

BELIEVERS' COMFORT.

LYONS. 10s & 11s. 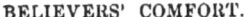 Francis Joseph Haydn (1732—1809).

204 *The Lord Will Provide.*

1 Though troubles assail, and dangers affright;
Though friends should all fail, and foes all unite;
Yet one thing secures us, whatever betide;
The Scripture assures us, the Lord will provide.

2 No strength of our own, or goodness we claim,
Yet since we have known the Saviour's great name,
In this, our strong tower, for safety we hide;
The Lord is our power, the Lord will provide.

3 When life sinks apace, and death is in view,
This word of His grace shall comfort us through,
No fearing or doubting, with Christ on our side,
We hope to die shouting, the Lord will provide.

Rev. John Newton (1725 – 1807).

SPOHR. C. M. Adapted from Louis Spohr.

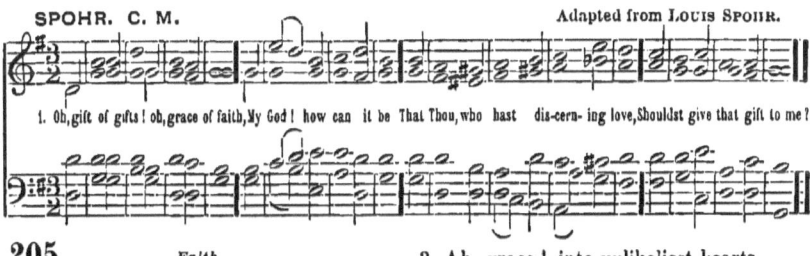

205 *Faith.*

1 Oh, gift of gifts! oh, grace of faith,
My God! how can it be
That Thou, who hast discerning love,
Shouldst give that gift to me?

2 How many hearts Thou mightst have
More innocent than mine!
How many souls more worthy far
Of that sweet touch of Thine!

3 Ah, grace! into unlikeliest hearts
It is Thy boast to come;
The glory of Thy light to find
In darkest spots a home.

4 Oh, happy, happy that I am!
If Thou canst be, O Faith,
[had The treasure that Thou art in life,
What wilt Thou be in death!

Rev. F. W. Faber, D. D. (1814 – 1863).

BELIEVERS' COMFORT.

ST. PETERSBURG. 8s, 6l. DIMITRI BORTUIANSKI.

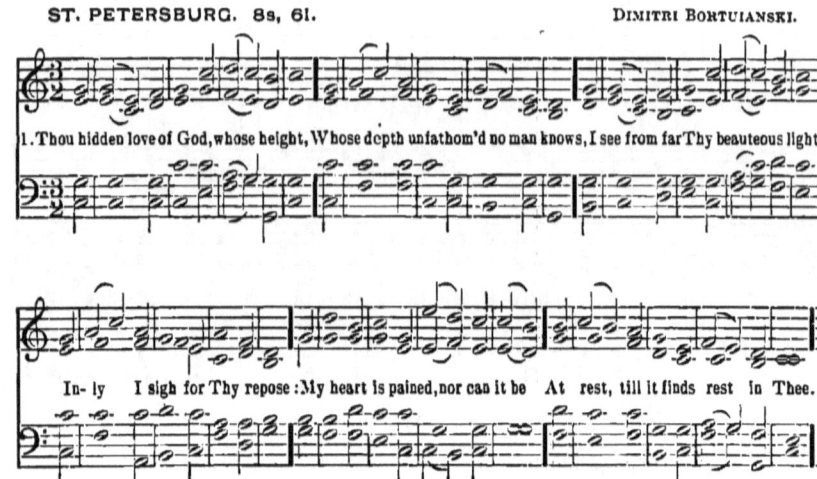

206   *Able to Comprehend.*

1 Thou hidden love of God, whose height,
  Whose depth unfathomed no man knows,
I see from far Thy beauteous light,
  Inly I sigh for Thy repose:
My heart is pained, nor can it be
At rest, till it finds rest in Thee.

2 Thy secret voice invites me still
  The sweetness of Thy yoke to prove;
And fain I would, but though my will
  Seems fixed, yet wide my passions rove;
Yet hindrances strew all the way:
I aim at Thee, yet from Thee stray.

3 'T is mercy all,—that Thou hast brought
  My mind to seek its peace in Thee:
Yet while I seek but find Thee not,
  No peace my wandering soul shall see:
O, when shall all my wanderings end,
And all my steps to Thee-ward tend?

4 O Lord, Thy sovereign aid impart,
  And hear Thy humble suppliant's prayer;
Chase this self-will through all my heart,
  Through all its latent mazes there:
Make me Thy duteous child, that I
Ceaseless may " Abba, Father " cry.
Gerhard Tersteegen (1687—1769).
Tr. John Wesley.

SUBMISSION. 10s, & 4s. GEORGE LOMAS.

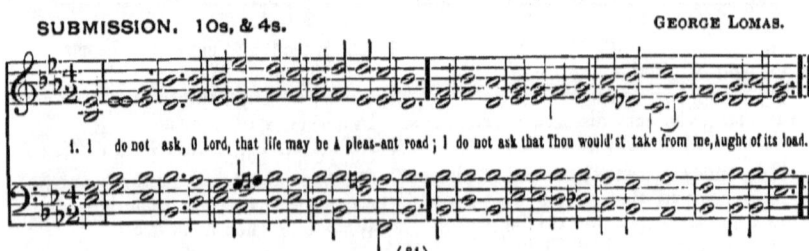

(84)

BELIEVERS' COMFORT.

RESIGNATION. L. M. 6l. JOHANN MICHAEL HAYDN (1737—1803).

1. When gathering clouds around I view, And days are dark, and friends are few, On Him I lean who not in vain Ex-peri-enced ev-'ry hu-man pain; He sees my wants, al-lays my fears, And counts and treas-ures up my tears.

207 *Christ Able to Succor the Tempted.*
1 When gathering clouds around I view,
And days are dark, and friends are few,
On Him I lean who, not in vain
Experienced every human pain;
He sees my wants allays my fears,
And counts and treasures up my tears.

2 If aught should tempt my soul to stray
From heavenly wisdom's narrow way;
To fly the good I would pursue,
Or do the sin I would not do;
Still He who felt temptation's power,
Shall guard me in that dangerous hour.

3 When sorrowing o'er some stone I bend
Which covers what was once a friend,
And from his voice, his hand, his smile,
Divides me for a little while;
Thou, Saviour, mark'st the tears I shed,
For Thou didst weep o'er Lazarus dead.

4 And O, when I have safely past
Through every conflict but the last,
Still, still unchanging, watch beside
My painful bed, for Thou hast died;

Then point to realms of cloudless day,
And wipe the latest tear away.
Sir Robert Grant (1785—1838).

208 *I Do Not Ask, O Lord.* Tune, SUBMISSION.
1 I do not ask, O Lord, that life may be
  A pleasant road;
I do not ask that Thou wouldst take from me
  Aught of its load.

2 I do not ask that flowers should always
  Beneath my feet;   [spring
I know too well the poison and the sting
  Of things too sweet.

3 I do not ask, O Lord, that Thou shouldst
  Full radiance here;   [shed
Give but a ray of peace, that I may tread
  Without a fear.

4 I do not ask my cross to understand,
  My way to see;
Better in darkness just to feel Thy hand,
  And follow Thee.

5 Joy is like restless day; but peace divine
  Like quiet night.
Lead me, O Lord, till perfect day shall shine,
  Through peace to light.

Miss Adelaide Proctor (—1864).

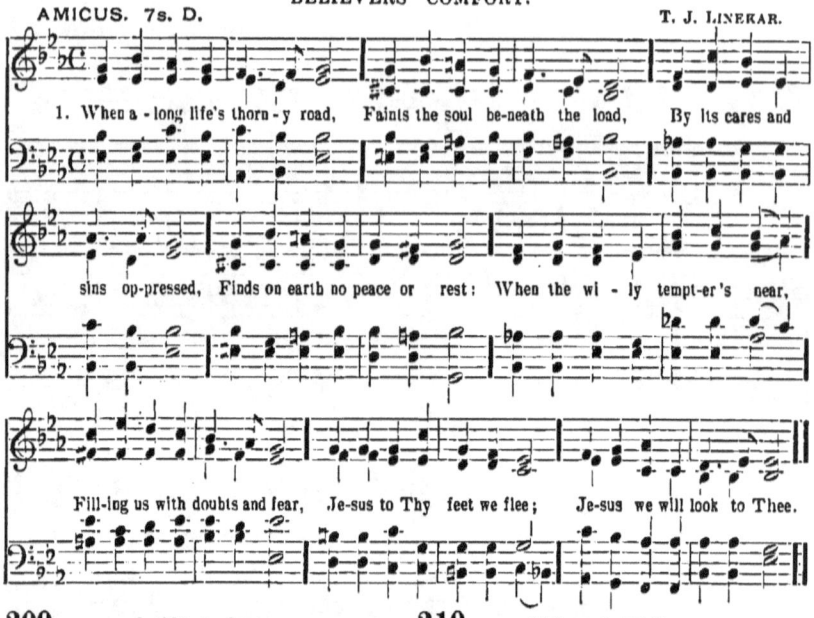

209 *Looking to Jesus.*

1 When, along life's thorny road,
Faints the soul beneath the load,
By its cares and sins oppressed,
Finds on earth no peace or rest:
When the wily tempter's near,
Filling us with doubts and fear,
Jesus, to Thy feet we flee;
Jesus we will look to Thee.

2 Thou, our Saviour, from the throne
Listening to Thy people's moan;
Thou, the living Head, dost share
Every pang Thy members bear;
Full of tenderness Thou art,
Thou wilt heal the broken heart;
Full of power, Thine arms shall quell
All the rage and might of hell.

3 Mighty to redeem and save,
Thou hast overcome the grave;
Thou the bars of death hast riven,
Opened wide the gate of heaven;
Soon in glory Thou shalt come,
Taking Thy poor pilgrims home:
Jesus, then we all shall be
Ever, ever, Lord, with Thee!

J. G. Deck (1802—).

210 *Welcome to the Cross.*

1 'T is my happiness below,
Not to live without the cross;
But the Saviour's power to know,
Sanctifying every loss.
Trials must and will befall;
But with humble faith to see
Love inscribed upon them all,
This is happiness to me.

2 God, in Israel, sows the seeds
Of affliction, pain and toil;
These spring up and choke the weeds
Which would else o'erspread the soil.
Trials make the promise sweet,
Trials give new life to prayer;
Trials bring me to His feet,
Lay me low, and keep me there.

3 Did I meet no trials here,
No chastisement by the way;
Might I not, with reason, fear
I should prove a cast-away?
Aliens may escape the rod,
Sunk in earthly, vain delight;
But the true-born child of God,
Must not, would not, if he might.

Wm. Cowper (1731—1800).

MISCELLANEOUS AND OCCASIONAL.

BENEVENTO. 7s. D. SAMUEL WEBBE (1803—1887).

1. While, with ceaseless course the sun Hast-ed thro' the form-er year, Ma-ny souls their race have run,
D.S. We a lit-tle long-er wait;
Nev-er-more to meet us here; Fixed in an e-ter-nal state, They have done with all be-low;
But how lit-tle none can know.

211 *New Year.*

1 While with ceaseless course, the sun
Hasted through the former year,
Many souls their race have run,
Nevermore to meet us here:
Fixed in an eternal state,
They have done with all below;
We a little longer wait;
But how little none can know.

2 As the wingéd arrow flies
Speedily the mark to find;
As the lightening from the skies
Darts and leaves no trace behind,—
Swiftly thus our fleeting days
Bear us down life's rapid stream;
Upward, Lord, our spirits raise,
All below is but a dream.

3 Thanks for mercies past receive;
Pardon of our sins renew;
Teach us henceforth how to live,
With eternity in view:
Bless Thy word to old and young;
Fill us with a Saviour's love;
When our life's short race is run,
May we dwell with Thee above.
Rev. J. Newton (1725—1807).

212 *Thanksgiving.*

1 Praise to God, immortal praise,
For the love that crowns our days!
Bounteous Source of every joy,
Let Thy praise our tongues employ.
For the blessings of the field,
For the stores the gardens yield;
For the fruits in full supply,
Ripened 'neath the summer sky;—

2 All that spring with bounteous hand
Scatters o'er the smiling land;
All that liberal autumn pours
From her rich o'erflowing stores;
These to Thee, my God, we owe,
Source whence all our blessings flow;
And for these my soul shall raise
Grateful vows and solemn praise.
Mrs. Anne L. Barbauld (1743—1825).

213 *General Thanksgiving.*

1 Swell the anthem, raise the song;
Praises to our God belong;
Saints and angels join to sing
Praises to the heavenly King.
Blessings from His liberal hand
Flow around this happy land:
Kept by Him, no foes annoy;
Peace and freedom we enjoy.

2 Here, beneath a virtuous sway
May we cheerfully obey;
Never feel oppression's rod,
Ever own and worship God.
Hark! the voice of nature sings
Praises to the King of kings;
Let us join the choral song,
And the grateful notes prolong.
Rev. Nathan Strong, D. D. (—1816).

(87)

MISCELLANEOUS AND OCCASIONAL.

MELCOMBE. L. M. SAMUEL WEBBE (1740—1816).

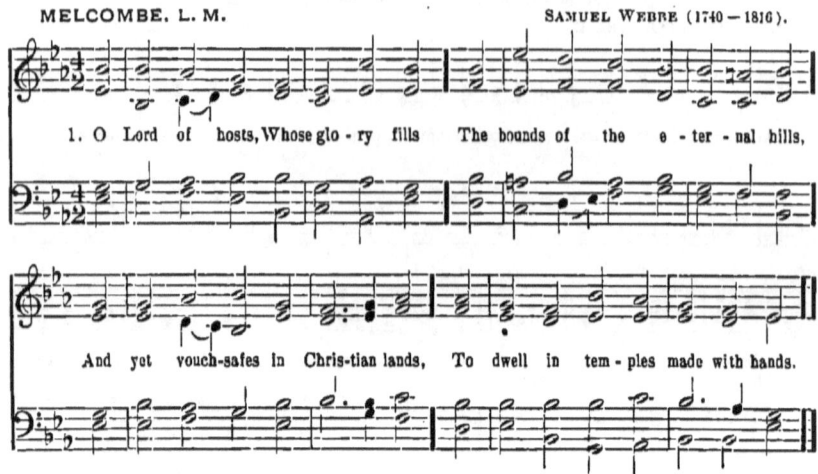

1. O Lord of hosts, Whose glo-ry fills The bounds of the e-ter-nal hills, And yet vouch-safes in Chris-tian lands, To dwell in tem-ples made with hands.

214 *Laying a Corner Stone.*

1 O Lord of hosts, Whose glory fills
The bounds of the eternal hills,
And yet vouchsafes, in Christian lands,
To dwell in temples made with hands:

2 Grant that all we, who here to-day,
Rejoicing this foundation lay,
May be in very deed Thine own,
Built on the precious Corner-stone.

3 Endue the creatures with Thy grace,
That shall adorn Thy dwelling-place;
The beauty of the oak and pine,
The gold and silver, make them Thine.

4 To Thee they all belong: to Thee
The treasures of the earth and sea;
And when we bring them to Thy Throne,
We but present Thee with Thine own.

5 The heads that guide endue with skill,
The hands that work preserve from ill,
That we, who these foundations lay,
May raise the topstone in its day.

6 Both now and ever, Lord, protect
The temple of Thine own elect;
Be Thou in them, and they in Thee,
O Ever-blessèd Trinity.
Rev. John Mason Neale (1818—1866).

215 *Hymn of Dedication.*
Tune, AUTUMN.

1 Unto Thee, Triune Jehovah,
"Glorious in Thy works and ways,"
We now dedicate this temple;

May each stone here voice Thy praise !
Built on Thee, our sure foundation,
Faith supreme o'er human fears,
Consecrates her all, rejoicing
Thus to serve through coming years.

2 We are weak, abide Thou with us,
Give to us Thy strength divine,
Purge from self, then like the stars,
Shall our work eternal shine.
Guard this church, Lord, with Thy spirit;
Let no error creep within;
But Thy truth, Thy word incarnate,
Pierce the mists of death and sin.

3 Draw Thou nigh, until Thy glory
At this mercy seat appears,
And the wings of waiting seraphs
Bear to Thee our contrite tears.
Oh, baptize us, Lord, with fire !
Let unnumbered souls be won,
That shall witness bear in heaven
What this church on earth hath done.

4 Still remember our dear children,
At baptismal altar blest,
Lord, we covenant with Thee for them;
May their lifes our faith attest.
Let Thy peace, Thy constant presence,
Make this spot a holy place.
Grant our church that here we give Thee,
Deathless service through Thy grace.
Mrs. Sophie F. Sea, 1891.

(88)

MISCELLANEOUS AND OCCASIONAL.

BROOKLYN. H. M.   J. ZUNDEL (1815—1882).

1. We can-not build alone; To rear, Great God, to Thee, A House which Thou wilt own, Thou must the Builder be.
Not by our might, But by Thy pow'r Must dome and tow'r Take upward flight, Must dome and tow'r Take upward flight.

216   *Hymn of Dedication.*
(Used by per.)

1 We cannot build alone;
To rear, Great God, to Thee,
A House which Thou wilt own,
Thou must the Builder be.
   Not by our might,
   But by Thy power
   Must dome and tower
   Take upward flight.

2 Were all the stones that lie
Unquarried 'neath the sod
Piled up against the sky,
It were not worthy God.
   To make this dear,
   Lord, condescend
   Thy head to bend,
   And enter here.

3 Let Faith here rear to God!
Here Love erect her thrones!
A House for Thine abode
Be built of lively stones!
   We do not err,
   O Holy Ghost!
   Pure hearts Thou dost
   To fanes prefer.

4 The heavenly only stands:
Earth briefly typifies
The House not made with hands,
Eternal in the skies —
   We see its towers:
   How sweet to know,
   When hence we go,
   That House is ours!

A. Coles, M.D., LL. D., (1813 — 1891).

AUTUMN. 8s & 7s, D.   Spanish Melody.

1. Un-to Thee, Triune Jehovah, "Glorious in Thy works and ways," We now ded-i-cate this tem-ple;
D.S. *Consecrates her all rejoicing,*

May each stone here voice Thy praise! Built on Thee, our sure foundation, Faith supreme o'er human fears,
Thus to serve thro' coming years.

MISCELLANEOUS AND OCCASIONAL.

COME, LET US ANEW. 11s, 5s.   SAMUEL WEBBE (1740—1816).

217   *New Year's Day.*

1 Come, let us anew
Our journey pursue,
Roll round with the year,
And never stand still, till the Master appear.
His adorable will
Let us us gladly fulfil,
And our talents improve
By the patience of hope and the labor of love.

2 O that each in the day
Of His coming might say,
"I have fought my way through,
I have finished the work Thou didst give me to do."
O that each from the Lord
May receive the glad word,
"Well and faithfully done,
Enter into My joy, and sit down on my throne." *Rev. Chas. Wesley* (1708—1788).

DUNDEE. C. M.   G. FRANC, 1545. Scotch Psalter, 1615.

218   *Dedication.*

1 O Thou whose own vast temple stands,
Built over earth and sea,
Accept the walls that human hands
Have raised to worship Thee.

2 Lord, from Thine inmost glory send,
Within these courts to bide,
The peace that dwelleth without end,
Serenely by Thy side.

3 May erring minds that worship here,
Be taught the better way;
And they who mourn and they who fear,
Be strengthened as they pray.

4 May faith grow firm, and love grow warm,
And pure devotion rise,
While round these hallowed walls the storm
Of earth-born passion dies.

Wm. Cullen Bryant (1794—1878).

MISCELLANEOUS AND OCCASIONAL.

219 *They Joy before Thee.*

1 Come, ye thankful people, come,
Raise the song of Harvest-home;
All is safely gather'd in,
Ere the winter storms begin;
God, our Maker, doth provide
For our wants to be supplied;
Come to God's own temple, come,
Raise the song of Harvest-home.

2 All this world is God's own field,
Fruit unto His praise to yield;
Wheat and tares therein are sown,
Unto joy or sorrow grown;
Ripening with a wondrous power,
Till the final Harvest-hour;
Grant, O Lord of life, that we
Holy grain and pure may be.

3 Come then, Lord of mercy, come,
Bid us sing Thy Harvest-home;
Let Thy saints be gather'd in,
Free from sorrow, free from sin;
All upon the golden floor,
Praising Thee for evermore;
Come, with all Thine angels come;
Bid us sing Thy Harvest-home.

Rev. Henry Alford (1810—1881).

220 *The Close of the Year.*

1 Thou who roll'st the year around,
Crowned with mercies large and free,
Rich Thy gifts to us abound,
Warm our praise shall rise to Thee.
Kindly to our worship bow,
While our grateful thanks we tell,
That, sustained by Thee we now,
Bid the parting year — farewell!

2 All its numbered days are sped,
All its busy scenes are o'er,
All its joys forever fled,
All its sorrows felt no more.
Mingled with the eternal past,
Its remembrance shall decay;
Yet to be revived at last
At the solemn judgment-day.

3 All our follies, Lord, forgive!
Cleanse us from each guilty stain;
Let Thy grace within us live,
That we spend not years in vain.
Then, when life's last eve shall come,
Happy spirits, may we fly
To our everlasting home,
To our Father's house on high!

Rev. Ray Palmer (1808—1887)

PRAYER FOR THOSE AT SEA.

MELITA. L. M. 6l.   Rev. J. B. Dykes (1823—1876).

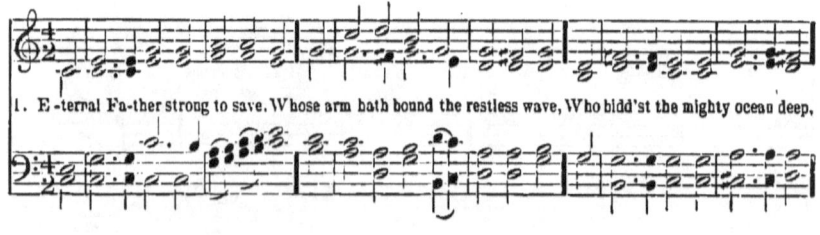

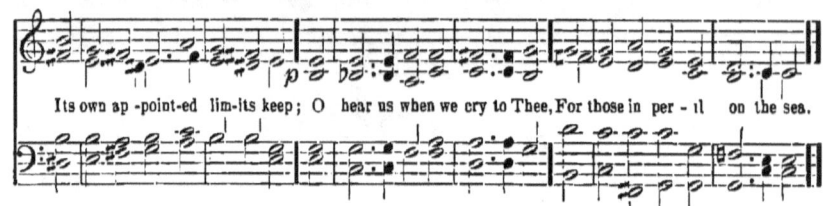

221 *These Men See the Works of the Lord.*
1 Eternal Father, strong to save,
Whose arm hath bound the restless wave,
Who bidd'st the mighty ocean deep
Its own appointed limits keep;
　Oh hear us when we cry to Thee
　For those in peril on the sea.

2 O Christ, whose voice the waters heard
And hushed their raging at Thy word,
Who walkedst on the foaming deep,
And calm amidst the storm didst sleep;
　O hear us when we cry to Thee
　For those in peril on the sea.

3 O Holy Spirit, who didst brood
Upon the waters dark and rude,
And bid their angry tumult cease,
And give, for wild confusion, peace;
　O hear us when we cry to Thee
　For those in peril on the sea.

O Trinity of love and power,
Our brethren shield in danger's hour;
From rock and tempest, fire and foe,
Protect them wheresoe'er they go;
　Thus evermore shall rise to Thee
　Glad hymns of praise from land and sea.
　　　　Wm. Whiting (1825—1878).

222 *The Confidence of all the Ends of the Earth.*
1 Great ruler of the land and sea,
Almighty God, we come to Thee,
Able to succor and to save
From perils of the wind and wave.
　Keep by Thy mighty hand, O keep
　The dwellers on the homeless deep!

2 Speak to the shadows of the night,
And turn their darkness into light;
Smooth down the breaker's rising crest,
Say to the billow, "Be at rest!"
　Keep by thy mighty hand, O keep
　The dwellers on the homeless deep!

3 Soothe the rough ocean's troubled face,
And bid the hurricane give place
To the soft breeze that wafts the bark
Safely alike through light and dark.
　Keep by Thy mighty hand, O keep
　The dwellers on the homeless deep.

4 Good Pilot of the awful main,
Let us not plead Thy love in vain;
Jesus, draw near with kindly aid,—
Say, " It is I, be not afraid."
　Keep by Thy mighty hand, O keep
　The dwellers on the homeless deep.
　　　　Rev. Horatius Bonar (1808—1890).

PRAYER FOR THOSE AT SEA.

223 *Far at Sea.*
1 Star of peace to wanderers weary,
  Bright the beams that smile on me;
  Cheer the pilot's vision dreary,
      Far, far at sea.

2 Star of hope, gleam o'er the billow,
  Bless the soul that sighs for Thee,
  Bless the sailor's lonely pillow,
      Far, far at sea.

3 Star of faith, when winds are mocking
  All his toil, he flies to Thee;
  Save him, on the billows rocking,
      Far, far at sea.

4 Star divine, Oh! safely guide him,
  Bring the wanderer home to Thee;
  Sore temptations long have tried him,
      Far, far at sea.
            Mrs. J. B. C. Simpson, 1830.

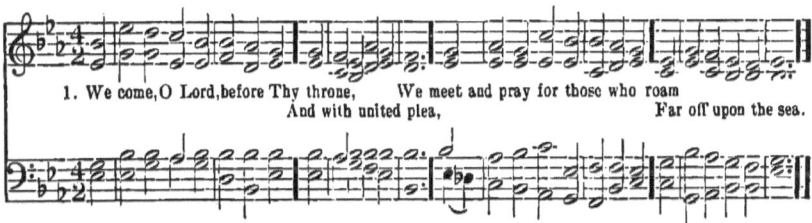

224 *Prayer for Seamen.*
1 We come, O Lord, before Thy throne,
    And with united plea,
  We meet and pray for those who roam
    Far off upon the sea.

2 Oh! may the Holy Spirit bow
    The sailor's heart to Thee,
  Till tears of deep repentance flow
    Like rain-drops on the sea.

3 Then may a Saviour's dying love
    Pour peace into his breast,
  And waft him to the port above,
    Of everlasting rest.
            Mrs. P. H. Brown (1783—1861).

OPENING AND CLOSING HYMNS.

SABBATH. 7s, 6l.   Dr. L. Mason (1792—1872).

225   *Sabbath Worship.*
1 Safely, through another week,
   God has brought us on our way:
Let us now a blessing seek,
   Waiting in His courts to-day;
Day of all the week the best,
   Emblem of eternal rest.

2 While we seek supplies of grace,
   Through the dear Redeemer's name,
Show Thy reconciling face,
   Take away our sin and shame:
From our worldly cares set free,
   May we rest this day in Thee.

3 Here we 're come Thy name to praise;
   Let us feel Thy presence near;
May Thy glory meet our eyes,
   While we in Thy house appear:
Here afford us, Lord, a taste
   Of our everlasting feast.

4 May the gospel's joyful sound
   Conquer sinners, comfort saints;
Make the fruits of grace abound,
   Bring relief for all complaints:
Such let all our Sabbaths prove,
   Till we join the church above.
          Rev. John Newton (1725—1807).

BROWN. C. M.   W. B. Bradbury (1816—1868).

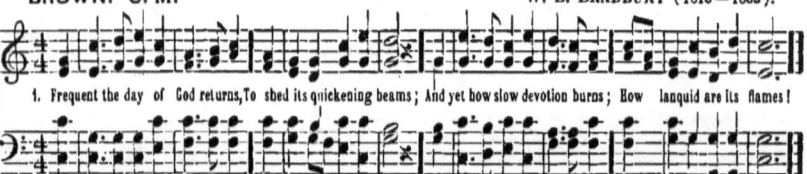

226   *Lord's Day Evening.*
1 Frequent the day of God returns,
   To shed its quickening beams;
And yet how slow devotion burns;
   How languid are its flames!

2 Accept our faint attempts to love;
   Our frailties, Lord, forgive:
We would be like Thy saints above,
   And praise Thee while we live.

3 Increase, O Lord, our faith and hope,
   And fit us to ascend,
Where the assembly ne'er breaks up,
   The Sabbaths ne'er shall end.

4 Where we shall breathe in heavenly air,
   With heavenly lustre shine;
Before the throne of God appear,
   And feast on love divine.
          Rev. Simon Browne (1680—1732).

OPENING AND CLOSING HYMNS.

WARWICK. C. M.   S. Stanley (1767—1822).

1. Lord in the morn-ing Thou shalt hear My voice as-cend-ing high; To Thee will I di-rect my pray'r, To Thee lift up mine eye;—

227   *For the Lord's Day Morning.*

1 Lord, in the morning Thou shalt hear
   My voice ascending high;
To Thee will I direct my prayer,
   To Thee lift up mine eye;—

2 Up to the hills, where Christ has gone
   To plead for all His saints,
Presenting, at His Father's throne,
   Our songs and our complaints.

3 Thou art a God, before whose sight
   The wicked shall not stand;
Sinners shall ne'er be Thy delight,
   Nor dwell at Thy right hand.

4 Oh, may Thy Spirit guide my feet,
   In ways of righteousness;
Make every path of duty straight,
   And plain before my face.
              Rev. Isaac Watts (1674—1748).

228   *Confident Hope.*

1 My God, the spring of all my joys,
   The life of my delights,
The glory of my brightest days,
   And comfort of my nights!

2 In darkest shades if He appear,
   My dawning is begun;
He is my soul's bright morning star,
   And He my rising sun.

3 The opening heavens around me shine
   With beams of sacred bliss;
While Jesus shows His heart is mine,
   And whispers, I am His.

4 My soul would leave this heavy clay,
   At that transporting word;
Run up with joy the shining way,
   To embrace my dearest Lord.
              Rev. Isaac Watts (1674—1748).

229   *Psalm 118.*

1 This is the day the Lord hath made,
   He calls the hours His own;
Let heaven rejoice, let earth be glad,
   And praise surround the throne.

2 To-day He rose and left the dead,
   And Satan's empire fell;
To-day the saints His triumph spread,
   And all His wonders tell.

3 Hosanna to th' anointed King,
   To David's holy Son;
Help us, O Lord, descend and bring
   Salvation from Thy throne.

4 Blest is the Lord who comes to men
   With messages of grace;
Who comes in God His Father's name,
   To save our sinful race.

5 Hosanna in the highest strains
   The Church on earth can raise;
The highest heavens, in which He reigns,
   Shall give Him nobler praise.
              Rev. Isaac Watts (1674—1748).

230   *Doxology.*

Let God the Father, and the Son,
   And Spirit, be adored,
Where there are works to make Him known,
   Or saints to love the Lord.

OPENING AND CLOSING HYMNS.

LISCHER. H. M. F. SCHNEIDER (1786—1853). Arr. by L. MASON.

231 *Welcome Worship.*
1 Welcome, delightful morn,
  Thou day of sacred rest;
I hail Thy kind return;—
  Lord, make these moments blest;
From the low train | I soar to reach
Of mortal toys | Immortal joys.

2 Now may the King descend
    And fill His throne of grace;
  Thy sceptre, Lord, extend,
    While saints address Thy face:
Let sinners feel | And learn to know
Thy quickening word. | And fear the Lord.

3 Descend, celestial Dove,
    With all Thy quickening powers;
  Disclose a Saviour's love,
    And bless these sacred hours:
Then shall my soul | Nor Sabbaths be
New life obtain, | Enjoyed in vain.
  Hayward in John Dobell's Col., 1806.

232 *Sabbath Morning.*
1 Awake, ye saints, awake!
  And hail this sacred day;
In loftiest songs of praise
  Your joyful homage pay!
Come bless the day that God hath blest,
The type of heaven's eternal rest

2 On this auspicious morn
  The Lord of life arose;
He burst the bars of death,
  And vanquished all our foes;
And now he pleads our cause above,
And reaps the fruits of all His love.

3 All hail, triumphant Lord!
  Heaven with hosannas rings,
And earth in humbler strains
  Thy praise responsive sings:
Worthy the Lamb that once was slain,
Through endless years to live and reign.
  Rev. Thos. Cotterill (—1823).

233 *Psalm 43.*
1 Now to Thy sacred house,
  With joy I turn my feet,
Where saints with morning-vows,
  In full assembly meet:
Thy power divine shall there be shown,
And from Thy throne Thy mercy shine.

2 Oh, send Thy light abroad;
  Thy truth, with heavenly ray,
Shall lead my soul to God,
  And guide my doubtful way;
I'll hear Thy word with faith sincere,
And learn to fear and praise the Lord.

3 Here reach Thy bounteous hand,
  And all my sorrows heal,
Here health and strength divine,
  Oh, make my bosom feel;
Like balmy dew, shall Jesus' voice
My heart rejoice, my strength renew.

4 Now in Thy holy hill,
  Before Thine altar, Lord!
My harp and song shall sound
  The glories of Thy word:
Henceforth, to Thee, O God of grace!
A hymn of praise my life shall be.
  Rev. T. Dwight (1752—1817).

OPENING AND CLOSING HYMNS,

234 *Thine Altars, my God.*

1 Pleasant are Thy courts above,
In the land of light and love;
Pleasant are Thy courts below,
In this land of sin and woe.
Oh, my spirit longs and faints
For the converse of Thy saints,
For the brightness of Thy face,
For Thy fullness, God of grace.

2 Happy birds that sing and fly
Round Thy altars, O Most High!
Happier souls that find a rest
In their Heavenly Father's breast!
Like the wandering dove that found
No repose on earth around,
They can to their ark repair,
And enjoy it ever there.

3 Happy souls! their praises flow,
Even in this vale of woe;
Waters in the desert rise,
Manna feeds them from the skies;
On they go from strength to strength,
Till they reach Thy throne at length;

At Thy feet adoring fall,
Who hast led them safe through all.
Rev. H. F. Lyte (1793 — 1847).

235 *Divine Worship.*
Tune, LISCHER.

1 Lord of the worlds above!
How pleasant, and how fair,
The dwellings of Thy love
Thine earthly temples are!
To Thine abode my heart aspires,
With warm desires to see my God.

2 Oh, happy souls who pray,
Where God appoints to hear!
Oh, happy men who pay
Their constant service there!
They praise Thee still; and happy they,
Who love the way to Zion's hill.

3 They go from strength to strength,
Through this dark vale of tears,
Till each arrives at length,
Till each in heaven appears;
Oh, glorious seat, when God, our King,
Shall thither bring our willing feet.
Rev. Isaac Watts (1674 — 1748.)

OPENING AND CLOSING HYMNS.

ITALIAN HYMN. 6s, 4s. — FELICE GIARDINI (1716—1796).

236 *One in Three.*
1 Come, Thou Almighty King,
 Help us Thy name to sing,
  Help us to praise:
Father all-glorious,
O'er all victorious,
Come and reign over us,
 Ancient of Days !

2 Come, Thou incarnate Word,
Gird on Thy mighty sword;
 Our prayer attend;
Come and Thy people bless,
And give Thy word success:
Spirit of holiness!
 On us descend.

3 Come, holy Comforter !
Thy sacred witness bear,
 In this glad hour;
Thou, who almighty art,
Now rule in every heart,
And ne'er from us depart,
 Spirit of power !

4 To the great One in Three,
The highest praises be,
 Hence evermore !
His sovereign majesty
May we in glory see,
And to eternity
 Love and adore.
  Rev. Chas. Wesley (1708—1788).

237 *Invocation.*
1 O Holy Lord, our God,
By heavenly hosts adored,
 Hear us, we pray;
To Thee the cherubim,
Angels and seraphim,
Unceasing praises hymn—
 Their homage pay.

2 Here give Thy word success,
And this Thy servant bless,
 His labors own;
And while the sinners Friend
His life and words commend,
Thy Holy Spirit, send
 And make Him known.

3 May every passing year
More happy still appear
 Than this glad day;
With numbers fill the place,
Adorn Thy saints with grace,
Thy truth may all embrace,
 O Lord, we pray.
  Anon.

AMERICA. 6s & 4s. — H. CAREY (1663—1743).

(98)

OPENING AND CLOSING HYMNS.

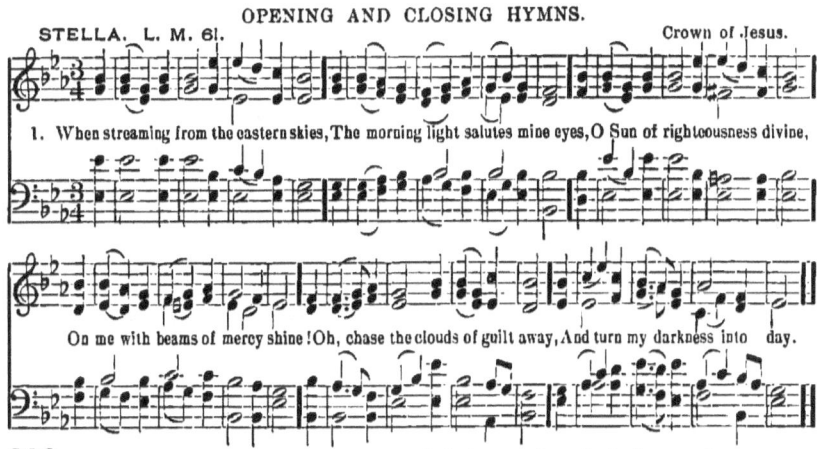

STELLA. L. M. 6l.   Crown of Jesus.

1. When streaming from the eastern skies, The morning light salutes mine eyes, O Sun of righteousness divine, On me with beams of mercy shine! Oh, chase the clouds of guilt away, And turn my darkness into day.

238 *Constant Devotion.*

1 When streaming from the eastern skies,
  The morning light salutes mine eyes,
  O Sun of righteousness divine,
  On me with beams of mercy shine!
  Oh, chase the clouds of guilt away,
  And turn my darkness into day.

2 And when to heaven's all-glorious King
  My morning sacrifice I bring,
  And, mourning o'er my guilt and shame,
  Ask mercy in my Saviour's name;
  Then, Jesus, cleanse me with Thy blood,
  And be my advocate with God.

3 When each day's scenes and labors close,
  And wearied nature seeks repose,
  With pardoning mercy richly blest,
  Guard me, my Saviour, while I rest;
  And as each morning sun shall rise,
  Oh, lead me onward to the skies!
                    Sir Robert Grant (1785—1838).

239 *Come, Condescending Spirit.*

1 Eternal Spirit, Source of light,
  Enlivening, consecrating Fire,
  Descend, and with celestial heat
  Our dull, our frozen hearts inspire;
  Our souls refine, our dross consume:
  Come condescending Spirit, come.

2 In our cold breast, Oh, strike a spark,
  Of the pure flame which seraphs feel;
  Nor let us wander in the dark,
  Or lie benumbed and stupid still;
  Come vivifying Spirit, come,
  And make our hearts Thy constant home.

3 Let pure devotion's fervors rise;
  Let every pious passion glow;
  Oh, let the raptures of the skies
  Kindle in our cold hearts below:
  Come condescending spirit, come,
  And make our souls Thy constant home.
                    Rev. Samuel Davies (1724—1761).

240 *The Good Shepherd.*

1 The Lord my pasture shall prepare,
  And feed me with a shepherd's care;
  His presence shall my wants supply,
  And guard me with a watchful eye;
  My noonday walks he shall attend,
  And all my midnight hours defend.

2 When in the sultry glebe I faint,
  Or on the thirsty mountain pant,
  To fertile vales and dewy meads,
  My weary, wandering steps He leads;
  Where peaceful rivers soft and slow,
  Amid the verdant landscape flow.

3 Though in the paths of death I tread,
  With gloomy horrors overspread,
  My steadfast heart shall fear no ill,
  For Thou, O Lord, art with me still;
  Thy friendly rod shall give me aid,
  And guide me through the dreadful shade.

4 Though in a bare and rugged way,
  Through devious lonely wilds I stray,
  Thy presence shall my pains beguile;
  The barren wilderness shall smile,
  With sudden greens and herbage crowned,
  And streams shall murmur all around.
                    Joseph Addison (1672—1719).

OPENING AND CLOSING HYMNS.

RATISBON. 7s, 6l.   HYMNS ANCIENT AND MODERN.

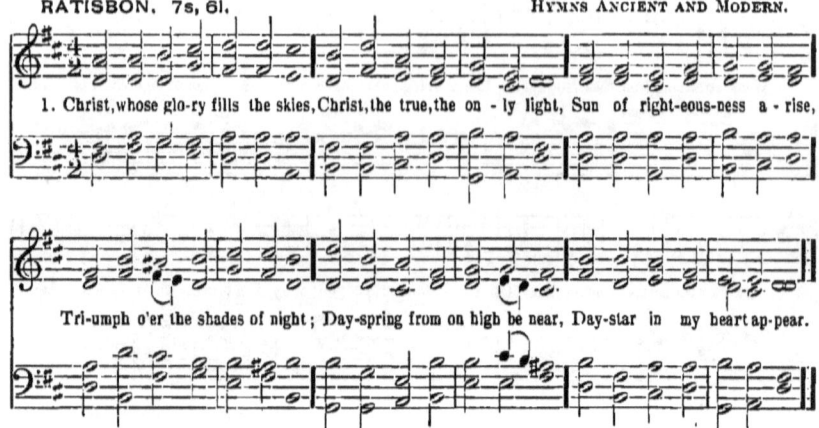

1. Christ, whose glory fills the skies, Christ, the true, the on-ly light, Sun of right-eous-ness a-rise, Tri-umph o'er the shades of night; Day-spring from on high be near, Day-star in my heart ap-pear.

241   *Christ, the only Light.*

1 Christ, whose glory fills the skies,
  Christ, the true, the only Light,
 Sun of Righteousness arise,
  Triumph o'er the shades of night;
 Dayspring from on high, be near;
 Daystar in my heart appear.

2 Dark and cheerless is the morn
  Unaccompanied by Thee;
 Joyless is the day's return,
  Till Thy mercy's beams I see;
 Till they inward light impart,
 Glad my eyes, and warm my heart.

3 Visit then this soul of mine,
  Pierce the gloom of sin and grief;
 Fill me, Radiancy Divine,
  Scatter all my unbelief;
 More and more Thyself display,
 Shining to the perfect day.

Rev. Chas. Wesley (1708—1788).

VESPER.   HYMNS ANCIENT AND MODERN.

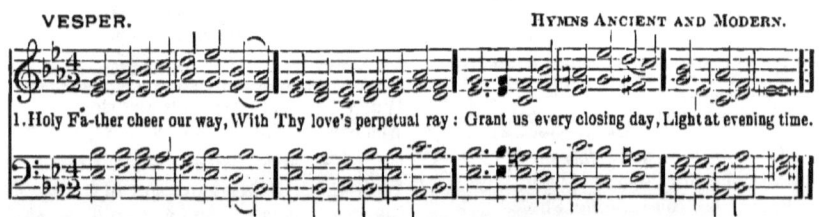

1. Holy Fa-ther cheer our way, With Thy love's perpetual ray : Grant us every closing day, Light at evening time.

242   *At Evening Time it shall be Light.*

1 Holy Father, cheer our way
  With Thy love's perpetual ray;
 Grant us every closing day
  Light at evening time.

2 Holy Saviour, calm our fears,
  When earth's brightness disappears;
 Grant us in our latter years
  Light at evening time.

3 Holy Spirit, be Thou nigh
  When in mortal pains we lie;
 Grant us, as we come to die,
  Light at evening time.

4 Holy, Blessèd Trinity!
  Darkness is not dark with Thee;
 Those Thou keepest always see
  Light at evening time.

Rev. R. H. Robinson (1842—).

OPENING AND CLOSING HYMNS.

LOVING-KINDNESS. L. M. Western Melody.

243 *Praise for Loving-kindness.*

1 Awake, my soul, in joyful lays
And sing thy great Redeemer's praise;
He justly claims a song from thee;
His loving-kindness, oh, how free!

2 He saw me ruined in the fall,
Yet loved me notwithstanding all;
He saved me from my lost estate;
His loving-kindness, oh, how great!

3 Though numerous hosts of mighty foes,
Though earth and hell my way oppose,
He safely leads my soul along;
His loving-kindness, oh, how strong!

4 Often I feel my sinful heart,
Prone from my Saviour to depart;
But though I oft have him forgot,
His loving-kindness changes not.

5 Soon shall I pass the gloomy vale,
Soon all my mortal powers must fail;
O may my last expiring breath,
His loving-kindness sing in death.

6 Then, let me mount and soar away,
To the bright world of endless day;
And sing, with rapture and surprise,
His loving-kindness in the skies.

Rev. S. Medley (1738—1799).

TALLIS' EVENING HYMN. L. M. THOMAS TALLIS (1529—1585).

244 *All Praise to Thee.*

1 All praise to Thee, my God, this night,
For all the blessings of the light,
Keep me, oh, keep me, King of kings!
Beneath Thine own almighty wings.

2 Forgive me, Lord! for Thy dear Son,
The ill that I this day have done,
That with the world, myself and Thee
I, ere I sleep, at peace may be.

3 Teach me to live that I may dread
The grave as little as my bed,
To die that this vile body may
Rise glorious at the awful day.

4 Oh, when shall I in endless day
Forever chase dark sleep away,
And praise with the angelic choir,
Incessant sing, and never tire?

Bishop Thos. Ken (1637—1721).

OPENING AND CLOSING HYMNS.

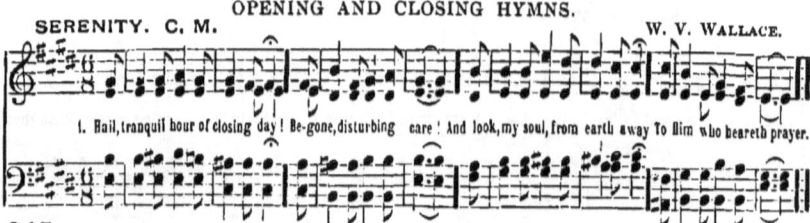
SERENITY. C. M. — W. V. WALLACE.
1. Hail, tranquil hour of closing day! Be-gone, disturbing care! And look, my soul, from earth away To Him who heareth prayer.

245 *Hail, Tranquil Hour.*
1 Hail, tranquil hour of closing day!
  Begone, disturbing care !
  And look, my soul, from earth away
  To Him who heareth prayer.

2 How sweet, through long-remembered
  His mercies to recall,   [years,
  And pressed with wants, and griefs, and
  To trust His love for all.   [fears,

3 How sweet to look, in thoughtful hope,
  Beyond this fading sky,
  And hear Him call His children up
  To His fair home on high.

4 Calmly the day forsakes our heaven
  To dawn beyond the west;
  So let my soul in life's last even,
  Retire to glorious rest.
  Rev. Leonard Bacon (1802—1881).

246 *Evening Song.*
1 Dread Sovereign, let my evening song
  Like holy incense rise;
  Assist the offerings of my tongue
  To reach the lofty skies.

2 Through all the dangers of the day
  Thy hand was still my guard;
  And still to drive my wants away,
  Thy mercy stood prepared.

3 Perpetual blessings from above
  Encompass me around;
  But oh, how few returns of love
  Hath my Creator found !

4 Lord, with this guilty heart of mine,
  To Thy dear cross I flee,
  And to Thy grace my soul resign
  To be renewed by Thee.
  Rev. Isaac Watts (1674—1748).

247 *Call To Prayer.*
1 Approach, my soul, the mercy seat,
  Where Jesus answers prayer;
  There humbly fall before His feet,
  For none can perish there.

2 Thy promise is my only plea,
  With this I venture nigh;
  Thou callest burdened souls to Thee,
  And such, O Lord, am I.

3 Bowed down beneath a load of sin,
  By Satan sorely pressed,
  By war without, and fear within,
  I come to Thee for rest.

4 Be Thou my shield and hiding-place,
  That, sheltered near Thy side,
  I may my fierce accuser face,
  And tell Him, "Thou hast died."

5 Oh, wondrous love ! to bleed and die,
  To bear the cross and shame,
  That guilty sinners, such as I
  Might plead Thy gracious name.
  Rev. J. Newton (1725—1807).

248 *Thou Art My Hiding-place.*
1 Thou art my Hiding-place, O Lord !
  On Thee I fix my trust,
  Encouraged by Thy holy word,
  A feeble child of dust.

2 I have no argument beside,
  I urge no other plea;
  And 't is enough the Saviour died,
  The Saviour died for me.

3 'Mid trials heavy to be borne,
  When mortal strength is vain,
  A heart with grief and anguish torn,
  A body racked with pain;

4 And when Thine awful voice commands
  This body to decay,
  And life, in its last lingering sands,
  Is ebbing fast away;

5 Then, though it be in accents weak,
  And faint and tremblingly,
  O give me strength in death to speak,
  " My Saviour, died for me."
  Rev. Thos. Raffles (—1863).

OPENING AND CLOSING HYMNS.

SEYMOUR. 7s. Arr. from Von Weber (1786—1826).

1. Soft-ly fades the twi-light ray Of the ho-ly Sab-bath day; Gen-tly as life's set-ting sun, When the Christ-ian's course is run.

249 *Sabbath Evening.*

1 Softly fades the twilight ray
  Of the holy Sabbath day;
Gently as life's setting sun,
  When the Christian's course is run.

2 Night her solemn mantle spreads
  O'er the earth as daylight fades;
All things tell of calm repose,
  At the holy Sabbath's close.

3 Peace is on the world abroad;
  'Tis the holy peace of God —

Symbol of the peace within
  When the spirit rests from sin.

4 Still the Spirit lingers near,
  Where the evening worshiper
Seeks communion with the skies,
  Pressing onward to the prize

5 Saviour! may our Sabbaths be
  Days of joy and peace in Thee,
Till in heaven our souls repose,
  Where the Sabbath ne'er shall close.

Rev. S. F. Smith (1808—).

THERMUTIS. 7s, D.

1. { Soft-ly now the light of day Fades up-on our sight away; } Thou, whose all pervading eye Naught escapes without, within;
   { Free from care from labor free, Lord, I would commune with Thee. }

D.C. *Pardon each infirmity, Open fault, and secret sin.*

250 *Softly Now the Light of Day.*

1 Softly now the light of day
  Fades upon our sight away;
Free from care, from labor free,
  Lord, I would commune with Thee.
Thou, whose all pervading eye
  Naught escapes without, within;
Pardon each infirmity,
  Open fault, and secret sin.

2 Soon, for me the light of day
  Shall for ever pass away;
Then from sin and sorrow free,
  Take me, Lord, to dwell with Thee.
Thou, who sinless, yet hast known
  All of man's infirmity;
Then, from Thine eternal throne,
  Jesus, look with pitying eye.

Bp. G. W. Doane (1799—1859).

OPENING AND CLOSING HYMNS.

NUREMBURGH. 7s, 6l.   JOHANN RUDOLF AHLE (1625—1673).

251   *Sinners Exhorted.*
1 Ye that in His courts are found,
  Listening to the joyful sound,
Lost and helpless as ye are,
Full of sorrow, sin and care,
  Glorify the King of kings,
  Take the peace the gospel brings.

2 Turn to Christ your longing eyes,
  View His bleeding sacrifice;
See in Him your sins forgiven,
Pardon, holiness and heaven;
  Glorify the King of kings,
  Take the peace the gospel brings.
Anon.

252   *Evening Hymn.*
1 Now from labor and from care,
  Evening shades have set me free;
In the work of praise and prayer,
  Lord I would converse with Thee;
Oh, behold me from above.
Fill me with a Saviour's love.

2 Sin and sorrow, guilt and woe,
  Wither all my earthly joys;
Naught can charm me here below,
  But my Saviour's loving voice:
Lord, forgive; Thy grace restore;
Make me Thine for evermore.

3 For the blessings of this day,
  For the mercies of this hour;
For the gospel's cheering ray,
  For the Spirit's quickening power,
Grateful notes to Thee I raise,
Oh, accept my song of praise.
Thos. Hastings (1784—1872).

CAPETOWN. 7s & 5s.   FRIEDRICH FILITZ (1804—1860).

253   *Three in One, and One in Three.*
1 Three in One and One in Three,
  Ruler of the earth and sea,
Hear us, while we lift to Thee
  Holy chant and psalm.

2 Light of lights, with morning shine:
  Lift on us Thy light divine;
And let charity benign
  Breathe on us her balm.

3 Light of light, when falls the even,
  Let it close on sin forgiven;
Fold us in the peace of heaven,
  Shed a holy calm.

4 Three in One, and One in Three,
  Dimly here we worship Thee:
With the saints hereafter we
  Hope to bear a palm.
Rev. Gilbert Rorison (1821—1869).

(104)

OPENING AND CLOSING HYMNS.

SESSIONS. L. M. L. O. Emerson.

1. Bless, O my soul! the living God; Call home thy tho'ts that rove abroad. Let all the pow'rs within me join In work and worship so divine.

254 *Psalm 103.*

1 Bless, O my soul! the living God;
Call home thy thoughts that rove abroad;
Let all the powers within me join
In work and worship so divine.

2 Bless, O my soul! the God of grace;
His favors claim thy highest praise;
Why should the wonders He hath wrought
Be lost in silence and forgot?

3 'Tis He, my soul! that sent His Son
To die for crimes which thou hast done;
He owns the ransomed and forgives
The hourly follies of our lives.

4 Let the whole earth His power confess,
Let the whole earth adore His grace;
The Gentile with the Jew shall join
In work and worship so divine.
Rev. Isaac Watts (1674—1748).

255 *God is Here.*

1 Lo, God is here: Let us adore,
And own how dreadful is this place;
Let all within us feel His power,
And silent bow before His face.

2 Lo, God is here: Him day and night
United choirs of angels sing;
To Him, enthroned above all height,
Let saints their humble worship bring.

3 Lord God of hosts, O may our praise
Thy courts with grateful incense fill;
Still may we stand before Thy face,
Still hear and do Thy sovereign will.
Gerhard Tersteegen (1697—1769).
Tr. by Rev. John Wesley (1703—1791).

256 *Parting.*

1 Come, Christian brethren, ere we part,
Join every voice and every heart:
One solemn hymn to God we raise,
One final song of grateful praise.

2 Christians, we here may meet no more,
But there is yet a happier shore;
And there released from toil and pain,
Dear brethren we shall meet again.
H. K. White.

257 *The Mercy Seat.*

1 What various hindrances we meet,
In coming to a mercy seat!
Yet who that knows the worth of prayer,
But wishes to be often there?

2 Prayer makes the darkened cloud withdraw;
Prayer climbs the ladder Jacob saw,
Gives exercise to faith and love,
Brings every blessing from above.

3 Restraining prayer we cease to fight;
Prayer makes the Christian's armor bright;
And Satan trembles when he sees
The weakest saint upon his knees.

4 Have you no words? Ah! think again,
Words flow apace when you complain,
And fill your fellow-creature's ear
With the sad tale of all your care.

5 Were half the breath thus vainly spent,
To heaven in supplication sent,
Our cheerful song would oftener be,
"Hear what the Lord has done for me."
Wm. Cowper (1731—1800).

OPENING AND CLOSING HYMNS.

BENTLEY. 7s & 6s, D.   JOHN HULLAH (1812—).

1. O day of rest and gladness, O day of joy and light, O balm of care and sadness, Most beautiful, most bright;
On Thee the high and low-ly, Thro' ages join'd in tune, Sing holy, ho-ly, ho -ly, To the Great God Triune.

258   *The Day Which the Lord Hath Made.*

1 O day of rest and gladness,
   O day of joy and light,
O balm of care and sadness,
   Most beautiful, most bright;
On thee, the high and lowly,
   Through ages joind in tune,
Sing holy, holy, holy,
   To the Great God Triune.

2 On thee, at the creation,
   The light first had its birth;
On thee, for our salvation,
   Christ rose from depths of earth;
On thee, our Lord, victorious,
   The Spirit sent from heaven,
And thus on thee most glorious,
   A triple light was given.

3 To-day on weary nations
   The heavenly manna falls; ·
To holy convocations
   The silver trumpet calls,
Where gospel light is glowing
   With pure and radiant beams,
And living water flowing
   With soul refreshing streams.

4 New graces ever gaining
   From this our day of rest,
We reach the rest remaining
   To spirits of the blest;

To Holy Ghost be praises,
   To Father, and to Son;
The Church her voice upraises
   To Thee blest Three in One.
     Bp. Christopher Wordsworth (1807 — 1:85).

259   *The Day of Resurrection.*

1 The day of resurrection,
   Earth tell it out abroad:
The Passover of gladness,
   The Passover of God.
From death to life eternal,
   From earth unto the sky,
Our Christ hath brought us over,
   With hymns of victory.

2 Our hearts be pure from evil,
   That we may see aright
The Lord in rays eternal
   Of resurrection light;
And, listening to His accents,
   May hear so calm and plain,
His own "All hail!" and hearing,
   May raise the victor-strain.

3 Now let the heavens be joyful;
   Let earth her song begin;
Let the round world keep triumph,
   And all that is therein;
Invisible and visible,
   Their notes let all things blend,
For Christ the Lord hath risen,
   Our Joy that hath no end.
     John of Damascus, 780.
   Tr. by Rev. John Mason Neale (1818 — 1866).

OPENING AND CLOSING HYMNS.

HENLEY. 11s & 10s.   Dr. L. Mason, (1792–1872).

260   *Trust, Strength, Calmness.*

1 Father! in Thy mysterious presence
    kneeling,   [kindling love;
  Fain would our souls feel all Thy
For we are weak, and need some deep re-
    vealing   [from above.
Of trust, and strength and calmness

2 Lord! we have wandered forth through
    doubt and sorrow,   [ward one;
And Thou hast made each step an on-
And we will ever trust each unknown mor-
    row;
Thou wilt sustain us till its work is done.

3 In the heart's depths, a peace serene
  and holy   [her will,
Abides; and, when pain seems to have
Or we despair, oh, may that peace rise
  slowly,
Stronger than agony! and we be still.

4 Now, Father! now in Thy dear presence
  kneeling,   [love;
Our spirits yearn to feel Thy kindling
Now make us strong; we need Thy deep
  revealing   [from above.
Of trust, and strength, and calmness
                         S Johnson (—1882).

BENEDICTION. 10s.   E. J. Hopkins (1818–).

261   *Go in Peace.*

1 Saviour, again to Thy dear name we raise
With one accord our parting hymn of praise;
We rise to bless Thee ere our worship cease,
And now, departing, wait Thy word of
    peace.

2 Grant us Thy peace upon our homeward
    way;   [day;
With Thee began, with Thee shall end the
Guard Thou the lips from sin, the hearts
    from shame,   [name.
That in this house have called upon Thy

3 Grant us Thy peace, Lord, through the
  coming night;
Turn Thou for us its darkness into light;
From harm and danger keep Thy children
  free,
For dark and light are both alike to Thee.

4 Grant us Thy peace throughout our
  earthly life,
Our balm in sorrow, and our stay in strife;
Then, when Thy voice shall bid our con-
  flict cease,
Call us, O Lord, to Thine eternal peace.
                         Rev. J. Ellerton, 1826.

OPENING AND CLOSING HYMNS.

ST. MATTHIAS. L. M. 6l.
W. H. Monk (1823–).

262 *Ere we go.*

1 Dear Saviour, bless us ere we go:
  Thy word into our minds instill;
  And make our lukewarm hearts to glow
  With lowly love and fervent will.
  Ref.—Through life's long day,
    And death's dark night,
    O gentle Saviour, be our light.

2 The day is gone, its hours have run,
  And Thou hast taken count of all,
  The scanty triumphs grace hath won,
  The broken vow, the frequent fall.–Ref.

3 Grant us, dear Lord, from evil ways
  True absolution and release;
  And bless us more than in past days
  With purity and inward peace.—Ref.

4 Do more than pardon, give us joy,
  Sweet fear, and sober liberty,
  And simple hearts without alloy
  That only long to be like Thee.—Ref.

5 For all we love, the poor, the sad,
  The sinful unto Thee we call;
  Oh, let Thy mercy make us glad:
  Thou art our Saviour and our all.–Ref.

Rev. F. W. Faber (1814 – 1863).

KYRIE ELEISON. 7s.
Mozart (1756—1791).

OPENING AND CLOSING HYMNS.

HORTON. 7s. Arr. from WARTENSEE.

1. Lord! I can-not let Thee go, Till a bless-ing Thou be-stow;
Do not turn a-way Thy face, Mine's an ur-gent press-ing case.

263 *An Urgent Call.*

1 Lord I cannot let Thee go,
Till a blessing Thou bestow;
Do not turn away Thy face,
Mine's an urgent, pressing case.

2 Once a sinner, near despair,
Sought Thy mercy-seat by prayer;
Mercy heard and set him free —
Lord, that mercy came to me.

3 Many days have passed since then,
Many changes I have seen;
Yet have been upheld till now;
Who could hold me up but Thou?

4 Thou hast helped in every need —
This emboldens me to plead;
After so much mercy past,
Canst Thou let me sink at last?

5 No — I must maintain my hold;
'T is Thy goodness makes me bold;
I can no denial take,
Since I plead for Jesus' sake.
Rev. John Newton (1725—1807).

264 *Invocation.*

1 Father, let Thy smiling face
Here within this holy place,
Sweetly shining on my heart,
Bid all sinful thoughts depart.

2 Jesus, Thou whose ceaseless love
Intercedes for us above,
Bend to me Thy listening ear,
Make my wayward heart sincere.

3 Comforter of all the saints,
Gently heal my soul's complaints,
May a foretaste now be given
Of the Sabbath day of heaven.
Rev. T. V. Moore (1818—1871).

265 *To Thy Temple.*

1 To Thy temple I repair;
Lord, I love to worship there,
When within the veil I meet
Christ before the mercy-seat.

2 Thou, through Him art reconciled;
I, through Him became Thy child;
Abba, Father! give me grace
In Thy courts to seek Thy face!

3 While Thy glorious praise is sung,
Touch my lips, unloose my tongue,
That my joyful soul may bless
Thee, the Lord my righteousness!

4 While Thy ministers proclaim
Peace and pardon in Thy Name,
Through their voice, by faith, may I
Hear Thee speaking from the sky.
Rev. James Montgomery (1771—1854).

(109)

OPENING AND CLOSING HYMNS.

HURSLEY. L. M. Francis Joseph Haydn (1732—1809).
Arr. by William Henry Monk, 1861.

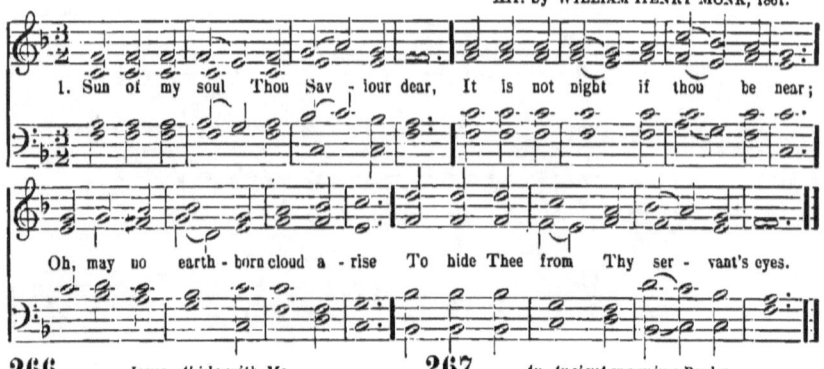

1. Sun of my soul Thou Sav-iour dear, It is not night if thou be near;
Oh, may no earth-born cloud a-rise To hide Thee from Thy ser-vant's eyes.

266 *Jesus, Abide with Me.*

1 Sun of my soul, Thou Saviour dear,
It is not night if Thou be near;
Oh, may no earth-born cloud arise
To hide Thee from Thy servant's eyes!

2 When soft the dews of kindly sleep
My wearied eyelids gently steep,
Be my last thought — how sweet to rest
Forever on my Saviour's breast.

3 Abide with me from morn till eve,
For without Thee I cannot live;
Abide with me when night is nigh,
For without Thee I dare not die.

4 Be near to bless me when I wake,
Ere through the world my way I take;
Abide with me till, in Thy love,
I lose myself in heaven above.
Rev. John Keble (1792—1866).

267 *An Ancient morning Psalm.*

1 O Christ! with each returning morn
Thine image to our heart be borne;
And may we ever clearly see
Our God and Saviour, Lord, in Thee!

2 All hallowed be our walk this day;
May meekness form our early ray,
And faithful love our noontide light,
And hope our sunset, calm and bright.

3 May grace each idle thought control,
And sanctify our wayward soul;
May guile depart, and malice cease,
And all within be joy and peace.

4 Our daily course, O Jesus, bless;
Make plain the way of holiness;
From sudden falls our feet defend,
And cheer at last our journey's end.
Latin.
Rev. Wm. S. Lacy, 1891.

HORACE'S CHANT. S. M.

1. Blest be Thy love, dear Lord, That taught us this sweet way, On-ly to love Thee for Thyself, And for that love o-bey. A-men.

268 *Love is the Fulfilling of the Commandment.*

1 Blest be Thy love, dear Lord,
 That taught us this sweet way,
 Only to love Thee for Thyself,
 And for that love obey.

2 O Thou, our soul's chief hope!
 We to Thy mercy fly;
 Where'er we are, Thou canst protect—
 Whate'er we need, supply.

3 Whether we sleep or wake,
 To Thee we both resign;
 By night we see as well as day,
 If Thy light on us shine.

4 Whether we live or die,
 Both we submit to Thee;
 In death we live as well as life,
 If Thine in death we be
John Austin.

OPENING AND CLOSING HYMNS.

SICILIAN HYMN. 8s & 7s, D. — Sicilian Melody.

269 *Before or After Sermon.*

1 Come, Thou soul-transforming Spirit,
  Bless the sower and the seed;
Let each heart Thy grace inherit,
  Raise the weak, the hungry feed;
    From the Gospel
  Now supply Thy people's need.

2 Oh, may all enjoy the blessing!
  Which Thy word's designed to give;
Let us all, Thy love possessing,
  Joyfully the truth receive;
    And for ever
  To Thy praise and glory live.
      Rev. J. Evans (1749 — 1809).

270 *Welcome to Christ.*

Welcome, welcome, dear Redeemer,
  Welcome to this heart of mine;
Lord, I make a full surrender,
  Ev'ry power and thought be Thine;
    Thine entirely,
  Through eternal ages Thine.

271 . *Close of Worship.*

1 Lord, dismiss us with Thy blessing,
  Fill our hearts with joy and peace;
Let us each, Thy love possessing,

Triumph in redeeming grace;
  Oh, refresh us!
Traveling through this wilderness.

2 Thanks we give and adoration,
  For Thy gospel's joyful sound;
May the fruits of Thy salvation
  In our hearts and lives abound;
    May Thy presence
  With us evermore be found.

3 So, when e'er the signal's given,
  Us from earth to call away;
Borne on angels' wings to heaven,
  Glad to leave our cumbrous clay,
    May we, ready,
  Rise and reign in endless day.
      Rev. Robert Hawker (1753 — 1827).

272 *Doxology.*

Great Jehovah! we adore Thee,
  God, the Father, God, the Son,
God, the Spirit, joined in glory
  On the same eternal throne;
    Endless praises
  To Jehovah, Three in One.

(111)

OPENING AND CLOSING HYMNS.

HURSLEY. L. M.
Francis Joseph Haydn (1752–1809.)
Arr. by William Henry Monk, 1861.

[Music: Hursley, L.M.]

1. A-wake, my soul, and with the sun Thy dai-ly stage of du-ty run;
Shake off dull sloth, and joy-ful rise To pay thy morn-ing sac-ri-fice.

273 *Awake, My Soul.*

1 Awake, my soul, and with the sun
Thy daily stage of duty run;
Shake off dull sloth, and joyful rise
To pay thy morning sacrifice.

2 Awake, lift up thyself, my heart,
And with the angels bear thy part,
Who all night long unwearied sing
High praises to the eternal King.

3 Glory to Thee, who safe hast kept,
And hast refreshed me when I slept;
Grant, Lord, when I from death shall wake,
I may of endless life partake.
Bp. Thomas Ken (1637–1711).

WARRINGTON. L. M.
Rev. Ralph Harrison.

[Music: Warrington, L.M.]

1. Come, dear-est Lord, de-scend and dwell, By faith and love, In ev-'ry breast;
Then shall we know, and taste, and feel The joys that can-not be ex-pressed.

274 *Come, Dearest Lord.*

1 Come, dearest Lord, descend and dwell,
By faith and love, in every breast;
Then shall we know, and taste, and feel
The joys that cannot be expressed.

2 Come, fill our hearts with inward strength,
Make our enlarged souls possess,
And learn the height, and breadth, and length
Of Thine unmeasurable grace.

3 Now to the God whose power can do
More than our thoughts and wishes know,
Be everlasting honors done,
By all the Church, through Christ the Son.
Rev. Isaac Watts (1674–1748).

(112)

OPENING AND CLOSING HYMNS.

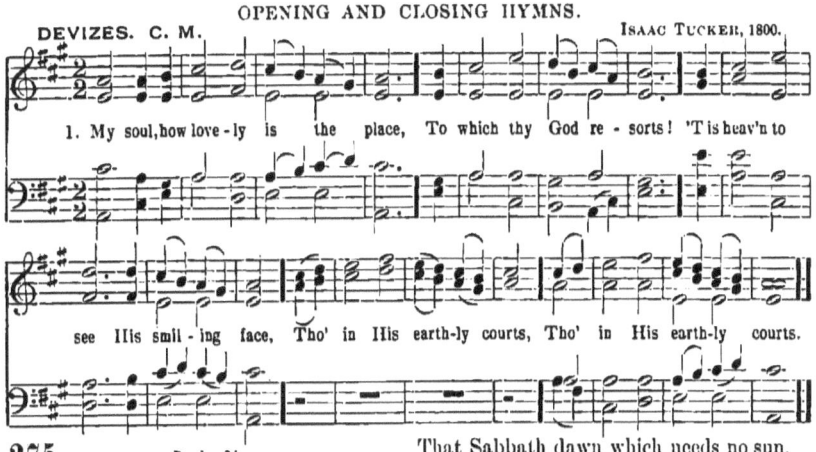

DEVIZES. C. M. — ISAAC TUCKER, 1800.

1. My soul, how love-ly is the place, To which thy God re-sorts! 'T is heav'n to see His smil-ing face, Tho' in His earth-ly courts, Tho' in His earth-ly courts.

275 *Psalm 84.*
1 My soul, how lovely is the place,
To which Thy God resorts!
'T is heaven to see His smiling face,
Though in His earthly courts.

2 There the great Monarch of the skies
His saving power displays;
And light breaks in upon our eyes,
With kind and quickening rays.

3 With His rich gifts the heavenly Dove
Descends and fills the place;
While Christ reveals His wondrous love,
And sheds abroad His grace.

4 There mighty God, Thy words declare
The secrets of Thy will;
And still we seek Thy mercy there,
And sing Thy praises still.
Rev. Isaac Watts (1674—1748).

276 *Yearning for Rest.*
1 When the worn spirit wants repose,
And sighs for God to seek,
How sweet to hail the evening's close
That ends the weary week.

2 How sweet will be the early dawn
That opens on the sight,
When first the soul-reviving morn
Shall shed new rays of light.

3 Blest day, thine hours too soon will cease,
Yet, while they gently roll,
Breathe, heavenly Spirit, source of peace,
A Sabbath o'er my soul.

4 When will my pilgrimage be done,
The world's long week be o'er,

That Sabbath dawn which needs no sun,
That day which fades no more?
James Edmeston (1791—1867).

277 *A Hymn before Sermon.*
1 In Thy great name, O Lord, we come
To worship at Thy feet;
Oh, pour Thy Holy Spirit down
On all that now shall meet.

2 We come to hear Jehovah speak,
To hear the Saviour's voice;
Thy face and favor, Lord, we seek;
Now make our hearts rejoice.

3 Teach us to pray, and praise — to hear
And understand Thy word;
To feel Thy blissful presence near,
And trust our living Lord. *Haskins.*

278 *An Evening Song.*
1 Now from the altar of our hearts
Let flames of love arise;
Assist us, Lord, to offer up
Our evening sacrifice.

2 Minutes and mercies multiplied
Have made up all this day;
Minutes came quick, but mercies were
More swift and free than they.

3 New time, new favor, and new joys,
Do a new song require;
Till we shall praise Thee as we would,
Accept our heart's desire.

4 Lord of our days whose hand hath set
New time upon our score;
Thee may we praise for all our time,
When time shall be no more.
Rev. John Mason (1634—1694).

(113)

OPENING AND CLOSING HYMNS.

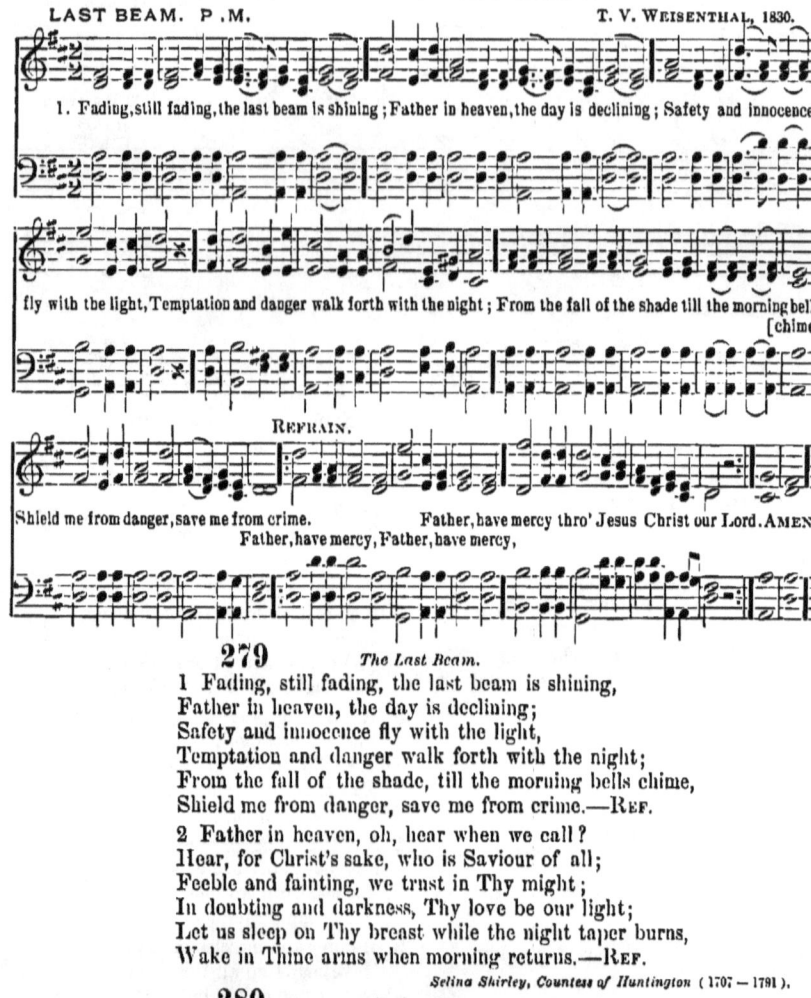

279   *The Last Beam.*

1 Fading, still fading, the last beam is shining,
Father in heaven, the day is declining;
Safety and innocence fly with the light,
Temptation and danger walk forth with the night;
From the fall of the shade, till the morning bells chime,
Shield me from danger, save me from crime.—REF.

2 Father in heaven, oh, hear when we call?
Hear, for Christ's sake, who is Saviour of all;
Feeble and fainting, we trust in Thy might;
In doubting and darkness, Thy love be our light;
Let us sleep on Thy breast while the night taper burns,
Wake in Thine arms when morning returns.—REF.

Selina Shirley, Countess of Huntington (1707 – 1791).

280   *Psalm 117.*
Tune, UXBRIDGE.

1 From all that dwell below the skies,
Let the Creator's praise arise;
Let the Redeemer's name be sung,
Through every land, by every tongue.

2 Eternal are Thy mercies, Lord;
Eternal truth attends Thy word;
Thy praise shall sound from shore to shore,
'Till suns shall rise and set no more.

Rev. Isaac Watts (1674 – 1748).

OPENING AND CLOSING HYMNS.

INVOCATION. L. M.   ENGLISH.

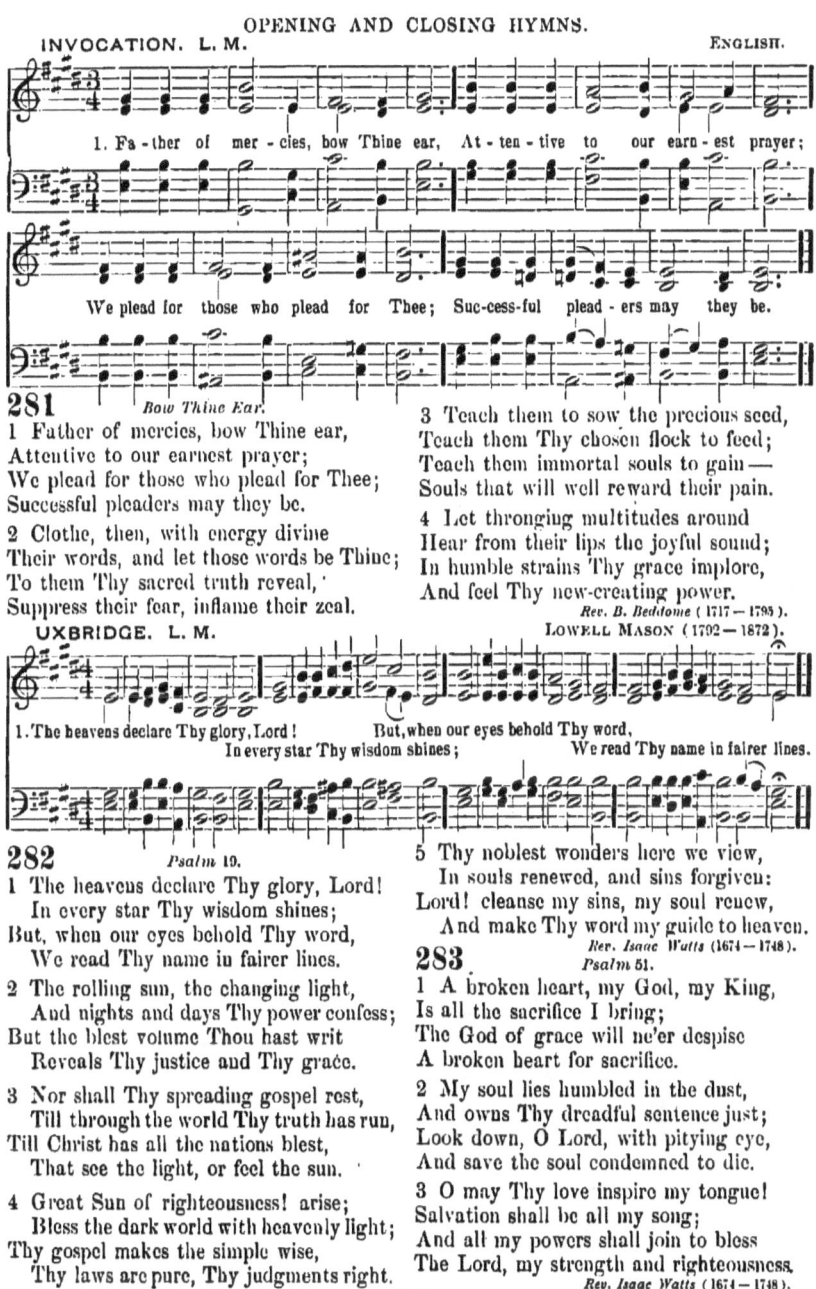

1. Fa-ther of mer-cies, bow Thine ear, At-ten-tive to our earn-est prayer;
We plead for those who plead for Thee; Suc-cess-ful plead-ers may they be.

281   *Bow Thine Ear.*

1 Father of mercies, bow Thine ear,
Attentive to our earnest prayer;
We plead for those who plead for Thee;
Successful pleaders may they be.

2 Clothe, then, with energy divine
Their words, and let those words be Thine;
To them Thy sacred truth reveal,
Suppress their fear, inflame their zeal.

3 Teach them to sow the precious seed,
Teach them Thy chosen flock to feed;
Teach them immortal souls to gain —
Souls that will well reward their pain.

4 Let thronging multitudes around
Hear from their lips the joyful sound;
In humble strains Thy grace implore,
And feel Thy new-creating power.
Rev. B. Beddome (1717 — 1795).

UXBRIDGE. L. M.   LOWELL MASON (1792 — 1872).

1. The heavens declare Thy glory, Lord!
In every star Thy wisdom shines;
But, when our eyes behold Thy word,
We read Thy name in fairer lines.

282   *Psalm 19.*

1 The heavens declare Thy glory, Lord!
In every star Thy wisdom shines;
But, when our eyes behold Thy word,
We read Thy name in fairer lines.

2 The rolling sun, the changing light,
And nights and days Thy power confess;
But the blest volume Thou hast writ
Reveals Thy justice and Thy grace.

3 Nor shall Thy spreading gospel rest,
Till through the world Thy truth has run,
Till Christ has all the nations blest,
That see the light, or feel the sun.

4 Great Sun of righteousness! arise;
Bless the dark world with heavenly light;
Thy gospel makes the simple wise,
Thy laws are pure, Thy judgments right.

5 Thy noblest wonders here we view,
In souls renewed, and sins forgiven:
Lord! cleanse my sins, my soul renew,
And make Thy word my guide to heaven.
Rev. Isaac Watts (1674 — 1748).

283   *Psalm 51.*

1 A broken heart, my God, my King,
Is all the sacrifice I bring;
The God of grace will ne'er despise
A broken heart for sacrifice.

2 My soul lies humbled in the dust,
And owns Thy dreadful sentence just;
Look down, O Lord, with pitying eye,
And save the soul condemned to die.

3 O may Thy love inspire my tongue!
Salvation shall be all my song;
And all my powers shall join to bless
The Lord, my strength and righteousness.
Rev. Isaac Watts (1674 — 1748).

OPENING AND CLOSING HYMNS.

SANQUHAR. L. M. ROBERT P. KERR, 1891.

1. How pleas-ant, how di-vine-ly fair, O Lord of hosts Thy dwell-ings are!
With long de-sire my spir-it faints To meet th' as-sem-blies of Thy saints.

Copyright by R. P. Kerr, 1891.

284 *Psalm 84.*

1 How pleasant, how divinely fair,
O Lord of hosts, Thy dwellings are !
With long desire my spirit faints
To meet th' assemblies of Thy saints.

2 My flesh would rest in Thine abode;
My panting heart cries out for God;
My God, my King, why should I be
So far from all my joys and Thee?

3 Blest are the saints who sit on high,
Around Thy throne, above the sky;
Thy brightest glories shine above,
And all their work is praise and love.

4 Blest are the saints who find a place
Within the temple of Thy grace;
There they behold Thy gentler rays,
And seek Thy face, and learn Thy praise.

Rev. Isaac Watts (1674—1748).

MIGDOL. L. M. Arr. L. MASON (1792—1872).

1. When Je-sus speaks, so sweet the sound, The harps of heav'n are hushed to hear;
And all His words go cir-cling round From lip to lip and ear to ear.

285 *When Jesus Speaks.*
From "The Light of the World," by per.

1 When Jesus speaks, so sweet the sound,
The harps of heaven are hushed to hear;
And all His words go circling round
From lip to lip and ear to ear.

2 But wondering seraph never heard,
In all the mighty years of heaven,
Music so sweet as that dear word;
"Thy many sins are all forgiven."

3 Sinners of earth, redeemed by blood,
How leaped your hearts, when first ye knew
Th' amazing grace, and understood
The gift of pardon was for you !

4 Adopted now, with spirits awed,
Knowing your privilege unpriced,
Ye claim the fatherhood of God
And brotherhood of Jesus Christ.

Abraham Coles, M.D. LL.D., (1813—1891).

(116)

OPENING AND CLOSING HYMNS.

GENTLE SHEPHERD. 8s & 7s. E. AUBREY YOUNG, 1891.

1. Hear my pray'r, O Heavenly Father, Ere I lay me down to sleep; Bid Thine angels, pure and holy, Round my bed their vigil keep.

286 *Evening Devotion.*

1 Hear my prayer, O Heavenly Father,
Ere I lay me down to sleep;
Bid Thine angels, pure and holy,
Round my bed their vigil keep.

2 Great my sins are, but Thy mercy
Far outweighs them every one;
Down before the cross I cast them,
Trusting in Thy help alone.

3 Keep me through this night of peril,
Underneath its boundless shade;
Take me to Thy rest, I pray Thee,
When my pilgrimage is made.

4 Pardon all my past transgressions,
Give me strength for days to come;
Guide and guard me with Thy blessing,
Till Thine angels bid me home.
Miss Harriet Parr, 1856.

ANGELUS. L. M. SCHEFFLER'S GEISTLICHE HIRTENLIEDER, 1657.

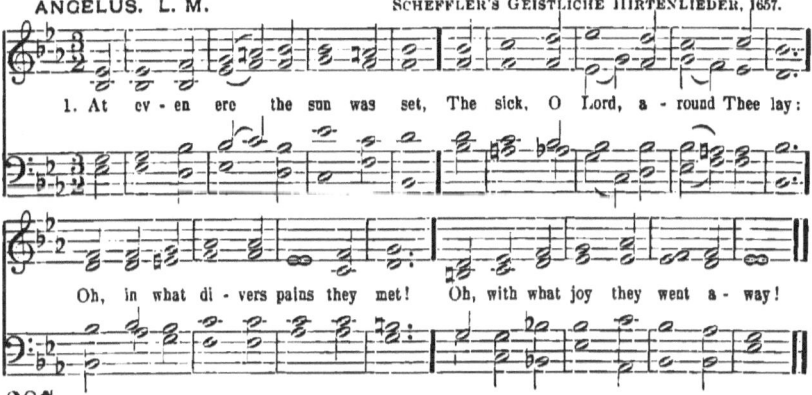

1. At ev-en ere the sun was set, The sick, O Lord, a-round Thee lay:
Oh, in what di-vers pains they met! Oh, with what joy they went a-way!

287 *And at Even when the Sun did Set.*

1 At even ere the sun was set,
The sick, O Lord, around Thee lay;
Oh, in what divers pains they met!
Oh, with what joy they went away!

2 Once more 't is eventide, and we
Oppress'd with various ills draw near;
What if Thy form we cannot see?
We know and feel that Thou art here.

3 O Saviour Christ, our woes dispel;
For some are sick, and some are sad,
And some have never loved Thee well,
And some have lost the love they had;

4 And some have found the world is vain,
Yet from the world they break not free;

And some have friends who give them pain,
Yet have not sought a friend in Thee;

5 And none, O Lord, have perfect rest,
For none are wholly free from sin;
And they who fain would serve Thee best,
Are conscious most of wrong within.

6 O Saviour Christ, Thou too art Man;
Thou hast been troubled, tempted, tried;
Thy kind but searching glance can scan
The very wounds that shame would hide.

7 Thy touch has still its ancient power;
No word from Thee can fruitless fall;
Hear, in this solemn evening hour,
And in Thy mercy heal us all.
Henry Twells.

OPENING AND CLOSING HYMNS.

EVENTIDE. 10s. WILLIAM HENRY MONK, 1861.

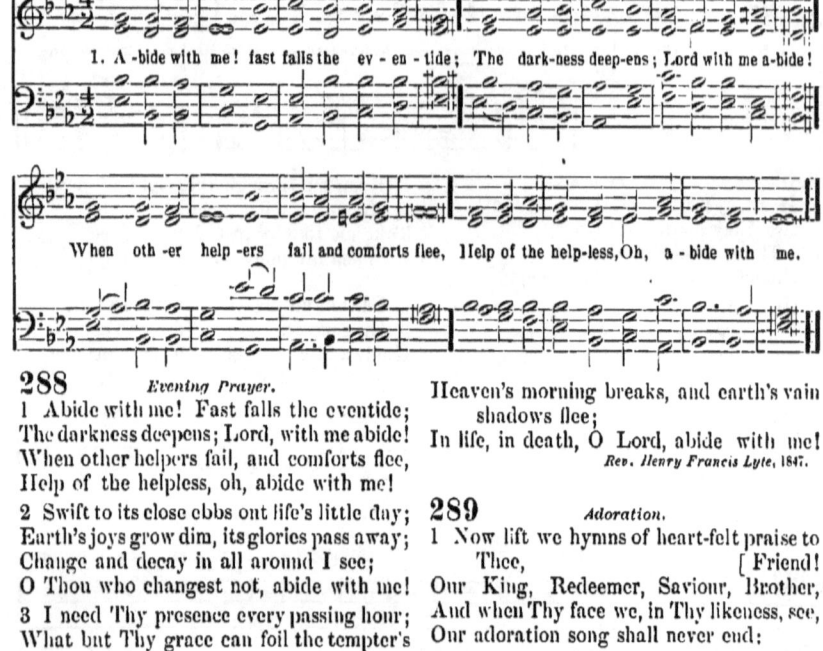

288 *Evening Prayer.*

1 Abide with me! Fast falls the eventide;
The darkness deepens; Lord, with me abide!
When other helpers fail, and comforts flee,
Help of the helpless, oh, abide with me!

2 Swift to its close ebbs out life's little day;
Earth's joys grow dim, its glories pass away;
Change and decay in all around I see;
O Thou who changest not, abide with me!

3 I need Thy presence every passing hour;
What but Thy grace can foil the tempter's power? [be
Who like Thyself my Guide and stay can
Through cloud and sunshine, oh, abide with me!

4 I fear no foe, with Thee at hand to bless;
Ills have no weight, and tears no bitterness;
Where is death's sting? where, grave, Thy victory?
I triumph still, if Thou abide with me!

5 Hold Thou Thy cross before my closing eyes; [the skies;
Shine through the gloom, and point me to
Heaven's morning breaks, and earth's vain shadows flee;
In life, in death, O Lord, abide with me!

Rev. Henry Francis Lyte, 1847.

289 *Adoration.*

1 Now lift we hymns of heart-felt praise to Thee, [Friend!
Our King, Redeemer, Saviour, Brother,
And when Thy face we, in Thy likeness, see,
Our adoration song shall never end:

2 Then shall we sing — when with our God we reign,
Serving Thee, ever, in most holy ways —
"Worthy the Lamb who once for us was slain!"
That song, forever new, of ceaseless praise.

3 While here we tarry in this world of need,
Seeking the lost ones who in darkness roam,
Thy little flock, Good Shepherd, gently lead,
And bear Thy lambs in safety to Thy Home.

Miss Emilie S. Coles.
From "The Mission Band Hymnal," by permission.

TROYTE'S CHANT, No. 1.

OPENING AND CLOSING HYMNS.

CORINA. L. M.   L. O. EMERSON.

1. My God, is a-ny hour so sweet, From blush of morn to ev'n-ing star, As that which calls me to Thy feet, The hour of prayer, The hour of prayer?

By per. of Oliver Ditson Company, owners of Copyright.

290   *The Hour of Prayer.*
1 My God, is any hour so sweet,
   From blush of morn to evening star,
As that which calls me to Thy feet,
   The hour of prayer?

2 Blest is that tranquil hour of morn,
   And blest that hour of solemn eve,
When, on the wings of prayer up-borne,
   The world I leave.

3 Then is my strength by Thee renewed;
   Then are my sins by Thee forgiven;
Then dost Thou cheer my longing soul
   With hopes of heaven.

4 No words can tell what sweet relief
   There for my every want I find;
What strength for warfare, balm for grief,
   What peace of mind.
          Miss Charlotte Elliott (1789–1871).

291   *Social Worship.*
1 May He, by whose kind care we meet,
Send His good Spirit from above;
Make our communications sweet,
And cause our hearts to burn with love.

2 Forgotten be each earthly theme,
When Christians see each other thus;
We only wish to speak of Him
Who lived, and died, and reigns, for us

3 We'll talk of all He did and said,
   And suffered for us here below;
The path He marked for us to tread,
   And what He's doing for us now.

4 Thus, as the moments pass away,
   We'll love, and wonder, and adore;
And hasten on the glorious day,
   When we shall meet — to part no more.
          Rev. John Newton (1725–1807).

292   *Thy Will Be Done.*
1 My God and Father, while I stray
   Far from my home, on life's rough way,
Oh! teach me from heart to say,
      Thy will be done.

2 Let but my fainting heart be blest.
   With Thy sweet Spirit for its guest,
My God, to Thee I leave the rest;
      Thy will be done.

3 Renew my will from day to day;
   Blend it with Thine; and take away
All that now makes it hard to say,
      Thy will be done!

4 Then, when on earth I breathe no more,
   The prayer, oft mixed with tears before,
I'll sing upon a happier shore,
      Thy will be done!
          Miss Charlotte Elliott (1789–1871).

OPENING AND CLOSING HYMNS.

RETREAT. L. M. T. HASTINGS (1784—1872).

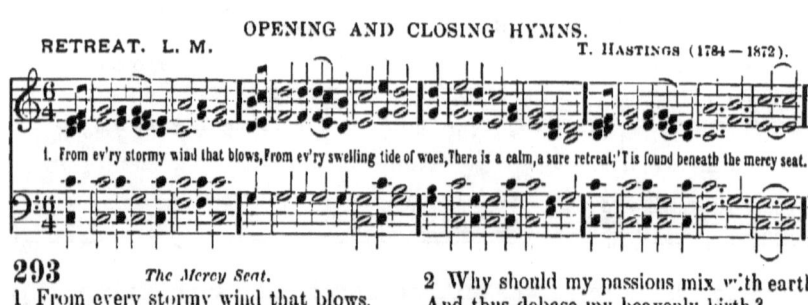

1. From ev'ry stormy wind that blows, From ev'ry swelling tide of woes, There is a calm, a sure retreat; 'Tis found beneath the mercy seat.

293 *The Mercy Seat.*

1 From every stormy wind that blows,
From every swelling tide of woes,
There is a calm, a sure retreat,
'Tis found beneath the mercy seat.

2 There is a place, where Jesus sheds
The oil of gladness on our heads;
A place than all besides more sweet,
It is the blood-bought mercy seat.

3 There is a scene where spirits blend,
Where friend holds fellowship with friend,
Though sundered far, by faith they meet,
Around one common mercy seat.

4 Ah! whither could we flee for aid,
When tempted, desolate, dismayed?
Or how the hosts of hell defeat,
Had suffering saints no mercy seat?

5 There, there on eagles' wings we soar,
And sin and sense seem all no more;
And heaven comes down our souls to greet,
And glory crowns the mercy seat.

6 Oh, let my hand forget her skill,
My tongue be silent, cold, and still,
This bounding heart forget to beat,
If I forget Thy mercy seat.
Rev. H. Stowell (1799—1865).

294 *Retirement and Meditation.*

1 My God, permit me not to be
A stranger to myself and Thee;
Amidst a thousand thoughts I rove,
Forgetful of my highest love.

2 Why should my passions mix with earth
And thus debase my heavenly birth?
Why should I cleave to things below,
And let my God, my Saviour go?

3 Call me away from flesh and sense;
One sovereign word can draw me thence;
I would obey the voice divine,
And all inferior joys resign.

4 Be earth, with all her scenes, withdrawn;
Let noise and vanity be gone;
In secret silence of the mind,
My heaven, and there my God, I find.
Rev. Isaac Watts (1674—1748).

295 *A Blessing Implored.*

1 Command Thy blessing from above,
O God! on all assembled here;
Behold us with a Father's love,
While we look up with filial fear.

2 Command Thy blessing, Jesus, Lord!
May we Thy true disciples be;
Speak to each heart the mighty word,
Say to the weakest, "Follow Me."

3 Command Thy blessing in this hour;
Spirit of Truth! and fill this place
With humbling and exalting power,
With quickening and confirming grace.

4 O Thou, our Maker, Saviour, Guide,
One true eternal God confest;
May naught in life or death divide
The saints of Thy communion blest.
Rev. J. Montgomery (1771—1854).

LACHRYMÆ. 7s, 3l. Sir ARTHUR SULLIVAN, Mus. D.

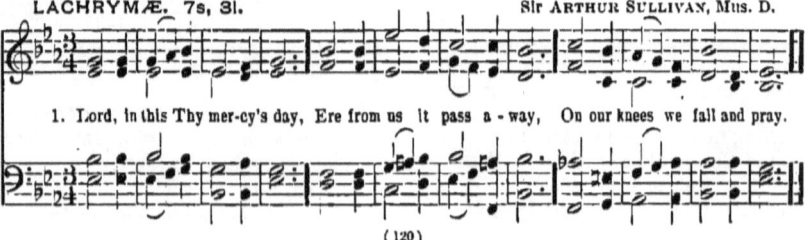

1. Lord, in this Thy mer-cy's day, Ere from us it pass a-way, On our knees we fall and pray.

OPENING AND CLOSING HYMNS.

GENEVA. C. M.   JOHN COLE, 1805.

1. When all Thy mercies, O my God! My rising soul surveys,
Transported with the view, I'm lost In wonder, love, and praise.

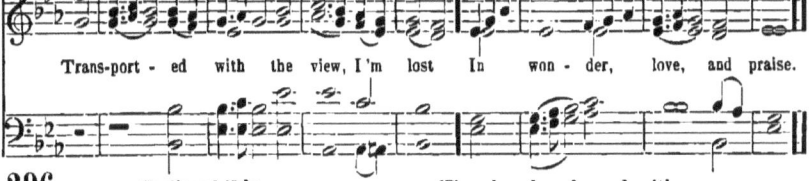

296   *Continued Help.*
1 When all Thy mercies, O my God!
My rising soul surveys,
Transported with the view, I'm lost
In wonder, love, and praise.

2 Unnumbered comforts, to my soul,
Thy tender care bestowed,
Before my infant heart conceived
From whom those comforts flowed.

3 When, in the slippery paths of youth,
With heedless steps, I ran,
Thine arm, unseen, coveyed me safe,
And led me up to man.

4 Ten thousand thousand precious gifts
My daily thanks employ;
Nor is the least a cheerful heart,
That tastes those gifts with joy.

5 Through every period of my life,
Thy goodness I'll pursue;
And after death, in distant worlds,
The glorious theme renew.

6 Through all eternity, to Thee
A joyful song I'll raise:
For, oh, eternity's too short
To utter all Thy praise!
Joseph Addison (1672—1719).

297   *Psalm 122.*
1 How did my heart rejoice to hear
My friends devoutly say,
In Zion let us all appear
And keep the solemn day.

2 I love her gates, I love the road;

The church, adorned with grace,
Stands like a palace built for God
To show His milder face.

3 Up to her courts, with joys unknown,
The holy tribes repair;
The Son of David holds His throne,
And sits in judgment there.

4 Peace be within this sacred place,
And joy a constant guest;
With holy gifts and heavenly grace
Be her attendants blest.
Rev. Isaac Watts (1674—1748).

298   Tune, LACHRYMÆ.
1 Lord, in this Thy mercy's day,
Ere it pass for aye away,
On our knees we fall and pray.

2 Holy Saviour, grant us tears,
Fill us with heart-searching fears,
Ere that awful doom appears.

3 Lord, on us Thy Spirit pour
Kneeling lowly at the door,
Ere it close for evermore.

4 By Thy night of agony,
By Thy supplicating cry,
By Thy willingness to die;

5 By Thy tears of bitter woe
For Jerusalem below,
Let us not Thy love forego.

6 Grant us 'neath Thy wings a place
Lest we lose this day of grace
Ere we shall behold Thy face.
I. Williams (—1865).

OPENING AND CLOSING HYMNS.

SHIRLAND, S. M.   S. STANLEY, 1800.

1. The day is past and gone, The even-ing shades ap-pear;
Oh, may we all re-mem-ber well The night of death draws near.

299   *On Going to Rest.*

1 The day is past and gone,
   The evening shades appear;
Oh, may we all remember well
   The night of death draws near.

2 Lord, keep us safe this night,
   Secure from all our fears;
May angels guard us while we sleep,
   Till morning light appears.

3 And when we early rise,
   And view the unwearied sun,
May we set out to win the prize,
   And after glory run.

4 And when our days are past,
   And we from time remove,

Oh, may we in Thy bosom rest,
   The bosom of Thy love.
     Rev. John Leland (1754—1841).

300   *The Sabbath a Delight.*

1 Welcome, sweet day of rest,
   That saw the Lord arise;
Welcome to this reviving breast,
   And these rejoicing eyes.

2 The King Himself comes near,
   And feasts His saints to-day;
Here we may sit, and see Him here,
   And love, and praise, and pray.

3 My willing soul would stay
   In such a frame as this,
And sit and sing herself away,
   To everlasting bliss.
     Rev. Isaac Watts (1674—1748).

EVENING PRAYER.   GEO. C. STEBBINS, by per.

1. Sav-iour breathe an even-ing bless-ing, Ere re-pose our spir-its seal:
Sin and want we come con-fess-ing, Thou canst save and Thou canst heal.

By per. of G. C. Stebbins, owner of copyright.

OPENING AND CLOSING HYMNS.

VESPER HYMN. 8s & 7s, D.   Russian Air, by DIMITRI BORTNIANSKI.

301   *Evening Song.*

1 Saviour, breathe an evening blessing,
   Ere repose our spirits seal;
Sin and want we come confessing,
   Thou canst save and Thou canst heal;
Though destruction walk around us,
   Though the arrow near us fly,
Angel-guards from Thee surround us,
   We are safe if Thou art nigh.

2 Though the night be dark and dreary,
   Darkness cannot hide from Thee;
Thou art He who, never weary,
   Watchest where Thy people be.
Should swift death this night o'ertake us,
   And our couch become our tomb;
May the morn in heaven awake us,
   Clad in light and deathless bloom.
        James Edmeston (1791 — 1867).

302   *Doxolgy.*

Praise the God of all creation;
   Praise the Father's boundless love;
Praise the Lamb, our expiation,
   Priest and King enthroned above;
Praise the Fountain of salvation,
   Him by whom our spirits live;
Undivided adoration
   To the one Jehovah give.

303   *Closing Prayer.*

May the grace of Christ, our Saviour,
   And the Father's boundless love,
With the Holy Spirit's favor,
   Rest upon us from above.
Thus may we abide in union
   With each other and the Lord,
And possess, in sweet communion,
   Joys which earth cannot afford.

THE SCRIPTURES.

AZMON. C. M.
Carl Gotthilf Gläser (1784—1829).
Arr. by Lowell Mason (1792—1872).

1. A glory gilds the sacred page, Majestic like the sun; It gives a light to ev'ry age; It gives, but borrows none.

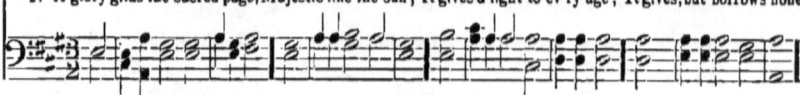

304   *The Bible.*

1 A glory gilds the sacred page,
   Majestic like the sun;
It gives a light to every age;
   It gives, but borrows none.

2 The hand that gave it still supplies
   The gracious light and heat;
His truths upon the nations rise,
   They rise, but never set.

3 Let everlasting thanks be Thine,
   For such a bright display,
As makes a world of darkness shine
   With beams of heavenly day.

4 My soul rejoices to pursue
   The steps of Him I love,
Till glory breaks upon my view
   In brighter worlds above.

Wm. Cowper (1731—1800).

305   *Godly Sincerity.*

1 Walk in the light! so shalt thou know
   That fellowship of love,
His Spirit only can bestow,
   Who reigns in light above.

2 Walk in the light! and thou shalt find
   Thy heart made truly His,
Who dwells in cloudless light enshrined,
   In whom no darkness is.

3 Walk in the light! and e'en the tomb
   No fearful shade shall wear;
Glory shall chase away its gloom,
   For Christ hath conquered there.

4 Walk in the light! and thou shalt see
   Thy path, though thorny, bright;
For God by grace shall dwell in thee,
   And God Himself is light.

R. Barton, 1820.

306   *Psalm* 119.

1 Oh, how I love Thy holy law!
   'T is daily my delight;
And thence my meditations draw
   Divine advice by night.

2 My waking eyes prevent the day
   To meditate Thy word;
My soul with longing melts away
   To hear Thy gospel, Lord.

3 Thy heavenly words my heart engage,
   And well employ my tongue;
And in my tiresome pilgrimage
   Yield me a heavenly song.

4 When nature sinks, and spirits droop,
   Thy promises of grace
Are pillars to support my hope;
   And there I write Thy praise.

Rev. Isaac Watts (1674—1748).

307   *Psalm* 119.

1 Lord, I have made Thy word my choice,
   My lasting heritage;
There shall my noblest powers rejoice,
   My warmest thoughts engage.

2 I'll read the histories of Thy love,
   And keep Thy laws in sight,
While through the promises I rove,
   With ever fresh delight.

3 'T is a broad land of wealth unknown,
   Where springs of life arise;
Seeds of immortal bliss are sown,
   And hidden glory lies.

4 The best relief that mourners have,
   It makes our sorrows blest;
Our fairest hope beyond the grave,
   And our eternal rest.

Rev. Isaac Watts (1674—1748).

THE SCRIPTURES.

AURELIA. 7s & 6s, D.   SAMUEL SEBASTIAN WESLEY, 1868.

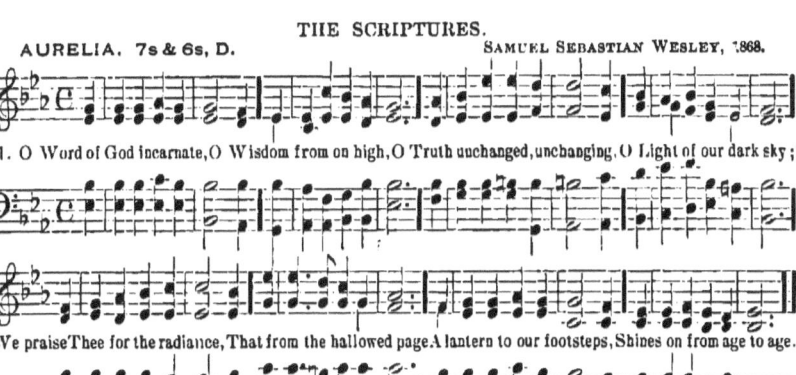

1. O Word of God incarnate, O Wisdom from on high, O Truth unchanged, unchanging, O Light of our dark sky;
We praise Thee for the radiance, That from the hallowed page A lantern to our footsteps, Shines on from age to age.

308   *The Word of God.*

1 O Word of God incarnate,
  O Wisdom from on high,
O Truth unchanged, unchanging,
  O Light of our dark sky;
We praise Thee for the radiance,
  That from the hallowed page
A lantern to our footsteps,
  Shines on from age to age.

2 The Church from Thee, her Master,
  Received the gift divine;
And still that light she lifteth
  O'er all the earth to shine.

It is the golden casket
  Where gems of truth are stored;
It is the heaven-drawn picture
  Of Thee, the living Word.

3 Oh, make Thy church, dear Saviour,
  A lamp of burnished gold,
To bear before the nations
  Thy true light, as of old.
Oh, teach Thy wandering pilgrims
  By this their path to trace,
Till, clouds and darkness ended,
  They see Thee face to face.

Bishop William Walsham How, 1867.

HAMBURG. L. M.

1. God in the gos-pel of His Son, Makes His eter-nal counsels known; Where love in all its glo-ry shines, And Truth is drawn in fairest lines.

309   *Fullness of the Gospel.*

1 God, in the gospel of His Son,
Makes His eternal counsels known;
Where love in all its glory shines,
And truth is drawn in fairest lines.

2 Here sinners, of a humble frame,
May taste His grace, and learn His name,
May read, in characters of blood,
The wisdom, power and grace of God.

3 The prisoner here may break his chains;
The weary rest from all his pains;

The captive feel his bondage cease;
The mourner find the way of peace.

4 Here faith reveals to mortal eyes
A brighter world beyond the skies;
Here shines the light which guides our way
From earth to realms of endless day.

5 Oh, grant us grace, almighty Lord,
To read and mark Thy holy word;
Its truths with meekness to receive,
And by its holy precepts live,

Rev. Benj. Beddome (17.7 — 1795).

THE SCRIPTURES.

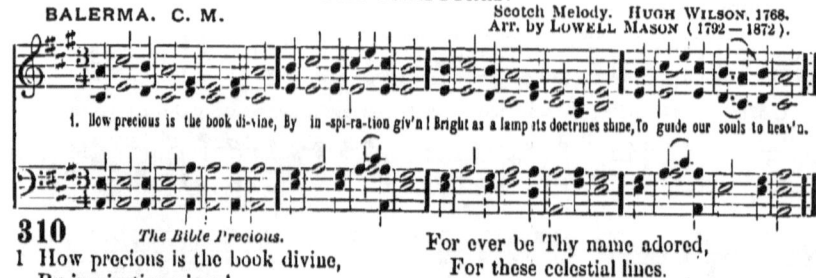

310 *The Bible Precious.*
1 How precious is the book divine,
By inspiration given!
Bright as a lamp its doctrines shine,
To guide our souls to heaven.

2 It sweetly cheers our drooping hearts,
In this dark vale of tears;
Life, light and joy, it still imparts,
And quells our rising fears.

3 This lamp through all the tedious night
Of life, shall guide our way,
Till we behold the clearer light
Of an eternal day.
Rev. John Fawcett (1739—1817).

311 *Richness of the Scriptures.*
1 Father of mercies, in Thy word,
What endless glory shines!
For ever be Thy name adored,
For these celestial lines.

2 Here the Redeemer's welcome voice
Spreads heavenly peace around;
And life and everlasting joys
Attend the blissful sound.

3 Oh, may these heavenly pages be
My ever dear delight;
And still new beauties may I see,
And still increasing light.

4 Divine Instructor, gracious Lord,
Be Thou for ever near!
Teach me to love Thy sacred word,
And view my Saviour there.
Miss Anne Steele (1717—1778).

312 *Christ's Glory Unveiled.*
1 Thou lovely Source of true delight,
Whom I unseen adore;
Unveil Thy beauties to my sight,
That I may love Thee more.

2 Thy glory o'er creation shines,
But in Thy sacred word,
I read in fairer, brighter lines,
My bleeding, dying Lord.

3 'Tis here, whene'er my comforts droop,
And sins and sorrows rise,
Thy love with cheerful beams of hope,
My fainting heart supplies.

4 Jesus, my Lord, my life, my light,
Oh, come with blissful ray,
Break radiant through the shades of night
And chase my fears away
Miss Anne Steele (1717—1778).

THE HOLY SPIRIT.

STEPHENS. C. M.   Rev. WILLIAM JONES (1726—1800).

1. Come, Ho-ly Spir-it, heav'n-ly Dove, With all Thy quickening pow'rs, Kin-dle a flame of sa - cred love, In these cold hearts of ours.

313 *Prayer for the Descent of the Spirit.*

1 Come, Holy Spirit, heavenly Dove,
With all Thy quickening powers,
Kindle a flame of sacred love,
In these cold hearts of ours.

2 Look how we grovel here below,
Fond of these trifling toys;
Our souls can neither fly nor go,
To reach eternal joys.

3 In vain we tune our formal songs,
In vain we strive to rise;
Hosannas languish on our tongues,
And our devotion dies.

4 Dear Lord, and shall we ever live
At this poor dying rate?
Our love so faint, so cold to Thee,
And Thine to us so great?

5 Come, Holy Spirit, Heavenly Dove,
With all Thy quickening powers,

Come, shed abroad a Saviour's Love,
And that shall kindle ours.
Rev. I. Watts (1674—1748).

314 *The Gift of God.*

1 Come, Holy Ghost, Creator, come,
Inspire these souls of Thine;
Till every heart which Thou hast made
Be filled with grace divine.

2 Thou art the Comforter, the gift
Of God, and fire of love;
The everlasting spring of joy,
And unction from above.

3 Enlighten our dark souls, till they
Thy sacred love embrace;
Assist our minds, by nature frail,
With Thy celestial grace.

4 Teach us the Father to confess,
And Son, from death revived,
And Thee, with both, O Holy Ghost,
Who art from both derived.
Latin of 12th Century. Tr. by Tate.

PRIERE, 7s, 3 l.   Arr. by WILLIAM HENRY MONK 1862.

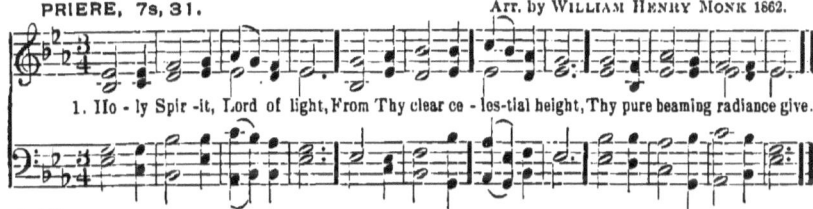

1. Ho - ly Spir -it, Lord of light, From Thy clear ce - les-tial height, Thy pure beaming radiance give.

315 *Veni Sancte Spiritus.*

1 Holy Spirit, Lord of light,
From Thy clear celestial height,
Thy pure beaming radiance give.

2 Come, Thou Father of the poor,
Come, with treasures which endure,
Come, Thou light of all that live.

3 Light immortal, Light divine,
Visit Thou these hearts of Thine,
And our inmost being fill.

4 If Thou take Thy grace away,
Nothing pure in man will stay;
All His good is turned to ill.

5 Thou, on those who evermore
Thee confess, and Thee adore,
In Thy sevenfold gifts descend.

6 Give them comfort when they die,
Give them life with Thee on high;
Give them joys which never end.
Robert II, King of France (972—1031).
Tr. by Rev. Edward Caswall, 1814.

THE HOLY SPIRIT.

NEW HAVEN. 6s, 4s. THOMAS HASTINGS (1784—1872).

316 *Veni Sancte Spiritus.*

1 Come, Holy Ghost, in love
Shed on us from above
Thine own bright ray!
Divinely good Thou art;
Thy sacred gifts impart
To gladden each sad heart:
Oh, come to day!

2 Come, tenderest Friend, and best,
Our most delightful guest,
With soothing power:
Rest, which the weary know,
Shade, 'mid the noontide glow,
Peace, where deep griefs o'erflow,
Cheer us, this hour!

3 Come, Light serene, and still
Our inmost bosoms fill;
Dwell in each breast;

We know no dawn but Thine;
Send forth Thy beams divine,
On our dark souls to shine,
And make us blest!

4 Exalt our low desires;
Extinguish passion's fires;
Heal every wound:
Our stubborn spirits bend;
Our icy coldness end;
Our devious steps attend,
While heavenward bound.

5 Come, all the faithful bless;
Let all who Christ confess,
His praise employ:
Give virtue's rich reward;
Victorious death accord,
And, with our glorious Lord,
Eternal joy!

Robert II., King of France (972—1031).
Tr. by Rev. Ray Palmer.

EVELYN. 7s & 6s. Sir ARTHUR S. SULLIVAN, Mus. D.

317 *The Spirit of Knowledge.*

1 Spirit blest, who art adored
With the Father and the Word.
One eternal God and Lord —
Hear us, Holy Spirit.

2 Spirit, showing us the way,
Warning when we go astray,
Pleading in us when we pray —
Hear us, Holy Spirit.

3 Spirit, strength of all the weak,
Giving courage to the meek,
Teaching faltering tongues to speak —
Hear us, Holy Spirit.

4 Spirit guiding to the right,
Spirit making darkness light,
Spirit of resistless might —
Hear us, Holy Spirit.

T. B. Pollock.

THE HOLY SPIRIT.

LAST HOPE. 7s.   L. M. GOTTSCHALK (1829 – 1869).

1. Ho-ly Ghost! with light di-vine, Shine up-on this heart of mine; Chase the shades of night a-way, Turn my dark-ness in-to day.

318   *Light, Power, Joy.*

1 Holy Ghost! with light divine,
Shine upon this heart of mine;
Chase the shades of night away,
Turn my darkness into day.

2 Holy Ghost, with power divine,
Cleanse this guilty heart of mine;
Long has sin, without control,
Held dominion o'er my soul.

3 Holy Ghost, with joy divine,
Cheer this saddened heart of mine,
Bid my many woes depart,
Heal my wounded, bleeding heart.

4 Holy Spirit, all divine,
Dwell within this heart of mine;
Cast down every idol throne,
Reign supreme — and reign alone.
                    Rev. A. Reed (1787 – 1862).

319   *Prayer to the Spirit.*

1 Gracious Spirit, love divine,
Let Thy light within me shine;
All my guilty fears remove,
Fill me full of heaven and love.

2 Speak Thy pardoning grace to me,
Set the burdened sinner free;
Lead me to the Lamb of God,
Wash me in His precious blood.

3 Life and peace to me impart,
Seal salvation on my heart;
Breathe Thyself into my breast,
Earnest of immortal rest.

4 Let me never from Thee stray,
Keep me in the narrow way;
Fill my soul with joy divine,
Keep me, Lord, for ever Thine.
                    John Stocker, 1726.

CONSOLATOR. 7s & 5s.   A. CROIL FALCONER.

1. Come to our poor nature's night, With Thy blessed inward light, Holy Ghost, the Infinite, Com-fort-er Divine.

320   *Comforter Divine.*

1 Come to our poor nature's night
With Thy blessed inward light,
Holy Ghost, the Infinite,
   Comforter Divine.

2 Like the dew, Thy peace distill;
Guide, subdue our wayward will,

Things of Christ unfolding still,
   Comforter Divine!

3 Gentle, loving, holy Guest,
Make Thy temple in each breast;
There Thy presence be confessed
   Comforter Divine!
                    Geo. Rawson (1807 – 1885).

THE HOLY SPIRIT.

WELLS. L. M.   Israel Holdroyd, 1740.

1. Sure the blest Comforter is nigh; 'Tis He sustains my fainting heart: Else would my hope forever die, And ev'ry cheering ray depart.

321   *Sure the Blest Comforter is Nigh.*

1 Sure the blest Comforter is nigh;
'T is He sustains my fainting heart:
Else would my hope for ever die,
And every cheering ray depart.

2 When some kind promise glads my soul,
Do I not find His healing voice
The tempest of my fears control,
And bid my drooping powers rejoice?

3 Whene'er to call the Saviour mine,
With ardent wish my heart aspires,
Can it be less than power divine,
That animates these strong desires?

4 And when my cheerful hope can say,
I love my God, and taste His grace,
Lord, is it not Thy blissful ray
Which brings this dawn of sacred peace?

5 Let Thy kind Spirit in my heart
For ever dwell, O God of love,
And light and heavenly peace impart,
Sweet earnest of the joys above.
Miss Anne Steele (1717 — 1778).

322   *Veni, Creator!*

1 Come, O Creator Spirit blest!
And in our souls take up Thy rest;
Come, with Thy grace and heavenly aid,
To fill the hearts which Thou hast made.

2 Great Comforter! to Thee we cry;
O highest gift of God most high!
O fount of life! O fire of love!
Send sweet anointing from above!

3 Kindle our senses from above,
And make our hearts o'erflow with love;
With patience firm, and virtue high,
The weakness of our flesh supply

4 Far from us drive the foe we dread,
And grant us Thy true peace instead;
So shall we not with Thee for guide,
Turn from the path of life aside.
Rabanus Maurus (776 — 856).
Tr. by Rev. Edward Caswall (1814 — 1878).

323   *Grieved Spirit Besought.*

1 Stay, Thou insulted Spirit, stay;
Though I have done Thee such despite,
Cast not the sinner quite away,
Nor take Thine everlasting flight.

2 Though I have most unfaithful been
Of all, who e'er Thy grace received,
Ten thousand times Thy goodness seen,
Ten thousand times Thy goodness grieved.

3 Yet O! the chief of sinners spare,
In honor of my great High Priest;
Nor in Thy righteous anger swear,
I shall not see Thy people's rest.

4 If yet Thou canst my sins forgive,
E'en now, O Lord, relieve my woes;
Into Thy rest of love receive,
And bless me with a calm repose.

5 E'en now my weary soul release,
And raise me by Thy gracious hand;
Guide me into Thy perfect peace,
And bring me to the promised land.
Rev. Charles Wesley (1708 — 1788).

THE HOLY SPIRIT.

FEDERAL STREET. L. M. H. K. Oliver (1800—1885).

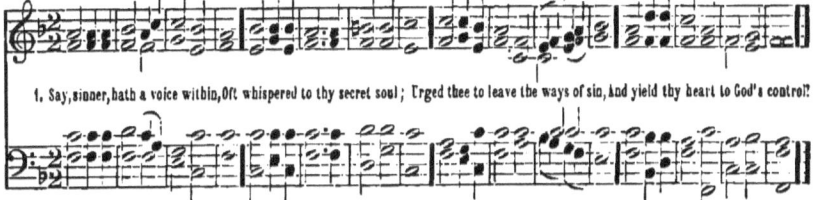

1. Say, sinner, hath a voice within, Oft whispered to thy secret soul; Urged thee to leave the ways of sin, And yield thy heart to God's control?

324 *Striving of the Spirit.*

1 Say, sinner, hath a voice within,
  Oft whispered to thy secret soul;
  Urged thee to leave the ways of sin,
  And yield thy heart to God's control?

2 Sinner, it was a heavenly voice,
  It was the Spirit's gracious call;
  It bade thee make the better choice,
  And haste to seek in Christ thine all.

3 Spurn not the call to life and light;
  Regard in time the warning kind:
  That call thou mayst not always slight,
  And yet the gate of mercy find.

4 God's Spirit will not always strive
  With hardened, self-destroying man;
  Ye, who persist His love to grieve,
  May never hear His voice again.

5 Sinner, perhaps this very day
  Thy last accepted time may be;
  Oh, shouldst thou grieve Him now away,
  Then hope may never beam on thee.
  Mrs. Ann Bradley Hyde (— 1872).

325 *Prayer for Rest in God.*

1 Come, Holy Spirit, calm my mind,
  And fit me to approach my God;
  Remove each vain, each worldly thought,
  And lead me to Thy blest abode.

2 Hast Thou imparted to my soul
  A living spark of heavenly fire?
  Oh, kindle now the sacred flame;
  Teach it to burn with pure desire.

3 A brighter faith and hope impart,
  And let me now the Saviour see;
  Oh, soothe and cheer my burdened heart,
  And bid my spirit rest in Thee.
  Rev. Henry Forster Burder's Coll., 1826.

TALLIS' ORDINAL. C. M. Thomas Tallis.
Archbishop Parker's Psalter, 1561.

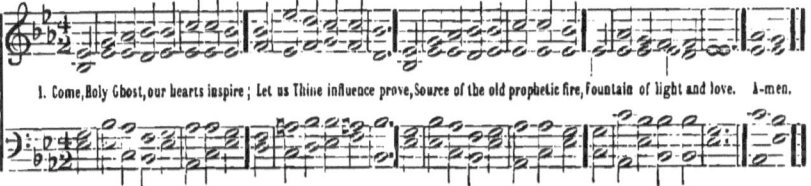

1. Come, Holy Ghost, our hearts inspire; Let us Thine influence prove, Source of the old prophetic fire, Fountain of light and love. A-men.

326 *They spake as they were moved by the Holy Ghost.*

1 Come, Holy Ghost, our hearts inspire;
  Let us Thine influence prove,
  Source of the old prophetic fire,
  Fountain of light and love.

2 Come, Holy Ghost, for moved by Thee
  The prophets wrote and spoke;
  Unlock the truth, Thyself the key,
  Unseal the sacred book.

3 Expand Thy wings, celestial Dove,
  Brood o'er our nature's night;
  On our disordered spirits move,
  And let there now be light.

4 God through Himself we then shall know
  If Thou within us shine,
  And sound, with all Thy saints below,
  The depths of love divine.
  Rev. Chas. Wesley (1708—1788).

THE HOLY SPIRIT.

DENNIS. S. M.   H. G. NAEGELI (1773—1836).

1. Blest Com-fort-er Di-vine, Whose rays of heavenly love A-mid our gloom and darkness shine, And point our souls a-bove.

327   *The Comforter.*

1 Blest Comforter Divine,
   Whose rays of heavenly love
Amid our gloom and darkness shine,
   And point our souls above.

2 Thou who with "still small voice"
   Dost stop the sinner's way,
And bid the mourning saint rejoice,
   Though earthly joys decay.

3 Thou whose inspiring breath
   Can make the cloud of care,
And e'en the gloomy vale of death,
   A smile of glory wear.

4 Thou who dost fill the heart
   With love to all our race,
Blest Comforter! to us impart
   The blessings of Thy grace.
   Mrs. Lydia Howard Huntley Sigourney (1791—1865).

328   *Grieving the Spirit.*

1 And canst thou, sinner, slight
   The call of love divine?
Shall God with tenderness invite,
   And gain no thought of thine?

2 Wilt thou not cease to grieve
   The Spirit from thy breast,
Till He thy wretched soul shall leave,
   With all thy sins oppressed?

3 To-day a pardoning God
   Will hear the suppliant pray;
To-day, a Saviour's cleansing blood
   Will wash thy guilt away.

4 But grace so dearly bought,
   If yet thou wilt despise,
Thy fearful doom with vengeance fraught,
   Will fill thee with surprise.
   Mrs. A. B. Hyde (—1872).

LEIGHTON. S. M.   HENRY WELLINGTON GREATOREX (1811—1858).

1. Come, Ho-ly Spir-it, come; Let Thy bright beams arise; Dispel the dark-ness from our minds, And o-pen Thou our eyes.

329   *The Spirit's Influences.*

1 Come, Holy Spirit, come;
   Let Thy bright beams arise;
Dispel the darkness from our minds,
   And open Thou our eyes.

2 Revive our drooping faith;
   Our doubts and fears remove;
And kindle in our breasts the flame
   Of never dying love.

3 Convince us of our sin,
   Then lead to Jesus' blood;
And to our wondering view reveal
   The gracious love of God.

4 'T is Thine to cleanse the heart,
   To sanctify the soul,
To pour fresh life on every part,
   And new create the whole.

5 Dwell, therefore, in our hearts;
   Our minds from bondage free;
Then shall we know, and praise, and love
   The Father, Son and Thee.
   Rev. Joseph Hart (1712—1768).

CHRISTIAN ACTIVITY.

THATCHER. S. M. GEO. FRED. HANDEL (1685—1759).

1. Sow in the morn thy seed, At eve hold not thy hand;
To doubt and fear give Thou no heed, Broad-cast it o'er the land.

330 *Sow Beside all Waters.*

1 Sow in the morn thy seed,
   At eve hold not thy hand;
To doubt and fear give thou no heed,
   Broad-cast it o'er the land.

2 The good, the fruitful ground,
   Expect not here nor there;
O'er hill and dale, by plots, 't is found:
   Go forth, then, everywhere.

3 Thou knowest not which may thrive,
   The late or early sown;
Grace keeps the precious germs alive,
   When and wherever strown.

4 Thou canst not toil in vain;
   Cold, heat, and moist, and dry,
Shall foster and mature the grain,
   For garners in the sky.

5 Thence, when the glorious end,
   The day of God, is come,
The angel reapers shall descend,
   And heaven sing "Harvest-home."

Rev. J. Montgomery (1771—1854).

SHIRLAND. S. M. S. STANLEY (1767—1822).

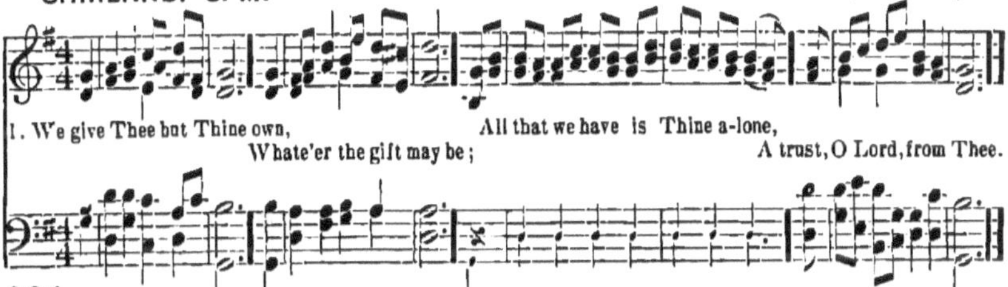

1. We give Thee but Thine own, Whate'er the gift may be;
All that we have is Thine a-lone, A trust, O Lord, from Thee.

331 *Contribution.*

1 We give Thee but Thine own,
   Whate'er the gift may be;
All that we have is Thine alone,
   A trust, O Lord, from Thee.

2 May we Thy bounties thus
   As stewards true receive,
And gladly, as Thou blessest us,
   To Thee our first-fruits give.

3 To comfort and to bless,
   To find a balm for woe,
To tend the lone and fatherless
   Is angel's work below.

4 The captive to release,
   To God the lost to bring,
To teach the way of life and peace—
   It is a Christ-like thing.

5 And we believe Thy word,
   Though dim our faith may be;
Whate'er for Thine we do, O Lord,
   We do it unto Thee.

Bp. W. W. How (1823—).

CHRISTIAN ACTIVITY.

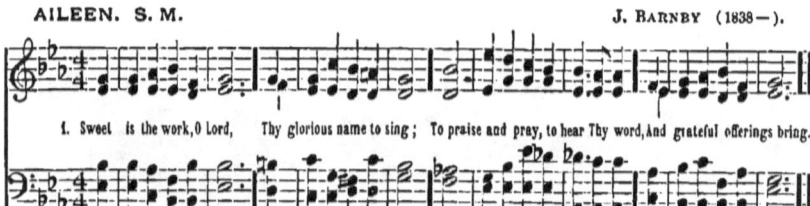

332   *Psalm 92.*

1 Sweet is the work, O Lord,
  Thy glorious name to sing;
To praise and pray—to hear thy word,
  And grateful offerings bring.

2 Sweet—at the dawning light,
  Thy boundless love to tell;
And when approach the shades of night,
  Still on the theme to dwell.

3 Sweet— on this day of rest,
  To join in heart and voice,
With those who love and serve Thee best,
  And in Thy name rejoice.

4 To songs of praise and joy
  Be every Sabbath given,
That such may be our blest employ
  Eternally in heaven.
            Miss Hariet Auber (1773 — 1862).

333   *Christian Warfare.*

1 Stand up, my soul, shake off thy fears,
  And gird the gospel armor on;
March to gates of endless joy,
  Where Jesus, thy great Captain's gone.

2 Hell and thy sins resist thy course,
  But hell and sin are vanquished foes;
Thy Jesus nailed them to the cross,
  And sung the triumph when He rose.

3 Then let my soul march boldly on,
  Press forward to the heavenly gate;
There peace and joy eternal reign,
  And glittering robes for conquerors wait.

4 There shall I wear a starry crown,
  And triumph in almighty grace;
While all the armies of the skies
  Join in my glorious Leader's praise.
            Rev. Isaac Watts (1674 — 1748).

CHRISTIAN ACTIVITY.

LABAN, S. M.   Dr. L. Mason. (1792—1872).

1. A charge to keep I have, A God to glo-ri-fy;
A nev-er-dy-ing soul to save, And fit it for the sky.

334 *A Charge To Keep.*

1 A charge to keep I have,
  A God to glorify;
  A never-dying soul to save,
  And fit it for the sky.

2 From youth to hoary age,
  My calling to fulfill;
  Oh, may it all my powers engage
  To do my Master's will.

3 Arm me with jealous care,
  As in Thy sight to live,
  And oh, Thy servant, Lord, prepare
  A strict account to give.

4 Help me to watch and pray,
  And on Thyself rely;
  Assured if I my trust betray,
  I shall for ever die.
    Rev. Chas. Wesley (1708—1788).

335 *Soldiers Of Christ.*

1 Soldiers of Christ, arise
  And put your armor on,
  Strong in the strength which God supplies
  Through His eternal Son.

2 Strong in the Lord of Hosts,
  And in His mighty power;
  Who in the strength of Jesus trusts,
  Is more than conqueror.

3 Stand, then, in His great might,
  With all His strength endued;
  But take to arm you for the fight,
  The panoply of God:—

4 That having all things done,
  And all your conflicts past,
  Ye may o'ercome through Christ alone,
  And stand entire at last.

5 From strength to strength go on,
  Wrestle, and fight, and pray;
  Tread all the powers of darkness down,
  And win the well-fought day.

6 Still let the Spirit cry
  In all His soldiers, "Come,"
  Till Christ the Lord descend from high,
  And take the conquerors home.
    Rev. Chas. Wesley (1708—1788).

336 *Watch And Pray.*

1 My soul, be on thy guard,
  Ten thousand foes arise;
  And hosts of sins are pressing hard,
  To draw thee from the skies.

2 Oh, watch and fight and pray,
  The battle ne'er give o'er;
  Renew it boldly every day,
  And help divine implore.

3 Ne'er think the victory won,
  Nor once at ease sit down;
  Thy arduous work will not be done,
  Till thou hast got the crown.

4 Fight on, my soul, till death
  Shall bring thee to thy God;
  He'll take thee, at thy parting breath,
  Up to His blest abode.
    Geo. Heath, 1781.

(135)

CHRISTIAN ACTIVITY.

ARLINGTON. C. M.   T. A. Arne (1710—1778).

1. Amazing grace! how sweet the sound, That saved a wretch like me! I once was lost, but now am found, Was blind, but now I see.

337   *Triumphant Grace.*

1 Amazing grace! how sweet the sound,
   That saved a wretch like me!
I once was lost, but now am found,
   Was blind, but now I see.

2 'T was grace that taught my heart to fear,
   And grace my fears relieved;
How precious did that grace appear,
   The hour I first believed!

3 Through many dangers, toils and snares,
   I have already come;
'Tis grace has brought me safe thus far,
   And grace will lead me home.

4 The Lord has promised good to me,
   His word my hope secures;
He will my shield and portion be,
   As long as life endures.

5 And when this flesh and heart shall fail,
   And mortal life shall cease;
I shall possess, within the veil,
   A life of joy and peace.
            Rev. John Newton (1725—1807).

338   *Christian Activity.*

1 Awake, my soul, stretch every nerve,
   And press with vigor on;
A heavenly race demands thy zeal,
   And an immortal crown.

2 A cloud of witnesses around
   Hold thee in full survey;
Forget the steps already trod,
   And onward urge thy way.

3 'Tis God's all-animating voice
   That calls thee from on high;
'Tis His own hand presents the prize
   To thine uplifted eye.

4 Then wake, my soul, stretch every nerve,
   And press with vigor on;
A heavenly race demands thy zeal,
   And an immortal crown.
       Rev. Philip Doddridge (1702—1751).

339   *The Christian Soldier.*

1 Am I a soldier of the cross,
   A follower of the Lamb,
And shall I fear to own His cause,
   Or blush to speak His name?

2 Must I be carried to the skies,
   On flowery beds of ease;
While others fought to win the prize,
   And sailed through bloody seas?

3 Are there no foes for me to face?
   Must I not stem the flood?
Is this dark world a friend to grace,
   To help me on to God?

4 Sure I must fight, if I would reign;
   Increase my courage, Lord;
I'll bear the toil, endure the pain,
   Supported by Thy word.

5 Thy saints in all this glorious war,
   Shall conquer though they die;
They see the triumph from afar,
   With faith's discerning eye.

6 When that illustrious day shall rise,
   And all Thine armies shine,
In robes of victory through the skies,
   The glory shall be Thine.
            Rev. Isaac Watts (1674—1748).

340   *Strive to Enter.*

1 Oh! speed thee, Christian, on thy way,
   And to thy armor cling;
With girded loins the call obey
   That grace and mercy bring.

2 There is a battle to be fought,
   An upward race to run;
A crown of glory to be sought,
   A victory to be won.

3 Oh! faint not, Christian, for thy sighs
   Are heard before His throne;
The race must come before the prize,
   The cross before the crown.
            Church Mel.

CHRISTIAN ACTIVITY.

ST. GERTRUDE. 6s, 5s, D. Sir ARTHUR SULLIVAN, 1842.

341 *Fight the Good Fight.*

1 Onward, Christian soldiers,
　Marching as to war,
With the cross of Jesus
　Going on before.
Christ the royal Master
　Leads against the foe;
Forward into battle,
　See, His banners go.
　　Onward, Christian soldiers,
　　　Marching as to war,
　　With the cross of Jesus
　　　Going on before.

2 At the sign of triumph
　Satan's host doth flee;
On, then, Christian soldiers,
　On to victory.
Hell's foundations quiver
　At the shout of praise;
Brothers, lift your voices,
　Loud your anthems raise. — CHO.

3 Like a mighty army
　Moves the Church of God;
Brothers, we are treading
　Where the saints have trod;

We are not divided,
　All one body we,
One in hope and doctrine,
　One in charity. — CHO.

4 Crowns and thrones may perish,
　Kingdoms rise and wane,
But the Church of Jesus
　Constant will remain;
Gates of hell can never
　'Gainst that Church prevail;
We have Christ's own promise,
　And that cannot fail. — CHO.

5 Onward, then, ye people,
　Join our happy throng,
Blend with ours your voices
　In the triumph-song;
Glory, laud, and honor,
　Unto Christ the King;
This through countless ages,
　Men and angels sing.
　　Onward, Christian soldiers,
　　　Marching as to war,
　　With the cross of Jesus
　　　Going on before.

Rev. Sabine Baring-Gould (1834—), 1865.

CHRISTIAN ACTIVITY.

ST. ALBAN'S. 6s, 5s, D. JOS. HAYDN (1732—1809).

342 *Christ our Leader.*

1 Brightly gleams our banner,
  Pointing to the sky,
Waving wanderers onward
  To their home on high!
Journeying o'er the desert,
  Gladly thus we pray,
Still with hearts united
  •Singing on our way.
Brightly gleams our banner, etc.

2 Jesus, Lord and Master,
  At Thy sacred feet,
Here, with hearts rejoicing,
  See Thy children meet.
Often have we left Thee,
  Often gone astray;
Keep us, mighty Saviour,
  In the narrow way.
Brightly gleams our banner, etc.

3 All our days direct us
  In the way we go,
Lead us on victorious
  Over every foe;
Bid Thine angels shield us
  When the storm clouds lour;
Pardon, Lord, and save us
  In the last dread hour.
Brightly gleams our banner, etc.

4 Then with saints and angels
  May we join above,
Offering prayers and praises
  At Thy throne of love.
When the toil is over,
  Then comes rest and peace,
Jesus in His beauty!
  Songs that never cease!
Brightly gleams our banner, etc.

Rev. T. J. Potter (—1873).

(138)

THE ADVENT.

CHELTENHAM. CALEB SIMPER.

343 *Christmas Carol.*

1 It came upon the midnight clear,
  That glorious song of old,
From angels bending near the earth,
  To touch their harps of gold:
"Peace on the earth, good-will to men
  From heaven's all-gracious King."
The world in solemn stillness lay
  To hear the angels sing.

2 Still through the cloven skies they come,
  With peaceful wings unfurled;
And still their heavenly music floats
  O'er all the weary world:
Above its sad and lowly plains
  They bend on hovering wing,
And ever o'er its Babel sounds
  The blessed angels sing.

3 But with the woes of sin and strife
  The world has suffered long;
Beneath the angel-strain have rolled
  Two thousand years of wrong;
And man, at war with man, hears not
  The love song which they bring:
Oh, hush the noise, ye men of strife,
  And hear the angels sing.

4 And ye, beneath life's crushing load
  Whose forms are bending low,
Who toil along the climbing way,
  With painful steps and slow,—
Look now; for glad and golden hours
  Come swiftly on the wing:
Oh, rest beside the weary road,
  And hear the angels sing.

5 For lo, the days are hastening on
  By prophet bards foretold,
When with the ever circling years
  Comes round the age of gold:
When Peace shall over all the earth
  Its ancient splendors fling,
And the whole world give back the song
  Which now the angels sing.
  Rev. Edmund Hamilton Sears (1810—1876).

THE ADVENT.

MEAR. C. M.   AARON WILLIAMS (1731—1776).

1. While shepherds watched their flocks by night, All seated on the ground;
The angel of the Lord came down, And glory shone around.

344   *The Nativity.*

1 While shepherds watched their flocks by night,
All seated on the ground;
The angel of the Lord came down,
And glory shone around.

2 "Fear not," said he,—for mighty dread
Had seized their troubled mind,—
"Glad tidings of great joy I bring,
To you and all mankind.

3 "To you in David's town this day,
Is born of David's line,
The Saviour, who is Christ, the Lord,
And this shall be the sign;—

4 "The heavenly Babe you there shall find
To human view displayed,
All meanly wrapped in swathing bands,
And in a manger laid"

5 Thus spake the seraph—and forthwith
Appeared a shining throng
Of angels, praising God, who thus
Addressed their joyful song:—

6 "All glory be to God on high,
And to the earth be peace;
Good-will henceforth from heaven to men
Begin, and never cease!"
                         Tate and Brady.

345   *The Angels' Song.*

1 Angels rejoiced and sweetly sung
At our Redeemer's birth;
Mortals! awake; let every tongue
Proclaim His matchless worth.

2 Glory to God, who dwells on high,
And sent His only Son

To take a servant's form, and die
For evils we had done!

3 Good-will to men; ye fallen race!
Arise, and shout for joy;
He comes, with rich abounding grace,
To save, and not destroy.

4 Lord! send the gracious tidings forth,
And fill the world with light,
That Jew and Gentile, through the earth,
May know Thy saving might.
                             Hurn.

346   *The Nativity of Christ.*

1 Mortals, awake, with angels join,
And chant the solemn lay;
Joy, love, and gratitude combine
To hail the auspicious day.

2 In heaven the rapturous song began,
And sweet seraphic fire
Through all the shining regions ran,
And strung and tuned the lyre.

3 O! for a glance of heavenly love!
Our hearts and songs to raise;
Sweetly to bear our souls above,
And mingle with their lays.

4 Hark, the cherubic armies shout,
And glory leads the song;
Good-will and peace are heard throughout
The harmonious heavenly throng.

5 With joy the chorus we repeat,
"Glory to God on high!
Good-will and peace are now complete;
Jesus was born to die."
                      Rev. Samuel Medley (1738—1799).

(140)

THE ADVENT.

MENDELSSOHN. 7s, D.   FELIX BARTHOLDY MENDELSSOHN (1809—1847).

1. Hark! the her-ald an-gels sing "Glo-ry to the new-born King; Peace on earth, and mer-cy mild, God and sin-ners re-con-ciled!" Joy-ful, all ye na-tions, rise, Join the tri-umph of the skies; With th' an-gel-ic host proclaim, Christ is born in Beth-le-hem! With th' angel-ic host pro-claim, Christ is born in Beth-le-hem.

347   *The Nativity.*

1 Hark! the herald angels sing
"Glory to the new-born King;
Peace on earth, and mercy mild,
God and sinners reconciled!"
Joyful, all ye nations, rise,
Join the triumph of the skies;
With the angelic host proclaim,
Christ is born in Bethlehem!

2 Christ, by highest heaven adored;
Christ, the everlasting Lord;
Late in time behold Him come,
Offspring of the Virgin's womb;
Vailed in flesh the Godhead see;
Hail the incarnate Deity,
Pleased as man with men to dwell;
Jesus, our Immanuel!

3 Hail! the heaven-born Prince of Peace!
Hail the Sun of Righteousness!
Light and life to all He brings,
Risen with healing in his wings;
Mild he lays his glory by,
Born that man no more may die;
Born to raise the sons of earth,
Born to give them second birth.
      Rev. Chas. Wesley (1709—1788).

348   *The Christ of God.*

1 He has come! the Christ of God
Left for us his glad abode;
Stooping from His throne of bliss,
To this darksome wilderness.
He has come! the Prince of Peace;
Come to bid our sorrows cease;
Come to scatter with his light
All the shadows of our night.

2 He, the mighty King, has come!
Making this poor earth his home;
Come to bear our sin's sad load;
Son of David, Son of God!
He has come, whose name of grace
Speaks deliverance to our race;
Left for us His glad abode;
Son of Mary, Son of God!

3 Unto us a child is born!
Ne'er has earth beheld a morn,
Among all the morns of time,
Half so glorious in its prime.
Unto us a Son is given!
He has come from God's own heaven,
Bringing with him from above
Holy peace and holy love.
      Rev. H. Bonar (1808—1890).

THE ADVENT.

ARMENIA. C. M. S. B. POND (1792—1871).

1. Calm on the listening ear of night, Come heavens melodious strains, Where wild Ju-de-a stretches far Her sil-ver-man-tled plains.

349 *Glory to God.*

1 Calm on the listening ear of night,
  Come heaven's melodious strains,
  Where wild Judea stretches far
  Her silver-mantled plains.

2 Celestial choirs, from courts above,
  Shed sacred glories there,
  And angels, with their sparkling lyres,
  Make music on the air.

3 The answering hills of Palestine
  Send back the glad reply;
  And greet, from all their holy heights,
  The day-spring from on high.

4 O'er the blue depths of Galilee
  There comes a holier calm,
  And Sharon waves, in solemn praise,
  Her silent groves of palm.

5 "Glory to God!" the sounding skies
  Loud with their anthems ring —
  "Peace to the earth, good-will to men,
  From heaven's eternal King!"
  Rev. E. H. Sears, 1835.

CHRISTMAS. C. M. GEORGE FREDERICK HANDEL (1685—1759).

1. Glo-ry to God! the loft-y strain The realm of eth-er fills; How sweeps the song of sol-emn joy O'er Ju-dah's sa-cred hills, O'er Ju-dah's sa-cred hills.

350 *The Nativity.*

1 Glory to God! the lofty strain
  The realm of ether fills;
  How sweeps the song of solemn joy
  O'er Judah's sacred hills!

2 "Glory to God!" the sounding skies
  Loud with their anthems ring:
  "Peace on the earth; good-will to men,
  From heaven's eternal King."

3 Light on thy hills, Jerusalem!
  The Saviour now is born;
  More bright on Bethlehem's joyous plains,
  Breaks the first Christmas morn.

4 And brighter on Moriah's brow,
  Crowned with her temple-spires,
  Which first proclaim the new-born light,
  Clothed with its orient fires.

5 This day shall Christian tongues be mute,
  And Christian hearts be cold?
  Oh, catch the anthem that from heaven
  O'er Judah's mountains rolled!

6 When nightly burst from seraph-harps
  The high and solemn lay,—
  "Glory to God; on earth be peace;
  Salvation comes to-day."
  Rev. Edmund Hamilton Sears, 1835.

THE ADVENT.

HARWELL. 8s, 7s, D. — Dr. LOWELL MASON (1792—1872).

351 *Song of the Angels.*

1 Hark! what mean those holy voices,
   Sweetly sounding through the skies!
Lo! the angelic host rejoices,
   Heavenly hallelujahs rise.
Listen to the wondrous story
   Which they chant in hymns of joy;
Glory in the highest, glory!
   Glory be to God most high!

2 Peace on earth, good-will from heaven,
   Reaching far as man is found;
Souls redeemed and sins forgiven,
   Loud our golden harps shall sound.
Christ is born, the great Anointed,
   Heaven and earth.His praises sing;
Oh! receive whom God appointed,
   For your Prophet, Priest, and King.

3 Hasten mortals to adore him,
   Learn His name and taste His joy;
Till in heaven ye sing before Him,
   Glory be to God most high.
Let us learn the wondrous story,
   Of our great Redeemer's birth,
Spread the brightness of His glory,
   Till it covers all the earth.
                    Rev. Jno. Cawood (1775—1852).

352 *Christ the New-Born King.*

1 Angels, from the realms of glory,
   Wing your flight o'er all the earth;
Ye who sang creation's story,
   Now proclaim Messiah's birth:
      Come and worship,
   Worship Christ, the new-born King.

2 Shepherds in the field abiding,
   Watching o'er your flocks by night,
God with man is now residing,
   Yonder shines the infant-light:
      Come and worship,
   Worship Christ, the new-born King.

3 Sages, leave your contemplations;
   Brighter visions beam afar;
Seek the great desire of nations,
   Ye have seen His natal star;
      Come and worship,
   Worship Christ, the new-born King.

4 Saints in humble prayer are bending,
   Watching long in hope and fear;
Suddenly the Lord, descending,
   In His temple shall appear;
      Come and worship,
   Worship Christ, the new-born King.
                    Rev. J. Montgomery (1771—1854).

THE ADVENT.

ZERAH. C. M. — Dr. L. Mason (1792–1872).

1. Lift up your heads, e-ter-nal gates! Un-fold, to en-ter-tain The King of glo-ry; see! He comes,
With His ce-les-tial train, The King of glo-ry; see! He comes, With His ce-les-tial train.

353 *Psalm 24.*

1 Lift up your heads, eternal gates !
  Unfold, to entertain
The King of glory; see! He comes,
  With his celestial train.

2 Who is this King of glory — who?
  The Lord, for strength renowned;
In battle mighty; o'er His foes
  Eternal victor crowned.

3 Lift up your heads, ye gates! unfold,
  In state to entertain
The King of glory; see! He comes,
  With all His shining train.

4 Who is the King of glory — who?
  The Lord of hosts renowned;
Of glory He alone is King,
  Who is with glory crowned.
  Anon.

354 *To Us a Child is Born.*

1 To us a Child of hope is born,
  To us a Son is given;
Him shall the tribes of earth obey,
  Him all the hosts of heaven.

2 His name shall be the Prince of Peace,
  For evermore adored,
The Wonderful, the Counsellor,
  The great and mighty Lord.

3 His power, increasing, still shall spread,
  His reign no end shall know;
Justice shall guard His throne above,
  And peace abound below.

4 To us a Child of hope is born,
  To us a Son is given,
The Wonderful, the Counsellor,
  The mighty Lord of heaven.
  Anon.

MANOAH. C. M. — Rossini, Arr. by H. W. Greatorex.

1. Hark! the glad sound, the Sav-iour comes, The Sav-iour prom-ised long:
Let ev-'ry heart pre-pare a throne, And ev-'ry voice a song.

THE ADVENT.

ANTIOCH. C. M.
From GEORGE FREDERICK HANDEL.
Arr. by LOWELL MASON (1792—1872).

355 *Joy to the World.*

1 Joy to the world, the Lord is come,
  Let earth receive her King;
  Let every heart prepare Him room,
  And heaven and nature sing.

2 Joy to the earth, the Saviour reigns,
  Let men their songs employ;
  While fields and floods, rocks, hills and plains
  Repeat the sounding joy.

3 No more let sins and sorrows grow,
  Nor thorns infest the ground;
  He comes to make His blessings flow,
  Far as the curse is found.

4 He rules the world with truth and grace,
  And makes the nations prove
  The glories of His righteousness,
  And wonders of His love.
  Rev. Isaac Watts (1674—1748).

356 *Advent of Christ.*
Tune, MANOAH.

1 Hark! the glad sound, the Saviour comes,
  The Saviour promised long;
  Let every heart prepare a throne,
  And every voice a song.

2 On Him the Spirit, largely poured,
  Exerts His sacred fire;
  Wisdom, and might, and zeal, and love
  His holy breast inspire.

3 He comes the prisoners to release,
  In Satan's bondage held,
  The gates of brass before Him burst,
  The iron fetters yield.

3 He comes from thickest films of vice,
  To clear the inward sight;
  And on the eyes obscured by sin,
  To pour celestial light.

5 He comes the broken heart to bind,
  The bleeding soul to cure;
  And with the treasures of his grace,
  To enrich the humble poor.

6 Our glad hosannas, Prince of Peace,
  Thy welcome shall proclaim,
  And heaven's eternal arches ring
  With Thy beloved name.
  Rev. Philip Doddridge (1702—1751).

THE ADVENT.

FOLSOM. 11s & 10s.   JOHANN C. W. A. MOZART (1756—1791).

1. Brightest and best of the sons of the morning, Dawn on our darkness and lend us thine aid;
Star of the East, the horizon adorning, Guide where our infant Redeemer is laid!

357   *Brightest and Best.*

1 Brightest and best of the sons of the
morning, [thine aid;
Dawn on our darkness, and lend us
Star of the East, the horizon adorning,
Guide where our infant Redeemer is laid!

2 Cold on His cradle the dew-drops are
shining, [stall;
Low lies His head with the beasts of the
Angels adore Him, in slumber reclining,
Maker, and Monarch, and Saviour of all!

3 Say, shall we yield Him in costly devotion,
Odors of Edom, and offerings divine,
Gems of the mountain, and pearls of the
ocean, [mine?
Myrrh from the forest, or gold from the

4 Vainly we offer each ample oblation;
Vainly with gifts would His favor secure;
Richer by far is the heart's adoration;
Dearer to God are the prayers of the poor.

Bp. Reg. Heber (1783 — 1826).

358   *Adeste Fideles.*

1 Oh, come, all ye faithful,
Joyfully triumphant,
To Bethlehem hasten now with glad accord;
Lo! in a manger
Lies the King of angels;
Oh, come, let us adore Him, Christ the Lord.

2 Raise, raise, choirs of angels,
Songs of loudest triumph,
Through heaven's high arches be your
praises poured:
Now to our God be
Glory in the highest;
Oh, come, let us adore Him, Christ the Lord.

Rev. Wm. Mercer, tr., 1873.

PORTUGUESE HYMN. 11s.   MARC ANTOINE PASTOGALLA (1763 — 1830.)

1. Oh, come, all ye faithful, Joyfully triumphant, To Bethlehem hasten now with glad accord; Lo! in a manger
Lies the King of angels; Oh, come, let us adore Him, Oh, come, let us adore Him, Oh, come, let us adore Him, Christ the Lord.

(146)

THE ADVENT.

AVISON. 11s, 10s.
CHORUS.
C. AVISON.

Shout the glad tidings, ex-ult-ing-ly sing; . . Je-ru-salem triumphs, Messi-ah is King. 1. Zion, the mar-velous sto-ry be telling, The Son of the Highest, how lowly His birth; The brightest archan-gel in glo-ry ex-cell-ing, He stoops to redeem thee, He reigns up-on earth.

Close with 1st chorus.

Chorus after last verse.

Shout the glad tidings, ex-ult-ing-ly sing, . . Je-ru-salem triumphs, Messiah is King, Mes-si-ah is King, Mes-si-ah is King.

359 *The Glad Tidings.*

Cho.—Shout the glad tidings, exultingly sing; [King.
Jerusalem triumphs, Messiah is

1 Zion, the marvelous story be telling,
The Son of the Highest, how lowly His birth;
The brightest archangel in glory excelling,
He stoops to redeem thee, He reigns upon earth.
Cho.— Shout the glad tidings, etc.
Cho.— Shout the glad tidings, etc.

2 Tell how He cometh; from nation to nation, [echo round;
The heart-cheering news let the earth

How free to the faithful He offers salvation!
How His people with joy everlasting are crowned!
Cho.— Shout the glad tidings, etc.

Cho.—Shout the glad tidings, etc.

3 Mortals, your homage be gratefully bringing, [arise;
And sweet let the gladsome hosanna
Ye angels, the full hallelujah be singing;
One chorus resound through the earth and the skies.
Cho.—Shout the glad tidings, etc.

Rev. W. A. Muhlenberg (1796–1877).

(147)

THE PASSION.

ETERNAL ROCK. 7s, 6l. Rev. R. P. KERR. 1890.

1. Son of God! to Thee I cry; By the ho-ly mys-ter-y
Of Thy dwell-ing here on earth, By Thy pure and ho-ly birth,—
Lord! Thy pres-ence let me see; Man-i-fest Thy-self to me!

By per. of J. M. Russell.

360 *The Manifestation Of Christ.*

1 Son of God! to Thee I cry;
By the holy mystery
Of Thy dwelling here on earth,
By Thy pure and holy birth,—
Lord! Thy presence let me see;
Manifest Thyself to me!

2 Lamb of God! to Thee I cry;
By Thy bitter agony,
By Thy pangs, to us unknown,
By Thy Spirit's parting groan,
Lord! Thy presence let me see;
Manifest Thyself to me!

3 Prince of life! to Thee I cry;
By Thy glorious majesty,
By Thy triumph o'er the grave,
Meek to suffer, strong to save,
Lord! Thy presence let me see;
Manifest Thyself to me!

4 Lord of glory, God most high,
Man exalted to the sky!
With Thy love my bosom fill;

Prompt me to perform Thy will;
Then Thy glory I shall see;
Thou wilt bring me home to Thee.
Rev. R. Mant, 1848.

361 *Christ our Pattern.*
TUNE, OLIVE'S BROW.

1 My dear Redeemer, and my Lord,
I read my duty in Thy word;
But in Thy life, the law appears
Drawn out in living characters.

2 Such was Thy truth, and such Thy zeal,
Such deference to Thy Father's will,
Such love, and meekness so divine,
I would transcribe and make them mine.

3 Cold mountains and the midnight air
Witnessed the fervor of Thy prayer;
The desert Thy temptations knew,
Thy conflict and Thy victory, too.

4 Be Thou my pattern; make me bear
More of Thy gracious image here;
Then God, the Judge, shall own my name
Amongst the followers of the Lamb.
Rev. Isaac Watts (1674—1748).

THE PASSION.

OLIVE'S BROW. L. M. WILLIAM BATCHELDER BRADBURY (1816—1868).

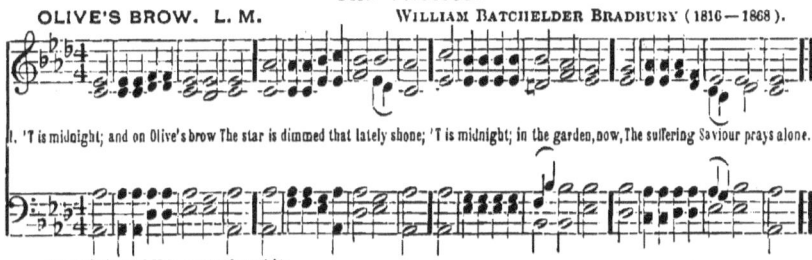

'T is midnight; and on Olive's brow The star is dimmed that lately shone; 'T is midnight; in the garden, now, The suffering Saviour prays alone.

By per. Biglow and Main, owners of copyright.

362 *Christ in Gethsemane.*

1 'T is midnight; and on Olive's brow
The star is dimmed that lately shone;
'T is midnight; in the garden, now,
The suffering Saviour prays alone.

2 'T is midnight; and from all removed,
The Saviour wrestles lone with fears;
E'en that disciple whom He loved
Heeds not his Master's grief and tears.

3 'T is midnight; and for others' guilt
The Man of Sorrows weeps in blood;
Yet He that hath in anguish knelt
Is not forsaken by His God.

4 'T is midnight; and from heavenly-plains
Is borne the song that angels know;
Unheard by mortals are the strains
That sweetly soothe the Saviour's woe.
Rev. William Bingham Tappan (1794—1849).

GETHSEMANE. 7s, 6l. RICHARD REDHEAD (1820—).

1. Go to dark Gethsem-a-ne, Ye that feel the tempter's pow'r; Your Redeemer's conflict see; Watch with Him one bit-ter hour; Turn not from His griefs away; Learn of Je-sus Christ to pray.

363 *Christ Our Example in Suffering.*

1 Go to dark Gethsemane,
Ye who feel the tempter's power;
Your Redeemer's conflict see;
Watch with Him one bitter hour;
Turn not from His griefs away,
Learn of Jesus Christ to pray.

2 Follow to the judgment-hall,
View the Lord of life arraigned;
Oh, the wormword and the gall!
Oh, the pangs His soul sustained!
Shun not suffering, shame or loss;
Learn of Him to bear the cross.

3 Calvary's mournful mountain climb:
There, adoring at His feet,
Mark that miracle of time,
God's own sacrifice complete:
"It is finished," hear Him cry;
Learn of Jesus Christ to die.

4 Early hasten to the tomb,
Where they laid His breathless clay;
All is solitude and gloom;
Who hath taken Him away?
Christ has risen, He meets our eyes;
Saviour, teach us so to rise.
Rev. J. Montgomery (1771—1854).

THE PASSION.

TOPLADY. 7s 6l.   Dr. THOS. HASTINGS, 1830.

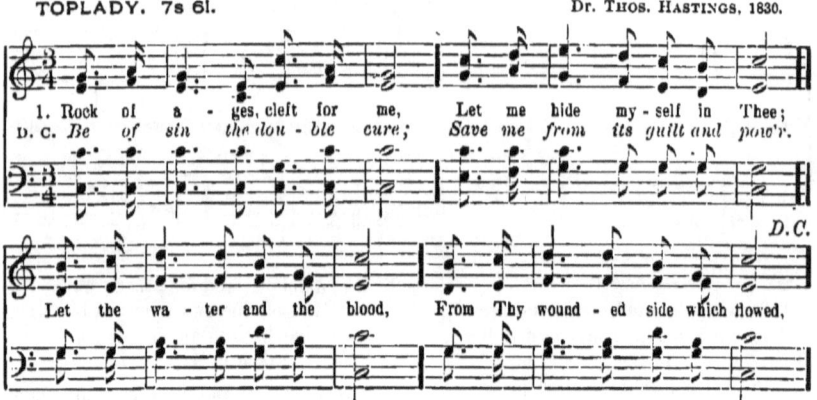

364   *Rock of Ages.*
1 Rock of ages, cleft for me,
   Let me hide myself in Thee;
Let the water and the blood,
   From Thy wounded side which flowed,
Be of sin the double cure;
   Save me from its guilt and pow'r.

2 Not the labors of my hands
   Can fulfil Thy law's demands;
Could my zeal no respite know,
Could my tears for ever flow,
All for sin could not atone;
Thou must save, and Thou alone.

3 Nothing in my hand I bring;
   Simply to Thy cross I cling;
Naked, come to Thee for dress;
Helpless, look to Thee for grace;
Vile, I to the fountain fly;
Wash me, Saviour, or I die.

4 While I draw this fleeting breath,
   When my eyelids close in death,
When I soar to worlds unknown,
See Thee on Thy judgment-throne,
Rock of ages, cleft for me,
Let me hide myself in Thee.
   Rev. Augustus Montague Toplady (1740 — 1778).

365   *The Lamb of God.*
1 Jesus, Lamb of God for me,
   Thou, the Lord of life, didst die;
Whither,—whither but to Thee,
   Can a trembling sinner fly?
Death's dark waters o'er me roll,
Save, O save, my sinking soul.

2 Never bowed a martyred head
   Weighed with equal sorrow down,
Never blood so rich was shed,
   Never king wore such a crown !
To Thy cross and sacrifice
Faith now lifts her tearful eyes.

3 All my soul, by love subdued,
   Melts in deep contrition there;
By Thy mighty grace renewed,
   New-born hope forbids despair;
Lord, Thou canst my guilt forgive,
Thou hast bid me look and live.

4 While with broken heart I kneel,
   Sinks the inward storm to rest;
Life,— immortal life I feel
   Kindled in my throbbing breast;
Thine,— for ever Thine I am,
Glory to the bleeding Lamb !
   Rev. Ray Palmer (1808 — 1887).

366   *Expostulation.*
1 Hearts of stone, relent, relent,
   Break, by Jesus' cross subdued;
See His body mangled, rent,
   Covered with His flowing blood.
Sinful soul, what hast thou done ?
Crucified the incarnate Son !

2 Will you let Him die in vain,
   Still to death pursue the Lord;
Open tear His wounds again,
   Trample on His precious blood ?
No, with all my sins I'll part,
Saviour, take my broken heart.
   Hor. Sac.

THE PASSION.

367 *Faith in the Sacrifice of Christ.*
1 Not all the blood of beasts
  On Jewish altars slain,
Could give the guilty conscience peace,
  Or wash away the stain.

2 But Christ, the heavenly lamb,
  Takes all our sins away;
A sacrifice of nobler name,
  And richer blood than they.

3 My faith would lay her hand
  On that dear head of Thine,
While like a penitent I stand,
  And there confess my sin.

4 My soul looks back to see
  The burdens Thou didst bear,
When hanging on the cursed tree,
  And hopes her guilt was there.

5 Believing, we rejoice
  To see the curse remove;
We bless the Lamb with cheerful voice,
  And sing His bleeding love.
  Rev. Isaac Watts (1674 — 1748).

368 *Doxology.*
Ye angels round the throne,
  And saints that dwell below,
Worship the Father, love the Son,
  And bless the Spirit too.

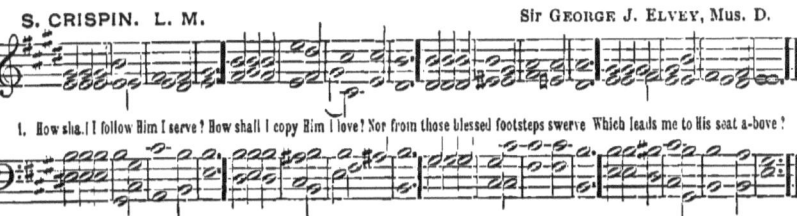

369 *The Fellowship of His Sufferings.*
1 How shall I follow Him I serve?
How shall I copy Him I love?
Nor from those blessèd footsteps swerve
Which lead me to His seat above?

2 Privations, sorrows, bitter scorn,
The life of toil, the mean abode,
The faithless kiss, the crown of thorn —
Are these the consecrated road?

3 'T was thus He suffered, though a Son,
Fore-knowing, choosing, feeling all,
Until the perfect work was done,
And drunk the cup of bitter gall.

4 Lord, should my path through suffering lie,
Forbid that I should e'er repine;
Still let me turn to Calvary,
Nor heed my griefs, remembering Thine.
  Josiah Conder (1789 — 1855).

(151)

THE PASSION.

AURELIA. 7s & 6s. D. S. S. WESLEY (1810–1876).

370 *At the Cross.*

1 O Sacred Head, once wounded,
  With grief and shame weighed down,
 How scornfully surrounded
  With thorns, Thine only crown;
 O sacred Head, what glory,
  What bliss, till now was Thine !
 Yet, though despised and gory,
  I joy to call Thee mine.

2 How art Thou pale with anguish,
  With sore abuse and scorn;
 How does that visage languish
  That once was bright as morn!
 What language shall I borrow
  To thank Thee, dearest Friend,
 For this Thy dying sorrow,
  Thy pity without end ?

3 Oh! make me Thine for ever;
  And should I fainting be,
 Lord, let me never, never
  Outlive my love to Thee.
 Be near when I am dying;
  Oh, show Thy cross to me!
 And, for my succor flying,
  Come Lord, and set me free.

Bernard of Clairvaux (1091–1153).
Rev. Paul Gerhardt (1606–1676), 1659.
Tr. by Rev. James Waddell Alexander (1804–1859).

371 *All-Forgiving!*

1 Life of the world! I hail Thee;
  Hail, Jesus, Saviour dear!
 I to Thy cross could yield me,
  Might I to Thee be near.
 Thyself, in all thy fullness,
  My Lord, to me impart;
 As Thee I seek, oh, help me
  To find Thee in my heart!

2 Look on me, All-Forgiving!
  Low at Thy feet I bow.
 Oh, all-divine Thou seemest,
  As I behold Thee now!
 I clasp with tender passion,
  Thy feet, so pierced for us,
 The cruel wounds deep graven,
  O'erwhelmed to see Thee thus!

3 While here with Thee I linger,
  Take me, dear Saviour mine!
 Oh, draw me to Thee closer,
  And make me wholly Thine;
 Say, "Be thou saved, O sinner!"
  And gladly at Thy call,
 On Thy sure word relying,
  To Thee I give my all.

Tr. by Rev. Ray Palmer.

THE PASSION.

THE EAGLE. L. M.   JAMES HOGG.

1. His are the thou-sand spark-ling rills, That from a thou-sand foun-tains burst, And fill with mu-sic all the hills; And yet He saith, "I thirst," "I thirst."

372   *I Thirst.*

1 His are the thousand sparkling rills,
  That from a thousand fountains burst,
And fill with music all the hills;
  And yet He saith, "I thirst."

2 All fiery pangs on battle-fields,
  On fever beds where sick men toss,
Are in that human cry He yields
  To anguish on the cross.

3 But more than pains that rack'd Him then
  Was the deep longing thirst divine,
That thirsted for the souls of men;
  Dear Lord! and one was mine.

4 O Love most patient, give me grace;
  Make all my soul athirst for Thee;
That parch'd dry lip, that fading face,
  That thirst were all for me.
                              Unknown.

373   *The Work Finished.*

1 'T is finished! so the Saviour cried,
  And meekly bowed His head and died;
'T is finished—yes, the race is run,
  The battle fought, the victory won.

2 'T is finished—all that heaven decreed,
  And all the ancient prophets said,
Is now fulfilled, as was designed,
  In Me the Saviour of mankind.

3 'T is finished—heaven is reconciled,
  And all the powers of darkness spoiled;
Peace, love, and happiness again
  Return and dwell with sinful men.

4 'T is finished—let the joyful sound
  Be heard through all the nations round;
'T is finished—let the echo fly
  Through heaven and hell, through earth and sky.
                          Rev. S. Stennett (1725 — 1795).

374   *Praise for Redemption.*

1 Blest Jesus, when Thy cross I view,
  That mystery to th' angelic host,
I gaze with grief and rapture too,
  And all my soul's in wonder lost.

2 What strange compassion filled Thy breast,
  That brought Thee from Thy throne on high,
To woes that cannot be expressed,
  To be despised, to groan and die!

3 Was it for man, rebellious man,
  Sunk by his crimes below the grave,
Who, justly doomed to endless pain,
  Found none to pity or to save?

4 For man didst Thou forsake the sky,
  To bleed upon the accursed tree?
And didst Thou taste of death, to buy
  Immortal life and bliss for me?

5 Had I a voice to praise Thy name
  Loud as the trump that wakes the dead,
Had I the raptured seraph's flame,
  My debt of love could ne'er be paid.

6 Yet, Lord, a sinner's heart receive,
  This burdened contrite heart of mine;
Thou knowest I've naught beside to give;
  And let it be forever Thine.
                Rev. Conrad Speece, D. D. (1776 – 1836).

THE PASSION.

THERE IS A GREEN HILL FAR AWAY. C. M. GEO. C. STEBBINS.

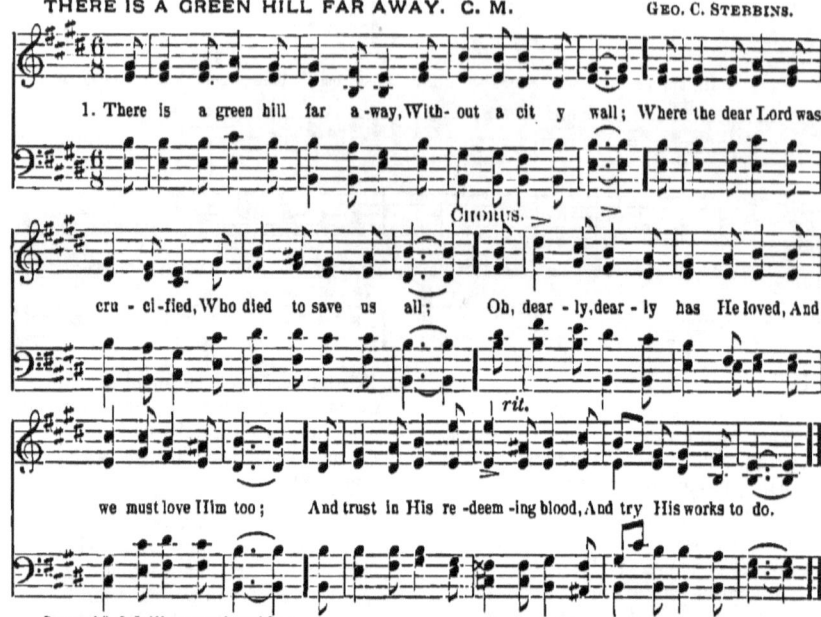

375 *And there They Crucified Him.*

1 There is a green hill far away,
  Without a city wall;
  Where the dear Lord was crucified,
  Who died to save us all.

2 We may not know, we cannot tell
  What pains He had to bear;
  But we believe it was for us
  He hung and suffered there.

3 He died that we might be forgiven,
  He died to make us good,
  That we might go at last to heav'n,
  Saved by His precious blood.

4 There was no other good enough,
  To pay the price of sin;
  He only could unlock the gate
  Of heaven and let us in.

  Mrs. Cecil F. Alexander (1823—).

376 *The Triumphs of Christ.*
  Tune, DRESDEN.

1 He dies, the Friend of sinners dies;
  Lo! Salem's daughters weep around;
  A solemn darkness veils the skies,
  A sudden trembling shakes the ground.
  Come, saints, and drop a tear or two,
  For Him who groaned beneath your load;
  He shed a thousand drops for you,
  A thousand drops of richer blood.

2 Here's love and grief beyond degree,
  The Lord of glory dies for men;
  But lo! what sudden joys we see,
  Jesus, the dead, revives again.
  The risen God forsakes the tomb,
  Up to His Father's courts He flies;
  Cherubic legions guard Him home,
  And shout Him welcome to the skies.

3 Dry up your tears, ye saints, and tell
  How high your great Deliverer reigns;
  Sing how He spoiled the hosts of hell,
  And led the monster death in chains.
  Say, "Live for ever, wondrous King!
  Born to redeem, and strong to save."
  Then ask the monster, "Where's thy sting,
  And where's thy victory, boasting, grave?"

  Rev. Isaac Watts (1674—1748).

THE PASSION.

PASSION CHORALE. 7s, 6s, D. Hans Leo Hasslee (1564—1612).
Arr. by Johann Sebastian Bach (1685—1750).

1. { O Jesus, we adore Thee, Up-on the cross, our King; } That name hath brought sal-va-tion,
    { We bow our hearts be-fore Thee; Thy gracious name we sing; }

That name, in life our stay; Our peace, our con-so-la-tion When life shall fade a-way.

377
We Adore Thee.

1 O Jesus, we adore Thee,
   Upon the cross, our King:
   We bow our hearts before Thee;
   Thy gracious name we sing;
   That name hath brought salvation,
   That name, in life our stay;
   Our peace, our consolation
   When life shall fade away.

2 Yet doth the world disdain Thee,
   Still passing by Thy cross:
   Lord, may our hearts retain The;
   All else we count but loss.

O glorious King, we bless Thee,
No longer pass Thee by;
O Jesus, we confess Thee
Our Lord, enthroned on high.

3 Thy wounds, Thy grief beholding,
   With Thee, O Lord, we grieve;
   Thee in our hearts enfolding,
   Our hearts Thy wounds receive;
   Lord, grant to us remission;
   Life through Thy death restore;
   Yea, grant us the fruition
   Of life for evermore.

Rev. Arthur Tozer Russell, 1851.

DRESDEN. C. M. D. A. William's Collection.
FINE.

1. { He dies, the Friend of sin-ners dies; Lo! Sa-lem's daught-ers weep a-round; }
    { A sol-emn dark-ness veils the skies, A cer-tain trembling shakes the ground; }
D.C.— He shed a thou-sand drops for you, A thou-sand drops of rich-er blood.

D.C.

Come, saints, and drop a tear or two For Him who groan'd be-neath your load.

(155)

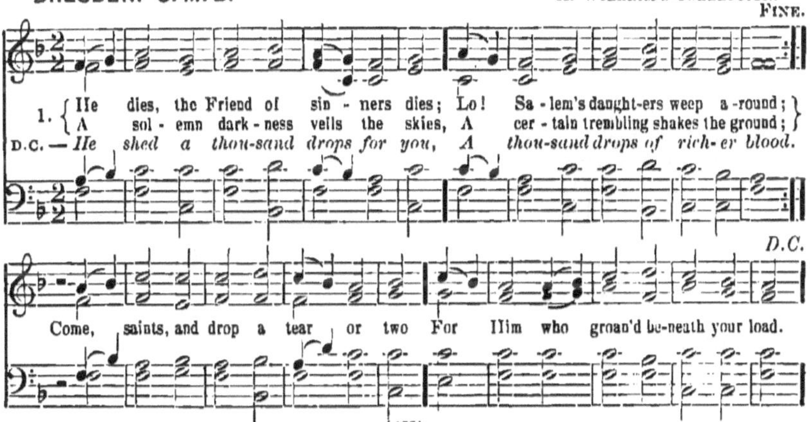

PRAISE TO THE RISEN LORD.

WARE. L. M. — George Kingsley (1811—1884).

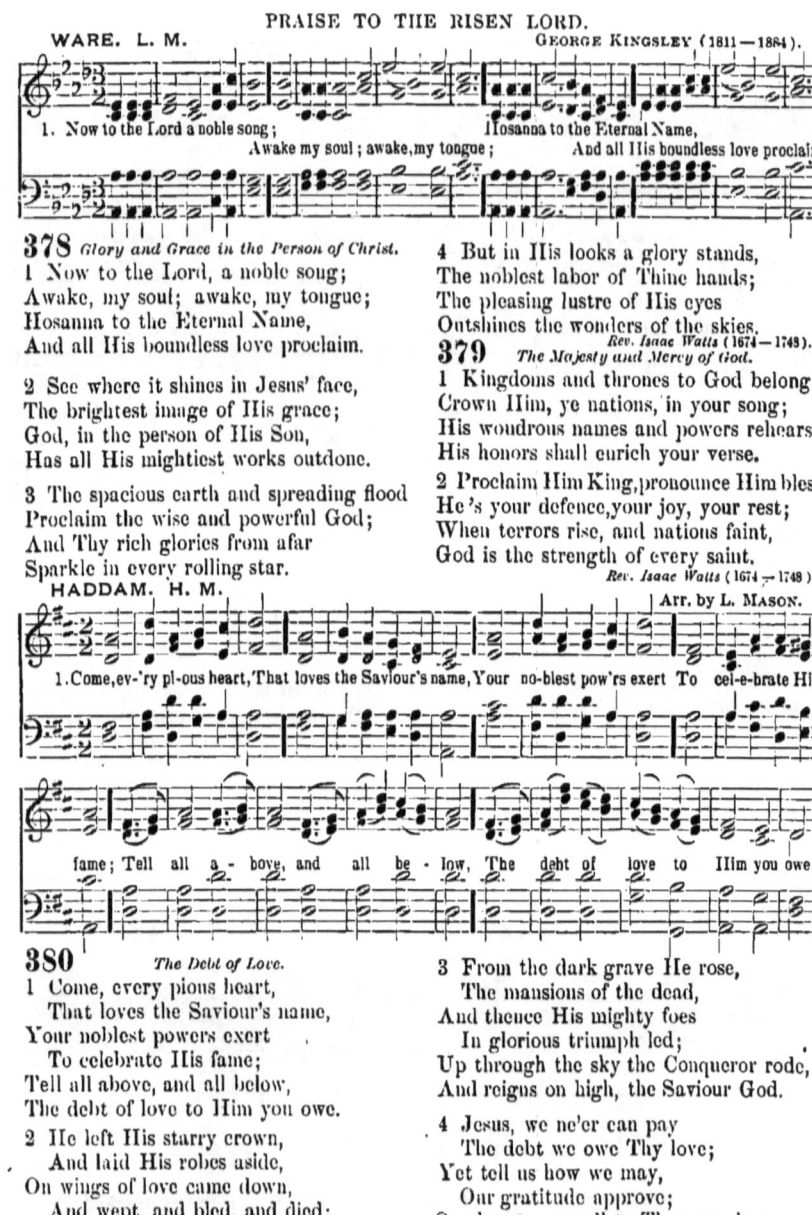

1. Now to the Lord a noble song;
Awake my soul; awake, my tongue;
Hosanna to the Eternal Name,
And all His boundless love proclaim.

378 *Glory and Grace in the Person of Christ.*

1 Now to the Lord, a noble song;
Awake, my soul; awake, my tongue;
Hosanna to the Eternal Name,
And all His boundless love proclaim.

2 See where it shines in Jesus' face,
The brightest image of His grace;
God, in the person of His Son,
Has all His mightiest works outdone.

3 The spacious earth and spreading flood
Proclaim the wise and powerful God;
And Thy rich glories from afar
Sparkle in every rolling star.

4 But in His looks a glory stands,
The noblest labor of Thine hands;
The pleasing lustre of His eyes
Outshines the wonders of the skies.
Rev. Isaac Watts (1674—1748).

379 *The Majesty and Mercy of God.*

1 Kingdoms and thrones to God belong;
Crown Him, ye nations, in your song;
His wondrous names and powers rehearse;
His honors shall enrich your verse.

2 Proclaim Him King, pronounce Him blest;
He's your defence, your joy, your rest;
When terrors rise, and nations faint,
God is the strength of every saint.
Rev. Isaac Watts (1674—1748).

HADDAM. H. M. — Arr. by L. Mason.

1. Come, ev-'ry pi-ous heart, That loves the Saviour's name, Your no-blest pow'rs exert To cel-e-brate His fame; Tell all a-bove, and all be-low, The debt of love to Him you owe.

380 *The Debt of Love.*

1 Come, every pious heart,
   That loves the Saviour's name,
Your noblest powers exert
   To celebrate His fame;
Tell all above, and all below,
The debt of love to Him you owe.

2 He left His starry crown,
   And laid His robes aside,
On wings of love came down,
   And wept, and bled, and died;
What He endured, oh, who can tell,
To save our souls from death and hell?

3 From the dark grave He rose,
   The mansions of the dead,
And thence His mighty foes
   In glorious triumph led;
Up through the sky the Conqueror rode,
And reigns on high, the Saviour God.

4 Jesus, we ne'er can pay
   The debt we owe Thy love;
Yet tell us how we may,
   Our gratitude approve;
Our hearts, our all to Thee we give;
The gift, though small, Thou wilt receive.
Samuel Stennett (1727—1795).

PRAISE TO THE RISEN LORD.

OAKSVILLE. C. M.   HEINRICH CHRISTOPHER ZEUNER (1795—1857).

1. Now let our cheerful eyes survey Our great High Priest above; And celebrate His constant care, And sympa-thet-ic love.

381   *Christ Interceding Above.*

1 Now let our cheerful eyes survey
   Our great High Priest above;
And celebrate His constant care,
   And sympathetic love.

2 Though raised to a superior throne,
   Where angels bow around,
And high o'er all the shining train,
   With matchless honors crowned;

3 The names of all His saints He bears,
   Deep graven on His heart;
Nor shall the meanest Christian say,
   That he hath lost his part.

4 Those characters shall fair abide
   Our everlasting trust,
When gems, and monuments, and crowns,
   Are mouldered down to dust.

5 So, gracious Saviour, on my breast
   May Thy dear name be worn,
A sacred ornament and guard,
   To endless ages borne.
          Rev. Isaac Watts (1674—1748).

382   *Christ's Intercession.*

1 Awake, sweet gratitude, and sing
   The ascended Saviour's love;
Sing how He lives to carry on
   His people's cause above.

2 With cries and tears, He offered up
   His humble suit below;
But with authority He asks,
   Enthroned in glory now.

3 For all that come to God by Him,
   Salvation He demands;
Points to their names upon His breast,
   And spreads His wounded hands.

4 His sweet atoning sacrifice
   Gives sanction to His claim:
"Father, I will that all My saints
   Be with Me where I am.

5 "By their salvation, recompense
   The sorrows I endured;
Just to the merits of Thy Son,
   And faithful to Thy word."

6 Eternal life, at His request,
   To every saint is given;
Safety on earth, and, after death,
   The plenitude of heaven.
          Rev. Augustus Montague Toplady (1740—1778).

BELMONT. C. M.   SAMUEL WEBBE (1740—1816).

1. A-wake, sweet grat-i-tude, and sing Th' as-cend-ed Sav-iour's love;
Sing how He lives to car-ry on His peo-ple's cause a-bove.

PRAISE TO THE RISEN LORD.

HASTINGS. C. H. M.   Dr. T. Hastings (1784—1872).

1. How calm and beau-ti-ful the morn That gilds the sa-cred tomb, Where once the Cru-ci-fied was borne, [*Omit* . . . . .] And veiled in midnight gloom!
Oh, weep no more the Sav-iour slain; The Lord is ris'n—He lives a-gain.

383   *The Sepulchre on Sabbath Morning.*

1 How calm and beautiful the morn
   That gilds the sacred tomb,
Where once the Crucified was borne,
   And veiled in midnight gloom!
Oh, weep no more the Saviour slain;
The Lord is ris'n — He lives again.

2 Ye mourning saints, dry every tear
   For your departed Lord;
"Behold the place, He is not here,"
   The tomb is all unbarred:
The gates of death were closed in vain,
The Lord is risen, He lives again.

3 Now cheerful to the house of prayer
   Your early footsteps bend;
The Saviour will Himself be there,
   Your Advocate and Friend:
Once by the law your hopes were slain,
But now in Christ ye live again.

4 How tranquil now the rising day!
   'T is Jesus still appears,
A risen Lord, to chase away
   Your unbelieving fears:
Oh, weep no more your comforts slain,
The Lord is risen, He lives again.

5 And when the shades of evening fall,
   When life's last hour draws nigh,
If Jesus shines upon the soul,
   How blissful then to die!

Since He has risen that once was slain,
Ye die in Christ to live again.

Dr. Thomas Hastings (1784—1872).

384   *Glory to God.*

1 The morning purples all the sky,
   The air with praises rings;
Defeated death stands sullen by,
   The world exulting sings:
Glory to God! our glad lips cry;
All glory be to God Most High!

2 While He, the King all strong to save,
   Rends the dark doors away,
And through the gateway of the grave
   Strides forth into the day:
Glory to God! our glad lips cry;
All glory be to God Most High!

3 The shining angels cry, "Away
   With grief; no spices bring;
Not tears, but songs, this joyful day,
   Should greet the rising King!"
Glory to God! our glad lips cry;
All glory be to God Most High!

4 That Thou our Paschal Lamb mayst be,
   And endless joy begin,
Jesus, Deliverer, set us free
   From the dread death of sin:
Glory to God! our glad lips cry;
All glory be to God Most High!

Ambrose of Milan (340—397).
Tr. by Rev. Alexander Ramsay Thompson, 1822.

PRAISE TO THE RISEN LORD.

STUTTGART. 8s & 7s. J. G. C. STORL (1676—1743).

1. "We shall see Him," in our nature, Seated on His lofty throne,
Loved, adored, by ev-'ry creature, Owned as God, and God alone!

385 *We Shall See His Face.*

1 "We shall see Him," in our nature,
 Seated on His lofty throne;
 Loved, adored, by every creature,
 Owned as God, and God alone!

2 There the hosts of shining spirits
 Strike their harps, and loudly sing
 To the praise of Jesus' merits,
 To the glory of their King.

3 When we pass o'er death's dark river,
 "We shall see Him as He is,"
 Resting in His love and favor,
 Owning all the glory His.

4 There to cast our crowns before Him,
 Oh, what bliss the thought affords!
 There for ever to adore Him,
 King of kings, and Lord of lords!

Miss Mary Pyper (1795—).
Hymns Ancient and Modern.

LINDISFARNE. P. M.

1. Jesus lives! no longer now Can thy terrors, death, appall us; Jesus lives! by this we know Thou, O grave, canst not enthral us. Alleluia!

386 *Jesus Lives!*

1 Jesus lives! no longer now
 Can thy terrors, death, appall us;
 Jesus lives! by this we know
  Thou, O grave, canst not enthral us,
   Alleluia!

2 Jesus lives! henceforth is death
 But the gate of life immortal;
 This shall calm our trembling breath
  When we pass its gloomy portal.
   Alleluia!

3 Jesus lives! for us He died;
 Then, alone to Jesus living;
 Pure in heart may we abide,
  Glory to our Saviour giving.
   Alleluia!

4 Jesus lives! our hearts know well
 Naught from us His love shall sever;
 Life, nor death, nor powers of hell
  Tear us from His keeping ever.
   Alleluia!

5 Jesus lives! to Him the throne
 Over all the world is given;
 May we go where He is gone,
  Rest and reign with Him in Heaven.
   Alleluia!

C. F. Gellert (1715—1769), *tr. Miss F. K. Cox.*

PRAISE TO THE RISEN LORD.

WILMOT. 7s.   C. M. VON WEBER (1786—1826).

1. Lo! the stone is rolled a-way, Death yields up his might-y prey;
Je-sus ris-ing from the tomb, Scat-ters all its fear-ful gloom.

387   *Praise to the Risen Saviour.*

1 Lo! the stone is rolled away,
Death yields up his mighty prey,
Jesus, rising from the tomb,
Scatters all its fearful gloom.

2 Praise Him, ye celestial choirs,
Praise and sweep your golden lyres;
Praise Him in the noblest songs,
From ten thousand thousand tongues.

3 Every note with rapture swell,
And the Saviour's triumph tell;
Where, O death is now thy sting?
Where thy terrors, vanquished king?

4 Let Immanuel be adored,
Ransom, Mediator, Lord!
To creation's utmost bound,
Let the eternal praise resound.
                     Scott.

388   *The Lord's Day.*

1 Hail the day that sees Him rise,
Glorious, to His native skies!
Christ, awhile to mortals given,
Enters now the gates of heaven.

2 There the glorious triumph waits;
Lift your heads, eternal gates!
Christ hath vanquished death and sin;
Take the King of glory in.

3 See, the heaven its Lord receives!
Yet He loves the earth He leaves;
Though returning to His throne,
Still He calls mankind His own.

4 Still for us He intercedes,
His prevailing death He pleads;
Near Himself prepares a place,
Great Forerunner of our race.
          Rev. Charles Wesley (1708—1788).

RESURRECTION. 7s.   BENJAMIN MILGROVE.

1. "Christ the Lord is risen to-day," Sons of men, and angels, say; Raise your songs of triumph high; Sing, ye heavens; and, earth, reply.

PRAISE TO THE RISEN LORD.

CROWN HIM. 8s, 7s, & 4s. Arr. by Geo. C. Stebbins.

By per. of G. C. Stebbins, owner of copyright.

389 *Crown Him.*

1 Look, ye saints, the sight is glorious,
See the "Man of sorrows" now,
From the fight returned victorious,
Every knee to Him shall bow.

2 Crown the Saviour! angels crown Him!
Rich the trophies Jesus brings;
In the seat of power enthrone Him,
While the vault of heaven rings.

3 Sinners in derision crowned Him,
Mocking thus the Saviour's claim;
Saints and angels crowd around Him,
Own His title, praise His name.

4 Hark! the bursts of acclamation!
Hark! those loud triumphant chords,
Jesus takes the highest station,
Oh, what joy the sight affords!
Rev. Thos. Kelly (1769—1855).

390 *He Has Risen, as He Said.*
Tune, Resurrection.

1 "Christ, the Lord, is risen to-day,"
Sons of men, and angels, say;
Raise your songs of triumph high;
Sing, ye heavens; and earth, reply.

2 Love's redeeming work is done,
Fought the fight, the battle won;
Lo, our Sun's eclipse is o'er!
Lo, He sets in blood no more!

3 Vain the stone, the watch, the seal;
Christ hath burst the gates of hell;
Death in vain forbids Him rise;
Christ hath opened Paradise.

4 Lives again our glorious King!
Where, O death, is now thy sting?
Once He died our souls to save;
Where's thy victory, O grave?

5 Soar we now where Christ hath led,
Following our exalted Head;
Made like Him, like Him we rise;
Ours the cross, the grave, the skies.

6 Hail the Lord of earth and heaven!
Praise to Thee by both be given;
Thee we greet triumphant now;
Hail, the Resurrection Thou!

7 King of glory, Soul of bliss,
Everlasting life is this,
Thee to know, Thy power to prove,
Thus to sing, and thus to love.
Rev. Chas. Wesley (1708—1788).

PRAISE TO THE RISEN LORD.

HOUGHTON. 10s & 11s.   HENRY JOHN GAUNTLETT (1806—1876).

391   *Praise to the Most High.*

1 Ye servants of God, your master proclaim,
And publish abroad His wonderful name;
The name all-victorious of Jesus extol;
His kingdom is glorious, He rules over all.

2 God ruleth on high, almighty to save;
And still He is nigh — His presence we have;
The great congregation His triumph shall sing,
Ascribing salvation to Jesus our King.

3 Salvation to God, who sits on the throne,
Let all cry aloud, and honor the Son;
The praises of Jesus the angels proclaim,
Fall down on their faces, and worship the Lamb.

4 Then let us adore, and give Him His right,
All glory and power, and wisdom and might,
All honor and blessing, with angels above,
And thanks never ceasing, for infinite love.

Rev. Chas. Wesley (1708—1788).

392   *Doxology.*

By angels in heaven of every degree,
And saints upon earth, all praise be addressed
To God in three Persons, one God ever blest,
As it has been, now is, and always shall be.

PRAISE TO THE RISEN LORD.

PERRY. 7s, D.
Arr. by J. P. Holbrook.

By per. est. J. P. Holbrook.

393 *The Lord God Reigneth.*

1 Hark! the song of jubilee,
 Loud as mighty thunders roar,
Or the fullness of the sea,
 When it breaks upon the shore!
Hallelujah! for the Lord
 God omnipotent shall reign!
Hallelujah! let the word
 Echo round the earth and main.

2 Hallelujah! hark, the sound,
 From the depths unto the skies,
Wakes above, beneath, around,
 All creation's harmonies!
See Jehovah's banners furled!
 Sheathed, His sword! He speaks — 't is [done!
And the kingdoms of this world
 Are the kingdoms of His Son!

3 He shall reign from pole to pole,
 With illimitable sway;
He shall reign, when, like a scroll,
 Yonder heavens have passed away
Then the end: beneath His rod
 Man's last enemy shall fall;
Hallelujah, Christ in God,
 God in Christ, is all in all!
Rev. James Montgomery (1771 – 1854).

394 *Resurrection and Ascension.*

1 Hark! the herald angels say
 Christ the Lord is risen to-day;
Raise your joys and triumphs high,
 Let the glorious tidings fly.

2 Love's redeeming work is done,
 Fought, the fight, the battle won;
Lo! the sun's eclipse is o'er;
 Lo! he sets in blood no more.

3 Vain the stone, the watch, the seal,
 Christ has burst the gates of hell;
Death in vain forbids him rise,
 Christ has opened paradise.

4 Lives again our glorious King;
 Where, O death, is now thy sting?
Once He died our souls to save;
 Where's thy victory, boasting grave?

5 Hail! Thou dear almighty Lord,
 Hail! Thou great incarnate Word,
Hail! Thou suffering Son of God,
 Take the trophies of thy blood.
Rev. Chas. Wesley (1708 – 1788).

Doxology.

Sing we to our God above
Praise eternal at His love:
Praise Him, all ye heavenly host,
Father, Son, and Holy Ghost.
Rev. Chas. Wesley, 1740.

PRAISE TO THE RISEN LORD.

ALLELUIA. 15s. Sir A. S. SULLIVAN (1842—).

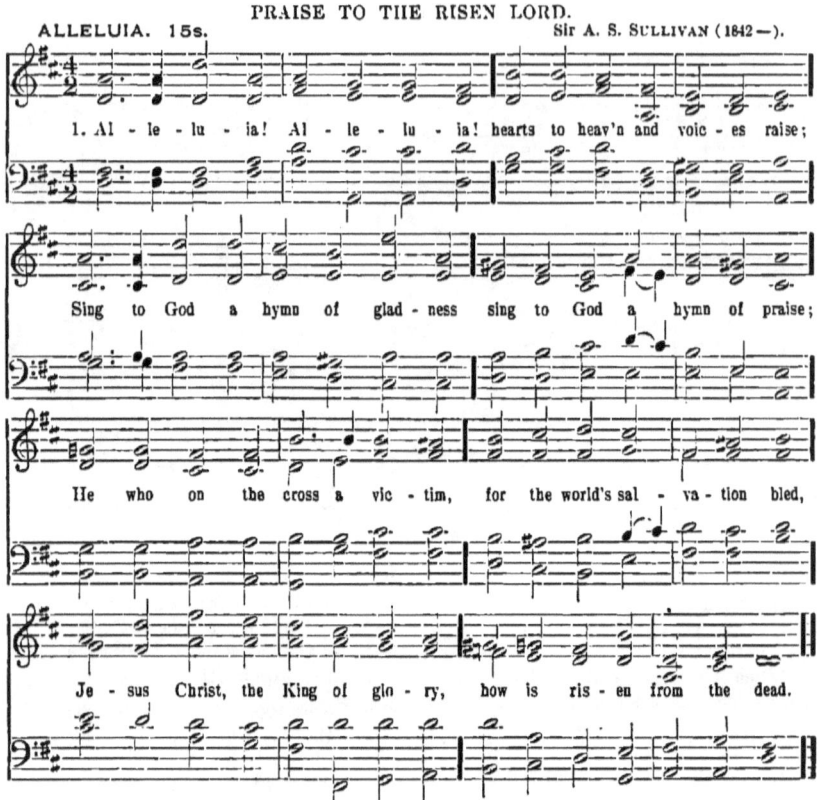

395 *Now is Christ risen from the dead, and become the first-fruits of them that slept.*

1 Alleluia! Alleluia! hearts to heav'n and voices raise;
Sing to God a hymn of gladness, sing to God a hymn of praise;
He, who on the cross a victim for the world's salvation bled,
Jesus Christ, the King of glory, now is risen from the dead.

2 Christ is risen, Christ the first-fruits of the holy harvest field,
Which will all its full abundance at his second coming yield;
Then the golden ears of harvest will their heads before Him wave,
Ripen'd by His glorious sunshine, from the furrows of the grave.

3 Christ is risen, we are risen; shed upon us heavenly grace,
Rain, and dew, and gleams of glory from the brightness of Thy face;
That we, with our hearts in heav'n, here on earth may fruitful be,
And by angel-hands be gather'd, and be ever, Lord, with Thee.

4 Alleluia! Alleluia! glory be to God on high;
Alleluia to the Saviour, who has gained the victory;
Alleluia to the Spirit, fount of love and sanctity;
Alleluia! Alleluia! to the Triune Majesty.

Hymns Ancient and Modern.

PRAISE TO THE RISEN LORD.

SPANISH HYMN. 7s, 6l.   Spanish Melody.

1. Shep-herd! with Thy ten-d'rest love, Guide me to Thy fold a-bove; Let me hear Thy gentle voice;
D.C. From Thy fullness, grace receive; Ever in Thy Spirit live. More and more in Thee rejoice;

396   *Psalm 23.*
1 Shepherd! with Thy tenderest love,
Guide me to Thy fold above;
Let me hear Thy gentle voice;
More and more in Thee rejoice;
From Thy fullness, grace receive;
Ever in Thy Spirit live.

2 Filled by Thee my cup o'erflows,
For Thy love no limit knows;
Guardian angels, ever nigh,
Lead and draw my soul on high;
Constant to my latest end,
Thou my footsteps wilt attend.

3 Jesus, with Thy presence blest,
Death is life, and labor rest;
Guide me while I draw my breath,
Guard me through the gate of death,

And at last, oh, let me stand,
With the sheep at Thy right hand.
Anon.

397   *Christ Risen.*
1 Angels, roll the rock away!
Death, yield up the mighty prey!
See, the Saviour quits the tomb,
Glowing with immortal bloom.
Alleluia! swell the lay!
Christ the Lord is risen to-day.

2 Shout, ye seraphs; angels, raise
Your eternal song of praise;
Let the earth's remotest bound
Echo to the blissful sound.
Alleluia! swell the lay!
Christ the Lord is risen to-day.
Rev. Thos. Scott (—1776).

PALMER. 7s, 6l.   Rev. Wm. S. Lacy, D.D., 1891.

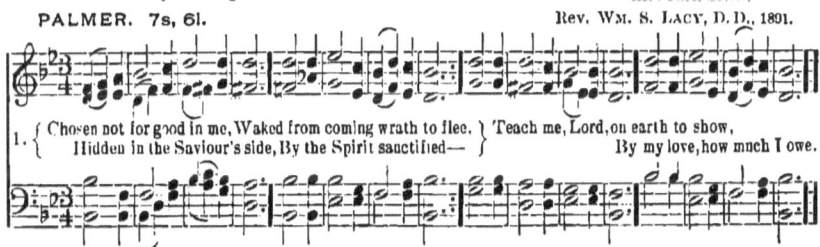

1. Chosen not for good in me, Waked from coming wrath to flee. Teach me, Lord, on earth to show,
Hidden in the Saviour's side, By the Spirit sanctified— By my love, how much I owe.

398   *How Much I Owe.*
1 Chosen not for good in me,
Waked from coming wrath to flee,
Hidden in the Saviour's side,
By the Spirit sanctified —
Teach me, Lord, on earth to show,
By my love, how much I owe.

2 Oft I walk beneath the cloud,
Dark as midnight's gloomy shroud;
But, when fear is at its height,
Jesus comes, and all is light;
Blessed Jesus! bid me show
Doubting saints how much I owe.

3 Oft the nights of sorrow reign —
Weeping, sickness, sighing, pain;
But a night Thine anger burns —
Morning comes, and joy returns;
God of comforts! bid me show
To Thy poor how much I owe.

4 When in flowery paths I tread,
Oft by sin I'm captive led;
Oft I fall, but still arise —
Jesus comes — the tempter flies;
Blessed Jesus! bid me show
Weary sinners all I owe.
Rev. Robert McCheyne (1813—1843).

PRAISE TO THE RISEN LORD.

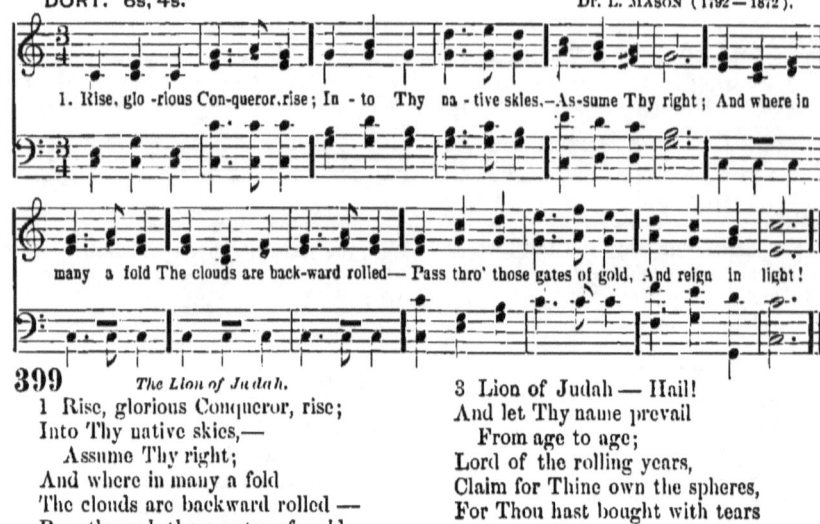

399 *The Lion of Judah.*

1 Rise, glorious Conqueror, rise;
Into Thy native skies,—
  Assume Thy right;
And where in many a fold
The clouds are backward rolled —
Pass through those gates of gold,
  And reign in light!

2 Victor o'er death and hell!
Cherubic legions swell
  Thy radiant train;
Praises all heaven inspire;
Each angel sweeps his lyre,
And waves his wings of fire,—
  Thou Lamb once slain!

3 Lion of Judah — Hail!
And let Thy name prevail
  From age to age;
Lord of the rolling years,
Claim for Thine own the spheres,
For Thou hast bought with tears
  Thy heritage!

4 And then was heard afar
Star answering to star—
  "Lo! these have come,
Followers of Him who gave
His life their lives to save;
And now their palms they wave,
  Brought safely home."
  Matthew Bridges (1800—).

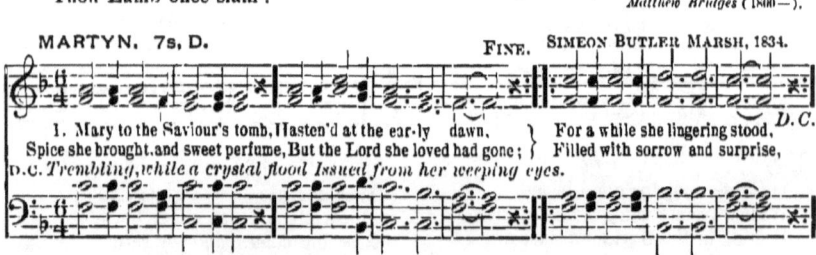

400 *Mary at the Tomb.*

1 Mary to the Saviour's tomb,
  Hastened at the early dawn,
Spice she brought, and sweet perfume,
  But the Lord she loved had gone;
For awhile she lingering stood,
  Filled with sorrow and surprise,
Trembling, while a crystal flood
  Issued from her weeping eyes.

2 But her sorrows quickly fled
  When she heard His welcome voice;
Christ had risen from the dead,
  Now He bids her heart rejoice;
What a change His word can make,
  Turning darkness into day!
Ye who weep for Jesus' sake,
  He will wipe your tears away.
  Rev. John Newton (1725—1807).

PRAISE TO THE RISEN LORD.

TOPAZ. P. M.   C. BEECHER.

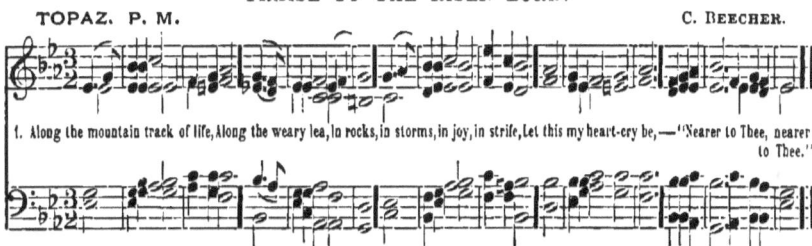

1. Along the mountain track of life, Along the weary lea, In rocks, in storms, in joy, in strife, Let this my heart-cry be,—"Nearer to Thee, nearer to Thee."

401   *Nearer to Thee.*

1 Along the mountain track of life,
Along the weary lea,
In rocks, in storms, in joy, in strife,
Let this my heart-cry be,—
"Nearer to Thee—nearer to Thee."

2 This pilgrim-path by Thee was trod,
Jesus,—my King, by Thee,
Traced by Thy tears, Thy feet, Thy blood,
In love, in death, for me;
Oh, bring my soul nearer to Thee.

3 Let every step, let every thought
Sweet memories bear of Thee;
And hear the soul Thy love hath bought,
Whose every cry shall be—
"Nearer to Thee—nearer to Thee."

4 Thou wilt! Thou dost!—a still small
Whispers of faith in Thee,   [voice
Of hope that might in grief rejoice,
If still the way-cry be,—
"Nearer to Thee—nearer to Thee."

Miss Phœbe Cary (1825—1871).

LANGTON. S. M.   C. STREETFIELD, arr.

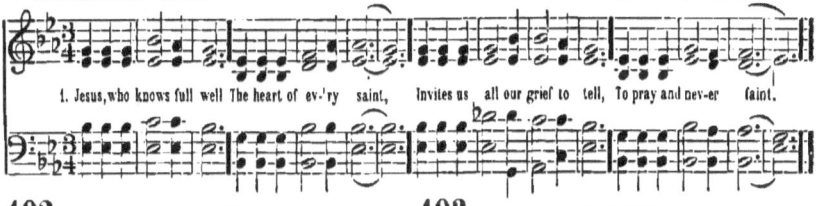

1. Jesus, who knows full well The heart of ev-'ry saint, Invites us all our grief to tell, To pray and nev-er faint.

402   *Importunity.*

1 Jesus, who knows full well
The heart of every saint,
Invites us all our grief to tell,
To pray and never faint.

2 He bows His gracious ear,—
We never plead in vain;
Then let us wait till He appear,
And pray, and pray again.

3 Jesus, the Lord, will hear
His chosen when they cry;
Yes, though He may a while forbear,
He'll help them from on high.

4 Then let us earnest cry,
And never faint in prayer;
He sees, He hears, and from on high,
Will make our cause His care.

Rev. J. Newton (1725—1807).

403   *Psalm 103.*

1 Oh, bless the Lord, my soul,
Let all within me join,
And aid my tongue to bless His name,
Whose favors are divine.

2 Oh, bless the Lord, my soul;
Nor let His mercies lie
Forgotten in unthankfulness,
And without praises die.

3 'T is He forgives thy sins,
'T is He relieves thy pain,
'T is He that heals thy sicknesses,
And makes thee young again.

4 He crowns thy life with love,
When ransomed from the grave;
He that redeemed my soul from hell
Hath sovereign power to save.

Rev. I. Watts (1674—1748).

PRAISE TO THE RISEN LORD.

LANSDOWN. 7s. D. G. Witts, 1890.

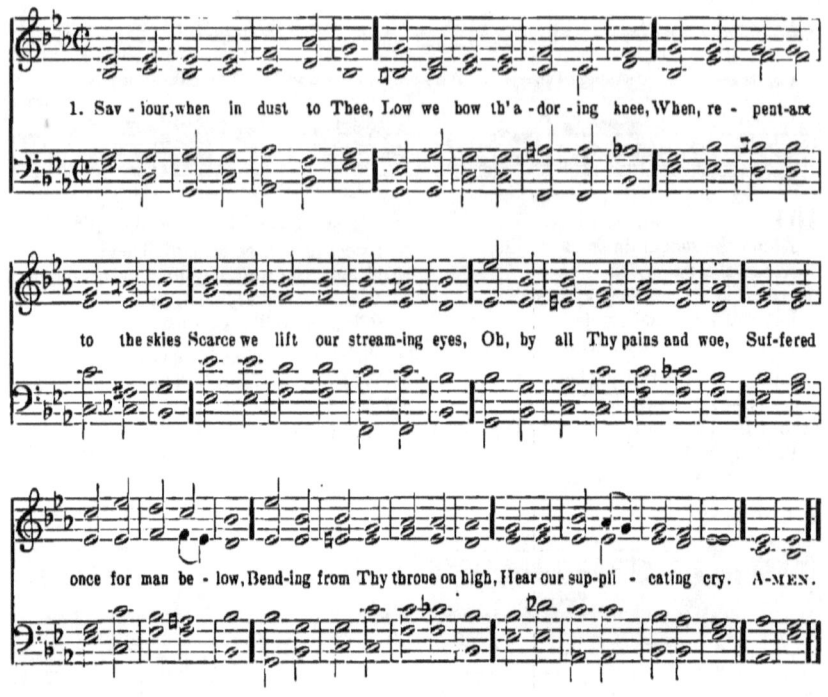

404 *Litany.*

1 Saviour, when in dust to Thee,
Low we bow th' adoring knee,—
When, repentant to the skies,
Scarce we lift our streaming eyes,
Oh, by all Thy pains and woe,
Suffered once for man below,
Bending from Thy throne on high,
Hear our supplicating cry.

2 By Thy birth and early years,
By Thy human griefs and fears,
By Thy fasting and distress
In the lonely wilderness,
By Thy vict'ry in the hour
Of the subtle tempter's power,—
Jesus, look with pitying eye,
Hear our deep, imploring cry.

3 By Thine hour of dark despair,
By Thine agony of prayer,
By the purple robe of scorn,
By Thy wounds, Thy crown of thorn,
By Thy cross, Thy pangs, and cries,
By Thy perfect sacrifice,—
Jesus, look with pitying eye,
Hear our sad, beseeching cry.

4 By Thy deep, expiring groan,
By the sealed sepulchral stone,
By Thy triumph o'er the grave,
By Thy power from death to save,—
Mighty God, ascended Lord,
To Thy throne in heaven restored,—
Saviour, Prince exalted high,
Hear our solemn litany.

Sir R. Grant (1788 – 1838).

PRAISE TO THE RISEN LORD.

MANOAH. C. M.   ROSSINI. Arr. by H. W. GREATOREX.

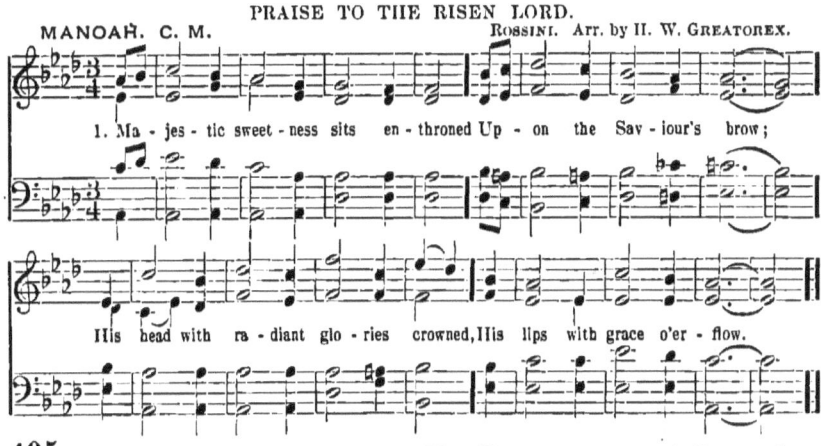

1. Ma - jes - tic sweet - ness sits en - throned Up - on the Sav - iour's brow; His head with ra - diant glo - ries crowned, His lips with grace o'er - flow.

405   *Glory of Christ.*
1 Majestic sweetness sits enthroned
  Upon the Saviour's brow;
His head with radiant glories crowned,
  His lips with grace o'erflow.

2 No mortal can with Him compare
  Among the sons of men;
Fairer is He than all the fair,
  Who fill the heavenly train.

3 He saw me plunged in deep distress
  And flew to my relief;
For me He bore the shameful cross,
  And carried all my grief.

4 To Him I owe my life and breath,
  And all the joys I have;
He makes me triumph over death,
  And saves me from the grave.

5 To heaven, the place of His abode,
  He brings my weary feet,
Shows me the glories of my God,
  And makes my joys complete.

6 Since from His bounty I receive
  Such proofs of love divine,
Had I a thousand hearts to give,
  Lord, they should all be Thine.
        Rev. S. Stennett (1727—1795).

406   *Repentance.*
1 O Thou, whose tender mercy hears
  Contrition's humble sigh;
Whose hand indulgent wipes the tears
  From sorrow's weeping eye.

2 See, low before Thy throne of grace,
  A wretched wanderer mourn;

Hast Thou not bid me seek Thy face?
  Hast Thou not said — return?

3 And shall my guilty fears prevail
  To drive me from Thy feet?
Oh, let not this dear refuge fail,
  This only safe retreat!

4 Oh, shine on this benighted heart!
  With beams of mercy shine!
And let Thy healing voice impart
  A taste of joys divine.
        Miss Anne Steele (1717—1778).

407   *The Glory of Christ.*
1 The Head, that once was crowned with
  Is crowned with glory now;   [thorns,
A royal diadem adorns
  The mighty Victor's brow.

2 The highest place that heaven affords
  Is Thine, is Thine by right,—
Thou King of kings, and Lord of lords,
  And heaven's eternal light.

3 The joy of all who dwell above,
  The joy of all below,
To whom Thou dost reveal Thy love,
  And grant Thy name to know.

4 To whom the cross, with all its shame,
  With all its grace, is given;
Their name, an everlasting name,
  Their joy, the joy of heaven.

5 They suffer with Thee, Lord, below,
  They reign with Thee above,
Their everlasting joy to know
  The mystery of Thy love.
        Rev. Thos. Kelly (1769—1855).

PRAISE TO THE RISEN LORD.

RATHBUN. 8s, 7s.   ITHAMAR CONKEY (1815—1867).

408
Glorying in the Cross.
1 In the cross of Christ I glory,
   Towering o'er the wrecks of time;
   All the light of sacred story
   Gathers round its head sublime.

2 When the woes of life o'ertake me,
   Hopes deceive, and fears annoy,
   Never shall the cross forsake me:
   Lo! it glows with peace and joy.

3 When the sun of bliss is beaming
   Light and love upon my way,
   From the cross the radiance, streaming,
   Adds more lustre to the day.

4 In the cross of Christ I glory,
   Towering o'er the wrecks of time;
   All the light of sacred story
   Gathers round its head sublime.
Sir John Bowring (1792—1872), 1825.

409
Progress.
1 Like the eagle, upward, onward,
   Let my soul in faith be borne;
   Calmly gazing, skyward, sunward,
   Let my eye unshrinking turn.

2 Where the cross, God's love revealing,
   Sets the fettered spirit free,
   Where it sheds its wondrous healing,
   There, my soul, thy rest shall be.

3 Oh, may I no longer, dreaming,
   Idly waste my golden day,
   But, each precious hour redeeming,
   Upward, onward, press my way.
Rev. Horatius Bonar (1809—1890).

410
The Paschal Lamb.
1 Hail, Thou once despised Jesus!
   Hail, Thou Galilean King!
   Thou didst suffer to release us;
   Thou didst free salvation bring.

2 Hail, Thou agonizing Saviour,
   Bearer of our sin and shame!
   By Thy merits we find favor;
   Life is given through Thy name.

3 Paschal Lamb, by God appointed,
   All our sins on Thee were laid;
   By Almighty Love anointed,
   Thou hast full atonement made.

4 All Thy people are forgiven
   Through the virtue of Thy blood;
   Opened is the gate of heaven,
   Peace is made 'twixt man and God.
Rev. Jno. Bakewell (1721—1819).

411
Jesus Interceding.
1 Jesus hail, enthroned in glory,
   There for ever to abide;
   All the heavenly hosts adore Thee,
   Seated at Thy Father's side.

2 There for sinners Thou art pleading,
   There Thou dost our place prepare;
   Ever for us interceding,
   Till in glory we appear.

3 Worship, honor, power and blessing,
   Thou art worthy to receive;
   Loudest praises, without ceasing,
   Meet it is for us to give.
Rev. John Bakewell (1721—1819).

PRAISE TO THE RISEN LORD.

ARIEL. C. P. M. — Dr. L. MASON (1792—1872).

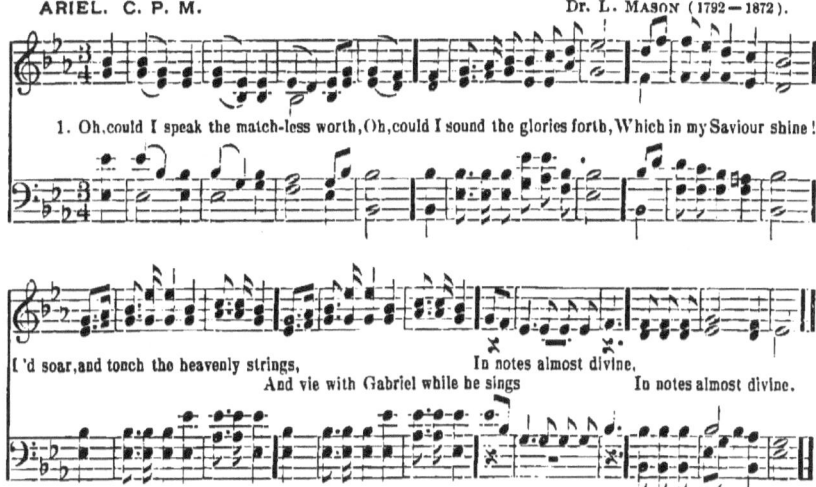

412 *Glory to Christ.*

1 Oh, could I speak the matchless worth,
Oh, could I sound the glories forth,
　Which in my Saviour shine!
I'd soar, and touch the heavenly strings,
And vie with Gabriel while he sings
　In notes almost divine.

2 I'd sing the precious blood He spilt,
My ransom from the dreadful guilt
　Of sin and wrath divine;
I'd sing His glorious righteousness,
In which all-perfect, heavenly dress
　My soul shall ever shine.

3 I'd sing the characters He bears,
And all the forms of love He wears,
　Exalted on His throne;
In loftiest songs of sweetest praise,
I would to everlasting days,
　Make all His glories known.

4 Soon the delightful day will come,
When my dear Lord will call me home,
　And I shall see His face;
Then, with my Saviour, Brother, Friend,
A blest eternity I'll spend,
　Triumphant in His grace.

Rev. S. Medley (1738—1799).

413 *Praise for Conversion.*
Tune, RATHBUN.

1 Hail! my ever blessed Jesus,
　Only Thee I wish to sing;
To my soul Thy name is precious,
　Thou my Prophet, Priest, and King.

2 Oh, what mercy flows from heaven!
　Oh, what joy and happiness!
Love I much? I'm much forgiven,
　I'm a miracle of grace.

3 Once with Adam's race in ruin,
　Unconcerned in sin I lay;
Swift destruction still pursuing,
　Till my Saviour passed that way.

4 Witness, all ye hosts of heaven,
　My Redeemer's tenderness;
Love I much? I'm much forgiven,
　I'm a miracle of grace.

5 Shout, ye bright angelic choir,
　Praise the Lamb enthroned above;
Whilst astonished I admire
　God's free grace and boundless love.

6 That blest moment I received Him,
　Filled my soul with joy and peace;
Love I much? I'm much forgiven;
　I'm a miracle of grace.

J. Wingrove (1720—1793).

PRAISE TO THE RISEN LORD.

IN CŒLO QUIES. 7s, D. — J. E. SMITH.

414 *Surrendering to Christ.*

1 People of the living God,
  I have sought the world around;
  Paths of sin and sorrow trod,
  Peace and comfort nowhere found.
 Now to you my spirit turns,
  Turns, a fugitive unblest;
  Brethren, where your altar burns,
  Oh, receive me into rest!

2 Lonely, I no longer roam,
  Like the cloud, the wind, the wave ;
  Where you dwell shall be my home,
  Where you die shall be my grave.

Mine the God whom you adore,
  Your Redeemer shall be mine;
  Earth can fill my soul no more,
  Every idol I resign.

3 Tell me not of gain or loss,
  Ease, enjoyment, pomp and power,
  Welcome poverty and cross,
  Shame, reproach, affliction's hour;
 "Follow me;" I know Thy voice;
  Jesus, Lord, Thy steps I see;
  Now I take Thy yoke by choice;
  Light, Thy burden, now to me.

Rev. J. Montgomery (1771 — 1854).

BENEVENTO. 7s, D. — S. WEBBE (1740—1816).

PRAISE TO THE RISEN LORD.

AUSTRIAN HYMN. 8s, 7s, D. Francis Joseph Haydn (1732—1809).

415 *Mounting in Triumph.*

1 See the Conqueror mounts in triumph,
  See the King in royal state,
  Riding on the clouds His chariot
    To His heavenly palace gate;
  Hark, the choirs of angel voices,
  Joyful hallelujahs sing;
  And the portals high are lifted,
    To receive their heavenly King.

2 Who is this that comes in glory,
    With the trump of jubilee?
  Lord of battles, God of armies,
    He has gained the victory;
  He who on the cross did suffer,
  He who from the grave arose,
  He has vanquished sin and Satan,
  He, by death, has spoiled His foes.

3 Lift us up from earth to heaven,
    Give us wings of faith and love,
  Gales of holy aspiration
    Wafting us to realms above;
  That, with hearts and minds uplifted,
  We with Christ our Lord may dwell,
  Where He sits enthroned in glory
    In the heavenly citadel.

4 So at last, when He appeareth,
    We from out our graves may spring,
  With our youth renewed like eagles',
    Flocking round our heavenly King,
  Caught up on the clouds of heaven,
  And may meet Him in the air,
  Rise to realms where He is reigning,
  And may reign forever there.
    Bp. Christopher Wordsworth, 1862.

416 *Redeeming Love.*
    Tune, Benevento.

1 Now begin the heavenly theme,
  Sing aloud in Jesus' name;
  Ye who Jesus' kindness prove,
  Triumph in redeeming love.

2 Ye who see the Father's grace
  Beaming in the Saviour's face,
  As to Canaan on ye move,
  Praise and bless redeeming love.

3 Mourning souls, dry up your tears;
  Banish all your guilty fears;
  See your guilt and curse remove,
  Canceled by redeeming love.

4 Hither, then, your music bring,
  Strike aloud each joyful string;
  Mortals, join the host above,
  Join to praise redeeming love.
    John Langford, 1761.

PRAISE TO THE RISEN LORD.

HARWELL. 8s, 7s, D. — Dr. L. Mason (1792—1872).

417   *King of Glory.*

1 Hark! ten thousand harps and voices
   Sound the note of praise above;
Jesus reigns, and heaven rejoices;
   Jesus reigns, the God of love;
See, He sits on yonder throne;
Jesus rules the world alone.

2 King of glory! reign for ever —
   Thine an everlasting crown;
Nothing, from Thy love, shall sever
   Those whom Thou hast made Thine own;
Happy objects of Thy grace,
Destined to behold Thy face.

3 Saviour! hasten Thine appearing;
   Bring, oh, bring the glorious day,
When the awful summons hearing,
   Heaven and earth shall pass away;—
Then, with golden harps, we'll sing,—
   "Glory, glory to our King!"
Rev. T. Kelly (1769—1855).

418   *Doxology.*

Praise the God of all creation;
   Praise the Father's boundless love;
Praise the Lamb, our expiation,
   Priest and King enthroned above;
Praise the Fountain of salvation,
   Him by whom our spirits live;
Undivided adoration
   To the one Jehovah give.

419   *Christ Coming in Triumph.*

1 Christ is coming! Let creation
   Bid her groans and travail cease;
Let the glorious proclamation
   Hope restore, and faith increase.
      Come, Lord Jesus!
   Come, Thou blessèd Prince of Peace!

2 Though once cradled in a manger,
   Oft no pillow but the sod;
Here an alien and a stranger,
   Mock'd of men, though Son of God,
      All creation
   Yet shall own Thy kingly rod.

3 Long Thine exiles have been pining,
   Far from rest, and home, and Thee;
But, in heavenly vestures shining,
   They shall soon Thy glory see.
      Come, Lord Jesus!
   Haste the joyous Jubilee!

4 With that blessèd hope before us,
   Let no harp remain unstrung;
Let the mighty advent-chorus
   Onward roll from tongue to tongue.
      Hallelujah!
   Come, Lord Jesus, quickly come.
Rev. J. R. McDuff (1818—).

LOVE TO CHRIST.

CORONATION. C. M.   OLIVER HOLDEN (1765—1844), 1793.

All hail the pow'r of Je-sus' name! Let an-gels prostrate fall; Bring forth the roy-al di - a - dem, And crown Him Lord of all. Bring forth the royal di - a - dem, And crown Him Lord of all.

420   *Jesus, Lord of All.*

1 All hail the power of Jesus' name!
   Let angels prostrate fall;
Bring forth the royal diadem,
   And crown Him Lord of all.

2 Ye chosen seed of Israel's race,
   Ye ransomed from the fall;
Hail Him, who saves you by His grace,
   And crown Him Lord of all.

3 Sinners, whose love can ne'er forget
   The wormwood and the gall;
Go, spread your trophies at His feet,
   And crown Him Lord of all.

4 Let every kindred, every tribe,
   On this terrestrial ball,
To Him all majesty ascribe,
   And crown Him Lord of all.

5 Oh, that with yonder sacred throng,
   We at His feet may fall!
We'll join the everlasting song,
   And crown Him Lord of all.

Rev. Edward Perronet (—1792).

CROSS AND CROWN. C. M.   GEO. N. ALLEN, 1849.

1. Must Je-sus bear the cross alone, And all the world go free? No, there's a cross for ev-'ry one, And there's a cross for me.

421   *Cross and Crown.*

1 Must Jesus bear the cross alone,
   And all the world go free?
No, there's a cross for every one,
   And there's a cross for me.

2 The consecrated cross I'll bear,
   Till death shall set me free;
And then go home my crown to wear,
   For there's a crown for me.

3 Upon the crystal pavement, down
   At Jesus' piercéd feet,
With joy I'll cast my golden crown,
   And His dear name repeat.

4 O precious cross! O glorious crown!
   O resurrection day!
Ye angels, from the stars come down,
   And bear my soul away.

Thos. Shepherd (1665—1739).

LOVE TO CHRIST.

ST. MATTHIAS. L. M. 6l. W. H. MONK (1823—).

1. Is there a thing beneath the sun That strives with Thee my heart to share?
Ah! tear it thence, and reign a-lone, The Lord of ev-'ry mo-tion there.
Then shall my heart from earth be free, When it hath found re-pose in Thee.

422   *Thou Hidden Love of God.*

1 Is there a thing beneath the sun
 That strives with Thee my heart to share?
Ah! tear it thence, and reign alone,
 The Lord of every motion there.
Then shall my heart from earth be free,
 When it hath found repose in Thee.

2 Oh, hide this self from me, that I
 No more, but Christ in me, may live;
My vile affections crucify,
 Nor let one darling lust survive;
In all things nothing may I see,
Nothing desire or seek, but Thee.

3 Each moment draw from earth away
 My heart that lowly waits Thy call:
Speak to my inmost soul, and say,
 I am thy Love, thy God, thy All;
To feel Thy power, to hear Thy voice,
To taste Thy love, be all my choice.
 Gerhard of Tersteegen (1697—1769).
  Tr. by *John Wesley.*

423   *Gloria Patri.*

To God the Father, God the Son,
And God the Spirit, Three in One,
Be glory in the highest given,
By all on earth, and all in heaven,
As was through ages heretofore,
Is now, and shall be evermore.

(176)

LOVE TO CHRIST.

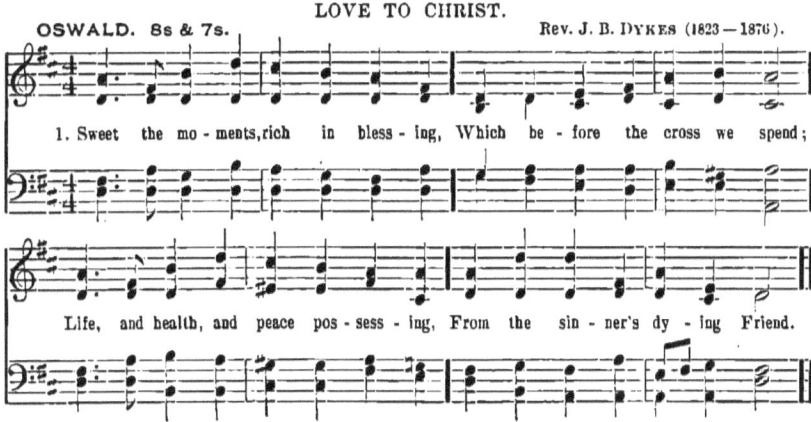

OSWALD. 8s & 7s. — Rev. J. B. Dykes (1823–1876).

1. Sweet the moments, rich in blessing, Which before the cross we spend; Life, and health, and peace possessing, From the sinner's dying Friend.

424 *Before the Cross.*

1 Sweet the moments, rich in blessing,
  Which before the cross we spend;
 Life, and health, and peace possessing,
  From the sinner's dying Friend.

2 Here I'll sit forever viewing,
  Mercy flow in streams of blood;
 Precious drops, my soul bedewing,
  Plead and claim my peace with God.

3 Truly blessed is this station,
  Low before His cross to lie;
 While I see divine compassion
  Beaming in His loving eye.

4 Here it is I find my heaven,
  While upon the cross I gaze;
 Love I much; I'm much forgiven,
  I'm a miracle of grace.

5 Love and grief my heart dividing,
  With my tears, His feet I bathe;
 Constant still in faith abiding,
  Life deriving from His death.
 Rev. James Allen (1734–1804).

BATTY. 8s & 7s. — German.

1. Jesus, full of all compassion, Hear Thy humble suppliant's cry; Let me know Thy great salvation: See, I languish, faint, and die.

425 *Repentance at the Cross.*

1 Jesus, full of all compassion,
  Hear Thy humble suppliant's cry;
 Let me know Thy great salvation;
  See, I languish, faint and die.

2 Guilty, but with heart relenting,
  Overwhelmed with helpless grief,
 Prostrate, at Thy feet repenting,
  Send, oh! send me quick relief!

3 Whither should a wretch be flying,
  But to Him who comfort gives?
 Whither, from the dread of dying,
  But to Him who ever lives?

4 While I view Thee, wounded, grieving,
  Breathless, on the cursed tree,
 Fain, I'd feel my heart believing
  That Thou sufferedst thus for me.

5 With Thy righteousness and Spirit,
  I am more than angels blest;
 Heir with Thee, all things inherit,
  Peace, and joy, and endless rest.

6 Saved!— the deed shall spread new glory
  Through the shining realms above;
 Angels sing the pleasing story,
  All enraptured with Thy love.
 Rev. Daniel Turner (1710–1798).

LOVE TO CHRIST.

MARGARET. 8s & 4s. Rev. Robert P. Kerr, D. D., 1883.

Copyright, 1891, by R. P. Kerr.

426   *Christ my All.*
1 Jesus, my Saviour! look on me,
For I am weary and opprest;
I come to cast myself on Thee:
   Thou art my Rest.

2 Look down on me, for I am weak;
I feel the toilsome journey's length;
From Thee, almighty aid I seek:
   Thou art my Strength.

3 I am bewilder'd on my way;
Dark and tempestuous is the night;
Oh, send Thou forth some cheering ray!
   Thou art my Light.

4 Standing alone on Jordan's brink,
In that tremendous latest strife,
Thou wilt not suffer me to sink:
   Thou art my Life.

5 Thou wilt my every want supply,
E'en to the end, whate'er befall;
Through life, in death, eternally,
   Thou art my All.
       Miss Charlotte Elliott (1789—1871).

WOODWORTH. L. M.   W. B. Bradbury (1816—1868).

427   *Just as I am.*
1 Just as I am, without one plea
But that Thy blood was shed for me,
And that Thou bid'st me come to Thee,
   O Lamb of God, I come.

2 Just as I am, and waiting not
To rid my soul of one dark blot,
To Thee, whose blood can cleanse each spot,
   O Lamb of God, I come.

3 Just as I am, though tossed about
With many a conflict, many a doubt,
Fightings within, and fears without,
   O Lamb of God, I come.

4 Just as I am, poor, wretched, blind,—
Sight, riches, healing of the mind,
Yea, all I need in Thee to find,
   O Lamb of God, I come.

5 Just as I am, Thou wilt receive,
Wilt welcome, pardon, cleanse, relieve;
Because Thy promise I believe,
   O Lamb of God, I come.

6 Just as I am, for love unknown
Has broken every barrier down;
Now to be Thine, and Thine alone,
   O Lamb of God, I come.
       Miss Charlotte Elliott (1789—1871).

LOVE TO CHRIST.

RAYNOLDS. 11s & 10s. Arr. from MENDELSSOHN (1809—1847).

1. We would see Jesus—for the shadows lengthen A-cross this lit-tle landscape of our life;
We would see Jesus, our weak faith to strengthen For the last wea-ri-ness—the fi-nal strife.

By per. of Oliver Ditson Company, owners of copyright.

428 *We would see Jesus.*

1 We would see Jesus — for the shadows lengthen
Across this little landscape of our life;
We would see Jesus, our weak faith to strengthen
For the last weariness — the final strife.

2 We would see Jesus — the great Rock Foundation,
Whereon our feet were set with sovereign grace;
Not life, nor death, with all their agitation,
Can thence remove us, if we see His face.

3 We would see Jesus — other lights are paling, [to see;
Which for long years we have rejoiced
The blessings of our pilgrimage are failing,
We would not mourn them for we go to Thee.

4 We would see see Jesus — this is all we're needing, [the sight;
Strength, joy, and willingness come with
We would see Jesus, dying, risen, pleading,
Then welcome day, and farewell mortal night!

Anon., 1858

JUST AS I AM. 8s & 6s. N. BOWDITCH CLAPP, 1801.

1. Just as I am, with-out one plea But that Thy blood was shed for me,
And that Thou bids't me come to Thee, O Lamb of God, I come.

(179)

LOVE TO CHRIST.

LUX MUNDI. 7s & 6s, D. J. BARNBY, 1838.

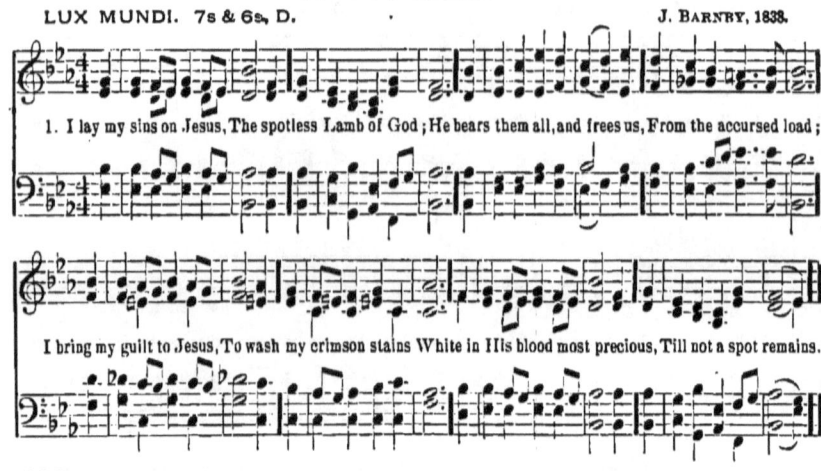

1. I lay my sins on Jesus, The spotless Lamb of God; He bears them all, and frees us, From the accursed load; I bring my guilt to Jesus, To wash my crimson stains White in His blood most precious, Till not a spot remains.

429 *Faith in Jesus.*

1 I lay my sins on Jesus,
　The spotless Lamb of God;
He bears them all, and frees us
　From the accursèd load;
I bring my guilt to Jesus,
　To wash my crimson stains
White in His blood most precious,
　Till not a spot remains.

2 I lay my wants on Jesus;
　All fullness dwells in Him;
He healeth my diseases,
　He doth my soul redeem;
I lay my griefs on Jesus,
　My burdens and my cares;
He from them all releases,
　He all my sorrows shares.

3 I long to be like Jesus,
　Meek, loving, lowly, mild;
I long to be like Jesus,
　The Father's holy child;

I long to be with Jesus,
　Amid the heavenly throng,
To sing with saints His praises,
　And learn the angel's song.

Rev. Horatius Bonar (1808 – 1890).

430 *I Do Believe.*

1 For ever here my rest shall be,
　Close to Thy bleeding side;
This all my hope and all my plea —
　For me the Saviour died.

2 My dying Saviour and my God,
　Fountain for guilt and sin,
Sprinkle me ever with Thy blood,
　And cleanse and keep me clean.

3 Wash me, and make me thus Thine own;
　Wash me, and mine Thou art;
Wash me, but not my feet alone —
　My hands, my head, my heart.

Rev. Chas. Wesley (1708 – 1788).

HORSLEY. C. M. WILLIAM HORSLEY, Mus. Bac. (1774 – 1858).

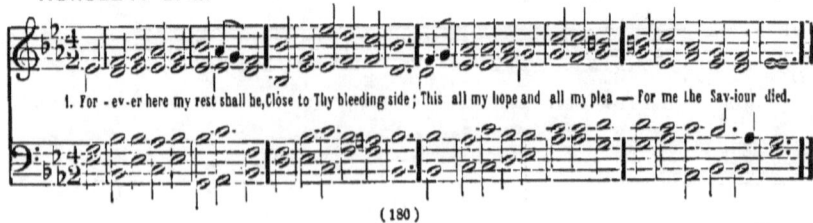

1. For-ev-er here my rest shall be, Close to Thy bleeding side; This all my hope and all my plea — For me the Sav-iour died.

LOVE TO CHRIST.

HOLLINGSIDE. 7s, D. — Rev. J. B. Dykes (1823—1876).

1. Jesus, lov-er of my soul! Let me to Thy bos-om fly While the rag-ing bil-lows roll,
D.S. Safe in-to the haven guide,

While the tempest still is high; Hide me, O my Saviour, hide, Till the storm of life is past:
Oh, re-ceive my soul at last.

---

431 *Jesus, Lover of my Soul.*

1 Jesus, lover of my soul!
  Let me to Thy bosom fly
While the raging billows roll,
  While the tempest still is high;
Hide me, O my Saviour, hide,
  Till the storm of life is past;
Safe into the haven guide,
  Oh, receive my soul at last.

2 Other refuge have I none;
  Hangs my helpless soul on Thee;
Leave, ah! leave me not alone,
  Still support and comfort me;
All my trust on Thee is stayed,
  All my help from Thee I bring;
Cover my defenceless head
  With the shadow of Thy wing.

3 Thou, O Christ! art all I want,
  All in all in Thee I find;
Raise the fallen, cheer the faint,
  Heal the sick and lead the blind;
Just and holy is Thy name,
  I am all unrighteousness:
Vile and full of sin I am,
  Thou art full of truth and grace.

4 Plenteous grace with Thee is found
  Grace to pardon all my sin;
Let the healing streams abound,
  Make and keep me pure within;
Thou, of life, the fountain art,
  Freely let me take of Thee;
Spring Thou up within my heart;
  Rise to all eternity.

        Rev. Charles Wesley (1709—1788).

MARTYN. 7s, D. — S. B. Marsh (1798—1875).

1. { Je-sus, lov-er of my soul! Let me to Thy bos-om fly } { Hide me, O my Sav-iour, hide,
* { While the rag-ing billows roll, While the tempest still is high; } { Till the storm of life is past;*
D.C. Safe into the haven guide, Oh, receive my soul at last.

LOVE TO CHRIST.

COOLING. C. M.   A. J. ABBEY (1825—1887).

432   *Love to Christ.*
1 To whom, my Saviour, shall I go,
  If I depart from Thee,
My guide through all this vale of woe,
  And more than life to me?

2 The world resists Thine easy reign.
  And pays Thy death with scorn;
Oh, they would plait Thy crown again,
  And sharpen every thorn.

3 But I have felt Thy dying love
  Steal sweetly through my heart,
To whisper hope of joys above,—
  And can we ever part?

4 Ah, no! with Thee I'll walk below,
  My journey to the grave;
To whom, my Saviour, shall I go,
  When only Thou canst save?
        Dr. William Maxwell (1784—1857).

433   *Old Things are Passed Away.*
1 Let worldly minds the world pursue,
  It has no charms for me;
Once I admired its trifles too,
  But grace has set me free.

2 Its pleasures now no longer please,
  No more content afford;
Far from my heart be joys like these,
  Now I have seen the Lord.

3 As by the light of opening day
  The stars are all concealed,

So earthly pleasures fade away,
  When Jesus is revealed.

4 Creatures no more divide my choice,
  I bid them all depart;
His name, and love, and gracious voice,
  Have fixed my roving heart.

5 Now, Lord, I would be Thine alone,
  And wholly live to Thee;
Yet worthless still myself I own,
  Thy worth is all my plea.
        Rev. John Newton (1725—1807).

434   *Psalm 71.*
1 My Saviour, my almighty Friend;
  When I begin Thy praise,
Where will the growing numbers end,—
  The numbers of Thy grace?

2 Thou art my everlasting trust;
  Thy goodness I adore;
And, since I knew Thy graces first,
  I speak Thy glories more.

3 My feet shall travel all the length,
  Of the celestial road;
And march, with courage in Thy strength,
  To see my Father God.

4 How will my lips rejoice to tell
  The victories of my King!
My soul, redeemed from sin and hell,
  Shall Thy salvation sing.
        Rev. I. Watts (1674—1748).

LOVE TO CHRIST.

EVAN. C. M. W. H. HAVERGAL (1793—1870).

1. Jesus, these eyes have never seen
That radiant form of Thine;
The veil of sense hangs dark between
Thy blessed face and mine.

435 *An Unseen Saviour.*

1 Jesus, these eyes have never seen
That radiant form of Thine;
The veil of sense hangs dark between
Thy blessed face and mine.

2 I see Thee not, I hear Thee not,
Yet art Thou oft with me;
And earth hath ne'er so dear a spot,
As where I meet with Thee.

3 Like some bright dream that comes unsought,
When slumbers o'er me roll,
Thine image ever fills my thought,
And charms my ravished soul.

4 Yet though I have not seen, and still
Must rest in faith alone;
I love Thee, dearest Lord, and will,
Unseen, but not unknown.

5 When death these mortal eyes shall seal,
And still this throbbing heart,
The rending veil shall Thee reveal,
All glorious as Thou art.
Rev. Ray Palmer (1808—1887).

436 *Love to Christ.*

1 How sweet the name of Jesus sounds,
In a believer's ear!
It soothes his sorrows, heals his wounds,
And drives away his fear.

2 It makes the wounded spirit whole,
And calms the troubled breast;
'T is manna to the hungry soul,
And to the weary, rest.

3 Dear Name, the rock on which I build,
My shield and hiding-place;
My never-failing treasury, filled
With boundless stores of grace!

4 Jesus, my Shepherd, Saviour, Friend,
My Prophet, Priest, and King;
My Lord, my Life, my Way, my End,
Accept the praise I bring.

5 Weak is the effort of my heart,
And cold my warmest thought;
But when I see Thee as Thou art,
I'll praise Thee as I ought.

6 Till then I would Thy love proclaim
With every fleeting breath;
And may the music of Thy name
Refresh my soul in death.
Rev. J. Newton (1725—1807).

GEER. C. M. HENRY WELLINGTON GREATOREX (1811—1858).

By per. Oliver Ditson Company, owners of copyright.

LOVE TO CHRIST.

MARLOW. C. M. — English. L. MASON. Arr.

1. Oh, for a thou-sand tongues to sing My dear Re-deem-er's praise!
The glo-ries of my God and King, The tri-umphs of His grace.

437 *Rejoicing in Christ.*

1 Oh, for a thousand tongues to sing
My dear Redeemer's praise!
The glories of my God and King,
The triumphs of His grace.

2 My gracious Master, and my God,
Assist me to proclaim,
To spread through all the earth abroad,
The honors of Thy name.

3 Jesus, the name that calms our fears,
That bids our sorrows cease;
'Tis music in the sinner's ears;
'Tis life, and health, and peace.

4 He breaks the power of reigning sin,
He sets the prisoner free;
His blood can make the foulest clean,
His blood availed for me.

5 Let us obey; we then shall know,
Shall feel our sins forgiven;
Anticipate our heaven below,
And own that love is heaven.
Rev. Charles Wesley (1708 — 1788).

438 *The Mystery of Grace.*

1 In evil, long I took delight,
Unawed by shame or fear,
Till a new object struck my sight,
And stopped my wild career.

2 I saw One hanging on a tree,
In agony and blood;
Who fixed His languid eyes on me,
As near the cross I stood.

3 Sure, never, till my latest breath,
Can I forget that look;

It seemed to charge me with His death,
Though not a word He spoke.

4 Alas! I knew not what I did, —
But now my tears are vain;
Where shall my trembling soul be hid,
For I the Lord have slain!

5 A second look He gave, that said,
"I freely all forgive;
This blood is for thy ransom paid;
I die that thou may'st live."

6 Thus while His death my sin displays
In all its blackest hue,
Such is the mystery of grace,
It seals my pardon too!
Rev. John Newton (1725 — 1807).

439 *Not Ashamed of Christ.*

1 I'm not ashamed to own my Lord,
Nor to defend His cause,
Maintain the honor of His word,
The glory of His cross.

2 Jesus, my God, I know His name,
His name is all my trust;
Nor will He put my soul to shame,
Nor let my hope be lost.

3 Firm as His throne His promise stands
And He can well secure
What I've committed to His hands,
Till the decisive hour.

4 Then will He own my worthless name
Before His Father's face,
And in the New Jerusalem,
Appoint my soul a place.
Rev. Isaac Watts (1674 — 1748).

LOVE TO CHRIST.

440 *We Have Left All.*

1 Jesus, I my cross have taken,
  All to leave and follow Thee;
Naked, poor, despised, forsaken,
  Thou, from hence, my all shalt be.
Let the world neglect and leave me;
  They have left my Saviour too;
Human hopes have oft deceived me;
  Thou art faithful, Thou art true.

2 Perish, earthly fame and treasure,
  Come, disaster, scorn, and pain;
In Thy service, pain is pleasure;
  With Thy favor, loss is gain.
Oh, 't is not in grief to harm me!
  While Thy bleeding love I see;
Oh, 't is not in joy to charm me!
  When that love is hid from me.
  Rev. Henry Francis Lyte (1793—1847).

441 *The Friend of Sinners.*

1 One there is above all others
  Well deserves the name of Friend;
His is love beyond a brother's,
  Costly, free and knows no end.

2 Which of all our friends to save us
  Could or would have shed His blood?
But our Saviour died, to have us
  Reconciled in Him to God.

3 When He lived on earth, abased,
  Friend of sinners was His name;
Now, above all glory raised,
  He rejoices in the same.

4 Oh, for grace our hearts to soften!
  Teach us, Lord! at length to love;
We, alas! forget too often
  What a Friend we have above.
  Rev. John Newton (1725—1807).

LOVE TO CHRIST.

GALILEAN HYMN. 8s & 7s, D. Rev. R. P. Kerr, D. D., 1891.

Copyright, 1891, by R. P. Kerr.

442 *Galilean King.*

1 Galilean King and Prophet!
  Thou who once bestrode the sea,
 Come across the troubled waters,
  Come, and bid our sorrows flee:
 Let us hear the mighty mandate
  Of Thine own resistless will;
 Calling calmness o'er the tempest,
  Let us hear Thy "peace be still."

2 Galilean King and Shepherd,
  Who Thy flock didst gently lead,
 Through the fields and by the seaside,
  Now Thy sheep on mercies feed.
 In the mountains and the desert,
  As the thousands followed Thee;
 We, the hungry, press the nearest,
  For Thy bounty, full and free.

3 Galilean King and Healer!
  There are many waiting here,
 Waiting with their wounded spirits
  Speaking but with sigh or tear;
 Wilt Thou guide Thy white-winged vessel
  Toward the sorrow-shaded strand?
 Come, and give new life and blessing;
  Touch us with Thy tender hand.

4 Galilean King and Saviour!
  Here we crave Thy pardoning grace;
 Wilt Thou not forgive us freely
  As we kneel before Thy face?
 Cleansing, righteousness, adoption,
  And renewing from Thy love,
 Give us all, that we may serve Thee,
  'Till we find our rest above.
                Rev. Robert P. Kerr, D. D., 1891.

443 *At the Door of Mercy.*

1 At the door of mercy singing
  With the burden of my sin,
 Day and night my soul is crying,
  "Open Lord, and let me in."
 Waiting 'mid the darkness dreary,
  Stretching out my hands to Thee,
 In the refuge for the weary
  Is there not a place for me?

2 Hark! what sounds mine ear receiveth,
  Sweet as songs of seraphim!
 "He that in the Lord believeth
  Life eternal hath in Him."
 At the outer door why staying?
  Nothing, soul! hast thou to pay:
 Christ in love to thee is saying,
  "Weary child come in to-day."
                Rev.-S. Medley (1738—1799).

LOVE TO CHRIST.

CALVARY. L. M. Rev. R. P. Kerr, D. D., 1890.

By per. of J. M. Russell.

444 *Not Ashamed of Christ.*

1 Jesus, and shall it ever be,
A mortal man ashamed of Thee?
Ashamed of Thee, whom angels praise,
Whose glories shine through endless days

2 Ashamed of Jesus! Sooner far
Let evening blush to own a star;
He sheds the beams of light divine,
O'er this benighted soul of mine.

3 Ashamed of Jesus! Just as soon
Let midnight be ashamed of noon;
'Tis midnight with my soul, till He,
Bright Morning Star, bid darkness flee.

4 Ashamed of Jesus! that dear Friend
On whom my hopes of heaven depend!
No, when I blush, be this my shame,
That I no more revere His name.

5 Ashamed of Jesus! Yes, I may,
When I've no guilt to wash away,
No tear to wipe, no good to crave,
No fears to quell, no soul to save.

6 Till then — nor is my boasting vain—
Till then, I boast a Saviour slain:
And oh, may this my glory be,
That Christ is not ashamed of me.

Rev. Joseph Grigg (—1768).

445 *Crucifixion by the Cross.*

1 When I survey the wondrous cross,
On which the Prince of glory died,
My richest gain I count but loss,
And pour contempt on all my pride.

2 Forbid it, Lord, that I should boast,
Save in the death of Christ, my God;
All the vain things that charm me most,
I sacrifice them to His blood.

3 See, from His head, His hands, His feet,
Sorrow and love flow mingled down;
Did e'er such love and sorrow meet,
Or thorns compose so rich a crown?

4 His dying crimson, like a robe,
Spreads o'er His body on the tree;
Then am I dead to all the globe,
And all the globe is dead to me.

5 Were the whole realm of nature mine,
That were a present far too small;
Love so amazing, so divine,
Demands my soul, my life, my all.

Rev. Isaac Watts (1674—1748).

LOVE TO CHRIST.

I HEAR THY WELCOME VOICE. S. M.   Lewis Hartsough.

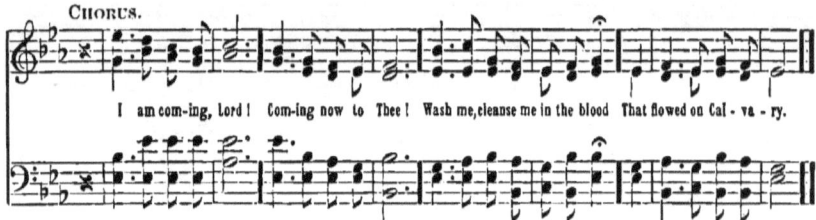

446   *Thy Face will I Seek.*

1 I hear Thy welcome voice,
   That calls me, Lord, to Thee;
For cleansing in Thy precious blood,
   That flowed on Calvary.

2 Though coming weak and vile,
   Thou dost my strength assure;
Thou dost my vileness fully cleanse,
   Till spotless all, and pure.

3 'T is Jesus calls me on
   To perfect faith and love,
To perfect hope, and peace, and trust,
   For earth and heaven above.

4 'T is Jesus who confirms
   The blessed work within,
By adding grace to welcomed grace,
   Where reigned the power of sin.

5 And He the witness gives
   To loyal hearts and free,
That every promise is fulfilled,
   If faith but brings the plea.

6 All hail! atoning blood!
   All hail! redeeming grace!
All hail! the gift of Christ, our Lord,
   Our Strength and Righteousness.
                Lewis Hartsough.

447   *Giving Ourselves Away.*
      Tune, Saviour.

1 Oh, sweetly breathe the lyres above,
   When angels touch the quivering string,
And wake, to chant Immanuel's love,
   Such strains as angel-lips can sing.

2 And sweet on earth the choral swell,
   From mortal tongues, of gladsome lays,
When pardoned souls their raptures tell,
   And, grateful, hymn Immanuel's praise.

3 Jesus, Thy name our souls adore;
   We own the bond that makes us Thine;
And carnal joys, that charmed before,
   For Thy dear sake we now resign.

4 Our hearts, by dying love subdued,
   Accept Thine offered grace to-day;
Beneath the cross, with blood bedewed,
   We bow and give ourselves away.

5 In Thee we trust, on Thee rely;
   Though we are feeble, Thou art strong;
Oh, keep us till our spirits fly
   To join the bright, immortal throng.
           Rev. Ray Palmer (1808—1887).

LOVE TO CHRIST.

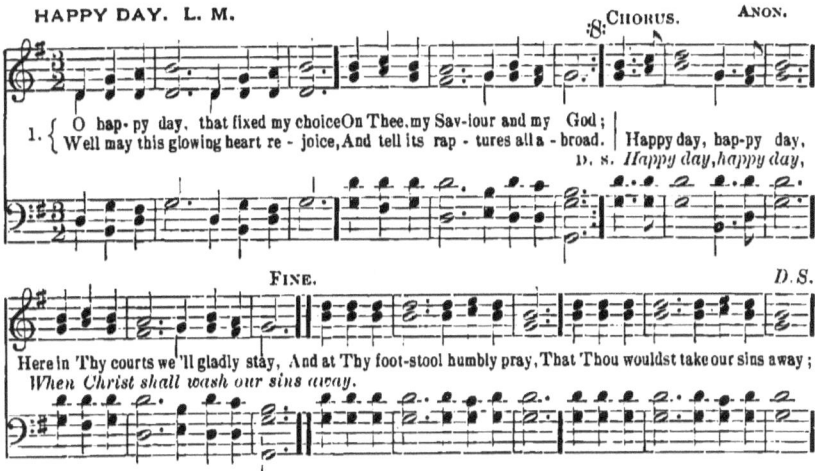

448 *Union with the Church.*

1 O happy day, that fixed my choice
 On Thee, my Saviour and my God;
Well may this glowing heart rejoice,
 And tell its raptures all abroad.

2 O happy bond, that seals my vows
 To Him, who merits all my love!
Let cheerful anthems fill His house,
 While to that sacred shrine I move.

3 'T is done! — the great transaction 's done;
 I am my Lord's, and He is mine!
He drew me, and I follow'd on,
 Charmed to confess the voice divine.

4 Now rest, my long-divided heart,
 Fixed on this blissful centre, rest;
With ashes who would grudge to part,
 When called on angel's bread to feast?

5 High heaven, that heard the solemn vow,
 That vow renew'd shall daily hear;
Till in life's latest hour I bow,
 And bless in death a bond so dear.
 Rev. Philip Doddridge (1702—1751).

LOVE TO CHRIST.

HENDON. 7s. Rev. C. MALAN (1787—1864).

449 *Jesus Christ, the Crucified.*

1 Ask ye what great thing I know
That delights and stirs me so?
What the high reward I win?
Whose the name I glory in?
Jesus Christ, the crucified.

2 What is faith's foundation strong?
What awakes my lips to song?
He who bore my sinful load,
Purchased for me peace with God,
Jesus Christ, the crucified.

3 Who defeats my fiercest foes?
Who consoles my saddest woes?
Who revives my fainting heart,
Healing all its hidden smart?
Jesus Christ, the crucified.

4 Who is life in life to me?
Who the death of death will be?
Who will place me on His right
With the countless hosts of light?
Jesus Christ, the crucified.

5 This is that great thing I know;
This delights and stirs me so;
Faith in Him, who died to save,
Him who triumphed o'er the grave,
Jesus Christ, the crucified.

Rev. B. H. Kennedy.

EVAN. C. M. Rev. W. H. HAVERGAL (1793—1870).

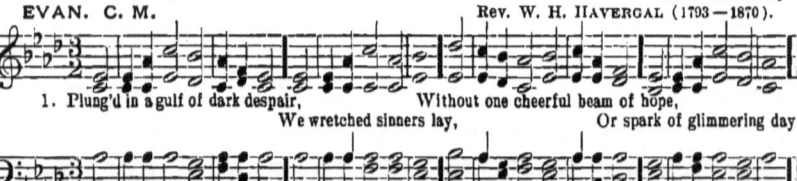

450 *Plunged in a Gulf.*

1 Plunged in a gulf of dark despair,
We wretched sinners lay,
Without one cheerful beam of hope,
Or spark of glimmering day.

2 With pitying eyes the Prince of grace
Beheld our helpless grief;
He saw,—and oh, amazing love!—
He ran to our relief.

3 Down from the shining seats above,
With joyful haste He fled,
Entered the grave in mortal flesh,
And dwelt among the dead.

4 Oh, for this love let rocks and hills
Their lasting silence break;
And all harmonious human tongues
The Saviour's praises speak.

5 Angels, assist our mighty joys;
Strike all your harps of gold;
But when you raise your highest notes,
His love can ne'er be told.

Rev. Isaac Watts (1674—1748).

LOVE TO CHRIST.

GREENVILLE. 8s & 7s, D.   J. J. ROUSSEAU (1712 — 1778).

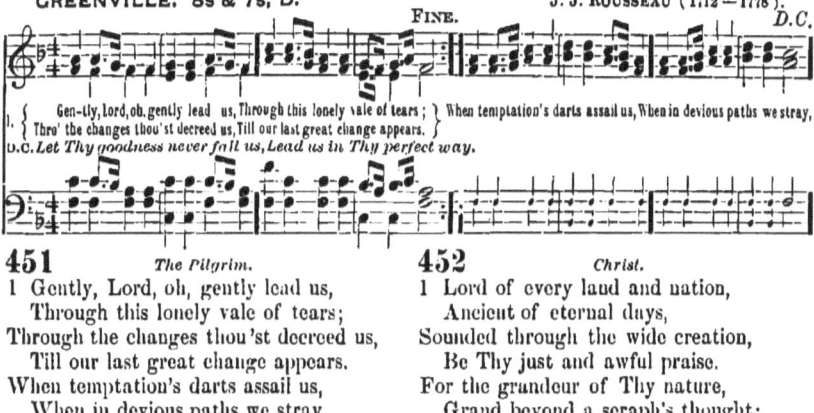

451   *The Pilgrim.*

1 Gently, Lord, oh, gently lead us,
Through this lonely vale of tears;
Through the changes thou'st decreed us,
Till our last great change appears.
When temptation's darts assail us,
When in devious paths we stray,
Let Thy goodness never fail us,
Lead us in Thy perfect way.

2 In the hour of pain and anguish,
In the hour when death draws near,
Suffer not our hearts to languish,
Suffer not our souls to fear.
And when mortal life is ended,
Bid us in Thine arms to rest,
Till by angel bands attended,
We awake among the blest.
Dr. T. Hastings (1784—1872).

452   *Christ.*

1 Lord of every land and nation,
Ancient of eternal days,
Sounded through the wide creation,
Be Thy just and awful praise.
For the grandeur of Thy nature,
Grand beyond a seraph's thought;
For created works of power,
Works with skill and kindness wrought.

2 For Thy providence, that governs
Through Thine empire's wide domain;
Wings an angel, guides a sparrow;
Blessed be Thy gentle reign.
Brightness of the Father's glory,
Shall Thy praise unuttered lie?
Fly, my tongue, such guilty silence;
Sing, the Lord, who came to die.
Robinson.

BRADEN. S. M.   WILLIAM BATCHELDER BRADBURY (1816 — 1868).

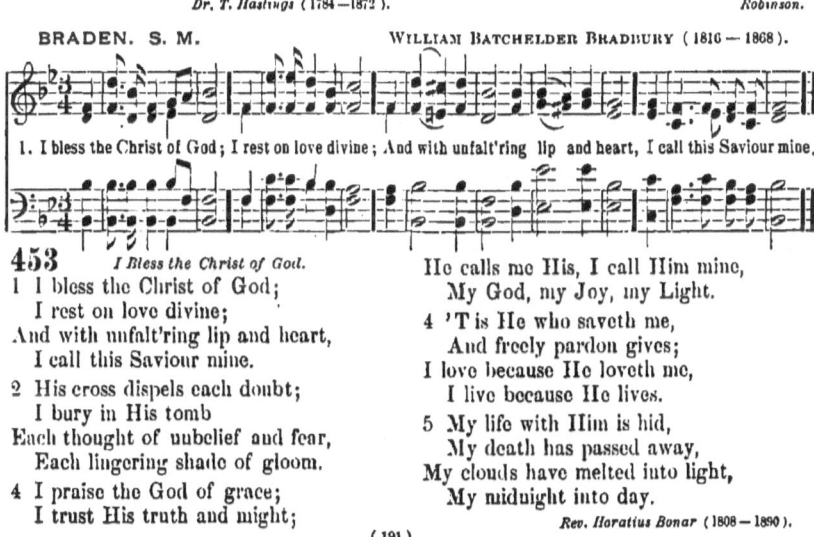

453   *I Bless the Christ of God.*

1 I bless the Christ of God;
I rest on love divine;
And with unfalt'ring lip and heart,
I call this Saviour mine.

2 His cross dispels each doubt;
I bury in His tomb
Each thought of unbelief and fear,
Each lingering shade of gloom.

4 I praise the God of grace;
I trust His truth and might;

He calls me His, I call Him mine,
My God, my Joy, my Light.

4 'T is He who saveth me,
And freely pardon gives;
I love because He loveth me,
I live because He lives.

5 My life with Him is hid,
My death has passed away,
My clouds have melted into light,
My midnight into day.
Rev. Horatius Bonar (1808—1890).

(191)

LOVE TO CHRIST.

INNOCENTS. 7s. The Parish Choir, 1851.

1. Jesus! name of wondrous love! Name, all other names above! Unto which must ev-'ry knee Bow in deep hu-mil-i-ty.

454 *Thou Shalt Call His Name, Jesus.*

1 Jesus! name of wondrous love!
Name, all other names above!
Unto which must every knee
Bow in deep humility.

2 Jesus! name of priceless worth
To the fallen sons of earth,
For the promise that it gave —
"Jesus shall His people save."

3 Jesus! name of mercy mild,
Given to the Holy Child,

When the cup of human woe
First He tasted here below.

4 Jesus! only name that's given
Under all the mighty heaven,
Whereby man, to sin enslaved,
Bursts his fetters, and is saved.

5 Jesus! name of wondrous love!
Human name of God above!
Pleading only this, we flee,
Helpless, O our God, to Thee.

Bp. W. W. How.

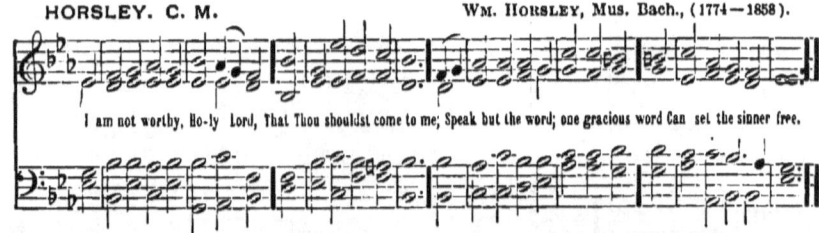

HORSLEY. C. M. WM. HORSLEY, Mus. Bach., (1774—1858).

I am not worthy, Ho-ly Lord, That Thou shouldst come to me; Speak but the word; one gracious word Can set the sinner free.

455 *Lord, I am not worthy that Thou shouldest come under my roof.*

1 I am not worthy, Holy Lord,
That Thou shouldst come to me;
Speak but the word; one gracious word
Can set the sinner free.

2 I am not worthy; cold and bare
The lodging of my soul;
How canst Thou deign to enter there?
Lord, speak, and make me whole.

3 I am not worthy; yet, my God,
How can I say Thee nay;
Thee, who didst give Thy flesh and blood
My ransom-price to pay?

4 O come! in this sweet morning hour
Feed me with food divine;
And fill with all Thy love and power
This worthless heart of mine.

Sir H. W. Baker (1821—1877).

(192)

LOVE TO CHRIST.

HEBER. C. M.   GEO. KINGSLEY (1811–1884).

1. Jesus, I love Thy charming name, 'Tis music to mine ear; Fain would I sound it out so loud, That earth and heaven should hear.

456   *Christ the Object of Love.*

1 Jesus, I love Thy charming name,
'Tis music to mine ear;
Fain would I sound it out so loud,
That earth and heaven should hear.

2 Yes, Thou art precious to my soul,
My joy, my hope, my trust;
Jewels, to Thee, are gaudy toys,
And gold is sordid dust.

3 All my capacious powers can wish,
In Thee most richly meet;
Nor to mine eyes is light so dear,
Nor friendship half so sweet.

4 Thy grace still dwells upon my heart,
And sheds its fragrance there;
The noblest balm of all its wounds,
The cordial of its care.

5 I'll speak the honors of Thy name,
With my last laboring breath;
Then speechless clasp Thee in mine arms,
The antidote of death.
                 Rev. P. Doddridge (1702–1751).

457   *Love to Christ.*

1 Do not I love Thee, O my Lord?
Behold my heart, and see;
And turn each hateful rival out,
That dares to rival Thee.

2 Do not I love Thee, from my soul?
Then let me nothing love;

Dead be my heart to every joy
Which Thou dost not approve.

3 Hast Thou a lamb in all Thy flock,
I would disdain to feed?
Hast Thou a foe, before whose face
I fear Thy cause to plead?

4 Thou knowest I love Thee, dearest Lord,
But oh, I long to soar,
Far from the sphere of mortal joys,
That I may love Thee more.
                 Rev. P. Doddridge (1702–1751).

458   *Joy in Christ.*

1 Jesus, the very thought of Thee
With gladness fills my breast;
But dearer far Thy face to see,
And in Thy presence rest.

2 Nor voice can sing, nor heart can frame,
Nor can the memory find
A sweeter sound than Thy blest name,
O Saviour of mankind!

3 O hope of every contrite heart,
O joy of all the meek,
To those who fall, how kind Thou art,
How good to those who seek!

4 And they who find Thee, find a bliss
Nor tongue nor pen can show;
The love of Jesus!— what it is,
None but His loved ones know.
             Bernard of Clairvaux (1091–1153).
        Tr. by Rev. Edward Caswall (1814–1878).

LOVE TO CHRIST.

NAZARETH. L. M. 6l.   Rev. CÆSAR MALAN (1787—1864).

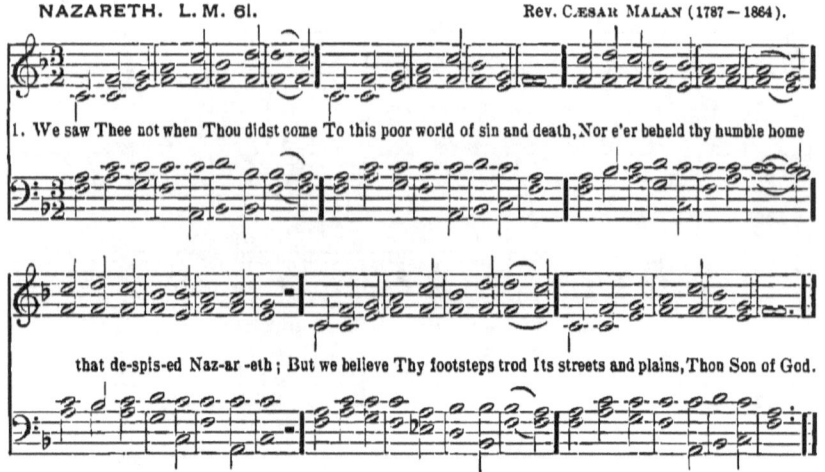

1. We saw Thee not when Thou didst come To this poor world of sin and death, Nor e'er beheld thy humble home that de-spis-ed Naz-ar-eth; But we believe Thy footsteps trod Its streets and plains, Thou Son of God.

459   *Blessed are They.*

1 We saw Thee not when Thou didst come
To this poor world of sin and death,
Nor e'er beheld Thy humble home
In that despiséd Nazareth;
But we believe Thy footsteps trod
Its streets and plains, Thou Son of God.

2 We did not see Thee lifted high
When foes were many, friends were few,
Nor heard Thy meek, imploring cry,
"Forgive, they know not what they do:"
Yet we believe the deed was done,
Which shook the earth and veiled the sun.

3 We stood not by the empty tomb
Where once Thy sacred body lay,
Nor sat within that upper room,
Nor met Thee in the open way;

But we believe that angels said,
"Why seek the living with the dead?"

4 We did not mark the chosen few,
When Thou didst through the clouds ascend,
First lift to heaven their wondering view,
Then to the earth all prostrate bend;
Yet we believe that mortal eyes
Beheld that journey to the skies.

5 And now that Thou dost reign on high,
And thence Thy waiting people bless,
No ray of glory from the sky
Doth shine upon our wilderness;
But we believe Thy faithful word,
And trust in our redeeming Lord.

J. H. Guerney.

POTSDAM. S. M.   Adapted from JOHANN SEBASTIAN BACH.

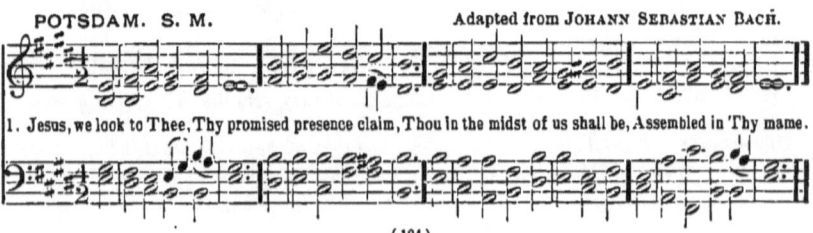

1. Jesus, we look to Thee, Thy promised presence claim, Thou in the midst of us shall be, Assembled in Thy name.

LOVE TO CHRIST.

STOCKWELL. 8s & 7s.   D. E. JONES (1815—1881).

1. Jesus only, when the morning Beams upon the path I tread; Jesus only, when the darkness Gathers round my weary head.

460
Jesus only.

1 Jesus only, when the morning
  Beams upon the path I tread;
Jesus only, when the darkness
  Gathers round my weary head.

2 Jesus only, when the billows
  Cold and sullen o'er me roll!
Jesus only, when the trumpet
  Rends the tomb and wakes the soul.

3 Jesus only, when adoring
  Saints their crowns before Him bring;
Jesus only, I will, joyous,
  Through eternal ages sing.
       Rev. Elias Nason (1811—).

461
Christ in the Midst.
Tune, POTSDAM.

1 Jesus, we look to Thee,
  Thy promised presence claim;
Thou in the midst of us shall be,
  Assembled in Thy name.

2 Thy name salvation is,
  Which here we come to prove;
Thy name is life, and health, and peace,
  And everlasting love.

3 Present we know Thou art,
  But, oh! Thyself reveal;
Now, Lord, let every longing heart
  The mighty comfort feel.

4 Oh, may Thy quickening voice
  The death of sin remove;
And bid our inmost souls rejoice,
  In hope of perfect love!
       Rev. Chas. Wesley (1708—1788).

462
Light of the World.

1 Light of those whose dreary dwelling
  Borders on the shades of death,
Come, and by Thy love revealing,
  Dissipate the clouds beneath.

2 The new heaven and earth's Creator,
  In our deepest darkness rise,
Scattering all the night of nature,
  Pouring eyesight on our eyes.

3 Still we wait for Thine appearing;
  Life and joy Thy beams impart,
Chasing all our fears, and cheering
  Every poor benighted heart.

4 Come, and manifest the favor
  God hath for our ransomed race;
Come, Thou glorious God and Saviour,
  Come, and bring the gospel-grace.
       Rev. Chas. Wesley (1708—1788).

463
We are Watching.

1 We are watching, we are waiting,
  For the bright prophetic day;
When the shadows, weary shadows,
  From the world shall roll away.

2 We are watching, we are waiting,
  For the star that brings the day;
When the night of sin shall vanish,
  And the shadows melt away.

3 We are watching, we are waiting,
  For the beauteous King of day;
For the Chiefest of ten-thousand,
  For the Light, the Truth, the Way.
       W. O. Cushing.

LOVE TO CHRIST.

SUNSET. 6s & 4s. KATE MACKINTOSH.

1. Fade, fade, each earthly joy; Jesus is mine. Break ev-'ry tender tie; Jesus is mine.
Dark is the wilderness, Earth has no resting-place, Jesus a-lone can bless; Jesus is mine.

464 *Jesus is Mine.*

1 Fade, fade, each earthly joy;
   Jesus is mine.
Break, every tender tie;
   Jesus is mine.
Dark is the wilderness,
Earth has no resting-place,
Jesus alone can bless;
   Jesus is mine.

2 Tempt not my soul away;
   Jesus is mine.
Here would I ever stay;
   Jesus is mine.
Perishing things of clay,
Born but for one brief day,
Pass from my heart away;
   Jesus is mine.

3 Farewell, ye dreams of night;
   Jesus is mine.
Lost in this dawning bright,
   Jesus is mine.
All that my soul has tried,
Left but a dismal void;
Jesus has satisfied;
   Jesus is mine.

4 Farewell, mortality;
   Jesus is mine.
Welcome, eternity;
   Jesus is mine.
Welcome, O loved and blest,
Welcome, sweet scenes of rest,
Welcome, my Saviour's breast;
   Jesus is mine.
                Mrs. Horatius Bonar (1808 —).

MORE LOVE. 6s & 4s. T. E. PERKINS.

1. { More love to Thee, O Christ! More love to Thee!
     Hear Thou the pray'r I make, (*Omit.*) On bended knee; This is my earnest plea,
D.C. More love, O Christ, to Thee, (*Omit.*) More love to Thee! More love, O Christ! to Thee,

By per. of T. E. Perkins owner of copyright.

(196)

LOVE TO CHRIST.

465 *More Love to Thee.*

1 More love to Thee, O Christ!
   More love to Thee!
   Hear Thou the prayer I make
   On bended knee;
   This is my earnest plea:
   More love, O Christ! to Thee,
   More love to Thee!

2 Once earthly joy I craved,
   Sought peace and rest;
   Now Thee alone I seek —
   Give what is best;
   This all my prayer shall be:
   More love, O Christ! to Thee,
   More love to Thee!

3 Let sorrow do its work,
   Send grief and pain;
   Sweet are Thy messengers,
   Sweet their refrain,
   When they can sing with me,
   More love, O Christ! to Thee,
   More love to Thee!

4 Then shall my latest breath
   Whisper Thy praise;
   This be the parting cry
   My heart shall raise,
   This still its prayer shall be:
   More love, O Christ! to Thee,
   More love to Thee!

   Mrs. Eliz. P. Prentiss (1819 — 1878).

466 *I Follow Thee.*

1 Saviour! I follow on,
   Guided by Thee,
   Seeing not yet the hand
   That leadeth me;

   Hushed be my heart, and still,
   Fear I no further ill,
   Only to meet Thy will
   My will shall be.

2 Riven the rock for me,
   Thirst to relieve,
   Manna from heaven falls
   Fresh every eve;
   Never a want severe
   Causeth my eye a tear,
   But Thou art whispering near:
   "Only believe."

3 Often to Marah's brink
   Have I been brought;
   Shrinking the cup to drink,
   Help I have sought;
   And with the prayer's ascent
   Jesus the branch has rent;
   Quickly relief He sent,
   Sweetening the draught.

4 Saviour! I long to walk
   Closer with Thee;
   Led by Thy guiding hand,
   Ever to be
   Constantly near Thy side,
   Quickened and purified,
   Living for Him who died
   Freely for me!

   Rev. C. S. Robinson, D. D. (1829 —).

467 *Doxology.*

Praise God, from whom all blessings flow;
Praise Him, all creatures here below;
Praise Him above, ye heavenly host;
Praise Father, Son, and Holy Ghost.

LOVE TO CHRIST.

THEODORA. 7s.   GEORGE F. HANDEL (1685—1759).

1. Ev-er-last-ing arms of love Are be-neath, a-round, a-bove;
He who left His throne of light, And un-num-bered an-gels bright.

468   *The Everlasting Arms.*

1 Everlasting arms of love
Are beneath, around, above;
He who left His throne of light,
And unnumbered angels bright; —

2 He who on the accursèd tree
Gave His precious life for me;
He it is that bears me on;
His the arm I lean upon.

3 All things hasten to decay,
Earth and sea will pass away;
Soon will yonder circling sun
Cease His blazing course to run.

4 Scenes will vary, friends grow strange,
But the Changeless cannot change;
Gladly will I journey on,
With His arm to lean upon.

Anon.

469   *Doxology.*

Sing we to our God above
Praise eternal as His love;
Praise Him, all ye heavenly host —
Father, Son, and Holy Ghost.

ST. AËLRED. 8s & 3s.   Rev. J. B. DYKES (1823—1876).

1. Fierce raged the tempest o'er the deep, Watch did Thine anxious servants keep, But Thou wast wrapped in guileless sleep, Calm and still.

470   *Peace, be Still.*

1 Fierce raged the tempest o'er the deep,
Watch did Thine anxious servants keep,
But Thou wast wrapped in guileless sleep,
   Calm and still.

2 "Save, Lord, we perish," was their cry,
"Oh, save us in our agony!"
Thy word above the storm rose high
   "Peace, be still."

3 The wild winds hushed; the angry deep
Sank, like a little child, to sleep;
The sullen billows ceased to leap,
   At Thy will.

4 So, when our life is clouded o'er,
And storm-winds drift us from the shore,
Say, lest we sink to rise no more,
   "Peace be still."

Rev. Godfrey Thring, 1866.

LOVE TO CHRIST.

BELIEF. C. M.   ANON.

1. Jesus, my Saviour, bind me fast, In cords of heavenly love; Then sweetly draw me to Thy breast, Nor let me thence re-move.

471   *Communion with Christ.*

1 Jesus, my Saviour, bind me fast,
In cords of heavenly love;
Then sweetly draw me to Thy breast,
Nor let me thence remove.

2 Draw me from all created good,
From self, the world and sin;
To the dear fountain of Thy blood,
And make me pure within.

3 Oh, lead me to Thy mercy seat,
Attract me nearer still;
Draw me, like Mary, to Thy feet,
To sit and learn Thy will.

4 Oh, draw me by Thy providence,
Thy Spirit and Thy word,
From all the things of time and sense,
To Thee, my gracious Lord.
               Rev. C. Wesley (1708—1788).

472   *Remember Me.*

1 Jesus! Thou art the sinner's Friend;
As such I look to Thee;
Now, in the fullness of Thy love,
O Lord! remember me.

2 Remember Thy pure word of grace,—
Remember Calvary;
Remember all Thy dying groans,
And, then, remember me.

3 Thou wondrous Advocate with God!
I yield myself to Thee:
While Thou art sitting on Thy throne,
Dear Lord! remember me.

4 Lord! I am guilty, I am vile,
But Thy salvation's free;
Then, in Thine all-abounding grace,
Dear Lord! remember me.

5 And, when I close my eyes in death,
When creature-helps all flee,
Then, O my dear Redeemer-God!
I pray, remember me.
               Rev. R. Burnham (1749—1810).

LANESBORO'. C. M.   English.

1. Je-sus! Thou art the sin-ner's Friend; As such I look to Thee; Now, in the full-ness of Thy love, Now, in the full-ness of Thy love, O Lord! re-mem-ber me.

INVITATIONS.

473 *From the Cross.*

1 From the cross uplifted high,
Where the Saviour deigns to die,
What melodious sounds I hear,
Bursting on my ravished ear!
Love's redeeming work is done,
Come and welcome, sinner, come.

2 Sprinkled now with blood the throne;
Why beneath thy burdens groan?
On My piercéd body laid,
Justice owns the ransom paid;
Bow the knee and kiss the Son,
Come and welcome, sinner, come.

3 Spread for thee the festal board,
See, with richest dainties stored;
To thy Father's bosom press'd,
Yet again a child confessed,
Never from His house to roam,
Come and welcome, sinner, come.

4 Soon the days of life will end,
Lo! I come, your Saviour, Friend!
Safe your spirits to convey
To the realms of endless day;
Up to My eternal home,
Come and welcome, sinner, come.
Rev. Thomas Haweis (1732—1820).

Doxology.
Praise the name of God most high,
Praise Him, all below the sky,
Praise Him, all ye heavenly host,
Father, Son, and Holy Ghost;
As through countless ages past,
Evermore His praise shall last.
A. CROIL FALCONER.

474 *Yet There is Room.*

1 "Yet there is room!" The Lamb's bright
    hall of song,
With its fair glory, beckons thee along;
    Room, room, still room!
    Oh, enter, enter now!

2 Day is declining, and the sun is low;
The shadows lengthen, light makes haste
    to go.

3 The bridal hall is filling for the feast;
Pass in, pass in, and be the Bridegroom's
    guest

4 It fills, it fills, that hall of jubilee:
Make haste, make haste; 't is not too full for
    thee.   [the gate,

5 "Yet there is room!" Still open stands
The gate of love; it is not yet too late.

6 Pass in, pass in! The banquet is for thee;
That cup of everlasting love is free.

7 All heaven is there, all joy! Go in, go in;
The angel's beckon thee the prize to win.

8 Louder and sweeter sounds the loving
    call;
Come, lingerer, come; enter that festal hall!
Rev. Horatius Bonar (1808—1890).

INVITATIONS.

ST. CRISPIN. L. M.   Sir GEORGE JOB ELVEY (1816—).

Just as thou art, with-out one trace Of love, or joy, or in-ward grace,
Or meet-ness for the heaven-ly place, O guilt-y sin-ner, come, O come.

475   *Just as Thou Art.*

1 Just as thou art, without one trace
Of love, or joy, or inward grace,
Or meetness for the heavenly place,
O guilty sinner, come, O come.

2 Thy sins I bore on Calvary's tree;
The stripes, thy due, were laid on Me,
That peace and pardon might be free;
O wretched sinner, come, O come.

3 Come, leave thy burden at the cross,
Count all thy gains but empty dross:
My grace repays all earthly loss;
O needy sinner, come, O come.
      Rev. Russell Sturgis Cook (1814—1864).

476   *Psalm 88.*

1 While life prolongs its precious light,
Mercy is found and peace is given;
But soon, ah, soon ! approaching night,
Shall blot out every hope of heaven.

2 While God invites, how blest the day!
How sweet the gospel's charming sound!
Come, sinners, haste, oh, haste away,
While yet a pardoning God he's found.

3 Soon borne on time's most rapid wing,
Shall death command you to the grave·
Before his bar your spirits bring,
And none be found to hear, or save.

4 In that lone land of deep despair,
No Sabbath's heavenly light shall rise;
No God regard your bitter prayer,
Nor Saviour call you to the skies.
      Rev. Isaac Watts (1674—1748).

477   *Invitation to the Heavy-laden.*

1 Come hither, all ye weary souls,
Ye heavy-laden sinners come;
I'll give you rest from all your toils,
And raise you to my heavenly home.

2 They shall find rest that learn of Me;
I'm of a meek and lowly mind;
But passion rages like the sea,
And pride is restless as the wind.

3 Blest is the man whose shoulders take
My yoke, and bear it with delight;
My yoke is easy to his neck,
My grace shall make the burden light.

4 Jesus, we come at Thy command,
With faith, and hope, and humble zeal;
Resign our spirits to Thy hand,
To mould and guide us at Thy will.
      Rev. Isaac Watts (1674—1748).

478   *All Things are Now Ready.*

1 Come, weary souls, with sin distrest,
Come, and accept the promised rest;
The Saviour's gracious call obey,
And cast your gloomy fears away.

2 Oppressed with guilt, a painful load,
Oh, come and bow before your God!
Divine compassion, mighty love,
Will all that painful load remove.

3 Here mercy's boundless ocean flows
To cleanse your guilt and heal your woes;
Pardon, and life, and endless peace;
How rich the gift, how free the grace!

4 Lord, we accept, with thankful heart,
The hope Thy gracious words impart;
We come with trembling, yet rejoice,
And bless the kind inviting voice.
      Miss Anne Steele (1717—1778).

INVITATIONS.

SCOTLAND. 12s.   JOHN CLARKE (1770—1818).

479
Glory to God.

1 The voice of free grace cries, "Escape to the mountain;
For Adam's lost race Christ hath opened a fountain:
For sin and uncleanness and every transgression,
His blood flows most freely in streams of salvation."
    Hallelujah to the Lamb, who has purchased our pardon!
    We will praise Him again when we pass over Jordan,
    We will praise Him again when we pass over Jordan.

2 Now glory to God in the highest is given;
Now glory to God is re-echoed in heaven;
Around the whole earth let us tell the glad story,
And sing of His love, His salvation and glory.
    Hallelujah to the Lamb, etc.

3 O Jesus, ride on,— Thy kingdom is glorious;
O'er sin, death, and hell Thou wilt make us victorious;
Thy name shall be praised in the great congregation,
And saints shall ascribe unto Thee their salvation.
    Hallelujah to the Lamb, etc.

4 When on Zion we stand, having gained the blest shore,
With our harps in our hands, we will praise evermore;
We'll range the blest fields on the banks of the river,
And sing of redemption forever and ever.
    Hallelujah to the Lamb, etc.

Rev. Richard Burdsall (1735—1824).

INVITATIONS.

SALVATION. C. M. D.   Old American Tune.

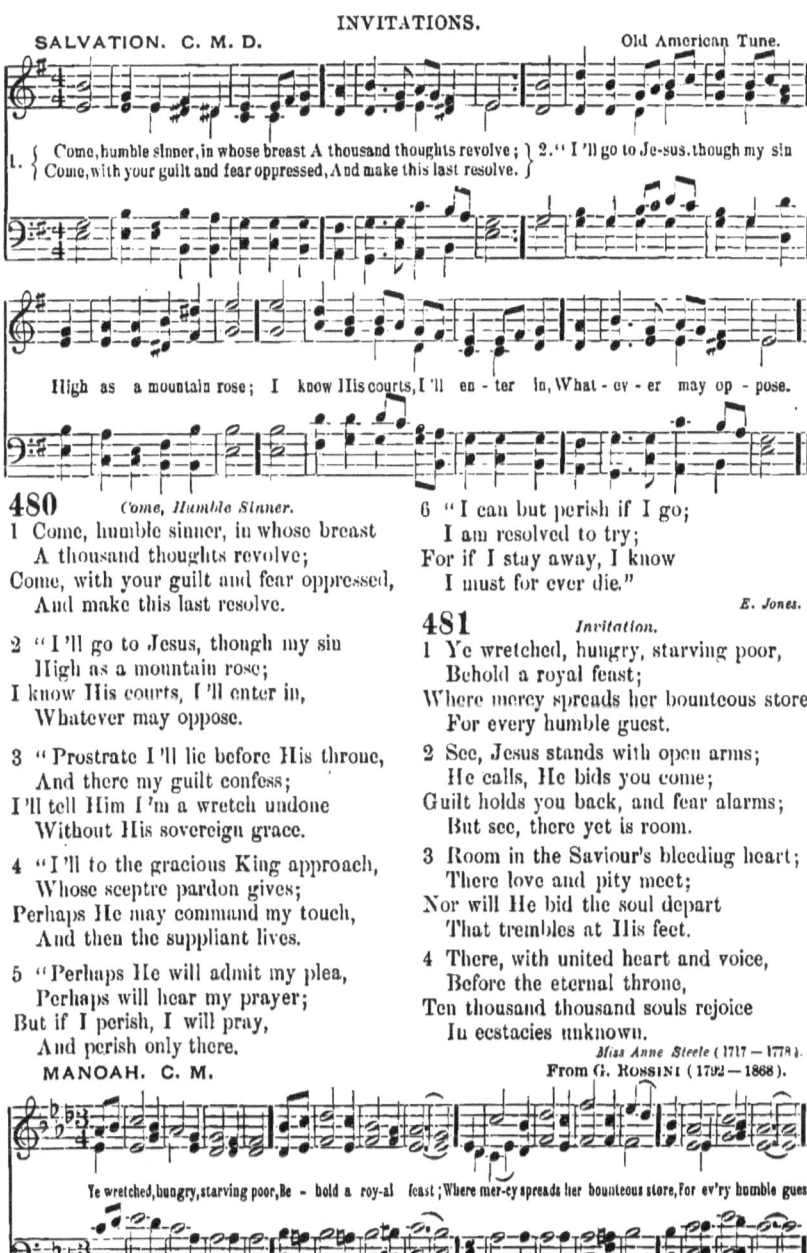

1. Come, humble sinner, in whose breast A thousand thoughts revolve;
Come, with your guilt and fear oppressed, And make this last resolve.
2. "I'll go to Jesus, though my sin High as a mountain rose; I know His courts, I'll enter in, Whatever may oppose.

480   *Come, Humble Sinner.*

1 Come, humble sinner, in whose breast
   A thousand thoughts revolve;
Come, with your guilt and fear oppressed,
   And make this last resolve.

2 "I'll go to Jesus, though my sin
   High as a mountain rose;
I know His courts, I'll enter in,
   Whatever may oppose.

3 "Prostrate I'll lie before His throne,
   And there my guilt confess;
I'll tell Him I'm a wretch undone
   Without His sovereign grace.

4 "I'll to the gracious King approach,
   Whose sceptre pardon gives;
Perhaps He may command my touch,
   And then the suppliant lives.

5 "Perhaps He will admit my plea,
   Perhaps will hear my prayer;
But if I perish, I will pray,
   And perish only there.

6 "I can but perish if I go;
   I am resolved to try;
For if I stay away, I know
   I must for ever die."
                           E. Jones.

481   *Invitation.*

1 Ye wretched, hungry, starving poor,
   Behold a royal feast;
Where mercy spreads her bounteous store,
   For every humble guest.

2 See, Jesus stands with open arms;
   He calls, He bids you come;
Guilt holds you back, and fear alarms;
   But see, there yet is room.

3 Room in the Saviour's bleeding heart;
   There love and pity meet;
Nor will He bid the soul depart
   That trembles at His feet.

4 There, with united heart and voice,
   Before the eternal throne,
Ten thousand thousand souls rejoice
   In ecstacies unknown.
                    Miss Anne Steele (1717–1778).

MANOAH. C. M.   From G. ROSSINI (1792–1868).

Ye wretched, hungry, starving poor, Behold a royal feast; Where mercy spreads her bounteous store, For ev'ry humble guest.

INVITATIONS.

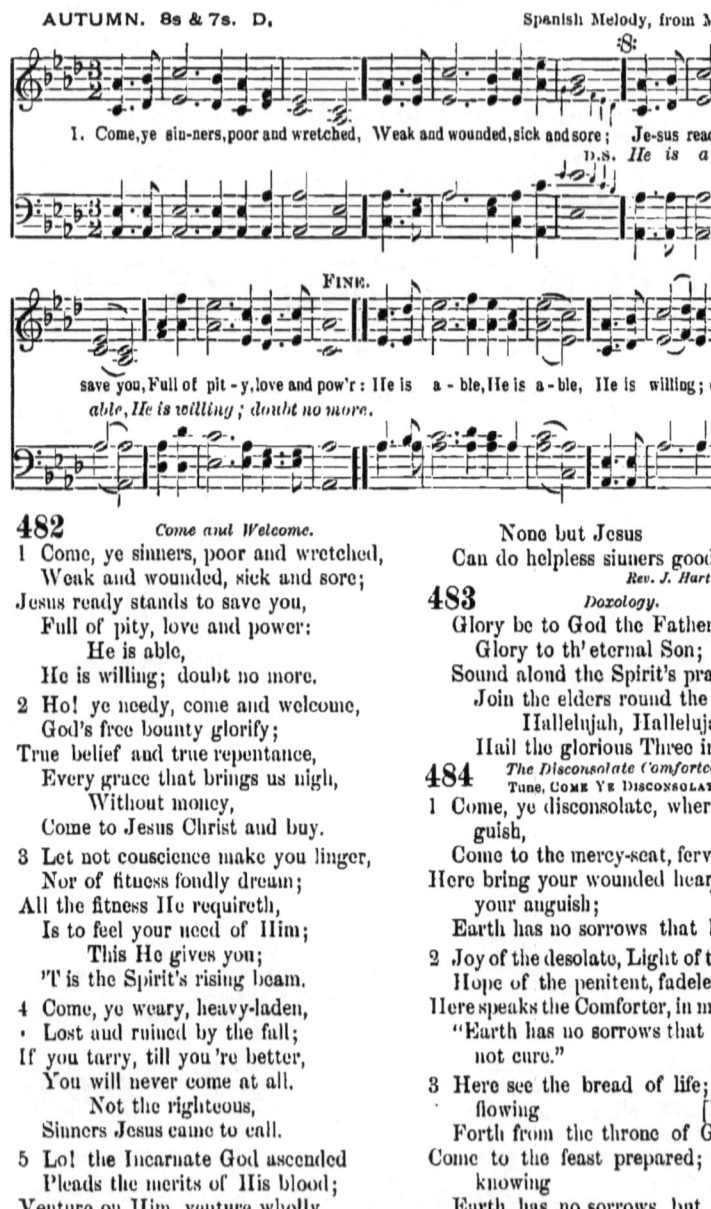

482 *Come and Welcome.*

1 Come, ye sinners, poor and wretched,
  Weak and wounded, sick and sore;
Jesus ready stands to save you,
  Full of pity, love and power:
    He is able,
  He is willing; doubt no more.

2 Ho! ye needy, come and welcome,
    God's free bounty glorify;
  True belief and true repentance,
    Every grace that brings us nigh,
      Without money,
    Come to Jesus Christ and buy.

3 Let not conscience make you linger,
    Nor of fitness fondly dream;
  All the fitness He requireth,
    Is to feel your need of Him;
      This He gives you;
    'T is the Spirit's rising beam.

4 Come, ye weary, heavy-laden,
    Lost and ruined by the fall;
  If you tarry, till you're better,
    You will never come at all.
      Not the righteous,
    Sinners Jesus came to call.

5 Lo! the Incarnate God ascended
    Pleads the merits of His blood;
  Venture on Him, venture wholly,
    Let no other trust intrude;

None but Jesus
  Can do helpless sinners good.
    Rev. J. Hart (1712—1768).

483 *Doxology.*
  Glory be to God the Father,
    Glory to th' eternal Son;
  Sound aloud the Spirit's praises;
    Join the elders round the throne;
      Hallelujah, Hallelujah,
    Hail the glorious Three in One.

484 *The Disconsolate Comforted.*
  Tune, COME YE DISCONSOLATE.

1 Come, ye disconsolate, where'er ye languish,
  Come to the mercy-seat, fervently kneel;
  Here bring your wounded hearts, here tell
    your anguish;   [not heal.
  Earth has no sorrows that heaven can-

2 Joy of the desolate, Light of the straying,
  Hope of the penitent, fadeless and pure,
  Here speaks the Comforter, in mercy saying,
    "Earth has no sorrows that heaven cannot cure."

3 Here is the bread of life; see waters
    flowing   [less in love;
  Forth from the throne of God, bound-
  Come to the feast prepared; come, ever
    knowing   [remove.
  Earth has no sorrows, but heaven can
    Thomas Moore (1779—1852).
    Thomas Hastings (1784—1872).

(204)

INVITATIONS.

485 *Matt. 11: 28.*

1 "Come unto Me, ye weary,
　And I will give you rest."
Oh, blessèd voice of Jesus,
　Which comes to hearts opprest;
It tells of benediction,
　Of pardon, grace, and peace,
Of joy that hath no ending,
　Of love which cannot cease.

2 "Come unto Me, ye fainting,
　And I will give you life."
Oh, peaceful voice of Jesus,
　Which comes to end our strife;
The foe is stern and eager,
　The fight is fierce and long;
But Thou hast made me mighty,
　And stronger than the strong.

3 "And whosoever cometh
　I will not cast Him out."
Oh, patient love of Jesus,
　Which drives away our doubt;
Which calls us,— very sinners,
　Unworthy though we be
Of love so free and boundless,—
　To come, dear Lord, to Thee.
　　　　　　　　　W. C. Dix (1837—).

INVITATIONS.

MORNINGTON. S. M. GARRET COLLEY WELLESLEY (1735—1781).
Arr. by LOWELL MASON (1792—1872).

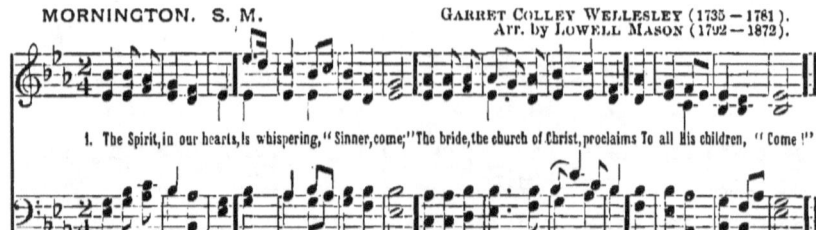

1. The Spirit, in our hearts, is whispering, "Sinner, come;" The bride, the church of Christ, proclaims To all His children, "Come!"

486 *The Gospel Call.*
1 The Spirit, in our hearts,
  Is whispering, " Sinner, come,"
The bride, the church of Christ proclaims;
  To all His children, " Come!"

2 Let him that heareth say
  To all about him, " Come,"
Let him that thirsts for righteousness
  To Christ, the Fountain, come!

3 Yes, whosoever will,
  Oh, let him freely come,
And freely drink the stream of life;
  'T is Jesus bids him come!

4 Lo! Jesus, who invites,
  Declares, " I quickly come;"
Lord, even so; we wait Thine hour;
  O blest Redeemer, come!
  Bp. H. U. Onderdonk (1789—1858).

487 *Burdens Cast on God.*
1 How gentle God's commands!
  How kind His precepts are!
" Come, cast your burdens on the Lord,
  And trust His constant care."

2 While Providence supports,
  Let saints securely dwell;
That hand which bears all nature up,
  Shall guide His children well.

3 Why should this anxious load
  Press down your weary mind?
Haste to your heavenly Father's throne,
  And sweet refreshment find.

4 His goodness stands approved,
  Down to the present day;
I'll drop my burden at His feet,
  And bear His song away.
  Rev. P. Doddridge D. D. (1702—1751).

STATE STREET. S. M. J. C. WOODMAN, 1813.

1. Now is the accepted time, Now is the day of grace; O sinners! come, without delay, And seek the Saviour's face.

488 *The Accepted Time.*
1 Now is the accepted time,
  Now is the day of grace;
O sinners! come, without delay,
  And seek the Saviour's face.

2 Now is the accepted time,
  The Saviour calls to-day;
To-morrow it may be too late; —
  Then why should you delay?

3 Now is the accepted time;
  The gospel bids you come;
And every promise in His word
  Declares there yet is room.

4 Lord, draw reluctant souls,
  And feast them with Thy love;
Then will the angels spread their wings,
  And bear the news above.
  John Dobell (1757—1840).

INVITATIONS.

ZEPHYR. L. M.   WILLIAM BATCHELDER BRADBURY (1816—1868).

1. Be-hold, a strang-er at the door: He gen-tly knocks, has knock'd be-fore, Has wait-ed long, is wait-ing still; You treat no oth-er friend so ill.

489   *Christ Knocking at the Door.*
1 Behold, a stranger at the door:
   He gently knocks, has knocked before;
Has waited long, is waiting still;
   You treat no other friend so ill.

2 But will He prove a friend indeed?
   He will, the very friend you need;
The friend of sinners, yes, 'tis He,
   With garments dyed on Calvary.

3 O lovely attitude! He stands
   With melting heart, and bleeding hands;
O matchless kindness! and He shows
   This matchless kindness to His foes.

4 Rise, touched with gratitude divine;
   Turn out His enemy and Thine,
That soul-destroying monster, Sin;
   And let the heavenly Stranger in.

5 Admit Him, ere His anger burn;
   His feet, departed, ne'er return!
Admit Him; or the hour's at hand
   You'll at His door rejected stand.
                   Rev. Joseph Grigg (—1768).

490   *Danger of Delay.*
1 Hasten, O sinner, to be wise,
   And stay not for to-morrow's sun!
The longer wisdom you despise,
   The harder is she to be won.

2 Oh, hasten mercy to implore,
   And stay not for to-morrow's sun!
For fear thy season should be o'er,
   Before this evening's course be run.

3 Hasten, O sinner, to return,
   And stay not for to-morrow's sun;
For fear thy lamp should fail to burn,
   Before the needful work is done.

4 Hasten, O sinner, to be blest,
   And stay not for to-morrow's sun;
For fear the curse should thee arrest,
   Before the morrow is begun.
                   Rev. Thos. Scott (1776—).

491   *Invitation to Wanderers.*
1 Return, O wanderer, return,
   And seek an injured Father's face;
Those warm desires that in thee burn
   Were kindled by reclaiming grace.

2 Return, O wanderer, return,
   And seek a Father's melting heart;
Whose pitying eyes thy grief discern,
   Whose hand can heal thine inward smart.

3 Return, O wanderer, return,
   Thy Saviour bids thy spirit live;
Go to His bleeding feet, and learn
   How freely Jesus can forgive.

4 Return, O wanderer, return,
   And wipe away the falling tear;
'Tis God who says, "No longer mourn,"
   'Tis mercy's voice invites thee near.
             Rev. William Bengo Collyer (1782—1854).

492   *One Thing Needful.*
1 Why will ye waste on trifling cares
   That life which God's compassion spares!
While, in the various range of thought,
   The one thing needful is forgot.

2 Shall God invite you from above?
   Shall Jesus urge his dying love?
Shall troubled conscience give you pain?
   And all these pleas be urged in vain?

3 Not so, your eyes will always view
   Those objects which you now pursue;
Not so will heaven and hell appear,
   When death's decisive hour is near.
                 Rev. P. Doddridge (1702—1751).

INVITATIONS.

GOSHEN. 11s. — Greek Melody.

1. De-lay not, de-lay not, O sin-ner, draw near; The wa-ters of
   life are now flow-ing for thee; No price is de-mand-ed, the Sav-iour is here,
   D.S. Re-demp-tion is pur-chased, sal-va-tion is free.

493 *Dangers of Delay.*

1 Delay not, delay not, O sinner, draw near;
The waters of life are now flowing for thee;
No price is demanded, the Saviour is here,
Redemption is purchased, salvation is free.

2 Delay not, delay not, why longer abuse
The love and compassion of Jesus Thy God?
A fountain is opened, how canst thou refuse
To wash and be cleansed in His pardoning blood!

3 Delay not, delay not, O sinner to come,
For mercy still lingers, and calls thee to-day;
Her voice is not heard in the vale of the tomb;
Her message unheeded will soon pass away.

4 Delay not, delay not, the Spirit of Grace,
Long grieved and resisted, may take His sad flight;
And leave thee in darkness to finish thy race,
To sink in the gloom of eternity's night,

5 Delay not, delay not, the hour is at hand;
The earth shall dissolve, and the heavens shall fade;
The dead, small and great, in the judgment shall stand;
What power then, O sinner, shall lend thee its aid?

Dr. Thos. Hastings (1784—1872).

INVITATIONS.

494 *The Weary Come to Christ.*

1 Come, ye weary sinners, come,
All who feel your heavy load;
Jesus calls the wanderers home;
Hasten to your pardoning God.

2 Jesus, full of truth and love,
We Thy kindest call obey;
Faithful let Thy mercies prove,
Take our load of guilt away.

3 Weary of this war within,
Weary of the endless strife,
Weary of ourselves and sin,
Weary of a wretched life.

4 Burdened with a world of grief,
Burdened with our sinful load,
Burdened with this unbelief,
Burdened with the wrath of God.

5 Lo! we come to Thee for peace,
True and gracious as Thou art;
Now our weary souls release,
Write forgiveness on our heart.
Rev. Charles Wesley (1708—1788).

495 *Strive to Enter in.*

1 Pilgrim, burdened with thy sin,
Haste to Sion's gate to-day;
There, till mercy let thee in,
Knock, and weep, and watch, and pray.

2 Knock, for mercy lends an ear;
Weep, she marks the sinner's sigh;
Watch, till heavenly light appear;
Pray, she hears the mourner's cry.

3 Mourning pilgrim, what for thee
In this world can now remain ?

Seek that world from which shall flee
Sorrow, shame, and tears, and pain.

4 Sorrow shall for ever fly;
Shame shall never enter there;
Tears be wiped from every eye;
Pain in endless bliss expire.
Rev. Geo. Crabbe (1754—1832).

496 *The Harvest Past.*
Tune, GOSHEN.

1 Lo! Jesus, the Saviour, in mercy draws
near,
Salvation He brings unto all who believe;
Ye mourners, dismiss all your doubting and
fear,   [ceive.
The gracious Redeemer with gladness re-

2 The day-star of promise illumines the sky,
And souls long benighted now welcome
the dawn;   [cry:
Embrace the glad season or soon you may
"The harvest is past and the summer is
gone."

3 The Spirit is striving with sinners to-day,
He graciously knocks at the door of your
heart;
He comes the compassion of God to display,
Your sins to remove, and His love to
impart.

4 Oh! welcome the Spirit, and grieve Him
no more,   [drawn,
Nor wait till His offers of life are with-
Lest then you may cry as your doom you
deplore: [gone."
"The harvest is past, and the summer is
Rev. E. F. Hatfield (1807—1883).

INVITATIONS.

497 *Atonement Accomplished.*

1 Hark! the voice of love and mercy
  Sounds aloud from Calvary;
  See, it rends the rocks asunder,
  Shakes the earth and veils the sky:
    "It is finished!"
  Hear the dying Saviour cry.

2 It is finished — oh, what pleasure
  Do these precious words afford!
  Heavenly blessings, without measure,
  Flow to us from Christ, the Lord.
    It is finished!
  Saints, the dying words record.

3 Finished — all the types and shadows
  Of the ceremonial law;
  Finished — all that God had promised;
  Death and hell no more shall awe;
    It is finished!
  Saints, from hence your comfort draw.

4 Tune your harps anew, ye seraphs;
  Join to sing the pleasing theme;
  All on earth and all in heaven,
  Join to praise Immanuel's name,
    Hallelujah!
  Glory to the bleeding Lamb!
        Rev. B. Francis (1734—1799).

498 *Hear, and Live.*

1 Sinners, will you scorn the message
  Sent in mercy from above?
  Every sentence, oh, how tender!
  Every line is full of love:
    Listen to it;
  Every line is full of love.

2 Hear the heralds of the gospel
  News from Zion's King proclaim:
  "Pardon to each rebel sinner,
  Free forgiveness in His name."
    How important!
  "Free forgiveness in His name."

3 Tempted souls, they bring you succor;
  Fearful hearts, they quell your fears,
  And, with news of consolation,
  Chase away the falling tears:
    Tender heralds!
  Chase away the falling tears.

4 O ye angels, hovering round us,
  Waiting spirits, speed your way;
  Haste ye to the court of heaven,
  Tidings bear without delay,
    Rebel sinners
  Glad the message will obey.
        Rev. Jonathan Allen, 1801.

INVITATIONS.

BENEVENTO. 7s, D.   S. WEBBE (1740—1816).

[Music notation]

1. Sin-ners, turn, why will ye die? God your Maker asks you why; God who did your be-ing give.
D.S. *Why, ye thankless creatures, why*

Made you with Him-self to live, He the fa-tal cause demands, Asks the work of His own hands;
Will ye cross His love and die?

499 *Sinners, Turn, Why will ye Die?*

1 Sinners, turn, why will ye die?
God your Maker asks you why;
God who did your being give,
Made you with Himself to live,
He the fatal cause demands;
Asks the work of His own hands;
Why, ye thankless creatures, why
Will ye cross His love and die?

2 Sinners, turn, why will ye die?
God your Saviour asks you why;
He who did your soul retrieve,
Died Himself that ye might live,
Will ye let Him die in vain,
Crucify your Lord again?
Why, ye rebel sinners, why
Will ye slight His grace and die?

3 Sinners, turn, why will ye die?
God the Spirit asks you why;
Many a time with you He strove,
Wooed you to embrace His love;
Will ye not His grace receive?
Will ye still refuse to live?
Why will ye forever die,
O ye guilty sinners, why?
Rev. C. Wesley (1708—1788).

TO-DAY. 6s & 4s.   Dr. L. MASON (1792—1872).

[Music notation]

1. To-day the Sav-iour calls! Ye wanderers, come; Oh, ye be-night-ed souls, Why long-er roam?

500 *To-day the Saviour calls!*

1 To-day the Saviour calls!
Ye wanderers, come;
Oh, ye benighted souls,
Why longer roam?

2 To-day the Saviour calls;
Oh, hear Him now!
Within these sacred walls
To Jesus bow.

3 To-day the Saviour calls;
For refuge fly;
The storm of justice falls,
And death is nigh.

4 The Spirit calls to-day:
Yield to His power;
Oh, grieve Him not away!
'Tis mercy's hour.
Rev. Samuel Francis Smith (1808—).
Dr. Thomas Hastings (1784—1872).

(211)

COMMUNION HYMNS.

ELIZABETHTOWN. C. M.   Geo. Kingsley (1811—1884).

1. How sweet and awful is the place, With Christ within the doors, While everlasting love displays The choicest of her stores.

501   *The Heavenly Feast.*

1 How sweet and awful is the place,
  With Christ within the doors,
While everlasting love displays
  The choicest of her stores.

2 While all our hearts, in this our song,
  Join to admire the feast,
Each of us cries with thankful tongue,
  "Lord, why was I a guest?"

3 "Why was I made to hear Thy voice,
  And enter while there's room;
When thousands make a wretched choice,
  And rather starve than come?"

4 'T was the same love that spread the feast,
  That sweetly forced us in;
Else we had still refused to taste,
  And perished in our sin.
          Rev. Isaac Watts (1674—1748).

502   *Gratitude Unto Jesus.*

1 If human kindness meets return,
  And owns the grateful tie;
If tender thoughts within us burn,
  To feel a Friend is nigh;

2 Oh, shall not warmer accents, tell
  The gratitude we owe
To Him who died, our fears to quell,
  Our more than orphan's woe!

3 While yet His anguish'd soul survey'd
  Those pangs He would not flee;
What love His latest words display'd,
  "Meet and remember Me!"

4 Remember Thee! Thy death, Thy shame,
  Our sinful hearts to share!
O memory, leave no other name
  But His recorded there.
          Rev. G. T. Noel (1782—1851).

503   *I Will Remember Thee.*

1 According to Thy gracious word,
  In meek humility,
This will I do, my dying Lord,
  I will remember Thee.

2 Thy body, broken for my sake,
  My bread from heaven shall be;
Thy testamental cup I take,
  And thus remember Thee?

3 Gethsemane, can I forget?
  Or there Thy conflict see,
Thine agony and bloody sweat,
  And not remember Thee?

4 When to the cross I turn mine eyes,
  And rest on Calvary,
O Lamb of God, my sacrifice!
  I must remember Thee:—

5 Remember Thee, and all Thy pains
  And all Thy love to me;
Yea, while a breath, a pulse remains,
  Will I remember Thee.

6 And when these failing lips grow dumb,
  And mind and memory flee,
When Thou shalt in Thy kingdom come,
  Then, Lord, remember me!
          Rev. J. Montgomery (1771—1854).

COMMUNION HYMNS.

COWPER. C. M. Dr. L. MASON (1792—1872).

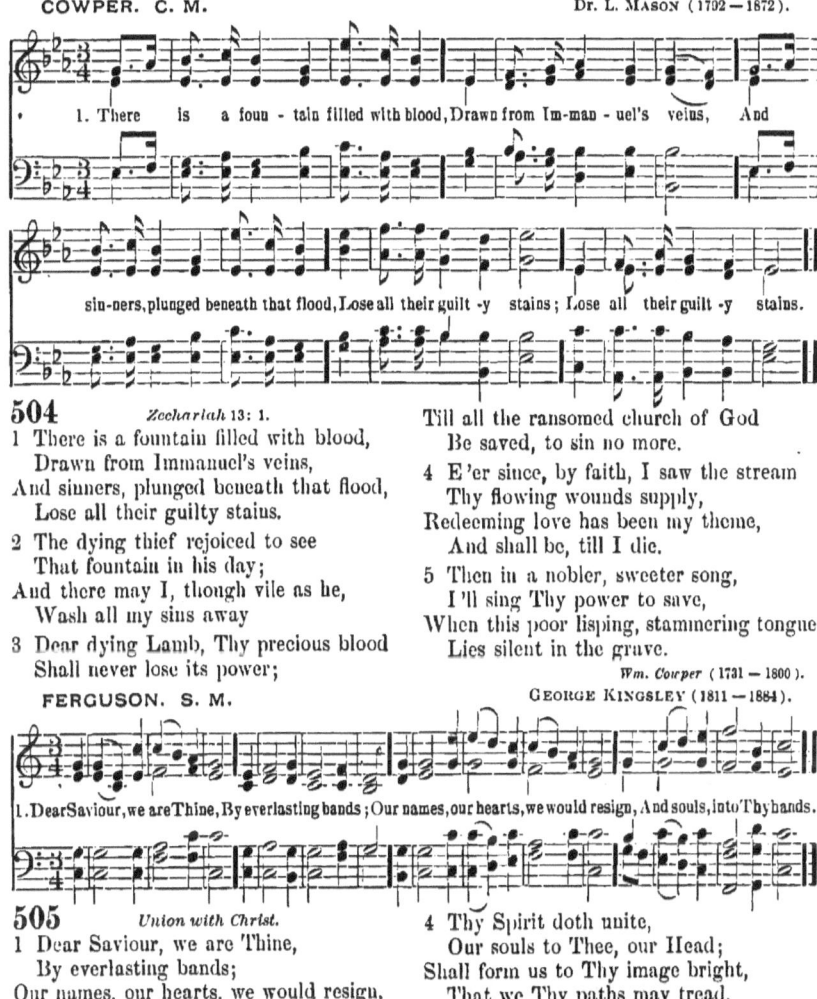

504 *Zechariah 13: 1.*

1 There is a fountain filled with blood,
  Drawn from Immanuel's veins,
  And sinners, plunged beneath that flood,
  Lose all their guilty stains.

2 The dying thief rejoiced to see
  That fountain in his day;
  And there may I, though vile as he,
  Wash all my sins away

3 Dear dying Lamb, Thy precious blood
  Shall never lose its power;
  Till all the ransomed church of God
  Be saved, to sin no more.

4 E'er since, by faith, I saw the stream
  Thy flowing wounds supply,
  Redeeming love has been my theme,
  And shall be, till I die.

5 Then in a nobler, sweeter song,
  I'll sing Thy power to save,
  When this poor lisping, stammering tongue
  Lies silent in the grave.

Wm. Cowper (1731—1800).

FERGUSON. S. M. GEORGE KINGSLEY (1811—1884).

505 *Union with Christ.*

1 Dear Saviour, we are Thine,
  By everlasting bands;
  Our names, our hearts, we would resign,
  And souls, into Thy hands.

2 Accepted for Thy sake,
  And justified by faith,
  We of Thy righteousness partake,
  And find in Thee our life.

3 To Thee we still would cleave,
  With ever growing zeal;
  If millions tempt us Christ to leave,
  Oh, let them ne'er prevail!

4 Thy Spirit doth unite,
  Our souls to Thee, our Head;
  Shall form us to Thy image bright,
  That we Thy paths may tread.

5 Death may our souls divide
  From these abodes of clay;
  But love shall keep us near Thy side,
  Through all the gloomy way.

6 Since Christ and we are one,
  Why should we doubt or fear?
  Since He in heaven has fixed His throne
  He'll fix His members there.

Rev. P. Doddridge (1702—1751).

COMMUNION HYMNS.

AURELIA. 7s & 6s, D.   S. S. WESLEY, Mus. Dr. (1810—1876).

1. O blessed feet of Jesus, Weary with seeking me Stand at God's bar of judgment, And intercede for me.

O knees, which bent in anguish In dark Gethsemane, Kneel at the throne of glo - ry And intercede for me.

506 *Jesus Intercessor.*

1 O blessed feet of Jesus,
   Weary with seeking me,
Stand at God's bar of judgmen ,
   And intercede for me
O knees, which bent in anguish
   In dark Gethsemane,
Kneel at the throne of glory
   And intercede for me

2 O hands, that were extended
   Upon the awful tree,
Hold up those precious nail-prints
   Which intercede for me
O side, from whence the spear-point
   Brought blood and water free,
For healing and for cleansing,
   Now intercede for me.

3 O head, so deeply pierced
   With thorns which sharpest be,
Bend low before Thy Father,
   And intercede for me.
O sacred heart, such sorrows
   This world may never see,
As those which are Thy warrant
   To intercede for me.

4 O body, scarred, and wounded,
   My sacrifice to be,
Present Thy perfect offering,
   And intercede for me.
O loving, risen Saviour,
   From death and sorrow free,

Though throned in endless glory,
   Still intercede for me.
Miss Margaret Elizabeth Winslow (1836 —).

507 *Bread and Water of Life.*

1 O Bread, to pilgrims given,
   O Food, that angels eat,
O Manna, sent from heaven,
   For heaven-born natures meet !
Give us, for Thee, long pining
   To eat till richly filled;
Till, earth's delights resigning,
   Our every wish is stilled !

2 O Water, life bestowing,
   From out the Saviour's heart,
A fountain purely flowing,
   A fount of love Thou art!
Oh, let us, freely tasting,
   Our burning thirst assuage!
Thy sweetness, never wasting,
   Avails from age to age.

3 Jesus, this feast receiving,
   We Thee unseen adore;
Thy faithful word believing,
   We take, and doubt no more:
Give us, Thou true and loving,
   On earth to live in Thee;
Then, death the veil removing,
   Thy glorious face to see!
Unknown mediæval author.
Tr. by Rev. Ray Palmer (1808 —1887).

COMMUNION HYMNS.

BENEDICTION. 10s.   E. J. HOPKINS (1818 —).

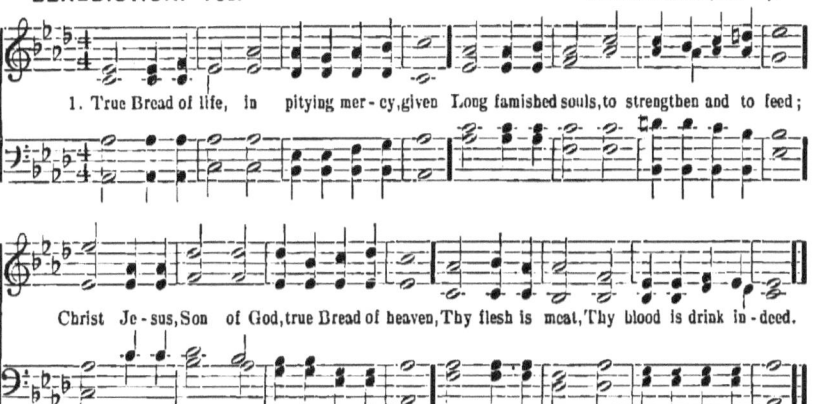

508   *The True Bread.*
1 True Bread of life, in pitying mercy, given
  Long famished souls, to strengthen and
      to feed;   [heaven,
  Christ Jesus, Son of God, true Bread of
  Thy flesh is meat, Thy blood is drink
      indeed.

2 I cannot famish, though this earth should
      fail,   [pine and die;
  Though life through all its fields should
  Though the sweet verdure should forsake
      each vale,
  And every stream of every land run dry.

3 True Tree of Life! of Thee I eat and live,
  Who eateth of Thy fruit shall never die;
  'T is Thine the everlasting health to give,
  The youth and bloom of immortality.

4 Feeding on Thee all weakness turns to
      power,
  This sickly soul revives, like earth in spring;
  Strength floweth on and in, each buoyant
      hour,
  This being seems all energy, all wing.

5 Jesus, our dying, buried, risen Head,
  Thy church's Life and Lord, Immanuel!
  At Thy dear cross we find the eternal bread,
  And in Thy empty tomb the living well.
      Rev. Horatius Bonar (1808 — 1890).

509   *Penitent Prayer.*
1 Not worthy, Lord, to gather up the
      crumbs   [table full,
  With trembling hand that from Thy
  A weary, heavy-laden sinner comes
  To plead Thy promise and obey Thy call.

2 I am not worthy to be thought Thy child;
  Nor sit the last and lowest at Thy board;
  Too long a wanderer and too oft beguiled,
  I only ask one reconciling word.

3 And is not mercy Thy prerogative —
  Free mercy, boundless, fathomless divine?
  Me, Lord! the chief of sinners, me forgive,
  And Thine the greater glory, only Thine.

4 I hear Thy voice; Thou bids't me come
      and rest;
  I come, I kneel, I clasp Thy pierced feet;
  Thou bids't me take my place, a welcome
      guest,   [eat.
  Among Thy saints, and of Thy banquet

5 My praise can only breathe itself in prayer,
  My prayer can only lose itself in Thee;
  Dwell Thou for ever in my heart, and there,
  Lord! let me sup with Thee; sup Thou
      with me.
      Bp. E. H. Bickersteth (1825 —).

COMMUNION HYMNS.

HAVERGAL. 7s, 6l.   Rev. J. B. DYKES, Mus. D. (1823—1876).

1. Bless-ed Sav-iour, Thee I love, All my oth-er joys a-bove; All my hopes in Thee a-bide, Thou my Hope, and naught be-side; Ev-er let my glo-ry be, On-ly, on-ly, on-ly Thee.

510   *Blessed Saviour.*

1 Blessèd Saviour, Thee I love,
All my other joys above;
All my hopes in Thee abide,
Thou my Hope, and naught beside;
Ever let my glory be,
Only, only, only Thee.

2 Once again beside the cross,
All my gain I count but loss;
Earthly pleasures fade away;
Clouds they are that hide my day:
Hence, vain shadows! let me see
Jesus, crucified for me.

3 From beneath that thorny crown
Trickle drops of cleansing down;
Pardon from Thy piercèd hand
Now I take, while here I stand;
Only then I live to Thee,
When Thy wounded side I see.

4 Blessèd Saviour, Thine am I,
Thine to live, and Thine to die;
Height or depth, or earthly power, (216)

Ne'er shall hide my Saviour more:
Ever shall my glory be,
Only, only, only Thee!

Rev. G. Duffield D. D. (1818—1888).

511   *Jesus, Master, whom I serve.*

1 Jesus, Master, whom I serve,
Though so feebly and so ill,
Strengthen hand and heart and nerve
All Thy bidding to fulfill;
Open Thou mine eyes to see
All the work Thou hast for me.

2 Lord, Thou needest not, I know
Service such as I can bring;
Yet I long to prove and show
Full allegiance to my King.
Thou an honor art to me;
Let me be a praise to Thee.

3 Jesus, Master, wilt Thou use
One who owes Thee more than all?
As Thou wilt! I would not choose;
Only let me hear Thy call.
Jesus, let me always be
In Thy service, glad and free!

Miss Frances R. Havergal (1836—1879).

COMMUNION HYMNS.

COMMUNION. L. M.   EDWARD MILLER, Mus. Doc. (1731—1807).

1. 'T was on that dark, that dole-ful night, When pow'rs of earth and hell a-rose A-gainst the Son of God's de-light, And friends be-trayed Him to His foes.

512   *Lord's Supper Instituted.*

1 'T was on that dark, that doleful night
   When powers of earth and hell arose
Against the Son of God's delight,
   And friends betrayed Him to His foes.

2 Before the mournful scene began,
   He took the bread, and blest, and brake;
What love through all His actions ran!
   What wondrous words of grace He spake.

3 "This is my body broke for sin;
   Receive and eat the living food;"
Then took the cup and blest the wine;
   'T is the new covenant in My blood."

4 "Do this, He cried, till time shall end,
   In memory of your dying Friend;
Meet at My table, and record
   The love of your departed Lord."

5 Jesus, Thy feast we celebrate,
   We show Thy death, we sing Thy name,
Till Thou return, and we shall eat
   The marriage supper of the Lamb.
                     Rev. Isaac Watts (1674—1748).

ROSEDALE. L. M.   GEORGE FREDERICK ROOT (1820—), 1843.

1. Behold the sin-atoning Lamb, With wonder, gratitude and love; To take away our guilt and shame, See Him descending from above!

513   *Christ the Lamb Slain.*

1 Behold the sin-atoning Lamb,
   With wonder, gratitude and love;
To take away our guilt and shame,
   See Him descending from above!

2 Our sins and griefs on Him were laid;
   He meekly bore the mighty load;
Our ransom-price He fully paid,
   In groans and tears, in sweat and blood.

3 To save a guilty world He dies;
   Sinners, behold the bleeding Lamb!
To Him lift up your longing eyes,
   And hope for mercy in His name.

4 Pardon and peace through Him abound
   He can the richest blessings give;
Salvation in His name is found,
   He bids the dying sinner live.

5 Jesus, my Lord, I look to Thee;
   Where else can helpless sinners go?
Thy boundless love shall set me free
   From all my wretchedness and woe.
                     Rev. John Fawcett (1739—1817).

COMMUNION HYMNS.

LOUVAN. L. M. — Virgil Corydon Taylor (1817–).

1. Behold the Man! how glorious He, Before His foes He stands unawed; And, without wrong or blasphemy, He claims equality with God.

514 *Behold the Man.*
1 Behold the Man! how glorious He!
  Before His foes He stands unawed;
  And, without wrong or blasphemy,
  He claims equality with God.

2 Behold the Man! by all condemned;
  Assaulted by a host of foes;
  His person and His claims contemned,
  A man of sufferings and of woes.

3 Behold the Man! He stands alone,
  His foes are ready to devour;
  Not one of all His friends will own
  Their Master in this trying hour.

4 Behold the Man! He knew no sin,
  Yet justice smites Him with her sword;
  He bears the stroke that else had been
  The sinner's portion from the Lord.

5 Behold the Man! so weak He seems,
  His awful word inspires no fear;
  But soon must he, who now blasphemes,
  Before His judgment-seat appear.

6 Behold the Man! though scorned below,
  He bears the greatest name above;
  The angels at His footstool bow,
  And all His royal claims approve.
  Rev. Thos. Kelly (1769–1855).

515 *Praise to Christ.*
1 Thou only Sovereign of my heart,
  My Refuge, my almighty Friend;—
  And can my soul from Thee depart,
  On whom alone my hopes depend?

2 Eternal life Thy words impart,
  On Thee my fainting spirit lives;
  Here, sweeter comfort cheers my heart,
  Than all the round of nature gives.

3 Let earth's alluring joys combine;
  While Thou art near, in vain they call;
  One smile, one blissful smile of Thine,
  My dearest Lord, outweighs them all.

4 Thy name, my inmost powers adore;
  Thou art my life, my joy, my care;
  Depart from Thee?—'t is death—'t is more!
  'T is endless ruin — deep despair!

5 Low at Thy feet my soul would lie;
  Here, safety dwells, and peace divine;
  Still let me live beneath Thine eye,
  For life, eternal life is Thine.
  Miss Anne Steele (1717–1773).

516 *Prayer for Divine Influence.*
Tune, SOLITUDE.
1 While the prayers of saints ascend,
  God of love! to mine attend;
  Hear me, for Thy Spirit pleads,
  Hear, for Jesus intercedes.

2 While I hearken to Thy law
  Fill my soul with humble awe,
  Till Thy gospel bring, to me
  Life and immortality.

3 From Thine house when I return
  May my heart within me burn,
  And at evening let me say,
  "I have walked with God to-day."
  Anon.

COMMUNION HYMNS.

HOLLEY. 7s.   GEORGE HEWS, 1835.

1. Hark, my soul, it is the Lord; 'T is thy Sav-iour, hear His word; Je-sus speaks, and speaks to thee: "Say, poor sin-ner, lov'st thou Me?"

517   *Constancy of Christ's Love.*
1 Hark, my soul, it is the Lord;
'T is thy Saviour, hear His word;
Jesus speaks, and speaks to thee:
"Say, poor sinner, lovest thou Me?

2 "I delivered thee when bound,
And, when wounded, healed thy wound,
Sought thee wandering, set thee right,
Turned Thy darkness into light.

3 "Can a woman's tender care
Cease toward the child she bare?
Yes, she may forgetful be,
Yet will I remember Thee.

4 "Mine is an unchanging love,
Higher than the heights above;
Deeper than the depths beneath,
Free and faithful, strong as death.

5 "Thou shalt see My glory soon,
When the work of grace is done;
Partner of My throne shalt be;
Say, poor sinner, lovest thou Me?"

6 Lord, it is my chief complaint,
That my love is weak and faint;
Yet I love Thee and adore,
Oh, for grace to love Thee more!
         Rev. Wm. Cowper (1731—1800).

518   *Sacramental Meditation.*
1 Jesus, Master, hear me now,
While I would renew my vow,
And record Thy dying love,
Hear, and help me from above.

2 Feed me, Saviour, with this bread,
Broken in Thy body's stead;
Cheer my spirit with this wine,
Streaming like that blood of Thine.

3 And, as now I eat and drink,
Let me truly, sweetly think,
Thou didst hang upon the tree,
Broken, bleeding there — for me.
         Dr. Wm. Maxwell (1784—1857).

519   *Doxology.*
1 Sing we to our God above
Praise eternal as His love;
Praise Him, all ye heavenly host—
Father, Son, and Holy Ghost.

SOLITUDE. 7s.   L. T. DOWNES, 1851.

1. While the prayers of saints ascend, God of love! to mine attend: Hear, for Je-sus intercedes.
Hear me, for Thy Spirit pleads,

By per. of Oliver Ditson Company, owners of copyright.

COMMUNION HYMNS.

COMMUNION. L. M.   EDWARD MILLER, Mus. D.

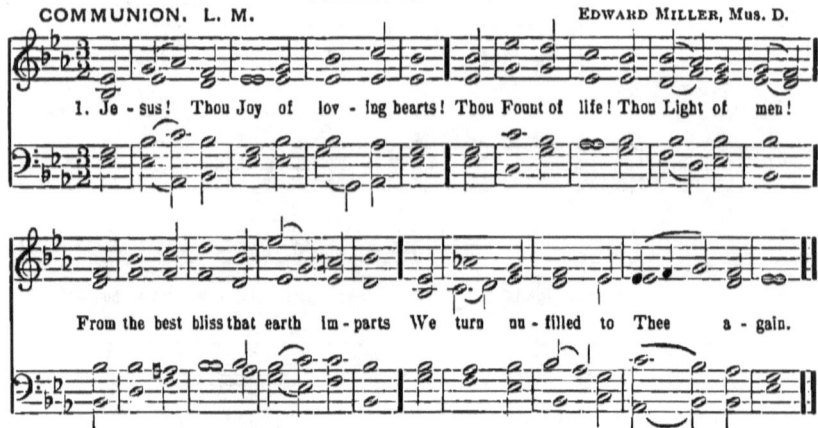

1. Je-sus! Thou Joy of lov-ing hearts! Thou Fount of life! Thou Light of men!
From the best bliss that earth im-parts We turn un-filled to Thee a-gain.

520 *Jesus! Thou Joy of Loving Hearts.*
1 Jesus! Thou Joy of loving hearts!
  Thou Fount of life! Thou Light of men!
From the best bliss that earth imparts
  We turn unfilled to Thee again.

2 Thy truth unchanged has ever stood;
  Thou savest those that on Thee call;
To them that seek Thee Thou art good,
  To them that find Thee all in all.

3 We taste Thee, O Thou living Bread!
  And long to feast upon Thee still;
We drink of Thee, the Fountain Head,
  And thirst our souls from Thee to fill.

4 Our restless spirits yearn for Thee,
  Where'er our changeful lot is cast,
Glad when Thy gracious smile we see,
  Blest when our faith can hold Thee fast.

5 O Jesus! ever with us stay;
  Make all our moments calm and bright;
Chase the dark night of sin away;
  Shed o'er the world Thy holy light.
        Bernard of Clairvaux (1091—1153).
        Tr. by Rev. Ray Palmer (1808—1887).

521 *Deep In Our Hearts Let Us Record.*
1 Deep in our hearts let us record
The deeper sorrows of our Lord;
Behold the rising billows roll
To overwhelm His holy soul.

2 Yet, gracious God! Thy power and love
Have made the curse a blessing prove;
Those dreadful sufferings of Thy Son
Atoned for sins that we have done.

3 The pangs of our expiring Lord
The honors of Thy law restored;
His sorrows made Thy justice known,
And paid for follies not His own.

4 Oh, for His sake, our guilt forgive,
And let the mourning sinner live;
The Lord will hear us in His name,
Nor shall our hope be turned to shame.
        Rev. Isaac Watts (1674—1748).

522 *Memorial of Our Risen Lord.*
1 Jesus is gone above the skies
  Where our weak senses reach Him not;
And carnal objects court our eyes,
  To thrust our Saviour from our thought.

2 He knows what wandering hearts we have,
  Apt to forget His glorious face;
And to refresh our minds, He gave
  These kind memorials of His grace.

3 The Lord of life this table spread,
  With His own flesh and dying blood;
We on the rich provision feed,
  We taste the wine, and bless our God.

4 Let sinful sweets be all forgot,
  And earth grow less in our esteem;
Christ and His love fill every thought,
  And faith and hope be fixed on Him.

5 While He is absent from our sight,
  'T is to prepare our souls a place;
That we may dwell in heavenly light,
  And live forever near His face.
        Rev. Isaac Watts (1674—1748).

COMMUNION HYMNS.

By per. of Oliver Ditson Company, owners of copyright.

523 *Cry of Penitence.*
1 Depth of mercy, can there be
Mercy still reserved for me?
Canst Thou still Thy wrath forbear,
And the chief of sinners spare?

2 We have long withstood Thy grace,
Long provoked Thee to Thy face,
Would not hear Thy gracious calls,
Grieved Thee by a thousand falls.

3 Jesus, answer from above,
Is not all Thy nature love?
Wilt Thou not our crimes forget?
Lo! we fall before Thy feet.

4 Lord, incline us to repent,
Help us now our fall lament,
Deeply our revolt deplore,
Weep, believe, and sin no more.
Rev. Charles Wesley (1708—1788).

524 *Prince of Peace, control my will.*
1 Prince of Peace, control my will,
Bid this struggling heart be still;
Bid my fears and doubtings cease,
Hush my spirit into peace.

2 Thou hast bought me with Thy blood,
Opened wide the gate to God;
Peace I ask,—but peace must be,
Lord, in being one with Thee.

3 May Thy will, not mine, be done,—
May Thy will and mine be one;
Chase these doubtings from my heart,
Now Thy perfect peace impart.

4 Saviour, at Thy feet I fall,
Thou my life, my God, my all!
Let Thy happy servant be
One for evermore with Thee.
Anon.

(221)

COMMUNION HYMNS.

LITANY. 7s & 6s. — ANONYMOUS. Harmonized by Sir ARTHUR S. SULLIVAN.

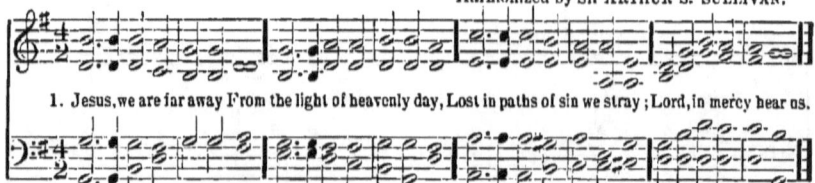

525 *Be Merciful unto Me.*

1 Jesus, we are far away
From the light of heavenly day,
Lost in paths of sin we stray;
   Lord, in mercy hear us.

2 Deeper has the darkness grown;
Saviour, come to seek Thine own,
Leave, oh, leave us not alone;
   Lord, in mercy hear us.

3 On our darkness shed Thy light,
Lead our wills to what is right,
Wash our evil nature white;
   Lord, in mercy hear us.

4 May Thy wisdom be our guide,
Comfort, rest, and peace provide
Near to Thy protecting side;
   Lord, in mercy hear us.

5 May the world seem only dross,
May we welcome shame and loss,
Willingly endure the cross;
   Lord, in mercy hear us.

6 When oppressed with trouble sore,
Teach our hearts to feel the more
For the pangs our Saviour bore;
   Lord, in mercy hear us.

7 May Thy grace within the soul
Nature's waywardness control,
Guiding towards the heavenly goal;
   Lord, in mercy hear us.

8 So at last, from sin set free,
What we long for, may we see,
And for ever blessèd be;
   Lord, in mercy hear us.

Rev. T. B. Pollock ('836—).

WESLEY. 11s & 10s. — LOWELL MASON (1792—1872).

THE CHURCH.

SAVANNAH. 10s. IGNACE PLEYEL (1757—1831).

1. Rise, crowned with light, imperial Sa-lem, rise! Ex-alt thy tow'ring head, and lift thine eyes;
See heaven its spark-ling portals wide dis-play, And break up-on thee in a flood of day.

526 *The Fullness of The Gentiles.*

1 Rise, crowned with light, imperial Salem, rise!
Exalt thy towering head, and lift thine eyes;
See heaven its sparkling portals wide display,
And break upon thee in a flood of day.

2 See barbarous nations at thy gates attend,
Walk in the light, and in thy temple bend;
See thy bright altars thronged with prostrate kings,
While every land its joyful tribute brings.

3 The seas shall waste, the skies to smoke decay,
Rocks fall to dust, and mountains melt away;
But fixed His word, His saving power remains;
Thy realms shall last, thy own Messiah reigns!

Alexander Pope (1683—1744).

527 *Daughter of Zion.*
Tune, WESLEY.

1 Daughter of Zion! awake from thy sadness;
Awake, for thy foes shall oppress thee no more;
Bright o'er thy hills dawns the day-star of gladness;
Arise! for the night of thy sorrow is o'er.

2 Strong were thy foes, but the arm that subdued them
And scattered their legions, was mightier far;
They fled, like the chaff from the scourge that pursued them,
For vain were their steeds and their chariots of war!

3 Daughter of Zion! the Power that hath saved thee,
Extolled with the harp and the timbrel should be:
Shout! for the foe is destroyed that enslaved thee,
Th' oppressor is vanquished, and Zion is free!

Anon. 1830.

528 *Doxology.*

Praise God, from whom all blessings flow
Praise Him, all creatures here below!
Praise Him above, ye heavenly host!
Praise Father, Son and Holy Ghost!

(223)

ST. THOMAS. S. M. THE CHURCH. WILLIAM TANSUR (1699—1744).

1. I love Thy kingdom, Lord, The house of Thine abode; The Church our blest Redeemer saved With His own precious blood.

529
Psalm 137.

1 I love Thy kingdom, Lord,
 The house of Thine abode;
The Church our blest Redeemer saved,
 With His own precious blood.

2 I love Thy Church, O God!
 Her walls before Thee stand,
Dear as the apple of Thine eye,
 And graven on Thy hand.

3 If e'er to bless Thy sons
 My voice or hands deny,
These hands let useful skill forsake,
 This voice in silence die.

4 If e'er my heart forget
 Her welfare or her woe,
Let every joy this heart forsake,
 And every grief o'erflow.

5 For her my tears shall fall;
 For her my prayers ascend:
To her my cares and toils be given,
 Till toils and cares shall end.

6 Beyond my highest joy
 I prize her heavenly ways,
Her sweet communion, solemn vows,
 Her hymns of love and praise.

7 Sure as Thy truth shall last,
 To Sion shall be given

The brightest glories earth can yield
 And brighter bliss of heaven.
Rev. T. Dwight, D. D. (1752 — 1817)

530
Psalm 117.

1 Thy name, almighty Lord,
 Shall sound through distant lands;
Great is Thy grace and sure Thy word;
 Thy truth for ever stands.

2 Far be Thine honor spread,
 And long Thy praise endure,
Till morning light and evening shade
 Shall be exchanged no more.
Rev. Isaac Watts (1674 — 1748).

531 *Hail the Glorious Dayspring.*

1 Christian, see, the orient morning
 Breaks along the heathen sky;
Lo! the expected day is dawning,
 Glorious dayspring from on high:
 Hallelujah!
Hail the dayspring from on high!

2 Lord of every tribe and nation,
 Spread Thy truth from pole to pole!
Spread the light of Thy salvation,
 Till it shine on every soul;
 Hallelujah!
Hail the dayspring from on high!
Anon., 1823.

REGENT SQUARE. 8s, 7s & 4 s. H. SMART (1812—1879).

1. Christian, see, the o-rient morning Breaks along the heath-en sky; Lo! th' expected day is dawning.

Glorious dayspring from on high; Hal-le-lu-jah! Hal-le-lu-jah! Hail the dayspring from on high!

THE CHURCH.

AURELIA. 7s & 6s. S. S. WESLEY (1810—1876).

532 *He is the Head of the Body, the Church.*

1 The Church's one foundation
　Is Jesus Christ her Lord;
She is His new creation
　By water and the Word:
From heaven He came and sought her
　To be His holy Bride;
With His own blood He bought her
　And for her life He died.

2 Elect from every nation,
　Yet one o'er all the earth,
Her charter of salvation,
　One Lord, one Faith, one Birth
One Holy Name she blesses,
　Partakes one Holy Food,
And to one hope she presses
　With every grace endued.

3 Though with a scornful wonder
　Men see her sore opprest,
By schisms rent asunder,
　By heresies distrest,

Yet saints their watch are keeping,
　Their cry goes up, "How long?"
And soon the night of weeping
　Shall be the morn of song.

4 Mid toil, and tribulation,
　And tumult of her war,
She waits the consummation
　Of peace forevermore;
Till with the vision glorious
　Her longing eyes are blest,
And the great Church victorious
　Shall be the Church at rest.

5 Yet she on earth hath union
　With God the Three in One,
And mystic sweet communion
　With those whose rest is won;
O happy ones and holy!
　Lord, give us grace that we,
Like them the meek and lowly,
　On high may dwell with Thee.

Rev. Samuel J. Stone (1839—).

(225)

MISSIONS.

533 *Missions.*

1 Ye Christian heralds, go, proclaim
Salvation through Immanuel's name;
To distant climes the tidings bear,
And plant the rose of Sharon there.

2 He'll shield you with a wall of fire,
With flaming zeal your breasts inspire,
Bid raging winds their fury cease,
And hush the tempest into peace.

3 And when your labors all are o'er,
Then we shall meet to part no more;
Meet with the blood-bought throng, to fall,
And crown our Jesus, Lord of all.
B. H. Draper (1778—1843).

534 *Psalm 113.*

1 Ye servants of th' Almighty King,
In every age His praises sing;
Where'er the sun shall rise or set,
The nations shall His praise repeat.

2 Above the earth, beyond the sky,
His throne of glory stands on high;
Nor time, nor place, His power restrain,
Nor bound His universal reign.

3 Which of the sons of Adam dare,
Or angels with their God compare?
His glories, how divinely bright,
Who dwells in uncreated light!

4 Behold His love! He stoops to view
What saints above, and angels do;
And condescends yet more to know
The mean affairs of men below.

5 From dust and cottages obscure
His grace exalts the humble poor!

Gives them the honor of His sons,
And fits them for their heavenly thrones.
Rev. Isaac Watts (1674—1748).

535 *Prayer for the Triumph of the Gospel.*

1 O Jesus, let Thy kingdom come;
Then sin and hell's terrific gloom
Shall, at Thy brightness, flee away,
The dawn of an eternal day.

2 Then shall the Jew and Gentile meet,
In pure devotion at Thy feet;
And earth shall yield Thee, as Thy due,
Her fullness and her glory too.

3 Oh, that from Zion now might shine
This heavenly light, this truth divine;
Till the whole universe shall be
But one great temple, Lord, for Thee.
Anon.

536 *Psalm 72.*

1 Jesus shall reign where'er the sun
Does his successive journeys run;
His kingdom stretch from shore to shore,
Till moons shall wax and wane no more.

2 For Him shall endless prayer be made,
And endless praises crown His head;
His name, like sweet perfume, shall rise
With every morning sacrifice.

3 People and realms of every tongue
Dwell on His love with sweetest song;
And infant voices shall proclaim
Their early blessings on His name.

4 Blessings abound where'er He reigns,
The joyful prisoner bursts his chains,
The weary find eternal rest,
And all the sons of want are blest.
Rev. Isaac Watts (1674—1748).

MISSIONS.

MISSIONARY HYMN. 7s & 6s. D. Dr. L. Mason, 1824.

537 *Missionary Hymn.*

1 From Greenland's icy mountains,
  From India's coral strand;
Where Afric's sunny fountains
  Roll down their golden sand;
From many an ancient river,
  From many a palmy plain,
They call us to deliver
  Their land from error's chain.

2 What, though the spicy breezes
  Blow soft o'er Ceylon's isle,
Though every prospect pleases,
  And only man is vile;
In vain, with lavish kindness,
  The gifts of God are strown;
The heathen, in His blindness,
  Bows down to wood and stone.

3 Shall we, whose souls are lighted
  With wisdom from on high,
Shall we, to men benighted,
  The lamp of life deny?
Salvation! O salvation!
  The joyful sound proclaim,
Till earth's remotest nation
  Has learned Messiah's name.

4 Waft, waft, ye winds, His story,
  And you, ye waters, roll,
Till, like a sea of glory,
  It spreads from pole to pole;
Till o'er our ransomed nature,
  The Lamb for sinners slain,
Redeemer, King, Creator,
  In bliss returns to reign
    Bp. Reginald Heber (1783 — 1826).

538 *The Day of Jubilee.*

1 How beauteous, on the mountains,
  The feet of Him that brings,
Like streams from living fountains,
  Good tidings of good things;
That publisheth salvation,
  And jubilee release,
To every tribe and nation,
  God's reign of joy and peace!

2 Lift up Thy voice, O watchman
  And shout, from Zion's towers,
Thy hallelujah chorus,—
  "The victory is ours!"
The Lord shall build up Zion
  In glory and renown,
And Jesus, Judah's lion,
  Shall wear His rightful crown.

3 Break forth in hymns of gladness
  O waste Jerusalem!
Let songs, instead of sadness,
  Thy jubilee proclaim;
The Lord, in strength victorious,
  Upon thy foes hath trod;
Behold, O earth! the glorious
  Salvation of our God!
    Benj. Gough (1805 — 1883).

MISSIONS.

WATCHMAN, TELL US. 7s, D. — Dr. L. Mason (1792—1872).

539 *Tell Us of the Night.*

1 Watchman ! tell us of the night,
What its signs of promise are;—
Traveler ! o'er yon mountain's height,
See that glory-beaming star !—
Watchman ! does its beauteous ray
Aught of joy or hope foretell ?—
Traveler ! yes; it brings the day,
Promised day of Israel. —

2 Watchman ! tell us of the night;
Higher yet that star ascends;
Traveler ! blessedness and light,
Peace and truth, its course portends;—

Watchman ! will its beams alone
Gild the spot that gave them birth ?—
Traveler ! ages are its own;
See, it bursts o'er all the earth !

3 Watchman ! tell us of the night,
For the morning seems to dawn;
Traveler ! darkness takes its flight;
Doubt and terror are withdrawn;—
Watchman ! let thy wanderings cease;
Hie thee to thy quiet home !—
Traveler ! lo ! the Prince of peace,
Lo ! the Son of God, is come !
Sir John Bowring, (1792—1872).

ELTHAM. 7s, D. — Dr. Lowell Mason.

540 *The World's Conversion.*

1 Hasten, Lord ! the glorious time
When, beneath Messiah's sway,
Every nation, every clime,
Shall the gospel's call obey.
Mightiest kings His power shall own,
Heathen tribes His name adore;
Satan and his hosts o'erthrown,
Bound in chains, shall hurt no more.

2 Then shall wars and tumults cease,
Then be banished grief and pain;
Righteousness and joy and peace
Undisturbed shall ever reign.
Bless we, then, our gracious Lord;
Ever praise His glorious name;
All His mighty acts record;
All His wondrous love proclaim.
Miss Harriet Auber, (1773—1862).

MISSIONS.

541 *The God of Sion.*

1 Sion stands with hills surrounded,—
Sion, kept by power divine;
All her foes shall be confounded,
Though the world in arms combine: —
Happy Sion !
What a favored lot is thine.

2 Every human tie may perish,
Friend to friend unfaithful prove,
Mothers cease their own to cherish,
Heaven and earth at last remove;
But no changes
Can attend Jehovah's love.

3 In the furnace God may prove thee,
Thence to bring thee forth more bright;
But can never cease to love thee;
Thou art precious in His sight:
God is with thee: —
God, thine everlasting light.
Rev. Thos. Kelly (1769—1855).

542 *Prayer for the Spread of the Gospel.*

1 O'er the gloomy hills of darkness,
Look, my soul, be still, and gaze;
All the promises do travail
With a glorious day of grace;
Blessed Jubilee,
Let thy glorious morning dawn.

2 Kingdoms wide, that sit in darkness,
Grant them, Lord, the glorious light;
And from eastern coast to western,
May the morning chase the night;
And redemption,
Freely purchased, win the day.

3 Fly abroad, thou mighty Gospel;
Win and conquer, never cease;
May thy lasting, wide dominions,
Multiply, and still increase !
Sway Thy sceptre,
Saviour, all the world around.
Rev. Wm. Williams (1717—1791).

543 *Home Missions.*

1 Saints of God ! the dawn is brightening,
Token of our coming Lord;
O'er the earth the field is whitening;
Louder rings the Master's word,—
" Pray for reapers
In the harvest of the Lord."

2 Now, O Lord ! fulfill Thy pleasure,
Breathe upon Thy chosen band,
And, with pentecostal measure,
Send forth reapers o'er our land,—
Faithful reapers,
Gathering sheaves for Thy right hand.

3 Broad the shadow of our nation,
Eager millions hither roam;
Lo ! they wait for Thy salvation;
Come, Lord Jesus ! quickly come !
By Thy Spirit,
Bring Thy ransomed people home.

4 Soon shall end the time of weeping,
Soon the reaping time will come,—
Heaven and earth together keeping
God's eternal Harvest Home:
Saints and angels !
Shout the world's great Harvest Home.
Mrs. Mary Maxwell, 1875.

MISSIONS.

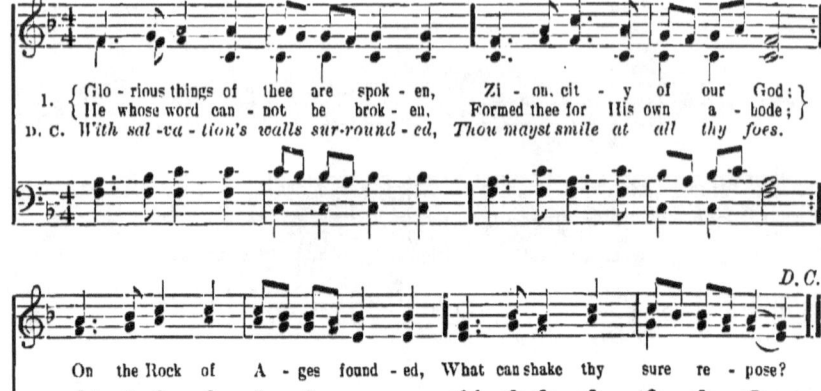

544 *Glorious Things.*

1 Glorious things of thee are spoken,
  Zion, city of our God;
He whose word cannot be broken
  Formed thee for His own abode;
On the Rock of Ages founded,
  What can shake thy sure repose?
With salvation's walls surrounded,
  Thou mayst smile at all thy foes.

2 See, the streams of living waters,
  Springing from eternal love,
Well supply thy sons and daughters,
  And all fear of want remove;
Who can faint while such a river
  Ever flows their thirst to assuage —
Grace, which, like the Lord, the giver,
  Never fails from age to age?

3 Round each habitation hovering,
  See the cloud and fire appear,
For a glory and a covering,
  Showing that the Lord is near;
Thus deriving from their banner
  Light by night and shade by day,
Safe they feed upon the manna
  Which he gives them when they pray.

Rev. John Newton (1725 – 1807).

545 *On the Mountain's Top Appearing.*

1 On the mountain top appearing,
  Lo! the sacred herald stands,
Welcome news to Zion bearing —
  Zion long in hostile lands;
    Mourning captive!
  God himself will loose thy bands.

2 Has thy night been long and mournful,
  All thy friends unfaithful proved?
Have thy foes been proud and scornful
  By thy sighs and tears unmoved?
    Cease thy mourning;
  Zion still is well beloved.

3 God, thy God, will now restore thee,
  He Himself appears thy friend;
All thy foes shall flee before thee,
  Here their boasts and triumphs end;
    Great deliverance
  Zion's King will quickly send.

4 Peace and joy shall now attend thee,
  All thy warfare now is past,
God, thy Saviour, shall defend thee,
  Peace and joy are come at last;
    All thy conflicts
  End in everlasting rest.

Rev. Thos. Kelly (1769 – 1855).

MISSIONS.

ANVERN. L. M.　　　　　　　　　German. Arr. by Dr. L. Mason.

546　*Spread of the Gospel.*
1 Ascend Thy throne, almighty King,
　And spread Thy glories all abroad;
　Let Thine own arm salvation bring,
　And be Thou known the gracious God.

2 Let millions bow before Thy seat;
　Let humble mourners seek Thy face;
　Bring daring rebels to Thy feet,
　Subdued by Thy victorious grace.

3 Oh, let the kingdoms of the world
　Become the kingdoms of the Lord;
　Let saints and angels praise Thy name,
　Be Thou through heaven and earth
　　adored.
　　　　　　Rev. B. Beddome (1717 — 1875).

547　*Conversion of the World.*
1 Sovereign of worlds! display Thy power;
　Be this Thy Zion's favored hour;
　Bid the bright morning Star arise,
　And point the nations to the skies.

2 Set up Thy throne where Satan reigns,—
　On Afric's shore, on India's plains,
　On wilds and continents unknown,—
　And make the nations all Thine own.

3 Speak! and the world shall hear Thy
　　voice;
　Speak! and the desert shall rejoice;

Scatter the gloom of heathen night,
　And bid all nations hail the light.
　　　　　　Mrs. Voke, 1833.

548　*He Shall Sprinkle.*
　　　　　Tune, MIDDLETON.
1 Saviour, sprinkle many nations,
　Fruitful let Thy sorrows be;
　By Thy pains and consolations,
　Draw the Gentiles unto Thee:
　Of Thy cross the wondrous story,
　Be it to the nations told;
　Let them see Thee in Thy glory,
　And Thy mercy manifold.

2 Far and wide, though all unknowing,
　Pants for Thee each mortal breast;
　Human tears for Thee are flowing,
　Human hearts in Thee would rest,
　Thirsting, as for dews of even,
　As the new-mown grass for rain;
　Thee, they seek, as God of Heaven,
　Thee, as Man, for sinners slain.

3 Saviour, lo, the isles are waiting,
　Stretched the hand, and strained the
　For Thy Spirit, new creating　　[sight,
　Love's pure flame and wisdom's light;
　Give the word, and of the preacher
　Speed the foot, and touch the tongue,
　Till on earth by every creature
　Glory to the Lamb be sung. *
　　　　　Bp. Arthur Cleveland Coxe (1818 —).

MISSIONS.

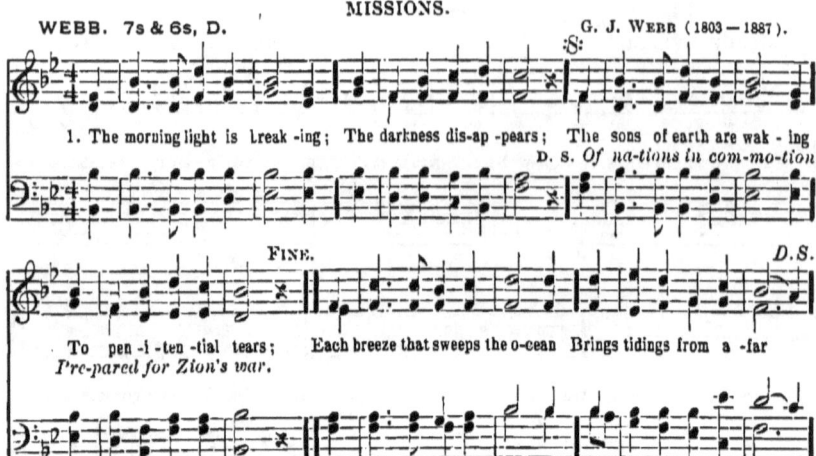

549   *Dawn of Day.*

1 The morning light is breaking;
  The darkness disappears;
The sons of earth are waking
  To penitential tears;
Each breeze that sweeps the ocean
  Brings tidings from afar
Of nations in commotion,
  Prepared for Zion's war.

2 Rich dews of grace come o'er us
  In many a gentle shower,
And brighter scenes before us
  Are opening every hour;
Each cry to heaven going
  Abundant answers brings,
And heavenly gales are blowing
  With peace upon their wings.

3 See heathen nations bending
  Before the God we love,
And thousand hearts ascending
  In gratitude above;
While sinners, now confessing,
  The gospel call obey,
And seek the Saviour's blessing,
  A nation in a day.

4 Blest river of salvation !—
  Pursue thine onward way;
Flow thou to every nation,
  Nor in thy richness stay —

Stay not till all the lowly
  Triumphant reach their home;
Stay not till all the holy
  Proclaim "The Lord is come."
S. F. Smith (1808 —).

550   *Christian Warfare.*

1 Now be the gospel banner
  In every land unfurled;
And be the shout, "Hosanna !"
  Re-echoed through the world,
Till every isle and nation,
  Till every tribe and tongue,
Receive the great salvation,
  And join the happy throng.

2 What though th' embattled legions
  Of earth and hell combine ?
His power throughout their regions
  Shall soon resplendent shine;
Ride on, O Lord ! victorious,
  Immanuel, Prince of peace !
Thy triumph shall be glorious,
  Thine empire shall increase.

3 Yes, Thou shalt reign for ever,
  O Jesus, King of kings !
Thy light, Thy love, Thy favor,
  Each ransomed captive sings;
The isles for Thee are waiting,
  The deserts learn Thy praise,
The hills and valleys greeting,
  The song responsive raise.
Thos. Hastings (1784 — 1872).

MISSIONS.

PARK STREET. L. M.   FREDERICK MARC ANTOINE VENUA (1788 —).

1. Arm of the Lord! a-wake, a-wake; Put on Thy strength, the na-tions shake; And let the world, a-dor-ing see Triumphs of mer-cy, wrought by Thee, Triumphs of mercy, wrought by Thee.

551   *Awake, Arm of the Lord.*
1 Arm of the Lord! awake, awake;
   Put on Thy strength, the nations shake;
   And let the world, adoring, see
   Triumphs of mercy wrought by Thee.

2 Say to the heathen, from Thy throne,
   "I am Jehovah — God alone!"
   Thy voice their idols shall confound,
   And cast their altars to the ground.

3 No more let human blood be spilt,
   Vain sacrifice for human guilt;
   But to each conscience be applied
   The blood that flowed from Jesus' side.

4 Almighty God! Thy grace proclaim,
   In every clime, of every name,
   Till adverse powers before Thee fall,
   And crown the Saviour — Lord of all.
                 Wm. Shrubsole (1759 — 1829).

552   *Prayer for the Jews.*
1 Disowned of Heaven, by man oppressed,
   Outcasts from Sion's hallowed ground,
   Oh! why should Israel's sons once blessed,
   Still roam the scorning world around?

2 Lord, visit Thy forsaken race,
   Back to Thy fold the wanderers bring;
   Teach them to seek Thy slighted grace,
   And hail in Christ their promised King.

3 The veil of darkness rend in twain,
   Which hides their Shiloh's glorious light;
   The severed olive branch again
   Firm to its parent stock unite.

4 Hail, glorious day, expected long,
   When Jew and Greek one prayer shall throng, [pour,
   With eager feet one people
   With grateful praise one God adore.
                               Anon.

553   *O Spirit.*
1 O Spirit of the living God,
   In all Thy plenitude of grace,
   Where'er the foot of man hath trod,
   Descend on our apostate race!

2 Give tongues of fire and hearts of love
   To preach the reconciling word;
   Give power and unction from above,
   Whene'er the joyful sound is heard.

3 Be darkness, at Thy coming, light;
   Confusion, order in Thy path;
   Souls without strength inspire with might;
   Bid mercy triumph over wrath.

4 O Spirit of the Lord, prepare
   All the round earth her God to meet;
   Breathe Thou abroad like morning air,
   Till hearts of stone begin to beat.

5 Baptize the nations far and nigh;
   The triumphs of the Cross record;
   The name of Jesus glorify
   Till every kindred call Him Lord.
               Rev. James Montgomery (1771 — 1854).

554   *Doxology.*
Praise God, from whom all blessings flow!
Praise Him, all creatures here below!
Praise Him above, ye heavenly host!
Praise Father, Son, and Holy Ghost!

(233)

YOUTH.

SILOAM. C. M.   I. B. WOODBURY, 1842.

1. By cool Siloam's shady rill, How sweet the lily grows; How sweet the breath beneath the hill Of Sharon's dewy rose.

By per. of Oliver Ditson Company, owners of copyright.

555   *Early Piety.*

1 By cool Siloam's shady rill,
   How sweet the lily grows;
How sweet the breath beneath the hill
   Of Sharon's dewy rose.

2 And such the child whose early feet
   The paths of peace have trod;
Whose secret heart, with influence sweet,
   Is upward drawn to God.

3 By cool Siloam's shady rill
   The lily must decay;
The rose that blooms beneath the hill
   Must shortly fade away.

4 And soon, too soon, the wintry hour,
   Of man's maturer age,
May shake the soul with sorrow's power,
   And stormy passion's rage.

5 O Thou, whose infancy was found
   With heavenly ray to shine, [crowned,
Whose years, with changeless virtue
   Were all alike divine;

6 Dependent on Thy bounteous breath,
   We seek Thy grace alone,
In childhood, manhood, and in death,
   To keep us still Thy own.
             Bp. Reg. Heber (1783 — 1826).

556   *Children Dedicated.*

1 Now let the children of the saints
   Be dedicate to God;
Pour out Thy Spirit on them, Lord,
   And wash them in Thy blood.

2 Thus to the parents and their seed
   Shall Thy salvation come;
And numerous households meet at last
   In one eternal home.
        Adapted by LOWELL MASON (1792 — 1872).

HAMBURG. (Gregorian.) L. M.

1. Dear Saviour, if these lambs should stray From Thy se-cure en-clos-ure's bound, And, lured by world-ly joys a-way. A-mong the thoughtless crowd be found;

557   *Prayer for the Children of the Church.*

1 Dear Saviour, if these lambs should stray
   From Thy secure enclosure's bound,
And, lured by worldly joys away,
   Among the thoughtless crowd be found;

2 Remember still that they are Thine,
   That Thy dear sacred name they bear;
Think that the seal of love divine,
   The sign of convenant grace, they wear.

3 In all their erring, sinful years,
   Oh, let them ne'er forgotten be;
Remember all the prayers and tears
   Which made them consecrate to Thee.

4 And when those lips no more can pray,
   These eyes can weep for them no more,
Turn Thou their feet from folly's way,
   The wanderers to Thy fold restore.
        Mrs. Ann Beadley Hyde (— 1872).

(234)

THE DEATH OF A CHILD.

EDEN. 8s, 7s & 6s. Samuel Smith.

558 *Of Such is the Kingdom of God.*

1 There 's a home for little children
  Above the bright blue sky,
  Where Jesus reigns in glory;
  A home of peace and joy;
No home on earth is like it
  Or can with it compare,
For every one is happy,
  Nor could be happier, there.

2 There 's a song for little children
  Above the bright blue sky,
A song that will not weary,
  Though sung continually;
A song which even angels
  Can never, never sing;
They know not Christ as Saviour,
  But worship Him as King.

3 There 's a crown for little children
  Above the bright blue sky,
A harp of sweetest music;
  A palm of victory.
All, all above is treasured
  And found in Christ alone;
Lord, grant Thy little children
  To know Thee as their own.
  Albert Mildane, 1825.

WOODLAND. C. M. 5l. Rev. N. D. Gould (1781—1864).

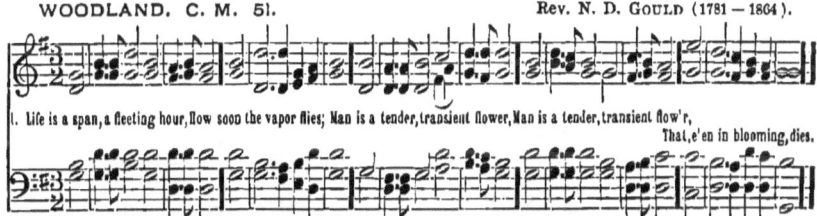

559 *The Death of A Child.*

1 Life is a span, a fleeting hour,
  How soon the vapor flies;
Man is a tender, transient flower,
  That, e'en in blooming, dies.

2 The once loved form, now cold and dead,
  Each mournful thought employs;
And nature weeps her comforts fled,
  And withered all her joys.

3 Hope looks beyond the bounds of time,
  When what we now deplore
Shall rise in full, immortal prime,
  And bloom to fade no more.

4 Cease, then, fond nature, cease thy tears,
  Religion points on high;
There everlasting spring appears,
  And joys that cannot die.
  Miss Anne Steele (1717—1778).

THE JUDGMENT.

TEMPLE BORO. 8s, 7s & 4s. F. PINDER.

560 *Lo! He Comes, With Clouds Descending.*

1 Lo! He comes, with clouds descending,
Once for favored sinners slain;
Thousand thousand saints attending
Swell the triumph of His train;
Hallelujah!
Jesus comes, He comes to reign.

2 Every eye shall now behold Him
Robed in dreadful majesty;
Those who set at naught and sold Him,
Pierced and nailed Him to the tree,
Deeply wailing,
Shall the true Messiah see.

3 Every island, sea and mountain,
Heaven and earth, shall flee away;
All who hate Him must, confounded,
Hear the trump proclaim the day;
Come to judgment!
Come to judgment! come away!

4 Answer thine own Bride and Spirit;
Hasten, Lord! and quickly come;
The new heaven, and earth to inherit
Take Thy pining exiles home;
All creation
Travails, groans and bids Thee come.

5 Yea, amen! let all adore Thee,
High on Thine eternal throne;
Saviour! take the power and glory,
Claim the kingdom for Thine own;
Oh, come quickly!
Hallelujah! come, Lord! come.

Rev. Charles Wesley (1708 — 1788).
Rev. Martin Madan (1726 — 1790).

561 *Lo, He Cometh!*

1 Lo! He cometh: countless trumpets
Blow to raise the sleeping dead;
Midst ten thousands saints and angels,
See their great exalted Head:
Hallelujah!
Welcome, welcome, Son of God.

2 Full of joyful expectation,
Saints, behold the Judge appear;
Truth and justice go before Him;
Now the royal sentence hear:
Hallelujah!
Welcome, welcome, Judge divine.

3 "Come, ye blessed of my Father,
Enter into life and joy;
Banish all your fears and sorrows;
Endless praise be your employ:"
Hallelujah!
Welcome, welcome, to the skies.

Rev. John Cennick (1717 — 1755).

THE JUDGMENT.

BREST. 8s, 7s & 4s. Dr. L. MASON (1792–1872).

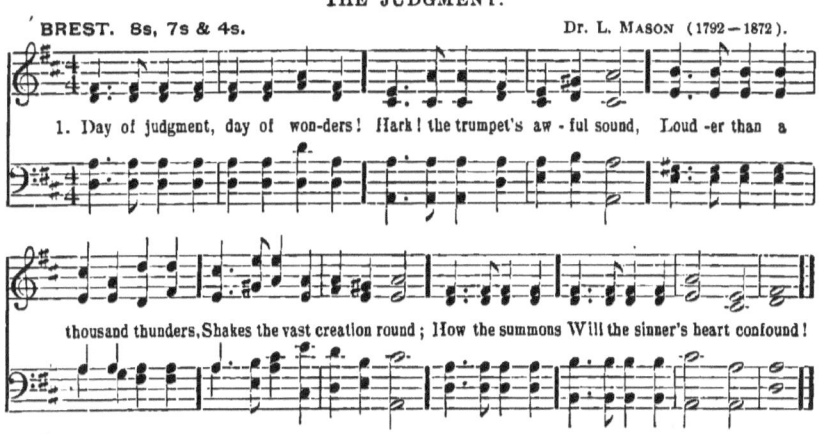

562 *The Day of Judgment.*

1 Day of judgment, day of wonders!
Hark! the trumpet's awful sound,
Louder than a thousand thunders,
Shakes the vast creation round!
How the summons
Will the sinner's heart confound!

2 At His call the dead awaken,
Rise to life from earth and sea;
All the powers of nature shaken
By His looks prepare to flee:
Careless sinner,
What will then become of thee?

3 See the Judge our nature wearing,
Clothed in majesty divine;
You who long for His appearing,
Then shall say, This God is mine!
Gracious Saviour,
Own me in that day for Thine.

Rev. John Newton (1725–1807).

TAMWORTH. 8s, 7s & 4s. C. LOCKHART.

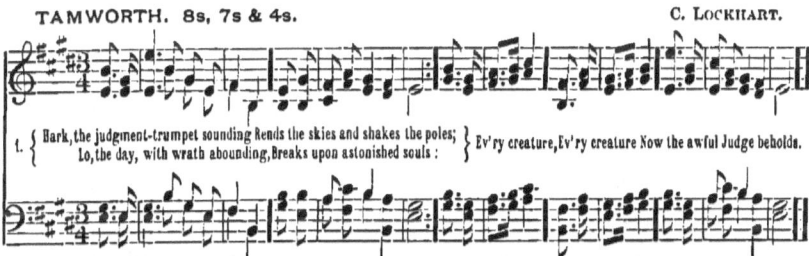

563 *The Judgment-Trumpet.*

1 Hark, the judgment-trumpet sounding
Rends the skies and shakes the poles;
Lo, the day, with wrath abounding,
Breaks upon astonished souls:
Every creature
Now the awful Judge beholds.

2 Jesus, Captain of salvation,
Leads His armies down the skies;
Every kindred, tribe and nation,
From the sleep of death, arise:
Heaven's loud summons
Fills the world with dread surprise.

3 Zion's King, His throne ascending,
Calls His saints before His face;
Crowns, with glory never-ending,
All the children of His grace:
Heaven shall echo;
Songs of triumph fill the place.

Rev. Nathan Sidney Smith Beman (1786–1871).

(237)

THE JUDGMENT.

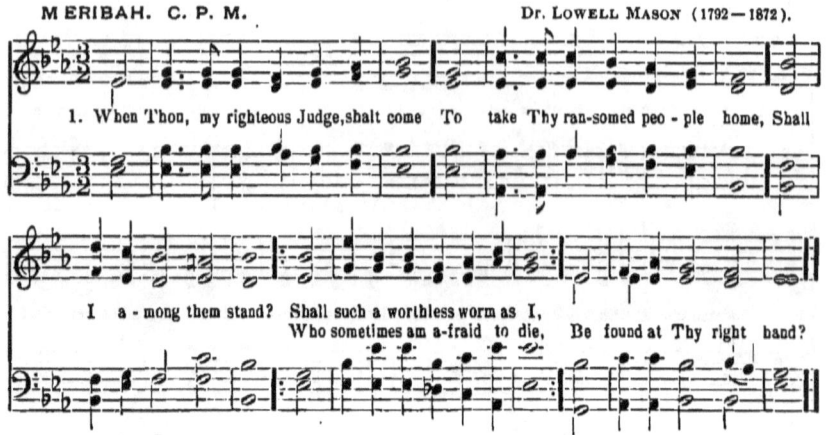

MERIBAH. C. P. M.   Dr. LOWELL MASON (1792—1872).

1. When Thou, my righteous Judge, shalt come To take Thy ransomed people home, Shall I among them stand? Shall such a worthless worm as I, Who sometimes am afraid to die, Be found at Thy right hand?

564 *Apprehension of Judgment.*

1 When Thou, my righteous Judge, shalt come
To take Thy ransomed people home,
 Shall I among them stand?
Shall such a worthless worm as I,
Who sometimes am afraid to die,
 Be found at Thy right hand?

2 I love to meet among them now,
Before Thy gracious feet to bow,
 Though vilest of them all:
But can I bear the piercing thought
What if my name should be left out,
 When Thou for me shalt call?

3 Prevent, prevent it by Thy grace;
Be Thou, dear Lord, my hiding-place,
 In this the accepted day;
Thy pardoning voice, oh, let me hear,
To still my unbelieving fear,
 Nor let me fall, I pray.

4 Let me among Thy saints be found,
Whene'er th' archangel's trump shall sound,
 To see Thy smiling face;
Then loudest of the crowd I'll sing,
While heaven's resounding mansions ring
 With shouts of sovereign grace.
Selina Shirley, Countess of Huntington (1707—1791).

565 *Fleeing to Christ as a Refuge.*

1 O Thou, that hearest the prayer of faith,
Wilt Thou not save a soul from death,
 That casts itself on Thee?
I have no refuge of my own,
But fly to what my Lord has done,
 And suffered, once for me.

2 Slain in the guilty sinner's stead,
His spotless righteousness I plead
 And His atoning blood:
Thy righteousness my robe shall be,
Thy merit shall avail for me,
 And bring me near to God.

3 Then snatch me from eternal death,
The Spirit of adoption breathe,
 His consolation send:
By Him some word of life impart,
And sweetly whisper to my heart,
 "Thy Maker is thy Friend."

4 The king of terrors then would be
A welcome messenger to me,
 To bid me come away:
Unclogged by earth, or earthly things,
I'd mount, I'd fly with eager wings,
 To everlasting day.
Rev. A. M. Toplady (1740—1778).

566 *Doxology.*

To Father, Son, and Holy Ghost,
Be praise amid the heavenly host,
 And in the church below;
From whom all creatures draw their breath,
By whom redemption blessed the earth,
 From whom all comforts flow.

THE JUDGMENT.

GANGES. C. P. M. Rev. John Chandler (1806—1876).

1. Awaked by Si-nai's aw-ful sound, My soul in bonds of guilt I found, And knew not where to go; E-ternal truth did loud proclaim, "The sin-ner must be born a-gain," Or sink to end-less woe.

567 *Necessity of Regeneration.*

1 Awaked by Sinai's awful sound,
My soul in bonds of guilt I found;
 And knew not where to go;
Eternal truth did loud proclaim,
"The sinner must be born again,"
 Or sink to endless woe.

2 When to the law I trembling fled,
It poured its curses on my head,
 I no relief could find;
This fearful truth increased my pain,
"The sinner must be born again,"
 And whelmed my tortured mind.

3 Again did Sinai's thunders roll,
And guilt lay heavy on my soul,
 A vast oppressive load;
Alas! I read and saw it plain,
"The sinner must be born again,"
 Or drink the wrath of God.

4 The saints I heard with rapture tell,
How Jesus conquered death and hell,
 And broke the fowler's snare;
Yet, when I found this truth remain,
"The sinner must be born again,"
 I sunk in deep despair.

5 But while I thus in anguish lay,
The gracious Saviour passed this way,
 And felt His pity move;

The sinner, by His justice slain,
Now by His grace is born again,
 And sings redeeming love.
 Rev. Sampson Occum (1723—1792).
 Rev. Asahel Nettleton (1783—1844).

568 *In Jeopardy Every Hour.*

1 Lo! on a narrow neck of land,
'Twixt two unbounded seas I stand,
 Yet how insensible!
A point of time, a moment's space,
Removes me to yon heavenly place,
 Or shuts me up in hell.

2 O God! my inmost soul convert,
And deeply on my thoughtful heart
 Eternal things impress:
Give me to feel their solemn weight,
And save me ere it be too late;
 Wake me to righteousness.

3 Be this my one great business here,—
With holy trembling, holy fear,
 To make my calling sure!
Thine utmost counsel to fulfill,
And suffer all Thy righteous will,
 And to the end endure!

4 Then Saviour, then my soul receive,
Then bid me in Thy presence live,
 And reign with Thee above;
Where faith is sweetly lost in sight,
And hope, in full, supreme delight,
 And everlasting love.
 Rev. Charles Wesley (1708—1788).

HEAVENLY ANTICIPATIONS.

GLORIA. 15s. Hymns Ancient and Modern.

569 *Hark! the Sound of Holy Voices.*

1 Hark! the sound of holy voices, chanting at the crystal sea —
Alleluia, Alleluia, Alleluia, Lord, to Thee;
Multitude, which none can number, like the stars in glory stands,
Clothed in white apparel, holding palms of victory in their hands.

2 They have come from tribulation, and have washed their robes in blood,
Washed them in the blood of Jesus; tried they were, and firm they stood;
Mock'd, imprison'd, stoned, tormented, sawn asunder, slain with sword,
They have conquer'd death and Satan by the might of Christ the Lord.

3 Marching with Thy Cross their banner, they have triumph'd following
Thee, the Captain of salvation, Thee their Saviour and their King;
Gladly, Lord, with Thee they suffer'd; gladly Lord with Thee they died;
And by death to life immortal they were born and glorified.

4 Now they reign in heavenly glory, now they walk in golden light,
Now they drink, as from a river, holy bliss and infinite;
Love and peace they taste for ever, and all truth and knowledge see
In the beatific vision of the Blessèd Trinity.

5 God of God, the One-begotten, Light of light, Emmanuel,
In whose Body join'd together all the saints forever dwell;
Pour upon us of Thy fullness, that we may for evermore
God the Father, God the Son, and God the Holy Ghost adore.

Bp. C. Wordsworth, D. D. (1807—1885).

HEAVENLY ANTICIPATIONS.

570   *Heavenly Hope.*
1 When I can read my title clear,
   To mansions in the skies,
I bid farewell to every fear,
   And wipe my weeping eyes.

2 Should earth against my soul engage,
   And hellish darts be hurled,
Then I can smile at Satan's rage,
   And face a frowning world.

3 Let cares like a wild deluge come,
   And storms of sorrow fall;
May I but safely reach my home,
   My God, my heaven, my all.

4 There shall I bathe my weary soul,
   In seas of heavenly rest,
And not a wave of trouble roll
   Across my peaceful breast.
Rev. Isaac Watts (1674—1748).

571   *The Father's House for Me.*
1 Thy Father's house! Thine own bright
   home!
And Thou hast there a place for me!
Though yet an exile here I roam,
   That distant home by faith I see.

2 I see its domes resplendent glow,
   Where beams of God's own glory fall,
And trees of life immortal grow,
   Whose fruits o'erhang the sapphire wall.

3 I know that Thou, who on the tree
   Didst deign our mortal guilt to bear,
Wilt bring Thine own to dwell with Thee,
   And waitest to receive them there.

4 Thy love will there array my soul
   In Thine own robe of spotless hue;
And I shall gaze, while ages roll,
   On Thee, with raptures ever new.

5 O welcome day, when Thou my feet
   Shalt bring the shining threshold o'er,
A Father's warm embrace to meet,
   And dwell at home for evermore.
Rev. Ray Palmer (1808—1887).

572   *Doxology.*
To God, the Father, God the Son,
And God the Spirit, Three in One,
Be honor, praise, and glory given,
By all on earth, and all in heaven.

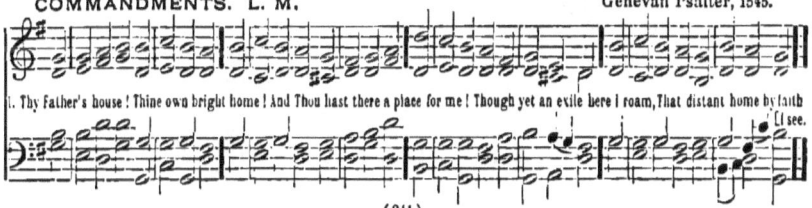

HEAVENLY ANTICIPATIONS.

ANGELS OF JESUS. P. M.   HENRY SMART (1812—1879).

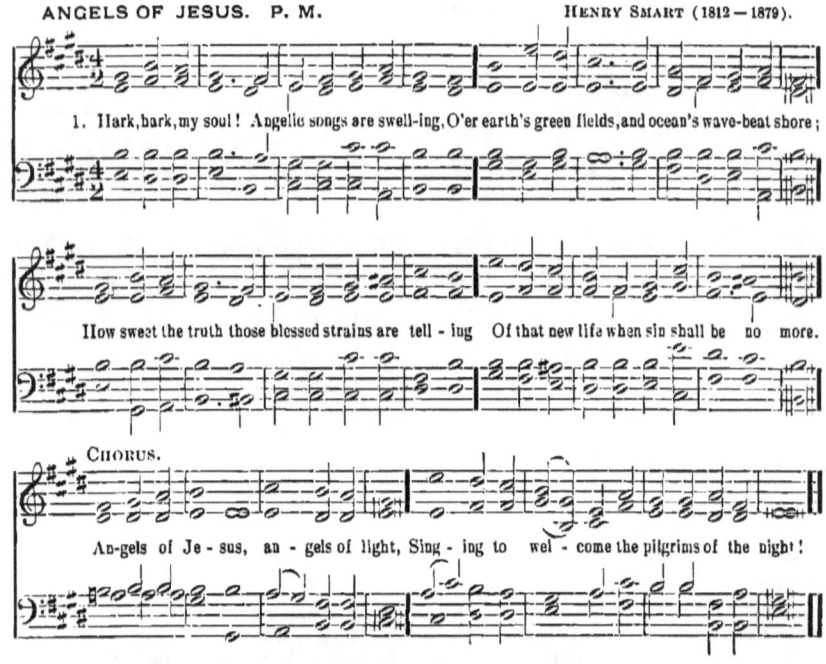

573   *The Night is Far Spent, The Day is at Hand.*

1 Hark, hark, my soul! angelic songs are swelling
    O'er earth's green fields, and ocean's wave-beat shore;
How sweet the truth those blessèd strains are telling
    Of that new life when sin shall be no more.

2 Onward we go, for still we hear them singing,
    "Come, weary souls, for Jesus bids you come;"
And through the dark, its echoes sweetly ringing,
    The music of the gospel leads us home.

3 Far, far away, like bells at evening pealing,
    The voice of Jesus sounds o'er land and sea,
And laden souls by thousands meekly stealing,
    Kind Shepherd, turn their weary steps to Thee.

4 Rest comes at length; though life be long and dreary,
    The day must dawn and darksome night be past;
Faith's journey ends in welcome to the weary,
    And Heav'n, the heart's true home, will come at last.

5 Angels! sing on, your faithful watches keeping,
    Sing us sweet fragments of the songs above;
Till morning's joy shall end the night of weeping,
    And life's long shadows break in cloudless love.

Rev. Frederick William Faber (1814—1863).

HEAVENLY ANTICIPATIONS.

574   *Thy Will be Done.*

1 " Thy will be | done!" ‖ In devious way The hurrying stream of | life may | run; ‖ Yet still our grateful hearts shall say, | " Thy will be | done."

2 " Thy will be | done!" ‖ If o'er us shine a gladdening and a | prosperous | sun, ‖ This prayer will make it more divine — | " Thy will be | done!"

3 " Thy will be | done!" ‖ Though shrouded o'er Our path with | gloom, ‖ one comfort — one ‖ is ours: — to breathe, while we adore, | " Thy will be | done."

Sir John Bowring (1792–1872).

(243)

HEAVENLY ANTICIPATIONS.

SIENNA. S. M.   W. H. DEANE.

1. Far from my heav'n-ly home, Far from my Fath-er's breast,
Faint-ing I cry, blest Spir-it, come, And speed me to my rest.

575   *Speed Me to My Rest.*
1 Far from my heavenly home,
   Far from my Father's breast,
Fainting I cry, blest Spirit, come,
   And speed me to my rest.

2 Upon the willows long
   My harp has silent hung;
How should I sing a cheerful song
   Till Thou inspire my tongue.

3 My spirit homeward turns,
   And fain would thither flee;
My heart, O Zion, droops and yearns
   When I remember thee.

4 To thee, to thee I press,
   A dark and toilsome road;
When shall I pass the wilderness,
   And reach the saints abode?

5 God of my life, be near;
   On Thee my hopes I cast;
Oh, guide me through the desert drear,
   And bring me home at last.
         Rev. Henry Francis Lyte (1793—1847).

576   *Give to the Winds Thy Fears.*
1 Give to the winds thy fears;
   Hope, and be undismayed:
God hears thy sighs, and counts thy tears;
   God shall lift up thy head.

2 Through waves and clouds and storms,
   He gently clears thy way;
Wait thou His time, so shall this night
   Soon end in joyous day.

3 Far, far above thy thought
   His counsel shall appear,
When fully He the work hath wrought
   That caused thy needless fear.
        Rev. Paul Gerhardt (1606—1676).
      Tr. by *Rev. John Wesley* (1703—1791).

577   *Forever with the Lord.*
1 Forever with the Lord:
   Amen, so let it be;
Life from the dead is in that word,
   'T is immortality.

2 Here in the body pent,
   Absent from Him I roam,
Yet nightly pitch my moving tent,
   A day's march nearer home.

3 My Father's house on high,
   Home of my soul, how near,
At times, to faith's far-seeing eye,
   Thy golden gates appear.

4 "Forever with the Lord;"
   Father, if 't is Thy will,
The promise of that faithful word
   E'en here to me fulfill.
        Rev. James Montgomery (1771—1854).

HEAVENLY ANTICIPATIONS.

578 *We Are Compassed About.*

1 For all the saints, who from their labors rest,
Who, Thee, by faith before the world con-
Thy name, O Jesus, be for ever blest. [fessed,
Hallelujah!

2 Thou wast their rock, their fortress, and
their might; [fight;
Thou, Lord, their captain in the well-fought
Thou, in the darkness drear, their one true
light.
Hallelujah!

3 Oh, may Thy soldiers, faithful, true and
bold,
Fight as the saints who nobly fought of old,
And win, with them, the victor's crown of
gold.
Hallelujah!

4 Oh, blest communion, fellowship divine!
We feebly struggle; they in glory shine!
Yet all are one in Thee, for all are Thine.
Hallelujah!

5 And when the strife is fierce, the warfare
long,
Steals on the ear the distant triumph-song,
And hearts are brave again, and arms are
strong!
Hallelujah!

6 The golden evening brightens in the west;
Soon, soon, to faithful warriors cometh rest;
Sweet is the calm of Paradise the blest.
Hallelujah!

7 But lo! there breaks a yet more glorious
day;
The saints triumphant rise in bright array;
The King of Glory passes on His way!
Hallelujah!

8 From earth's wide bounds, from ocean's
farthest coast, [less host,
Through gates of pearl streams in the count-
Singing to Father, Son, and Holy Ghost —
Hallelujah!

Bp. W. W. How (1823 –).

HEAVENLY ANTICIPATIONS.

LANGRAN. 10s. JAMES LANGRAN (1835—).

1. Weary of earth and lad-en with my sin, I look at heav'n and long to en-ter in, But there no e-vil thing may find a home: And yet I hear a voice that bids me "Come."

579 *Weary of Earth.*

1 Weary of earth and laden with my sin,
I look at heaven and long to enter in,
But there no evil thing may find a home;
And yet I hear a voice that bids me "Come."

2 So vile I am, how dare I hope to stand
In the pure glory of that holy land?
Before the whiteness of that throne appear?
Yet there are hands stretch'd out to draw me near.

3 The while I fain would tread the heavenly way,
Evil is ever with me, day by day;
Yet on mine ears the gracious tidings fall,
"Repent, confess, thou shalt be loosed from all."

4 It is the voice of Jesus that I hear,
His are the hands stretched out to draw me near,
And His the blood that can for all atone,
And set me faultless there before the throne.

5 'T was He Who found me on the deathly wild,
And made me heir of heaven, the Father's child,
And day by day, whereby my soul may live
Gives me His grace of pardon, and will give

6 Yea, Thou wilt answer for me, righteous Lord;
Thine all the merits, mine the great reward;
Thine the sharp thorns, and mine the golden crown.
Mine the life won, and Thine the life laid down.

Rev. S. J. Stone (1839—).

580 *Remember Me.*

1 Lord, when with dying lips my prayer is said,
Grant that in faith Thy kingdom I may see;
And, thinking on Thy cross and bleeding head,
May breathe my parting words, "Remember me."

2 Remember me, but not my shame or sin;
Thy cleansing blood hath washed them all away;
Thy precious death for me did pardon win;
Thy blood redeemed me in that awful day.

3 Remember me; yet how canst Thou forget
What pain and anguish I have caused to Thee,
The cross, the agony, the bloody sweat,
And all the sorrow Thou didst bear for me?

4 Remember me; and, ere I pass away,
Speak Thou the assuring word that sets us free,
And make Thy promise to my heart,"To-day,
Thou too shalt rest in Paradise with me."

Rev. W. D. Mac Lagan (1826—).

HEAVENLY ANTICIPATIONS.

NORTHFIELD. C. M. — JEREMIAH INGALLS (1764—1838).

1. Lo, what a glorious sight appears To our believing eyes; earth and seas are passed away, And the old rolling skies, The earth and seas are passed away. And the old rolling skies. The earth and seas are pass'd away, passed away, The earth and seas are passed away,

581 *A New Heaven, and a New Earth.*

1 Lo, what a glorious sight appears
  To our believing eyes;
The earth and seas are passed away,
  And the old rolling skies.

2 From the third heav'n where God resides,
  That holy, happy place,
The new Jerusalem comes down,
  Adorned with shining grace.

3 Attending angels shout for joy,
  And the bright armies sing,
Mortals, behold the sacred seat
  Of your descending King.

4 "The God of glory down to men
  Removes His blest abode;
Men, the dear objects of His grace,
  And He the loving God.

5 "His own soft hand shall wipe the tears
  From every weeping eye;
And pains, and groans, and griefs, and fears,
  And death itself shall die."

6 How long, dear Saviour, Oh, how long
  Shall this bright hour delay?
Fly swifter round, ye wheels of time,
  And bring the welcome day.
  Rev. Isaac Watts (1674—1748).

582 *The Resurrection.*

1 Lo, I behold the scattering shades,
  The dawn of heaven appears;
The sweet immortal morning spreads
  Its blushes round the spheres.

2 I see the Lord of glory come,
  And flaming guards around;
The skies divide to make Him room,
  The trumpet shakes the ground.

3 I hear the voice, "Ye dead arise,"
  And lo, the graves obey;
And waking, saints with joyful eyes,
  Salute the expected day.

4 Oh, may my humble spirit stand
  Amongst them clothed in white;
The meanest place at His right hand
  Is infinite delight.
  Rev. Isaac Watts (1674—1748).

583 *Dying Hymn.*

1 Earth, with its dark and dreadful ills,
  Recedes and fades away;
Lift up your heads, ye heavenly hills,
  Ye gates of death give way.

2 My soul is full of whispered song,
  My blindness is my sight;
The shadows that I feared so long
  Are all alive with light.

3 The while my pulses faintly beat,
  My faith doth so abound,
I feel grow firm beneath my feet
  The green, immortal ground.

4 The palace walls I almost see
  Where dwells my Lord and King;
O grave, where is thy victory,
  O death, where is thy sting!
  Miss Alice Cary (1820—1871).

TIME AND ETERNITY.

I'M A PILGRIM. 9s, 10s & 11s.   *Italian Melody.*

584   *The Christian Pilgrim.*

1 I'm a pilgrim, and I'm a stranger,
   I can tarry, I can tarry but a night;
Do not detain me, for I am going
To where the fountains are ever flowing.
   I'm a pilgrim, and I'm a stranger,
   I can tarry, I can tarry but a night.

2 There the sunbeams are ever shining,
   I am longing, I am longing for the sight.

Within a country unknown and dreary,
I have been wandering forlorn and weary.
   I'm a pilgrim, etc.

3 Of that country, to which I am going,
   My Redeemer, my Redeemer is the light;
There are no sorrows, nor any sighing,
Nor any sin there, nor any dying.
   I'm a pilgrim, etc.

Anon.

AMSTERDAM. 7s & 6s, D.   JAMES NARES (1715—1783).

TIME AND ETERNITY.

ALFORD. 7s & 6s, D. Rev. J. B. DYKES (1823–1876).

1. Ten thousand times ten thousand, In sparkling raiment bright, The armies of the ransom'd saints Throng up the steeps of light; 'T is finished, all is finished, Their fight with death and sin; Fling open wide the golden gates, And let the victors in.

585 *The Armies of God.*
1 Ten thousand times ten thousand,
  In sparkling raiment bright,
The armies of the ransomed saints
  Throng up the steeps of light;
'T is finished, all is finished,
  Their fight with death and sin;
Fling open wide the golden gates,
  And let the victors in.

2 What rush of hallelujahs
  Fills all the earth and sky!
What ringing of a thousand harps
  Bespeaks the triumph nigh!
O day, for which creation
  And all its tribes were made!
O joy, for all its former woes,
  A thousand fold repaid!

3 Bring near Thy great salvation,
  Thou Lamb for sinners slain;
Fill up the roll of Thine elect,
  Then take Thy power, and reign;
Appear, Desire of nations —
  Thine exiles long for home —
Show in the heaven Thy promised sign,
  Thou Prince and Saviour, come!
   Rev. Henry Alford (1810–1871).

586 *Aspiring After Heaven.*
   Tune, AMSTERDAM.
1 Rise, my soul, and stretch thy wings,
  Thy better portion trace;
Rise from transitory things,
  Towards heaven, thy native place;

Sun and moon and stars decay;
  Time shall soon this earth remove;
Rise, my soul, and haste away,
  To seats prepared above.

2 Rivers to the ocean run,
  Nor stay in all their course;
Fire ascending seeks the sun;
  Both speed them to their source:
So a soul that's born of God
  Pants to view His glorious face,
Upward tends to His abode,
  To rest in His embrace.

3 Cease, ye pilgrims, cease to mourn;
  Press onward to the prize;
Soon our Saviour will return,
  Triumphant in the skies.
Yet a season, and you know,
  Happy entrance will be given;
All our sorrows left below,
  And earth exchanged for heaven.
   Rev. Robert Seagrave (1693–).

587 *Doxology.*
   Tune, AMSTERDAM.
Father, Son, and Holy Ghost,
  One God, whom we adore,
Join we with the heavenly host
  To praise Thee evermore;
Live, by heaven and earth adored,
  Three in One, and One in Three,
Holy, holy, holy Lord,
  All glory be to Thee!

(249)

TIME AND ETERNITY.

ELTHAM. 7s, D.   Dr. LOWELL MASON (1792—1872).

588   *Till He Comes!*
1 "*Till He come!*"—Oh, let the words
Linger on the trembling chords;
Let the "little while" between
In their golden light be seen;
Let us think how heav'n and home
Lie beyond that "*till He come!*"

2 When the weary ones we love
Enter on that rest above;
When the words of love and cheer
Fall no longer on our ear:
Hush! be every murmur dumb,
It is only "*till He come!*"

3 Clouds and darkness round us press;
Would we have one sorrow less?
All the sharpness of the cross,
All that tells the world is loss.
Death, and darkness, and the tomb,
Pain us only "*till He come!*"

4 See! the feast of love is spread,
Drink the wine and eat the bread;
Sweet memorials, till the Lord
Call us round His heavenly board,
Some from earth, from glory some,
Severed only "*till He come!*"
           Bp. Ed. H. Bickersteth 1825.

589   *Praise of the Redeemed in Heaven.*
1 High, in yonder realms of light,
   Dwell the raptured saints above;
Far beyond our feeble sight,
   Happy in Immanuel's love;

Pilgrims in this vale of tears,
   Once they knew, like us below,
Gloomy doubts, distressing fears,
   Torturing pain, and heavy woe.

2 Oft the big unbidden tear,
   Stealing down the furrowed cheek
Told, in eloquence sincere,
   Tales of woe they could not speak.
But these days of weeping o'er,
   Past this scene of toil and pain,
They shall feel distress no more,
   Never, never weep again.

3 'Mid the chorus of the skies,
   'Mid the angelic lyres above,
Hark! their songs melodious rise,
   Songs of praise to Jesus' love,
Happy spirits, ye are fled
   Where no grief can entrance find;
Lulled to rest, the aching head,
   Soothed, the anguish of the mind.

4 All is tranquil and serene,
   Calm and undisturbed repose;
There no cloud can intervene.
   There no angry tempest blows.
Every tear is wiped away,
   Sighs no more shall heave the breast;
Night is lost in endless day,
   Sorrow, in eternal rest.
           Rev. Thomas Raffles (1788—1863).

TIME AND ETERNITY.

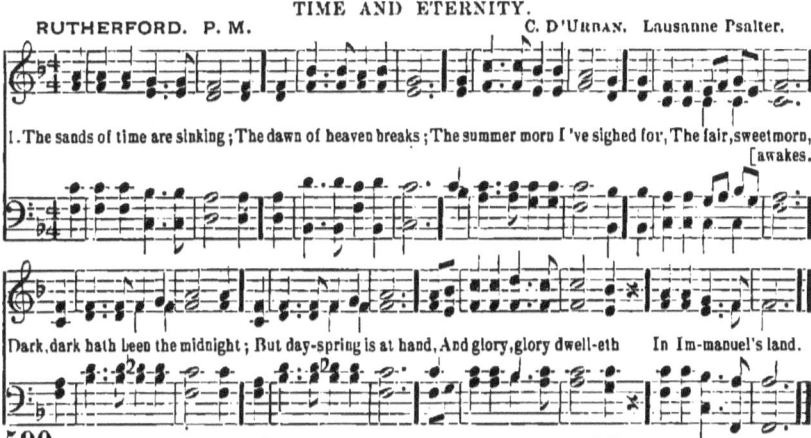

590 *Immanuel's Land.*

1 The sands of time are sinking;
  The dawn of heaven breaks;
  The summer morn I've sighed for,
  The fair, sweet morn awakes.
  Dark, dark hath been the midnight;
  But dayspring is at hand,
  And glory—glory dwelleth
  In Immanuel's land.

2 O Christ! He is the fountain,
  The deep, sweet well of love;
  The streams on earth I've tasted,
  More deep I'll drink above;
  There to an ocean fulness
  His mercy doth expand,
  And glory—glory dwelleth
  In Immanuel's land.

3 With mercy and with judgment
  My web of time He wove,
  And aye the dews of sorrow
  Were lustred by His love;
  I'll bless the hand that guided,
  I'll bless the heart that planned,
  When throned where glory dwelleth,
  In Immanuel's land.

Mrs. Anne R. Cousin, 1857.

591 *Rest in Heaven.*

1 And, is there, Lord! a rest,
  For weary souls designed,
  Where not a care shall stir the breast,
  Or sorrow entrance find?

2 Is there a blissful home,
  Where kindred minds shall meet,
  And live, and love, nor ever roam
  From that serene retreat?

3 Are there celestial streams,
  Where living waters glide,
  With murmurs sweet as angel dreams,
  And flowery banks beside?

4 For ever blessèd they,
  Whose joyful feet shall stand,
  While endless ages waste away,
  Amid that glorious land!

5 My soul would thither tend,
  While toilsome years are given;
  Then let me, gracious God! ascend
  To sweet repose in heaven.

Rev. Ray Palmer (1808—1887).

TIME AND ETERNITY.

SHINING SHORE. P. M. GEORGE FREDERICK ROOT (1820 –).

1. My days are glid-ing swift-ly by, And I, a pil-grim stranger, Would not detain them as they fly,
D. S. *just before the shining shore,*

Those hours of toil and dan-ger: For now we stand on Jor-dan's strand, Our friends are passing ov-er; And,
We may al-most dis-cov-er!

592 *Shining Shore.*

1 My days are gliding swiftly by,
And I, a pilgrim stranger,
Would not detain them as they fly,—
Those hours of toil and danger:
For now we stand on Jordan's strand,
Our friends are passing over;
And, just before, the shining shore
We may almost discover.

2 Our absent King, the watchword gave,—
"Let every lamp be burning;"
We look afar, across the wave,
Our distant home discerning.
For now, etc.

3 Should coming days be dark and cold,
We will not yield to sorrow,
For hope will sing, with courage bold,
"There's glory on the morrow!"
For now, etc.

4 Let storms of woe in whirlwinds rise,
Each cord on earth to sever,—
There — bright and joyous in the skies —
There — is our home forever.
For now, etc.

Rev. David Nelson (1793 – 1844).

HORSLEY. C. M.

593 *A Little While.*

1 And is it so ? "A little while,"
And then the life undying,
The light of God's unclouded smile,
The singing for the sighing ?
"A little while!"— O glorious word!
Sweet solace of our sorrow;
And then "forever with the Lord,"
The everlasting morrow.

2 Then be it ours to journey on
In paths that He decrees us,
Where His own feet before have gone,
Our strength, our hope, our Jesus;
In lowly fellowship with Him,
The cross appointed bearing;
For oh! a crown no grief can dim,
One day we shall be wearing.

3 Oh! 't will be passing sweet to gaze
On Him in all His glory;
And lost in love and glad amaze
To shout redemption's story;
Till angels bend to catch the strain
Our human lips are swelling,
And "worthy is the Lamb once slain,"
Resounds through heaven's high dwelling.

Songs of Zion.

WILLIAM HORSLEY (1774 – 1858).

TIME AND ETERNITY.

BEYOND THE SMILING AND THE WEEPING. P. M.   GEO. C. STEBBINS.

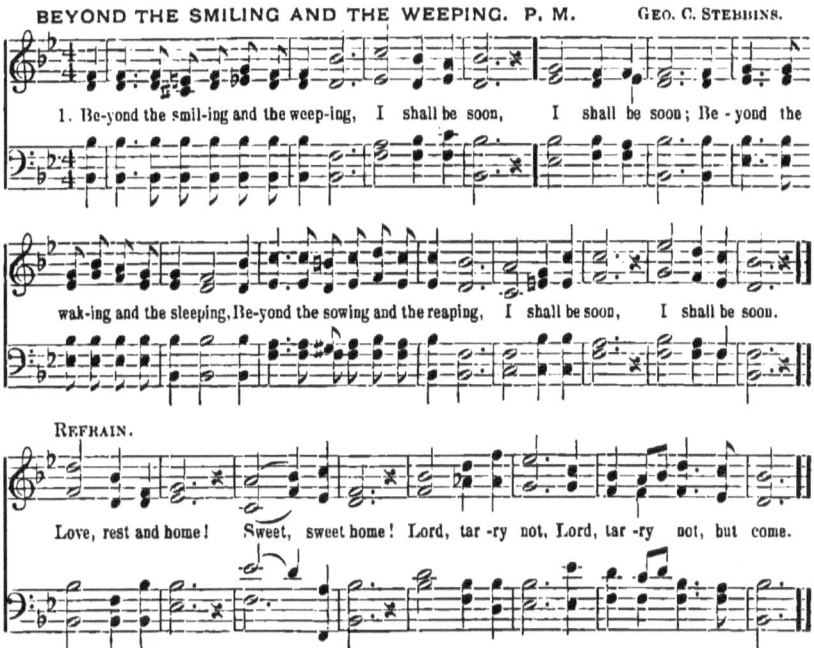

By per. of G. C. Stebbins, owner of copyright.

594   *Beyond.*

1 Beyond the smiling and the weeping,
   I shall be soon, I shall be soon;
Beyond the waking and the sleeping,
Beyond the sowing and the reaping,
   I shall be soon, I shall be soon.

2 Beyond the blooming and the fading,
   I shall be soon, I shall be soon;
Beyond the shining and the shading,
Beyond the hoping and the dreading,
   I shall be soon, I shall be soon.

3 Beyond the parting and the meeting,
   I shall be soon, I shall be soon;
Beyond the farewell and the greeting,
Beyond the pulse's fever beating,
   I shall be soon, I shall be soon.

4 Beyond the frost-chain and the fever,
   I shall be soon, I shall be soon;
Beyond the rock-waste and the river,

Beyond the ever and the never,
   I shall be soon, I shall be soon.
      Rev. Horatius Bonar, D. D. (1808 — 1890).

595   *I saw a New Heaven and a New Earth.*
       Tune, HORSLEY.

1 From heaven the new Jerusalem comes
   All worthy of her Lord:
See all things now at last renewed,
   And Paradise restored!

2 The God of glory down to men
   Removes His blest abode;
He dwells with men; His people, they,
   And He, His people's God.

3 His gracious hand shall wipe the tear
   From every weeping eye;
And pains and groans, and griefs and fears,
   And death itself, shall die.

4 Oh, may we stand before the Lamb
   When earth and seas are fled,
And hear the Judge pronounce our name,
   With blessings on our head.
      Rev. Isaac Watts (1674 — 1748).

TIME AND ETERNITY.

WOODLAND. C. M. 5 l.   Rev. N. D. GOULD (1781—1864).

1. There is an hour of peaceful rest, To mourning wand'rers given; There is a joy for souls distressed. A balm for ev-'ry wound-ed breast: 'T is found a-bove, in heaven.

596 *Heaven.*

1 There is an hour of peaceful rest,
  To mourning wanderers given;
  There is a joy for souls distressed,
  A balm for every wounded breast:
  'T is found above — in heaven.

2 There is a home for weary souls,
  By sin and sorrow driven,—
  When tossed on life's tempestuous shoals,
  Where storms arise, and ocean rolls,
  And all is drear — but heaven.

3 There faith lifts up her cheerful eye
  To brighter prospects given;
  And views the tempest passing by
  The evening shadows quickly fly,
  And all serene — in heaven.

4 There, fragrant flowers immortal bloom,
  And joys supreme are given;
  There, rays divine disperse the gloom;
  Beyond the confines of the tomb
  Appears the dawn of heaven!

  Rev. W. B. Tappan (1794 — 1849).

597 *Heaven and Home.*

1 The saints of God, from death set free,
  With joy shall mount on high;
  The heavenly hosts, with praises loud,
  Shall meet them in the sky.

2 Together to their Father's house
  With joyful hearts they go,

And dwell for ever with the Lord,
  Beyond the reach of woe.

3 A few short years of evil past,
  We reach the happy shore,
  Where death-divided friends at last
  Shall meet to part no more.

  M. Bruce (1746 — 1767).

598 *Give Me the Wings of Faith.*

1 Give me the wings of faith, to rise
  Within the veil, and see
  The saints above, how great their joys
  How bright their glories be.

2 Once they were mourning here below,
  And wet their couch with tears;
  They wrestled hard, as we do now,
  With sins, and doubts, and fears.

3 I ask them, whence their victory came.
  They, with united breath,
  Ascribe their conquest to the Lamb,
  Their triumph to His death.

4 They marked the footsteps that He trod,
  His zeal inspired their breast;
  And following their incarnate God,
  Possessed the promised rest.

5 Our glorious Leader claims our praise
  For His own pattern given;
  While the long cloud of witnesses
  Shows the same path to heaven.

  Rev. Isaac Watts (1674 — 1748).

TIME AND ETERNITY.

IRENE. 7s & 5s. From Rev. C. C. SCHOLEFIELD. Arr. by Sir A. SULLIVAN.

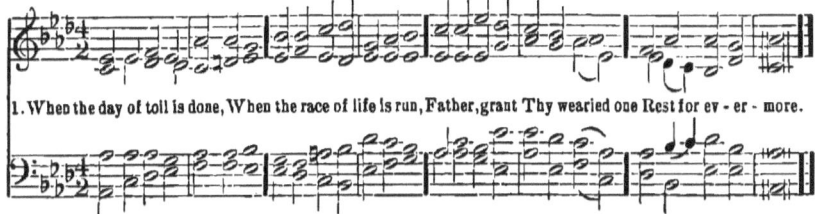

1. When the day of toil is done, When the race of life is run, Father, grant Thy wearied one Rest for ev - er - more.

599 *At Thy Right Hand There are Pleasures For Evermore.*

1 When the day of toil is done,
When the race of life is run,
Father, grant Thy wearied one
   Rest for evermore.

2 When the strife of sin is stilled,
When the foe within is killed,
Be Thy gracious word fulfilled —
   Peace for evermore.

3 When the darkness melts away
At the breaking of Thy day,
Bid us hail the cheering ray,
   Light for evermore.

4 When the heart, by sorrow tried,
Feels at length its throbs subside,
Bring us where all tears are dried —
   Joy for evermore.

5 When for vanished days we yearn,
Days that never can return,
Teach us in Thy love to learn
   Love for evermore.

6 When the breath of life is flown,
When the grave must claim its own,
Lord of life, be ours Thy crown,
   Life for evermore.

Rev. John Ellerton (1826 —).

NAUMANN. C. M. 5l. Arr. from NAUMANN.

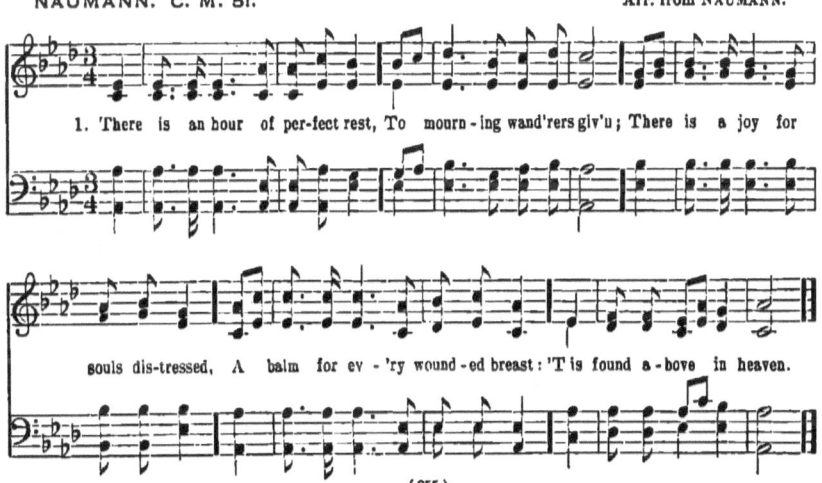

1. There is an hour of per-fect rest, To mourn-ing wand'rers giv'n; There is a joy for souls dis-tressed, A balm for ev - 'ry wound-ed breast: 'T is found a - bove in heaven.

TIME AND ETERNITY.

FREDERICK. 11s.   G. KINGSLEY (1811—1884).

I would not live al-way: I ask not to stay
Where storm aft-er storm ris-es [Omit . . .] dark o'er the way; The few lu-rid
morn-ings that dawn on us here, Are e-nough for life's woes, full e-nough for its cheer.

600   *Death Welcome to the Believer.*

1 I would not live alway; I ask not to stay
Where storm after storm rises dark o'er
    the way;   [here,
The few lurid mornings that dawn on us
Are enough for life's woes, full enough for
    its cheer.

2 I would not live alway, thus fettered by
    sin,
Temptation without, and corruption within;
E'en the rapture of pardon is mingled
    with fears,   [tears.
And the cup of thanksgiving with penitent

3 I would not live alway; no, welcome the
    tomb;   [gloom;
Since Jesus hath lain there, I dread not its
There, sweet be my rest, till He bid me
    arise,   [skies.
To hail Him in triumph descending the

4 Who, who would live alway, away from
    his God,
Away from yon heaven, that blissful abode,
Where the rivers of pleasure flow o'er the
    bright plains,
And the noontide of glory eternally reigns.

5 Where the saints of all ages in harmony
    meet   [greet;
Their Saviour and brethren, transported to

While the anthems of rapture unceasingly
    roll,   [the soul.
And the smile of the Lord is the feast of
    Rev. W. A. Muhlenberg (1796—1877).

601   *Looking to Jesus.*

1 O eyes that are weary, and hearts that
    are sore!
Look off unto Jesus, and sorrow no more;
The light of His countenance shineth so
    bright,   [night.
That here, as in heaven, there need be no

2 When looking to Jesus, I go not astray,
My eyes are upon Him, He shows me the
    way;   [along,
The path may seem dark, as He leads me
But following Jesus, I cannot go wrong.

3 Still looking to Jesus, oh! may I be
    found,   [round;
When Jordan's dark waters encompass me
They'll bear me away in His presence to be,
And see Him still nearer, whom always I
    see.

4 Then, then shall I know the full beauty
    and grace   [face—
Of Jesus my Lord, when I stand face to
Shall know how His love went before me
    each day,
And wonder that ever my eyes turned away.
    Sab. Hy. Book.

TIME AND ETERNITY.

RHINE. C. M. — German.

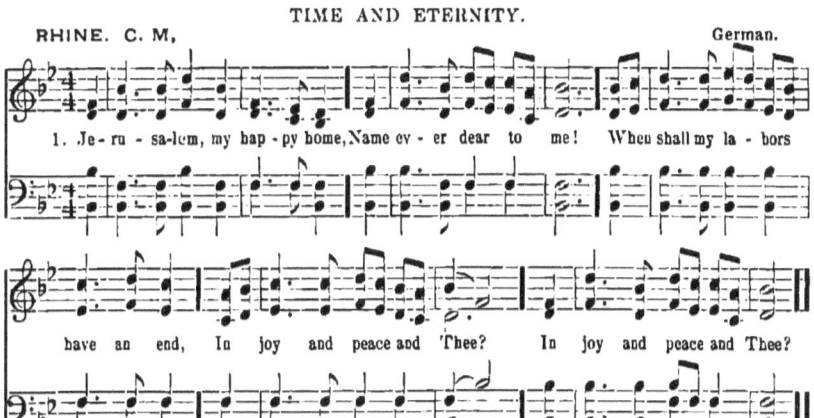

602 *The New Jerusalem.*

1 Jerusalem, my happy home,
    Name ever dear to me!
When shall my labors have an end,
    In joy and peace and thee?

2 When shall these eyes thy heaven-built
        And pearly gates behold? [walls,
Thy bulwarks, with salvation strong,
    And streets of shining gold?

3 Oh, when, thou city of my God!
    Shall I thy courts ascend,
Where congregations ne'er break up,
    And Sabbaths have no end?

4 There happier bowers than Eden's bloom,
    Nor sin nor sorrow know;   [scenes,
Blest seats, through rude and stormy
    I onward press to you.

5 Why should I shrink at pain and woe,
    Or feel at death dismay?
I've Canaan's goodly land in view,
    And realms of endless day.
Williams and Boden's Collection. 1801.

AZMON. C. M. — CARL GOTTHILF GLASER (1784 — 1829).
Arr. by LOWELL MASON.

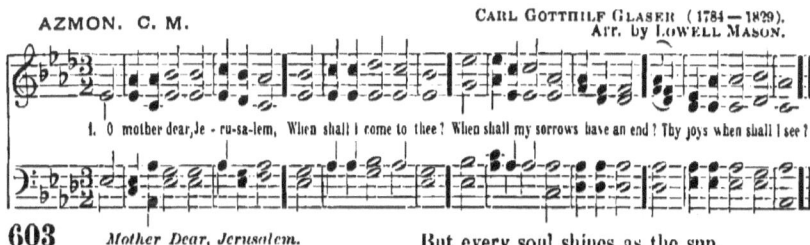

603 *Mother Dear, Jerusalem.*

1 O mother dear, Jerusalem,
    When shall I come to thee?
When shall my sorrows have an end!
    Thy joys when shall I see?

2 O happy harbor of the saints!
    O sweet and pleasant soil!
In thee no sorrow may be found,
    No grief, no care, no toil.

3 No dim'ning cloud o'ershadows thee,
    No gloom, nor darksome night;
But every soul shines as the sun,
    For God Himself gives light.

4 Quite through the streets, with silver
    The flood of Life doth flow,   [sound,
Upon whose banks, on either side,
    The tree of Life doth grow.

5 Those trees each month yield ripened
    For evermore they spring,   [fruit
And all the nations of the earth,
    To thee their honors bring.
Rev. David Dickson (1583 — 1663).

(257)

TIME AND ETERNITY.

TAPPAN. C. M. 5l. GEORGE KINSLEY (1811—1884).

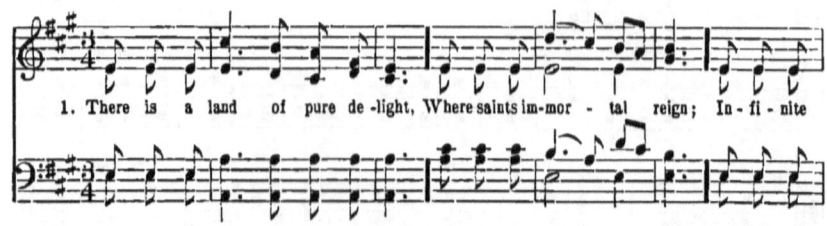

604 *Death Welcome in Prospect of Heaven.*
1 There is a land of pure delight,
  Where saints immortal reign;
  Infinite day excludes the night,
  And pleasures banish pain.

2 There, everlasting spring abides,
  And never-withering flowers;
  Death, like a narrow sea, divides
  This heavenly land from ours.

3 Sweet fields, beyond the swelling flood,
  Stand dressed in living green;
  So to the Jews old Canaan stood,
  While Jordan rolled between.

4 But timorous mortals start and shrink,
  To cross this narrow sea;
  And linger, shivering on the brink,
  And fear to launch away.

5 Oh, could we make our doubts remove
  Those gloomy doubts that rise!
  And see the Canaan that we love
  With unbeclouded eyes;

6 Could we but climb where Moses stood,
  And view the landscape o'er,
  Not Jordan's stream, nor death's cold flood
  Should fright us from the shore.
  Rev. Isaac Watts (1674—1748).

605 *Rest in Heaven.*
1 O land of rest, for thee I sigh;
  When will the moment come,
  That I shall lay my armor by,
  And dwell in peace at home?

2 No tranquil joys on earth I know,
  No peaceful sheltering dome;
  This world's a wilderness of woe,
  This world is not my home.

3 To Jesus Christ I flee for rest;
  He bids me cease to roam,
  And lean for succor on His breast,
  And He'll conduct me home.

4 Weary of wandering round and round
  This vale of sin and gloom,
  I long to quit th' unhallowed ground,
  And dwell with Christ at home.
  Hunter's Sel. Mel.

TIME AND ETERNITY.

REST FOR THE WEARY. 8s & 7s.   J. W. DADMUN. Arr., 1860.

606   *Rest for the Weary.*
1 In the Christian's home in glory
   There remains a land of rest,
There my Saviour's gone before me,
   To fulfill my soul's request.—Cho.

2 This is not my place of resting,
   Mine's a city yet to come;
Onward to it I am hasting,
   On to my eternal home.—Cho.

3 In it all is light and glory,
   O'er it shines a nightless day;
Ev'ry trace of sin's sad story,
   All the curse hath passed away.—Cho.

4 There the Lamb, our Shepherd, leads us
   By the streams of life along,
On the freshest pastures feed us,
   Turns our sighing into song:—Cho.
                 Rev. H. Bonar (1808—1890).

607   *Thy Will be Done.*
1 Jesus, while our hearts are bleeding
   O'er the spoils that death has won,
We would at this solemn meeting,
   Calmly say, "Thy will be done."—Cho.

2 Though cast down, we're not forsaken;
   Though afflicted, not alone;
Thou didst give, and Thou hast taken;
   Blesséd Lord, "Thy will be done."—Cho.

3 Tho' to-day we're filled with mourning,
   Mercy still is on the throne;
With Thy smiles of love returning,
   We can sing—"Thy will be done."—Cho.

4 By Thy hands the boon was given,
   Thou hast taken but Thine own;
Lord of earth, and God of heaven,
   Evermore—"Thy will be done."—Cho.
               Thomas Hastings (1784—1872).

TIME AND ETERNITY.

FEDERAL STREET. L. M. H. K. OLIVER (1800—1885).

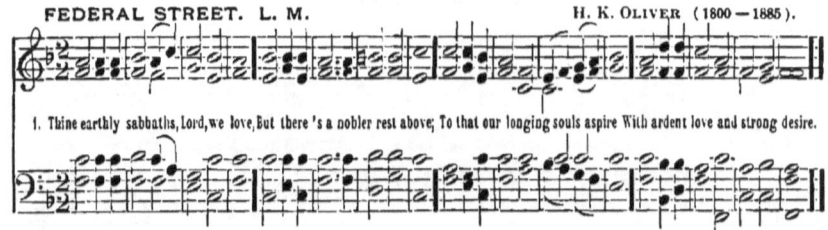

1. Thine earthly sabbaths, Lord, we love, But there's a nobler rest above; To that our longing souls aspire With ardent love and strong desire.

608 *The Eternal Sabbath.*

1 Thine earthly sabbaths, Lord, we love,
But there's a nobler rest above;
To that, our longing souls aspire
With ardent love and strong desire.

2 In Thy blest kingdom, we shall be
From every mortal trouble free;
No groans shall mingle with the songs,
Which warble from immortal tongues.

3 No rude alarms of raging foes,
No cares to break the long repose,
No m'dnight shade, no clouded sun,
But sacred, high, eternal noon.

4 Oh, long expected day, begin;
Dawn on this world of woe and sin;
Fain would we leave this weary road,
And sleep in death, and rest in God.
  Rev. Philip Doddridge (1702—1751).

609 *Home in Heaven.*

1 As when the weary traveler gains
The height of some o'erlooking hill,
His heart revives, if 'cross the plains,
He eyes his home, though distant still.

2 While he surveys the much-loved spot,
He slights the space that lies between;
His past fatigues are now forgot,
Because his journey's end is seen.

3 Thus when the Christian pilgrim views,
By faith, his mansion in the skies,
The sight his fainting strength renews,
And wings his speed to reach the prize.

4 The thought of home his spirit cheers,
No more he grieves for troubles past;
Nor any future trial fears,
So he may safe arrive at last.

5 'T is there, he says, I am to dwell,
With Jesus, in the realms of day;
Then I shall bid my cares farewell,
And he will wipe my tears away.

6 Jesus, on Thee, our hope depends,
To lead us on to Thine abode;
Assured our home will make amends
For all our toil while on the road.
  Rev. John Newton (1725—1807).

WARD. L. M. Dr. L. MASON (1792—1872).

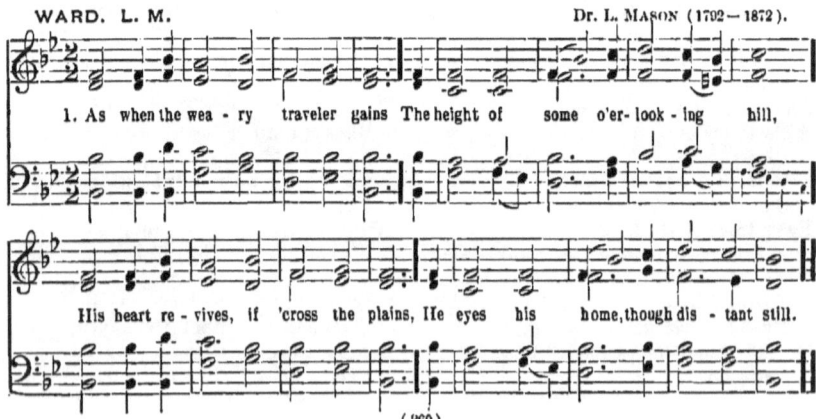

1. As when the weary traveler gains The height of some o'er-look-ing hill,
His heart re-vives, if 'cross the plains, He eyes his home, though dis-tant still.

(260)

TIME AND ETERNITY.

DE FLEURY. 8s, D. JONATHAN EDSON, 1782.

610   *Philippians 1: 23.*

1 Ye angels! who stand round the throne,
    And view my Immanuel's face,—
In rapturous songs make Him known,
    Oh, tune your soft harps to His praise:
He formed you the spirits you are,
    So happy, so noble, so good;
When others sank down in despair,
    Confirmed by His power, ye stood.

2 Ye saints! who stand nearer than they
    And cast your bright crowns at His feet
His grace and His glory display,
    And all His rich mercy repeat;
He snatched you from hell and the grave
    He ransomed from death and despair;
For you He was mighty to save,
    Almighty to bring you safe there.

3 Oh, when will the period appear
    When I shall unite in your song?
I'm weary of lingering here,
    And I to your Saviour belong!

I want — oh, I want to be there,
    To sorrow and sin bid adieu —
Your joy and your friendship to share —
    To wonder, and worship with you.
Miss Maria De Fleury, 1791.

611   *What Must It Be to Be There.*

1 We speak of the realms of the blest,
    That country so bright and so fair;
And oft are its glories confessed;
    But what must it be to be there!
We speak of its pathways of gold,
    Its walls decked with jewels most rare;
Its wonders and pleasures untold;
    But what must it be to be there.

2 We speak of its freedom from sin,
    From sorrow, temptation, and care;
From trials without and within;
    But what must it be to be there!
We speak of its service of love,
    The robes which the glorified wear;
The Church of the First-born above;
    But what must it be to be there!
Mrs. Elizabeth Mills (1805—1829)

(261)

TIME AND ETERNITY.

OLIVET. 6s & 4s.   Dr. L. Mason (1792—1872).

1. My faith looks up to Thee, Thou Lamb of Cal-va-ry, Sav-iour di-vine! Now hear me while I pray, Take all my guilt a-way, Oh, let me from this day Be whol-ly Thine.

612 *My Faith Looks Up.*

1 My faith looks up to Thee,
Thou Lamb of Calvary,
　Saviour divine!
Now hear me while I pray,
Take all my guilt away,
Oh, let me from this day
　Be wholly Thine!

2 May Thy rich grace impart
Strength to my fainting heart;
　My zeal inspire;
As Thou hast died for me,
Oh, may my love to Thee
Pure, warm, and changeless be,
　A living fire.

3 While life's dark maze I tread,
And griefs around me spread,
　Be Thou my guide;
Bid darkness turn to day,
Wipe sorrow's tears away,
Nor let me ever stray
　From Thee aside.

4 When ends life's transient dream,
When death's cold, sullen stream
　Shall o'er me roll,
Blest Saviour! then, in love,
Fear and distrust remove;
Oh, bear me safe above,
　A ransomed soul!

Rev. Ray Palmer (1808—1887).

BEULAH. 6s, 4s & 7s.

614

1. There is a hap-py land, Far, far a-way, Where saints in glo-ry stand, Bright, bright as day; Oh, how they sweet-ly sing, Wor-thy is our Sav-iour King, Loud let His prais-es ring, Praise, praise for aye.

TIME AND ETERNITY.

OAK. 6s, 4s & 6s.   Dr. L. MASON (1792—1872).

1. I'm but a stranger here, Heav'n is my home: Earth is a des-ert drear, Heav'n is my home:
Dan-gers and sorrows stand Round me on ev-'ry hand, Heav'n is my Fatherland, Heav'n is my home.

By per. of Oliver Ditson Company, owners of copyright.

613   *Heaven the Christian's Home.*

1 I'm but a stranger here,
   Heav'n is my home;
Earth is a desert drear,
   Heav'n is my home;
Dangers and sorrows stand
Round me on ev'ry hand;
Heav'n is my Fatherland,
   Heav'n is my home.

2 What though the tempests rage,
   Heav'n is my home;
Short is my pilgrimage,
   Heav'n is my home;
And time's wild wintry blast
Soon will be over, past,
I shall reach home at last,—
   Heav'n is my home.

3 Therefore, I murmur not,
   Heav'n is my home;
Whate'er my earthly lot,
   Heav'n is my home;
And I shall surely stand
There at my Lord's right hand;
Heav'n is my Fatherland,—
   Heav'n is my home.

4 There, at my Saviour's side,
   Heav'n is my home;
I shall be glorified,
   Heav'n is my home;
There are the good and blest:

Those I love most and best;
There, too, I soon shall rest,
   Heaven is my home.

Rev. Thomas Rawson Taylor (1807—1835).

614   *Happy Land.*
        Tune, BEULAH.

1 There is a happy land,
   Far, far away,
Where saints in glory stand,
   Bright, bright as day;
Oh! how they sweetly sing,
Worthy is our Saviour King;
Loud let His praises ring,
   Praise, praise for aye.

2 Come to that happy land,
   Come, come away;
Why will ye doubting stand,
   Why still delay?
Oh, we shall happy be,
When from sin and sorrow free,
Lord, we shall live with Thee,
   Blest, blest for aye!

3 Bright, in that happy land,
   Beams every eye;
Kept by a Father's hand,
   Love cannot die.
Oh! then to glory run,
Be a crown and kingdom won;
And bright above the sun,
   We reign for aye.

Anon.

TIME AND ETERNITY.

PARADISE. P. M. J. BARNBY (1838—).

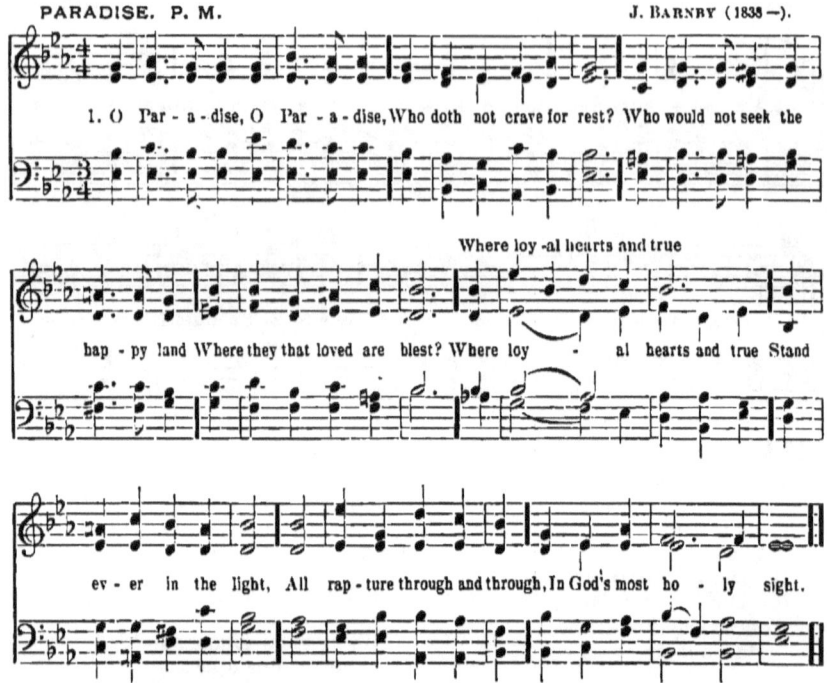

615 *O Paradise.*

1 O Paradise, O Paradise,
  Who doth not crave for rest?
Who would not seek the happy land
  Where they that loved are blest?
    Where loyal hearts and true,
    Stand ever in the light,
    All rapture through and through,
    In God's most holy sight.

2 O Paradise, O Paradise,
  The world is growing old;
Who would not be at rest and free
  Where love is never cold?
    Where loyal hearts and true, etc.

3 O Paradise, O Paradise,
  'T is weary waiting here;
I long to be where Jesus is,
  To feel, to see Him near;
    Where loyal hearts and true, etc.

4 O Paradise, O Paradise,
  I want to sin no more,
I want to be as pure on earth
  As on thy spotless shore;
    Where loyal hearts and true, etc.

5 O Paradise, O Paradise,
  I greatly long to see
The special place my dearest Lord
  In love prepares for me;
    Where loyal hearts and true, etc.

6 Lord Jesus, King of Paradise,
  Oh, keep me in Thy love,
And guide me to that happy land
  Of perfect rest above;
    Where loyal hearts and true,
    Stand ever in the light,
    All rapture through and through,
    In God's most holy sight.
            Rev. F. W. Faber (1814—1863).

HOME SWEET HOME. 11s.
TIME AND ETERNITY.
Sir HENRY ROWLEY BISHOP (1780–1855).

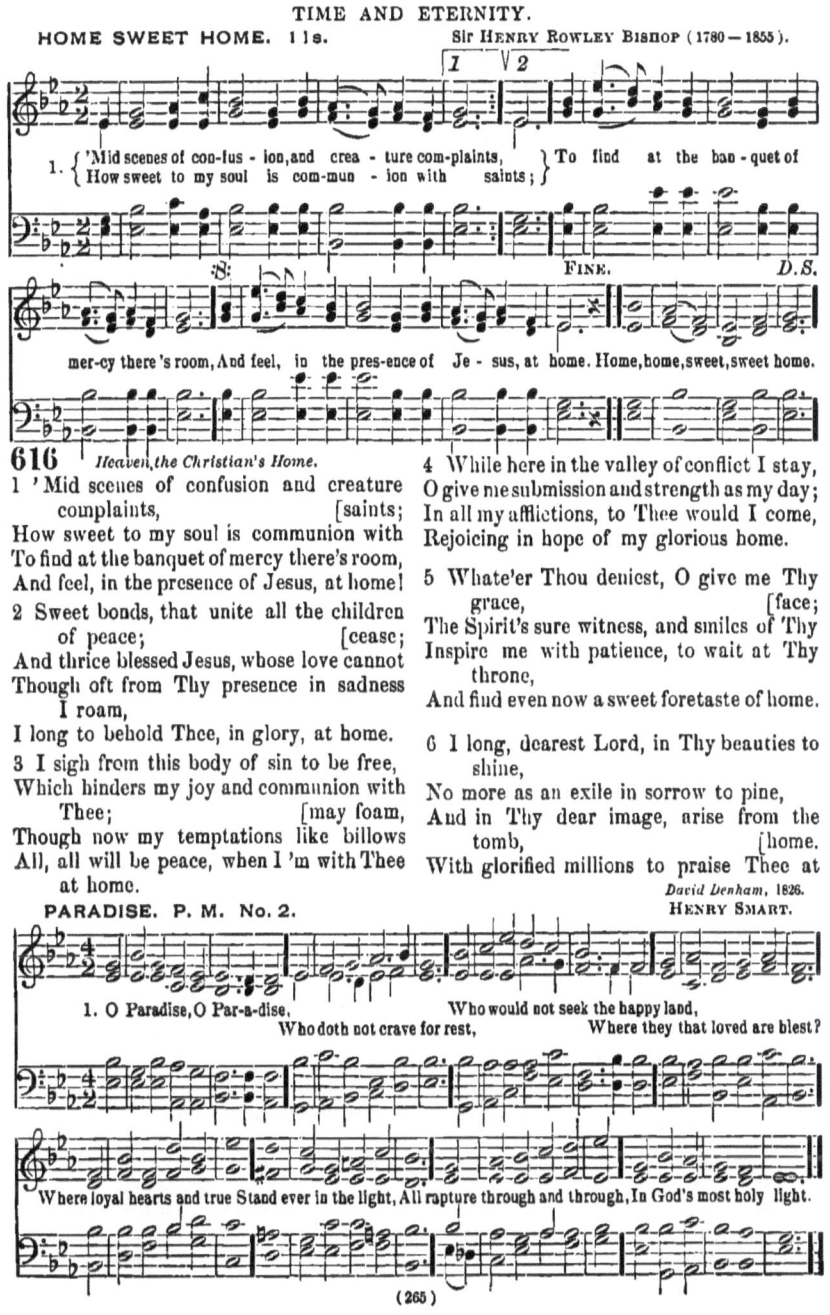

1. 'Mid scenes of confusion, and creature complaints, To find at the banquet of mercy there's room,
How sweet to my soul is communion with saints; And feel, in the presence of Jesus, at home. Home, home, sweet, sweet home.

616 *Heaven, the Christian's Home.*

1 'Mid scenes of confusion and creature complaints, [saints;
How sweet to my soul is communion with
To find at the banquet of mercy there's room,
And feel, in the presence of Jesus, at home!

2 Sweet bonds, that unite all the children of peace; [cease;
And thrice blessed Jesus, whose love cannot
Though oft from Thy presence in sadness I roam,
I long to behold Thee, in glory, at home.

3 I sigh from this body of sin to be free,
Which hinders my joy and communion with Thee; [may foam,
Though now my temptations like billows
All, all will be peace, when I 'm with Thee at home.

4 While here in the valley of conflict I stay,
O give me submission and strength as my day;
In all my afflictions, to Thee would I come,
Rejoicing in hope of my glorious home.

5 Whate'er Thou deniest, O give me Thy grace, [face;
The Spirit's sure witness, and smiles of Thy
Inspire me with patience, to wait at Thy throne,
And find even now a sweet foretaste of home.

6 I long, dearest Lord, in Thy beauties to shine,
No more as an exile in sorrow to pine,
And in Thy dear image, arise from the tomb, [home.
With glorified millions to praise Thee at

David Denham, 1826.

PARADISE. P. M. No. 2.
HENRY SMART.

1. O Paradise, O Paradise, Who would not seek the happy land,
Who doth not crave for rest, Where they that loved are blest?
Where loyal hearts and true Stand ever in the light, All rapture through and through, In God's most holy light.

(265)

TIME AND ETERNITY.

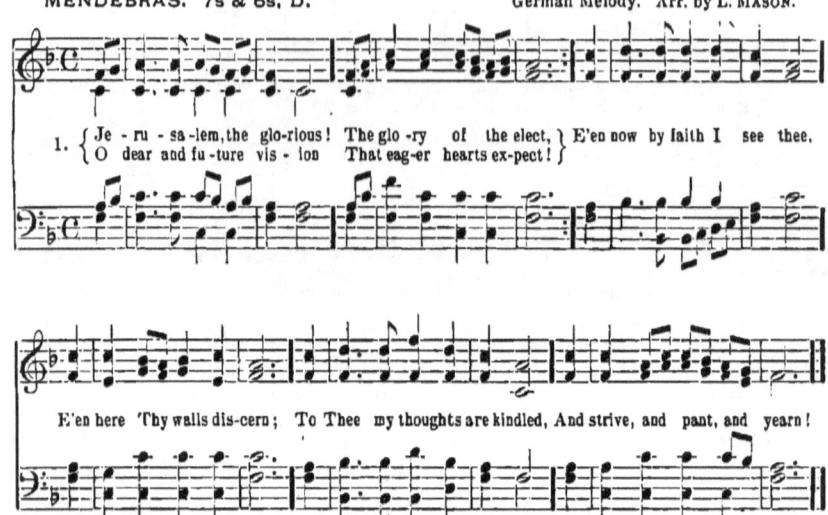

MENDEBRAS. 7s & 6s, D. — German Melody. Arr. by L. MASON.

1. Jerusalem, the glorious! The glory of the elect, O dear and future vision That eager hearts expect! E'en now by faith I see thee, E'en here Thy walls discern; To Thee my thoughts are kindled, And strive, and pant, and yearn!

617 *The Heavenly City.*

1 Jerusalem, the glorious!
　The glory of the elect,—
O dear and future vision
　That eager hearts expect!
Ev'n now by faith I see thee,
　Ev'n here thy walls discern;
To thee my thoughts are kindled,
　And strive, and pant, and yearn.

2 With jasper glow thy bulwarks,
　Thy streets with emeralds blaze;
The sardius and the topaz
　Unite in thee their rays;
Thine ageless walls are bonded
　With amethyst unpriced;
The saints build up its fabric,
　The corner-stone is Christ.

3 O sweet and blessèd Country,
　The home of God's elect!
O sweet and blessèd Country,
　That eager hearts expect!
Jesus, in mercy bring us,
　To that dear land of rest;

Who art, with God the Father,
　And Spirit, ever blest.
Bernard of Cluny. c. 1145
Tr. by Rev. John Mason Neale, 1851. *Alt.*

618 *On Jordan's Rugged Banks.*
　　Tune, HOWARD.

1 On Jordan's rugged banks I stand,
　And cast a wishful eye
To Canaan's fair and happy land,
　Where my possessions lie.

2 O'er all those wide extended plains
　Shines one eternal day;
There God the Son forever reigns,
　And scatters night away.

3 When shall I reach that happy place,
　And be forever blest?
When shall I see my Father's face,
　And in His bosom rest?

4 Filled with delight, my raptured soul
　Would here no longer stay;
Tho' Jordan's waves around me roll,
　Fearless I'd launch away.
Rev. Samuel Stennet (1727 — 1795).

TIME AND ETERNITY.

MIRIAM. 7s, & 6s, D. J. P. HOLBROOK (1822—).

1. O God, the Rock of Ages, Who ev-er-more hast been, What time the tempest ra-ges.
D.S.—*To end-less gen-er - a -tions,*

Our dwell-ing-place se-rene: Be-fore Thy first cre - a - tions, O Lord, the same as now,
The Ev -er-last-ing Thou.

By per. est. of J. P. Holbrook.

619 *Our Dwelling-place in all Generations.*

1 O God, the Rock of Ages,
Who evermore hast been,
What time the tempest rages,
Our dwelling-place serene;
Before Thy first creations,
O Lord, the same as now,
To endless generations
The everlasting Thou!

2 Our years are like the shadows
On sunny hills that lie,
Or grasses in the meadows
That blossom but to die;
A sleep, a dream, a story
By strangers quickly told,
An unremaining glory
Of things that soon are old.

3 O Thou, who canst not slumber,
Whose light grows never pale,
Teach us aright to number
Our years before they fail.
On us Thy mercy lighten!
On us Thy goodness rest!
And let Thy spirit brighten
The hearts Thyself hast blessed!

4 Lord, crown our faith's endeavor
With beauty and with grace,
Till, clothed in light for ever,
We see Thee face to face:
A joy no language measures;
A fountain brimming o'er;
An endless flow of pleasures;
An ocean without shore.
Bp. Edward Henry Bickersteth (1825—), 1862.

HOWARD. C. M. SAMUEL HOWARD (1710—1782).

1. On Jor-dan's rugged banks I stand, And cast a wish-ful eye To Canaan's fair and happy land, Where my pos-ses - sions lie.

(267)

TIME AND ETERNITY.

BONA PATRIA. 7s & 6s, D.  Rev. R. P. KERR, 1890.

620 *Paradise of Joy.*

1 For thee, O dear, dear country,
  Mine eyes their vigils keep;
 For very love, beholding
  Thy happy name, they weep;
 The mention of Thy glory
  Is unction to the breast,
 And medicine in sickness,
  And love, and light, and rest.

2 O one, O only mansion!
  O Paradise of joy!
 Where tears are ever banished,
  And smiles have no alloy;
 The Lamb is all Thy splendor,
  The Crucified Thy praise;
 His laud and benediction
  Thy ransomed people raise.

3 Thou hast no shore, fair ocean!
  Thou hast no time, bright day!
 Dear fountain of refreshment
  To pilgrims far away!
 Upon the Rock of Ages,
  They raise thy holy tower;
 Thine is the victor's laurel,
  And thine the golden dower,
    Bernard of Cluny, c. 1145.
   Tr. by Rev. John Mason Neale, 1851.

621 *The Land Immortal.*

1 There is a land immortal,
  The beautiful of lands;

  Beside its ancient portal
   A sentry grimly stands;
  He only can undo it,
   And open wide the door;
  And mortals who pass through it
   Are mortal nevermore.

2 That glorious land is heaven,
   And Death the sentry grim;
  The Lord thereof has given
   The opening keys to him;
  And ransom'd spirits, sighing
   And sorrowful for sin,
  Pass through the gate in dying,
   And freely enter in.

3 Though dark and drear the passage
   That leads unto the gate,
  Yet grace attends the message
   To souls that watch and wait;
  And at the time appointed
   A messenger comes down,
  And guides the Lord's anointed
   From cross to glory's crown.

4 Their sighs are lost in singing;
   They're blessed in their tears;
  Their journey heavenward winging,
   They leave on earth their fears.
  Death, like an angel seeming,
   "We welcome thee!" they cry;
  Their eyes with glory gleaming,
   'T is life for them to die.
    Thomas McKellar, Ph. D., 1845.

TIME AND ETERNITY.

EWING. 7s & 6s.   Bp. A. EWING (1830 —).

1. Jerusalem, the golden, With milk and honey blest! Beneath thy contemplation, Sink heart and voice oppressed; I know not, oh, I know not What joys await me there! What radiancy of glo-ry, What light beyond compare.

622 *The Golden City.*

1 Jerusalem, the golden,
  With milk and honey blest!
Beneath thy contemplation
  Sink heart and voice oppressed,
I know not, oh, I know not
  What joys await me there!
What radiancy of glory,
  What light beyond compare.

2 They stand, those halls of Zion,
  All jubilant with song,
And bright with many an angel,
  And all the martyr throng;
The Prince is ever in them,
  The daylight is serene;
The pastures of the blessèd
  Are decked in glorious sheen.

3 There is the throne of David;
  And there, from care released,
The song of them that triumph,
  The shout of them that feast;
And they, who, with their Leader,
  Have conquered in the fight,
For ever and for ever
  Are clad in robes of white.

4 O sweet and blessèd country,
  The home of God's elect;
O sweet and blessèd country,
  That eager hearts expect!
Exult, O dust and ashes!
  The Lord shall be thy part:

His only, His for ever,
  Thou shalt be, and thou art!
  Bernard of Cluny, c. 1145.
  Tr. by Rev. John M. Neale (1813 — 1866).

623 *Short Toil.*

1 Brief life is here our portion;
  Brief sorrow, short-lived care;
The life, that knows no ending,
  The tearless life, is there;
Oh, happy retribution!
  Short toil, eternal rest;
For mortals and for sinners,
  A mansion with the blest.

2 And there is David's fountain,
  And life in fullest glow;
And there the life is golden,
  And milk and honey flow;
The light, that hath no evening,
  The health, that hath no sore,
The life, that hath no ending,
  But lasteth evermore.

3 There Jesus shall embrace us,
  There Jesus be embraced,—
That spirit's food and sunshine,
  Whence earthly love is chased;
Yes! God, my King and Portion,
  In fullness of His grace,
We then shall see for ever,
  And worship face to face.
  Bernard of Cluny, c. 1145.
  Tr. Rev. J. N. Neale (1818 — 1866).

(269)

TIME AND ETERNITY.

SELVIN. S. M.   Arr. by Dr. L. Mason.

1. If, through un-ruffled seas, Tow'rd heaven we calm-ly sail, With grateful hearts, O God, to Thee, We'll own the fav-'ring gale, With grateful hearts, O God, to Thee, We'll own the fa-voring gale.

624   *"We Walk By Faith."* — 2 Cor. 5: 7.

1 If, through unruffled seas,
   Toward heaven we calmly sail,
With grateful hearts, O God, to Thee,
   We'll own the favoring gale.

2 But should the surges rise,
   And rest delay to come,
Blest be the sorrow — kind the storm,
   Which drives us nearer home.

3 Soon shall our doubts and fears
   All yield to Thy control;
Thy tender mercies shall illume
   The midnight of the soul.

4 Teach us, in every state,
   To make Thy will our own;
And when the joys of sense depart,
   To live by faith alone.
Rev. A. M. Toplady (1740—1778).

625   *Rest Only Found in God.*

1 Oh, where shall rest be found,
   Rest for the weary soul?
'T were vain the ocean's depths to sound,
   Or pierce to either pole.

2 The world can never give
   The bliss for which we sigh;
'T is not the whole of life to live,
   Nor all of death to die.

3 Beyond this vale of tears
   There is a life above,
Unmeasured by the flight of years;
   And all that life is love.

4 There is a death whose pang
   Outlasts the fleeting breath;
Oh, what eternal horrors hang
   Around "the second death!"

5 Lord God of truth and grace,
   Teach us that death to shun,
Lest we be banished from Thy face
   And evermore undone.

6 Here would we end our quest;
   Alone are found in Thee,
The life of perfect love, the rest
   Of immortality.
Rev. James Montgomery (1771—1854).

SHEFFIELD. S. M.   THOS. HASTINGS (1784—1872).

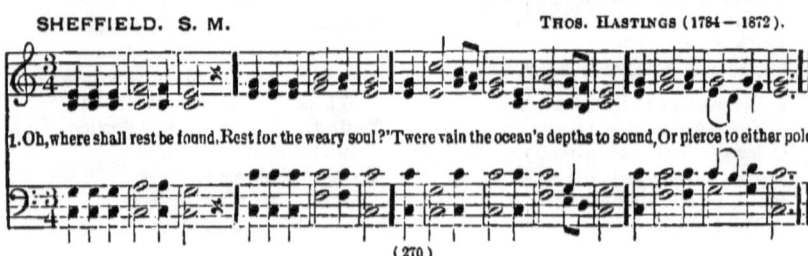

1. Oh, where shall rest be found, Rest for the weary soul? "Twere vain the ocean's depths to sound, Or pierce to either pole

TIME AND ETERNITY.

ROSEFIELD. 7s, 6l. Rev. CÆSAR HENRI ABRAHAM MALAN (1787—1864).

626   *The Forgiven Debt.*
1 When this passing world is done,
When has sunk yon glaring sun,
When we stand with Christ in glory,
Looking o'er life's finished story;
Then, Lord, shall I fully know,
Not till then, how much I owe.

2 When I stand before the throne,
Dressed in beauty not my own;
When I see Thee as Thou art,

Love Thee with unsinning heart;
Then, Lord, shall I fully know,
Not till then, how much I owe.

3 When the praise of heaven I hear,
Loud as thunders to the ear,
Loud as many waters' noise,
Sweet as harp's melodious voice;
Then, Lord, shall I fully know,
Not till then, how much I owe.
  Rev. Robert Murray McCheyne (1813--1843).

WALTON. L. M. LUDWIG VAN BEETHOVEN (1770—1827).

627   *Now Let Our Souls.*
1 Now let our souls, on wings sublime,
Rise from the vanities of time,
Draw back the parting vail, and see
The glories of eternity.

2 Born by a new, celestial birth,
Why should we grovel here on earth?
Why grasp at vain and fleeting toys,
So near to heaven's eternal joys?

3 Shall aught beguile us on the road,
While we are walking back to God?

For strangers into life we come,
And dying is but going home.

4 Welcome, sweet hour of full discharge,
That sets our longing souls at large,
Unbinds our chains, breaks up our cell,
And gives us with our God to dwell.

5 To dwell with God, to feel His love,
Is the full heaven enjoyed above;
And the sweet expectation now
Is the young dawn of heaven below.
  Rev. Thomas Gibbons (1720—1785).

DEATH OF THE CHRISTIAN.

628 *Funeral Hymn.*

1 Thou art gone to the grave, but we will not deplore Thee;
   Though sorrows and darkness encompass the tomb,
The Saviour has passed through its portals before thee,
   And the lamp of His love is thy guide through the gloom.

2 Thou art gone to the grave, we no longer behold thee,
   Nor tread the rough path of the world by thy side;
But the wide arms of mercy are spread to enfold thee,
   And sinners may hope, since the Sinless hath died.

3 Thou art gone to the grave, and its mansions forsaking,
   Perhaps thy tried spirit in doubt lingered long;
But the sunshine of heaven beamed bright on thy waking,
   And the song that thou heardst was the seraphim's song.

4 Thou art gone to the grave, but 'twere wrong to deplore thee,
   When God was thy ransom, thy guardian and guide;
He gave thee, and took thee, and soon will restore thee,
   Where death has no sting, since the Saviour has died.
                                                    Bp. Reginald Heber (1783 – 1826).

DEATH OF THE CHRISTIAN.

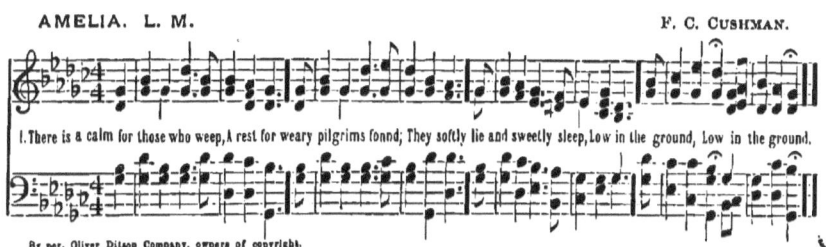

AMELIA. L. M. F. C. CUSHMAN.

629 *There is a Calm.*
1 There is a calm for those who weep,
A rest for weary pilgrims found;
They softly lie, and sweetly sleep,
Low in the ground.

2 The storm that sweeps the wintry sky,
No more disturbs their deep repose,
Than summer evening's latest sigh
That shuts the rose.

3 Then, traveler, in the vale of tears,
To realms of everlasting light,
Thro' time's dark wilderness of years,
Pursue thy flight.
Rev. James Montgomery (1771—1854).

EVENTIDE. 10s. W. H. MONK, 1861.

630 *Death at Prime.*
1 Go to the grave in all Thy glorious prime!
In full activity of zeal and power;
A Christian cannot die before his time;
The Lord's appointment is the servant's hour.

2 Go to the grave; at noon from labor cease;
Rest on thy sheaves, thy harvest task is done;
Come from the heat of battle, and in peace,
Soldier! go home; with thee the fight is won.

3 Go to the grave, for there thy Saviour lay
In death's embraces, ere He rose on high;
And all the ransomed, by that narrow way,
Pass to eternal life beyond the sky.

4 Go to the grave? no, take thy seat above!
Be Thy pure spirit present with the Lord, [love,
Where thou for faith and hope hast perfect
And open vision for the written word.
Rev. James Montgomery (1771—1854).

DEATH OF THE CHRISTIAN.

DEPARTURE. S. H. M. Dr. Thos. Hastings (1784—1872).

1. Friend after friend departs; Who has not lost a friend? There is no union here of hearts, That finds not here an end. Were this frail world our final rest, Living or dying none were blest.

631 *Separations in Time.*

1 Friend after friend departs;
  Who has not lost a friend?
 There is no union here of hearts,
  That finds not here an end.
 Were this frail world our final rest,
  Living or dying none were blest.

2 Beyond the flight of time,
  Beyond the weight of death,
 There surely is some blesséd clime
  Where life is not a breath;
 Nor life's affections, transient fire,
 Whose sparks fly upward and expire.

3 There is a world above,
  Where parting is unknown;
 A long eternity of love,
  Formed for the good alone;
 And faith beholds the dying here,
 Translated to that glorious sphere.

4 Thus star by star declines,
  Till all are passed away,
 As morning high and higher shines
  To pure and perfect day;
 Nor sink those stars in empty night,
 But hide themselves in heaven's own light.
  Rev. J. Montgomery (1771—1854).

MOCCAS. S. M. A. R. Reinagle.

1. It is not death to die; To leave this weary road, And 'midst the brotherhood on high To be at home with God. Amen.

632 *Not Death to Die.*

1 It is not death to die;
  To leave this weary road,
 And 'midst the brotherhood on high
  To be at home with God.

2 It is not death to close
  The eye long dimmed by tears,
 And wake, in glorious repose
  To spend eternal years.

3 It is not death to bear
  The wrench that set us free
 From dungeon chain, to breathe the air
  Of boundless liberty.

4 It is not death to fling
  Aside this sinful dust,
 And rise, on strong, exulting wing,
  To live among the just.

5 Jesus, Thou Prince of life!
  Thy chosen cannot die;
 Like Thee, they conquer in the strife,
  To reign with Thee on high.
  Rev. Cæsar Henri A. Malan (1787—1864).

633 *Doxology.*

 To Father, Son, and Holy Ghost,
  The God whom we adore,
 Be glory, as it was, is now,
  And shall be ever more.

DEATH OF THE CHRISTIAN.

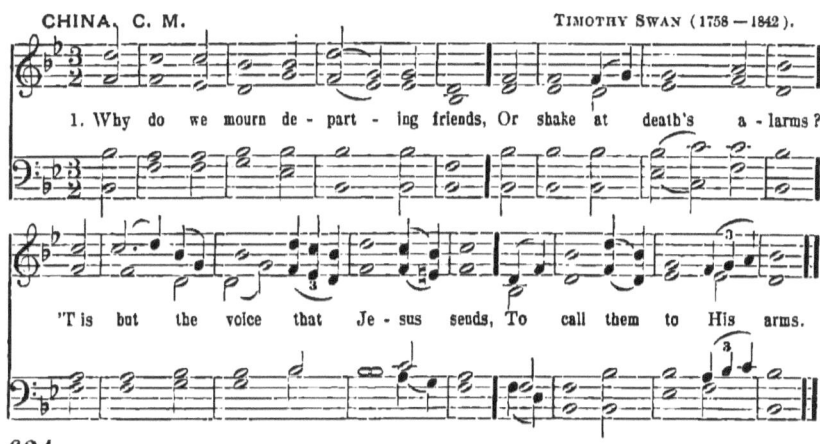

CHINA. C. M. — Timothy Swan (1758—1842).

1. Why do we mourn departing friends, Or shake at death's alarms?
'T is but the voice that Jesus sends, To call them to His arms.

634 *We are Confident.*

1 Why do we mourn departing friends,
    Or shake at death's alarms?
'T is but the voice that Jesus sends,
    To call them to His arms.

2 Are we not tending upward, too,
    As fast as time can move?
Nor would we wish the hours more slow,
    To keep us from our love.

3 Why should we tremble to convey
    Their bodies to the tomb?
There the dear flesh of Jesus lay,
    And scattered all the gloom.

4 The graves of all the saints He blessed,
    And softened every bed;
Where should the dying members rest,
    But with the dying Head?

5 Thence he arose, ascending high,
    And showed our feet the way;
Up to the Lord we, too, shall fly,
    At the great rising day.
            Rev. Isaac Watts (1674—1748).

635   *Peaceful Death.*
            Tune, MOCCAS.

1 Oh, for the death of those,
    Who slumber in the Lord!
Oh, be like theirs, my last repose,
    Like theirs, my last reward!

2 Their bodies in the ground
    In silent hope may lie,
Till the last trumpet's joyful sound
    Shall call them to the sky.

3 Their ransomed spirits soar
    On wings of faith and love,
To meet the Saviour they adore,
    And reign with Him above.

4 With us their names shall live
    Through long succeeding years,
Embalmed with all our hearts can give,
    Our praises and our tears.

5 Oh, for the death of those,
    Who slumber in the Lord!
Oh, be like theirs, my last repose,
    Like theirs, my last reward!
            Dr. Wm. Maxwell (1784—1857).

636   *How Still and Peaceful.*

1 How still and peaceful is the grave!
    Where, life's vain tumults past,
The appointed house, by heaven's decree,
    Receives us all at last.

2 The wicked there from troubling cease;
    Their passions rage no more;
And there the weary pilgrim rests
    From all the toils he bore.

3 There, servants, masters, small and great,
    Partake the same repose;
And there, in peace, the ashes mix
    Of those who once were foes.

4 All, leveled by the hand of death,
    Lie sleeping in the tomb,
Till God in judgment calls them forth,
    To meet their final doom.
            Anon.

(275)

DEATH OF THE CHRISTIAN.

REST. L. M. W. B. Bradbury (1816—1868).

637 *Asleep in Jesus.*

1 Asleep in Jesus! blessed sleep!
From which none ever wakes to weep!
A calm and undisturbed repose,
Unbroken by the last of foes!

2 Asleep in Jesus! oh, how sweet
To be for such a slumber meet!
With holy confidence to sing
That death hath lost its venomed sting.

3 Asleep in Jesus! peaceful rest!
Whose waking is supremely blest;
No fear — no woe, shall dim that hour,
That manifests the Saviour's power.

4 Asleep in Jesus! oh, for me
May such a blissful refuge be!
Securely shall my ashes lie,
Waiting the summons from on high.

5 Asleep in Jesus! time nor space
Debars this precious "hiding-place;"
On Indian plains, or Lapland snows,
Believers find the same repose.

6 Asleep in Jesus! far from Thee
Thy kindred and their graves may be;
But there is still a blessed sleep,
From which none ever wakes to weep.
Mrs. Margaret Mackay (1801—), 1832.

638 *The Dying Christian.*

1 Gently, my Saviour! let me down,
To slumber in the arms of death;
I rest my soul on Thee alone,
E'en till my last expiring breath.

2 Bid me possess sweet peace within;
Let child like patience keep my heart;
Then shall I feel my heaven begin,
Before my spirit hence depart.

3 Oh, speed Thy chariot, God of love!
And take me from this world of woe;
I long to reach those joys above,
And bid farewell to all below.

4 There shall my raptured spirit raise
Still louder notes than angels sing,—
High glories to Immanuel's grace,
My God, my Saviour, and my King!
Rev. Rowland Hill (1744—1833).

639 *Burial of Believers.*

1 Unvail thy bosom, faithful tomb!
Take this new treasure to thy trust,
And give these sacred relics room
To seek a slumber in the dust.

2 Nor pain, nor grief, nor anxious fear,
Invade Thy bounds;— no mortal woes
Can reach the peaceful sleeper here,
While angels watch the soft repose.

3 So Jesus slept;— God's dying Son
Passed through the grave and blessed
  the bed! [throne,
Rest here, blest saint! — till, from His
The morning break, and pierce the shade

4 Break from His throne, illustrious morn!
Attend, O earth! His sovereign word;
Restore Thy trust;— a glorious form
Shall then arise to meet the Lord.
Rev. Isaac Watts (1674—1748).

(276)

DEATH OF THE CHRISTIAN.

ZEPHYR. L. M. W. B. BRADBURY (1816—1868).

640 *Death of the Righteous.*

1 How blest the righteous when he dies!
 When sinks a weary soul to rest;
 How mildly beam the closing eyes,
 How gently heaves the expiring breast!

2 So fades a summer cloud away,
 So sinks the gale when storms are o'er;
 So gently shuts the eye of day,
 So dies a wave along the shore.

3 A holy quiet reigns around,
 A calm which life nor death destroys;
 Nothing disturbs that peace profound,
 Which his unfettered soul enjoys.

4 Farewell, conflicting hopes and fears,
 Where lights and shades alternate dwell;
 How bright the unchanging morn appears
 Farewell, inconstant world, farewell!

5 Life's duty done, as sinks the clay,
 Light from its load the spirit flies;
 While heaven and earth combine to say,
 "How blest the righteous when he dies."
 Mrs. Anna Laetitia Barbauld (1743—1825).

641 *Death Swallowed Up in Victory.*

1 We sing His love who once was slain,
 Who soon o'er death revived again,
 That all His saints through Him might have
 Eternal conquests o'er the grave.

2 The saints who now in Jesus sleep,
 His own almighty power shall keep,
 Till dawns the bright illustrious day,
 When death itself shall pass away.

3 When Jesus we in glory meet,
 Our utmost joys shall be complete;
 When landed on that heavenly shore,
 Death and the curse will be no more.

4 Hasten, dear Lord, the glorious day,
 And that delightful scene display;
 When all Thy saints from death shall rise,
 Raptured in bliss beyond the skies.
 Rev. Rowland Hill (1744—1833).

HAYDN. L. M. FRANCIS JOS. HAYDN (1732—1809).

DEATH OF THE CHRISTIAN.

642 *The Soldier's Discharge.*

1 Servant of God, well done!
Rest from Thy loved employ;
The battle fought, the victory won,
Enter thy Master's joy.

2 At midnight came the cry,
" To meet thy God prepare! "
He woke, and caught his captain's eye,
Then, strong in faith and prayer,

3 His spirit with a bound
Left its encumbering clay;
His tent, at sunrise, on the ground
A darkened ruin lay.

4 The pains of death are past;
Labor and sorrow cease;
And life's long warfare closed at last,
His soul is found in peace.

5 Soldier of Christ, well done!
Praise be thy new employ;
And while eternal ages run,
Rest in thy Saviour's joy.
Rev. J. Montgomery (1771 — 1854).

643 *Nearer Home.*

1 One sweetly solemn thought
Comes to me o'er and o'er,
Nearer my parting hour am I
Than e'er I was before.

2 Nearer my Father's house,
Where many mansions be;
Nearer the throne where Jesus reigns;
Nearer the crystal sea.

3 Nearer my going home,
Laying my burden down,
Leaving my cross of heavy grief,
Wearing my starry crown.

4 Nearer that hidden stream,
Winding through shades of night,
Rolling its cold dark waves between
Me and the world of light.

5 Jesus, to Thee I cling;
Strengthen my arm of faith;
Stay near me while my way-worn feet
Press through the stream of death.
Miss Phebe Cary (1825 — 1871).

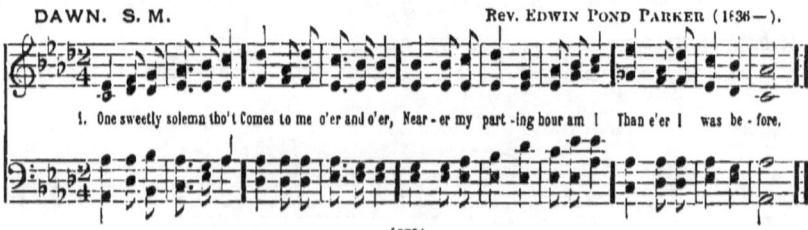

DEATH OF THE CHRISTIAN.

LEOMINSTER. S. M. D. — GEORGE WILLIAM MARTIN (1825—1881). Harmonized by Sir A. S. SULLIVAN.

1. A few more years shall roll, A few more seasons come, And we shall be with those that rest Asleep within the tomb;

REFRAIN.
Then, O my Lord, prepare My soul for that glad day; Oh, wash me in Thy precious blood, And take my sins away.

644 *A Little While.*

1 A few more years shall roll,
 A few more seasons come,
 And we shall be with those that rest
 Asleep within the tomb;

REF.—Then, O my Lord, prepare
 My soul for that glad day;
 Oh, wash me in Thy precious blood,
 And take my sins away.

2 A few more struggles here,
 A few more partings o'er,
 A few more toils, a few more tears,
 And we shall weep no more:—REF.

3 A few more storms shall beat
 On this wild rocky shore,
 And we shall be where tempests cease,
 And surges swell no more:—REF.

4 A few more Sabbaths here,
 Shall cheer us on our way,
 And we shall reach the endless rest,
 Th' eternal Sabbath day:—REF.

5 'T is but a little while
 And He shall come again,
 Who died that we might live, who lives
 That we with Him may reign:—REF.

Rev. Horatius Bonar (1808—1890).

CHALVEY. S. M. D. — Rev. LEIGHTON GEORGE HAYNE, Mus. D. (1836—1883).

1. A few more years shall roll, A few more seasons come, And we shall be with those that rest Asleep within the tomb;

REFRAIN.
Then, O my Lord, prepare My soul for that glad day; Oh, wash me in Thy precious blood, And take my sins away.

CHANTS.

GLORIA IN EXCELSIS.   Ancient English.

645
1 Glory be to | God on | high, ‖ and on earth | peace, good- | will toward | men.
2 We praise Thee, we bless Thee, we | worship | Thee, ‖ we glorify Thee, we give thanks to | Thee for | Thy great | glory.

   CHOIR.

3 O Lord God, | heavenly | King, ‖ God the | Father | al- | mighty,
4 O Lord, the only begotten Son, | Jesus | Christ; ‖ O Lord God, Lamb of | God, Son | of the | Father,

   CHOIR AND CONGREGATION ALTERNATELY.

5 That takest away the | sins · of the | world, ‖ have mercy | upon | us.
6 Thou that takest away the | sins · of the | world, | have mercy | upon | us.
7 Thou that takest away the | sins · of the | world, ‖ re- | ceive our | prayer.
8 Thou that sittest at the right hand of | God the | Father, ‖ have mercy | upon | us.

   FULL CHORUS.

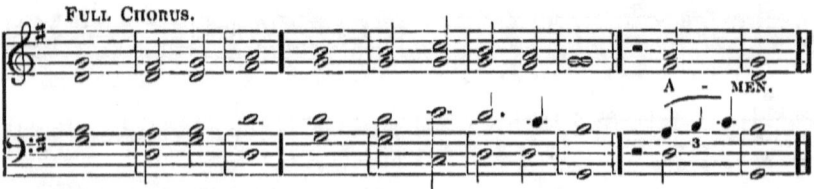

9 For Thou | only · art | holy; ‖ Thou | only | art the Lord;
10 Thou only, O Christ! with the | Holy | Ghost, ‖ art most high in the | glory of | God the | Father. ‖ A- | MEN.

(280)

CHANTS.

VENITE, EXULTEMUS DOMINO.   WILLIAM BOYCE (1710—1779).

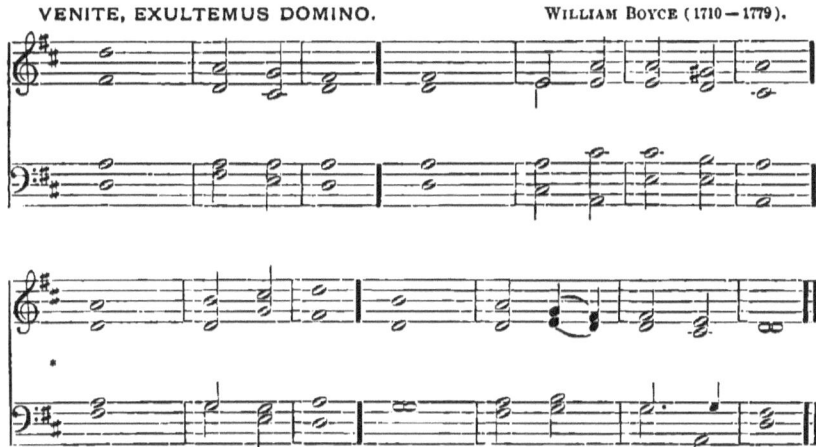

646
Psalm 95.

1 O come, let us sing | unto · the | Lord; ‖ Let us heartily rejoice in the | strength of | our sal- | vation

2 Let us come before His presence | with thanks- | giving; ‖ And show ourselves | glad in | Him with | psalms.

3 For the Lord is a | great — | God; ‖ And a great | King a - | bove all | gods.

4 In His hands are all the corners | of the | earth; ‖ And the strength of the | hills is | His — | also.

5 The sea is His | and He | made it; ‖ And His hands pre- | pared | —the dry | land

6 O come, let us worship | and fall | down; ‖ And kneel be- | fore the | Lord our | Maker.

7 For He is the | Lord our | God; ‖ And we are the people of His pasture, and the | sheep of | His — | hand.

8 O worship the Lord in the | beauty · of | holiness; ‖ Let the whole | earth · stand in | awe of | Him.

*9 For He cometh, for He cometh to | judge the | earth; ‖ And with righteousness to judge the world, and the | people | with His | truth.

10 Glory be to the Father, | and to · the | Son, ‖ And to the | Ho- | ly | Ghost;

11 As it was in the beginning, is now, and | ever · shall be, ‖ World | with-out | end, A- | men.

(281)

CHANTS.

DEUS MISEREATUR.

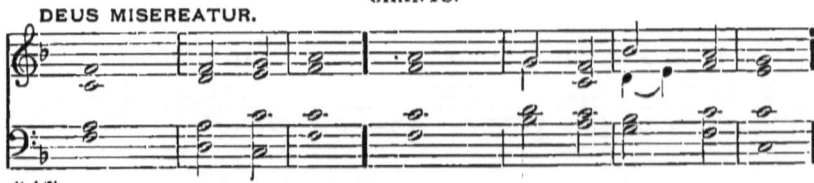

647 *Psalm 67.*

1 God be merciful unto | us, and | bless us ‖ and cause His | face · to | shine · up- | on us.
3 Let the people | praise Thee, · O | God! ‖ let all the | peo-ple | praise — | Thee.
5 Let the people | praise Thee, · O | God! ‖ let all the | peo-ple | praise — | Thee.
7 God shall | bless — | us, ‖ and all the ends of the | earth · shall | fear — | Him.
9 Blessed be the Lord God, the | God of | Israel ‖ who only | doeth | wondrous | things.

2 That Thy way may be | known up- | on | earth, ‖ Thy saving | health · a- | mong · all | nations.
4 Oh, let the nations be glad and | sing · for | joy, ‖ for Thou shalt judge the people righteously, and govern the | na-tions | up-on | earth.
6 Then shall the earth | yield · her increase, ‖ and God, even our own | God, · shall | bless — | us.
8 God shall | bless | us, ‖ and all the ends of the | earth · shall | fear — | Him.
10 And blessed be His glorious | name for ever: ‖ and let the whole earth be | filled with His | glory; A- | men.

648

GLORIA PATRI.   H. W. GREATOREX (1811—1858).

1. Glo - ry be to the Fa - ther, and to the Son, and to the Ho - ly Ghost; As it was in the be-gin-ning, is now, and ev - er shall be, world with-out end. A - men, A - men.

By per. of Oliver Ditson Company, owners of copyright.

CHANTS.

BEYOND THE SMILING AND THE WEEPING.

649

1 Beyond the smiling and the weeping | I shall be | soon:|| Beyond the waking and the sleeping, | Beyond the sowing and the reaping, | I shall be | soon.|| Love, rest and | home! | Sweet | home! | Lord! tarry | not, but | come.

2 Beyond the blooming and the fading | I shall be | soon:|| Beyond the shining and the shading, | Beyond the hoping and the dreading, | I shall be | soon : || Love, rest and | home! | Sweet | home! | Lord! tarry | not, but | come.

3 Beyond the parting and the meeting | I shall be | soon ; || Beyond the farewell and the greeting, | Beyond the pulse's fever beating, | I shall be | soon: || Love, rest and | home! | Sweet | home! | Lord! tarry | not, but | come.

4 Beyond the frost-chain and the fever | I shall be | soon;|| Beyond the rock-waste and the river, | Beyond the ever and the never, | I shall be | soon.|| Love, rest and | home! | Sweet | home! | Lord ! tarry | not, but | come.

Rev. H. Bonar (1808—1890).

WITH TEARFUL EYES.

650

1 With tearful eyes I look around; Life seems a dark and | stormy | sea;|| Yet 'midst the gloom I hear a sound, A heavenly | whisper, | Come to | me.

2 It tells me of a place of rest, It tells me where my | soul may | flee;|| Oh, to the weary, faint, opprest, How sweet the | bidding, | Come to | me!

3 Oh! voice of mercy! voice of love! In conflict, grief, and | ago- | ny, || Support me, cheer me from above! And gently | whisper, | "Come to | me."

4 I come; all else must fail and die; Earth has no resting- | place for | me; || To Christ I lift my weeping eye: Thou art my | hope; I | come to | Thee.

Miss Charlotte Elliott (1789—1871).

CHANTS.

DOMINE REFUGIUM.

651
Psalm 90.

1 Lord, Thou hast been our | dwelling- | place,|| In | all — | gener- | ations.

2 Before the mountains were brought forth, or ever Thou hadst formed the | earth · and the | world,|| Even from everlasting to ever- | lasting, | Thou art | God.

3 Thou turnest man | to de- | struction;|| And sayest, Re- | turn, ye | children · of | men.

4 For a thousand years in Thy sight are but as yesterday, | when · it is | past,|| And as a | watch — | in the | night.

5 Thou carriest them away as with a flood; they are | as a | sleep:|| In the morning they are like | grass which | groweth | up.

6 In the morning it flourisheth, and | groweth | up;|| In the evening it is cut | down, and | wither- | eth.

7 For we are consumed | by Thine | anger,|| And by Thy | wrath — | are we | troubled.

8 Thou hast set our iniquities | before | Thee,|| Our secret sins in the | light · of Thy | counte- | nance.

9 For all our days are passed away | in Thy | wrath:|| We spend our years as a | tale — | that is | told.

10 The days of our years are three-score years and ten; and if by reason of strength they be | four-score | years,|| Yet is their strength labor and sorrow; for it is soon cut off, | and we | fly a- | way.

11 Who knoweth the power | of Thine | anger?|| Even according to Thy fear, | so— | is Thy | wrath.

12 So teach us to | number · our | days,|| That we may apply our | hearts— | unto | wisdom.

Glory be to the Father, | and to · the | Son, || And to the | Ho- | ly | Ghost;

As it was in the beginning, is now, and | ever · shall | be, || World | with-out | end, A- | men.

(284)

CHANTS.

JUBILATE DEO.

652

1 Make a joyful noise unto the Lord, | all · ye | lands; ‖ Serve the Lord with gladness; come before His | pres - ence | with — | singing.
3 Enter into His gates with thanksgiving, and into His | courts · with | praise; ‖ be thankful unto Him, | and — | bless · His | name.
5 Glory be to the Father, | and to · the | Son, ‖ and to the | Ho - | ly | Ghost;

2 Know ye that the Lord | He · is | God; ‖ It is He that hath made us, and not we ourselves; we are His people, | and · the | sheep of · His | pasture.
4 For the Lord is good; His mercy is | ev - er - | lasting, ‖ and His truth endureth to | all — | gen - er - | ations.
6 As it was in the beginning, is now, and | ever · shall | be, ‖ world | with - out | end, A - | men.

NUNC DIMITTIS.

653

1 Lord, now lettest Thou Thy servant de - | part · in | peace ‖ ac - | cord - ing | to · Thy | word;
2 For mine | eyes · have | seen ‖ Thy | —· sal - | va -— | tion,
3 Which Thou | hast · pre - | pared ‖ before the | face · of | all — | people.
4 A light to | lighten · the | Gentiles ‖ and the glory | of · hy | peo - ple | Israel.
  Glory be to the Father, | and to · the | Son, ‖ and to the | Ho - | ly | Ghost;
  As it was in the beginning, is now, and | ever · shall | be, ‖ world | with - out | end, A - | men.

CHANTS.

BENEDIC ANIMA MEA.   CHARLES NORRIS (1740—1790).

654   *Psalm* 103.

1 Bless the Lord, | O my | soul: || And all that is within me, | bless His | holy | Name.
2 Bless the Lord, | O my | soul, || And for- | get not | all His | benefits:
3 Who forgiveth all | thine in- | iquities; || Who | healeth all | thy dis- | eases;
4 Who redeemeth thy life | from de- | struction; || Who crowneth thee with loving- | kindness · and | tender | mercies;
5 The Lord is merci - | ful and | gracious, || Slow to anger, and | plente | ous in | mercy.
6 He hath not dealt with us | after our | sins; || Nor rewarded us ac - | cording to | our in - | iquities.
7 For as the heaven is high a - | bove the | earth, || So great is His mercy toward | them that | fear— | Him.
8 As far as the east is | from the | west, || So far hath He removed | our trans - | gressions | from us.
9 Like as a father | pitieth · His | children, || So the Lord pitieth | them that | fear— | Him.
10 Glory be to the Father, | and to · the | Son, || And to · the | Ho- | ly | Ghost; As it was in the beginning, is now, and | ever · shall | be, || World | with-out | end, A- | men.

THE LORD'S PRAYER.

655   *Matt.* 6: 9-13.

1 Our Father, who art in heaven, | hallowed | be Thy | name; || Thy kingdom come, Thy will be done on | earth, as it | is in | heaven;
2 Give us this | day our | daily | bread; || and forgive us our trespasses, as we for- give | them that | trespass a - | gainst us.
3 And lead us not into temptation, but de- | liver | us from | evil; || for Thine is the kingdom, and the power, and the | glory, for- | ever. A - | men.

(286)

DOXOLOGIES.

656   *L. M.*

Praise God from whom all blessings flow;
Praise Him, all creatures here below;
Praise Him, above, ye heavenly host;
Praise Father, Son, and Holy Ghost.
Bp. Thomas Ken (1637—1711).

657   *L. M.*

To God the Father, God the Son,
And God the Spirit, Three in One,
Be honor, praise, and glory given,
By all on earth, and all in heaven.
Rev. Isaac Watts (1674—1748).

658   *L. C. M.*

To Father, Son, and Holy Ghost,
Be praise amid the heavenly host,
  And in the church below;
From whom all creatures draw their breath,
By whom redemption blessed the earth,
  From whom all comforts flow.

659   *L. P. M.*

Now to great and sacred Three,
The Father, Son, and Spirit be
  Eternal power and glory given,
Through all the worlds where God is known,
By all the angels near the throne,
  And all the saints in earth and heaven.
Rev. Isaac Watts (1674—1748).

660   *C. M.*

To Father, Son, and Holy Ghost,
  The God whom we adore,
Be glory as it was, is now,
  And shall be evermore.
Tate and Brady, 1696.

661   *C. M.*

Let God the Father, and the Son,
  And Spirit be adored,
Where there are works to make him known,
  Or saints to love the Lord.
Rev. Isaac Watts (1674—1748).

662   *S. M.*

To God the Father, Son,
  And Spirit, One and Three,
Be glory, as it was, is now,
  And shall forever be.
Rev. John Wesley (1703—1791).

663   *S. M.*

Give to the Father praise,
  Give glory to the Son,
And to the spirit of His grace
  Be equal honors done.
Rev. Isaac Watts (1674—1748).

664   *H. M.*

To God, the Father's throne,
  Perpetual honors raise;
Glory to God, the Son;
  To God, the Spirit, praise;
With all our powers, eternal King,
While faith adores Thy name we sing.

DOXOLOGIES

665   *7s.*
Sing we to our God above,
Praise eternal as His love;
Praise Him all ye heavenly host,
Father, Son, and Holy Ghost.
Rev. Chas. Wesley (1708—1788).

666   *7s.*
Holy Father, holy Son,
Holy Spirit, Three in One!
Glory as of old to Thee
Now and evermore shall be.

667   *7s, 6l.*
Praise the name of God most high,
Praise Him, all below the sky,
Praise Him, all ye heavenly host,
Father, Son, and Holy Ghost;
As through countless ages past,
Evermore His praise shall last.
Anon, 1827.

668   *7s, 6l.*
God the Father, God of grace,
Saviour, born of mortal race,
Comforter, our Life and Light,
One in essence, love and might;
Thee, whom all in heaven adore,
We would worship evermore.
Rev. Ray Palmer (1808—1887).

669   *7s, D.*
Praise our glorious King and Lord,
Angels waiting on His word,
Saints that walk with Him in white,
Pilgrims walking in His light;
Glory to the Eternal One,
Glory to His only Son,
Glory to the spirit be
Now, and through eternity.
Rev. Alexander Ramsay Thompson (1822—). 1869.

670   *7s & 6s, D. Trochaic.*
Father, Son, and Holy Ghost,
One God whom we adore,
Join we with the heavenly host,
To praise Thee evermore;
Live, by heaven and earth adored,
Three in One, and One in Three,
Holy, holy, holy Lord,
All glory be to Thee.
Rev. Chas. Wesley (1708—1788), 1746. Alt.

671   *8s.*
All praise to the Father, the Son,
And Spirit, thrice holy and bless'd,
Th' eternal, supreme Three in One,
Was, is, and shall still be address'd

672   *8s, 6s, & 8s, D.*
Father, Son, and Holy Ghost,
Thy Godhead we adore.
Join with the celestial host,
Who praise Thee evermore!
Live by earth and heaven adored,
The Three in One, the One in Three;
Holy, holy, holy Lord,
All glory be to Thee!
Rev. Chas. Wesley (1708—1788).

673   *8s & 7s.*
Praise the Father, earth, and heaven;
Praise the Son, the Spirit praise;
As it was, and is, be given
Glory through eternal days.

674   *8s & 7s, D.*
May the grace of Christ our Saviour,
And the Father's boundless love,
With the Holy Spirit's favor,
Rest upon us from above.
Thus may we abide in union
With each other and the Lord,
And possess in sweet communion,
Joys which earth cannot afford.
Rev. John Newton (1725—1807).

DOXOLOGIES.

675   8s & 7s, D.
Lord, dismiss us with Thy blessing,
  Bid us now depart in peace;
Still on heavenly manna feeding,
  Let our faith and love increase;
Fill each breast with consolation;
  Up to Thee our hearts we raise:
When we reach our blissful station,
  Then we 'll give Thee nobler praise.
Robert Hawker (1753 — 1827).

676   8s, 7s & 4s.
Glory be to God the Father,
  Glory be to God the Son,
Glory be to God the Spirit,
  Great Jehovah, Three in One.
    Glory, glory,
  While eternal ages run.
Rev. Horatius Bonar (1808 — 1890).

677   8s, 7s & 4s.
Great Jehovah! we adore Thee,
  God the Father, God the Son,
God the Spirit, joined in glory
  On the same eternal throne;
    Endless praises
  To Jehovah, Three in One.
Rev. William Grade (1762 — 1816).

678   10s.
All praise and glory to the Father be
And Son and Spirit, undivided Three,
As hath been alway, shall be, and is now,
To Thee, O God, the everlasting Thou.
Bp. Edward Henry Bickersteth (1825 —).

679   10s & 11s.
By all holy spirits that fill the wide
  heaven,
And saints upon earth, let praises be
  given
To God, in Three Persons, the God we
  adore,
As it has been; now is, and shall be
  e'ermore.

680   10s & 11s.
By angels in heaven of every degree,
And saints upon earth, all praise be ad-
  dressed
To God in Three Persons, one God ever
  blest,
As it has been, now is, and always shall be.

681   10s & 11s.
All glory to God, the Father, the Son,
And Spirit of grace the great Three and
  One;
Let highest ascriptions forever be given
By all the creation on earth and in
  heaven.
Rippon's Collection, 1778.

682   11s.
O Father Almighty, to Thee be address'd
With Christ and the Spirit, one God ever
  blest,
All glory and worship, from earth and
  from heaven,
As was, and is now, and shall ever be
  given.

GENERAL INDEX OF TUNES.

	HYMN		HYMN
Adger, P. M.	223	Brattle Street, C. M. D.	120
Adrian, S. M.	105	Brest, 8s, 7s and 4s	562
Aileen, S. M.	332	Brockway, C. M.	100
Alford, 7s and 6s, D.	585	Brooklyn	216
Alleluia, 15s	395	Brown, C. M.	226
Amelia, L. M.	629	Byefield, C. M.	179
America, 6s and 4s	237		
Amicus, 7s, D.	209	Calvary, L. M.	444
Amsterdam, 7s and 6s	586	Capetown, 7s and 5s	253
Angels of Jesus, P. M.	573	Chalvey, S. M. D.	644
Angelus, L. M.	287	Cheltenham, C. M. D.	343
Angel Voices, 8s, 5s, 4s and 3s	137	Chimes, C. M.	165
Antioch, C. M.	355	China, C. M.	634
Anvern, L. M.	546	Choral Song, C. M.	195
Ariel, C. P. M.	412	Christmas, C. M.	350
Arlington, C. M.	129, 337	Claremont, H. M.	16
Armenia, C. M.	349	Come Let Us Anew, 11s and 5s,	217
A Safe Stronghold, P. M.	4	Come Ye Disconsolate, 11s and 10s	484
Athens, C. M. D.	84	Comfort, 7s, D.	50
Aurelia, 7s and 6s, D.	82, 308, 370, 506, 532	Commandments, L. M.	571
Austrian Hymn, 8s and 7s, D.	415	Communion, L. M.	181, 512, 520
Autumn, 8s and 7s, D.	215, 482, 497	Consolator, 7s and 5s	320
Avison, 11s and 10s	359	Cooling, C. M.	432
Avon, C. M.	152	Corina, L. M.	290
Azmon, C. M.	117, 304, 603	Coronation, C. M.	420
		Cowper, C. M.	504
Bailey, 8s and 7s, D.	158	Creation, L. M. D.	7
Balerma, C. M.	310	Cross and Crown, C. M.	421
Barby, C. M.	23	Crown Him, 8s, 7s and 4s	389
Batty, 8s and 7s	425		
Belief, C. M.	471	Dallas, 7s	78
Belmont, C. M.	382	Dawn, S. M.	643
Benedic Anima Mea, (Chant)	654	De Fleury, 8s, D.	144, 610
Benediction, 10s	261, 508	Dennis, S. M.	53, 327
Benevento, 7s, D.	211, 414, 499	Departure, S. H. M.	631
Bently, 7s and 6s, D.	258	Deus Misereatur (Chant)	647
Bera, L. M.	30, 333	Devizes, C. M.	275
Bethany, 6s and 4s	132	Dominic Refugium, (Chant)	651
Bethlehem, L. M. D.	51	Dorrnance, 8s and 7s	441
Beulah, 6s, 4s and 6s	614	Dort, 6s and 4s	399
Beyond the Smiling, P. M.	594	Downs, C. M.	196
Beyond the Smiling, (Chant)	649	Dresden, C. M. D.	376
Bona Patria, 7s and 6s, D.	620	Duke Street, L. M.	197
Bowditch, 7s, 6l.	473	Dundee, C. M.	96, 218
Boylston, S. M.	148		
Braden, S. M.	453	Eden, 8s, 6s, 7s and 6s	558
Bradford, C. M.	66	Elizabethtown, C. M.	501

(290)

GENERAL INDEX OF TUNES.

	HYMN.		HYMN.
Ellesdie, 8s and 7s, D.	440	Howard, C. M.	618
Elswick, 6s and 4s	465	Hursley, L. M.	266, 273
Eltham, 7s, D.	540, 588		
Entreaty, 6s and 5s, D.	92	I Hear Thy Welcome Voice, S. M.	446
Ernan, L. M.	116	I'm a Pilgrim, 9s, 10s and 11s	584
Eternal Rock, 7s, 6l.	360	In Cœlo Quies, 7s, D.	414
Evan, C. M.	435, 450	Innocents, 7s	454
Evelyn, 7s and 6s	317	Invitation, 8s and 7s, D.	161
Evening Prayer, 8s and 7s	301	Invocation, L. M.	281
Even Me, 8s and 7s	180	Iona, L. M.	87
Eventide, 10s	288, 630	Irene, 7s and 5s	599
Everlasting Rest, 7s, D.	35	Italian Hymn, 6s and 4s	236
Ewing, 7s and 6s	622		
		Jubilate Deo, (Chant)	652
Federal Street, L. M.	324, 608	Just As I Am, 8s and 6s	427
Ferguson, S. M.	29, 505		
Flemming, 8s and 6s	174	Kyrie Eleison, 7s	265
Folsom, 11s and 10s	357		
Frederick, 11s	600	Laban, S. M.	334
		Lachrymæ, 7s, 3l.	298
		Land of Holy Light, 8s and 7s, D.	142
Galilean Hymn, 8s and 7s, D.	442	Lanesboro, C. M.	472
Ganges, C. P. M.	567	Langran, 10s	579
Geer, C. M.	436	Langton, S. M.	402
Gennesaret, 10s, 6l.	135	Lansdown, 7s, D.	404
Geneva, C. M.	296	Last Beam, P. M.	279
Gentle Shepherd, 8s and 7s	286	Last Hope, 7s	318, 523
Gera, S. M.	367	Lebanon, S. M. D.	28
Germany, L. M.	125	Leighton, S. M.	329
Gethsemane, 7s, 6l.	363	Lenox, H. M.	25
Gloria, 15s	569	Leominster, S. M. D.	644
Gloria In Excelsis, (Chant)	645	Lindisfarne, P. M.	386
Gloria Patri, (Chant)	648	Lischer, H. M.	231
Goshen, 11s	200, 493	Litany, 7s and 6s	525
Gratitude, L. M.	114	Louvan, L. M	514
Green Island, S. M.	104	Loving-kindness, L. M.	243
Greenport, C. M. D.	175	Lux Benigna, 10s and 4s	171
Greenville, 8s and 7s, D.	451	Lux Mundi, 7s and 6s, D.	429
Greenwood, S. M.	46	Lyons, 10s and 11s,	204
Gröningen, P. M.	190		
		Manopy, 8s	134
Haddam, H. M.	37, 380	Manoah, C. M.	356, 405, 481
Hamburg, L. M.	309, 557	Margaret, 8s and 4s	426
Hanover, 10s and 11s	18	Marlow, C. M.	437
Happy Day, L. M.	448	Martyn, 7s, D.	400, 431
Harwell, 8s and 7s, D.	351, 417	Mear, C. M.	344
Hastings, C. H. M.	383	Melcombe, L. M.	214
Havergal, 7s, 6l.	510	Melita, L. M. 6l.	221
Haydn, L. M.	641	Mendebras, 7s and 6s, D.	91, 617
Heber, C. M.	456	Mendelssohn, 7s, D.	347
Hebron, L. M.	123	Mendon, L. M.	7
Hendon, 7s	187, 449	Mercy Seat, L. M.	173
Henley, 11s and 10s,	260	Meribah, C. P. M.	504
Henry, C. M.	57	Merrial, 6s and 5s	189
Hesperus, L. M.	194	Merrill, 7s	110
Holley, 7s	517	Merton, C. M.	182
Hollingside, 7s, D.	85, 431	Messiah, 7s, D.	169
Home Sweet Home, 11s	616	Middleton, 8s and 7s, D.	5, 544
Horace's Chant, S. M.	268	Migdol, L. M.	285
Horsley, C. M.	430, 455, 595	Miriam, 7s and 6s, D	619
Horton, 7s	263	Missionary Chant, L. M.	533
Houghton, 10s and 11s	391	Missionary Hymn, 7s and 6s, D.	537

(291)

GENERAL INDEX OF TUNES.

	HYMN.		HYMN.
Moccas, S. M.	632	St. Aëlred, 8s and 3s,	470
More Love, 6s and 4s	465	St. Agnes, C. M.	119, 154
Mornington, S. M.	486	St. Albans, 6s and 5s, D.	342
Munich, 7s and 6s, D.	202	St. Bees, 7s	524
Naomi, C. M.	67	St. Crispin, L. M.	475
Nashville, L. P. M.	22	St. George, 7s, D.	219
Nazareth, L. M. 6l.	459	St. Gertrude, 6s and 5s, D.	341
Naumann, C. M.	598	St. Helen, 10s	36
Nettleton, 8s and 7s, D.	47	St. Johns, C. M.	74
New Haven, 6s and 4s	316	St. Jude, 6s, D.	40
Nicaea, P. M.	24	St. Margaret, 8s and 6s, 6l.	193
Northfield, C. M.	581	St. Martins, C. M.	570
Nottingham, C. M,	19	St. Matthias, L. M. 6l.	262, 422
Nunc Dimittis, (Chant)	653	St. Peter, C. M.	224
Nuremburgh, 7s, 6l	251	St. Petersburg, 8s, 6l.	206
		St. Regulus, 10s, 6s and 4s	474
Oak, 6s, 4s and 6s	613	St. Sylvester, 8s and 7s	138
Oaksville, C. M.	381	St. Thomas, S. M.	529
Old Hundred, L. M.	1	Sabbath, 7s, 6l.	225
Oliphant, 8s, 7s and 4s	155	Salvation, C. M. D.	480
Olivet, 6s and 4s	612	Sanquhar, L. M.	284
Olive's Brow, L. M.	362	Sarum, 10s and 4s	578
Olmutz, S. M.	642	Savannah, 10s	526
Olney, S. M.	106	Saviour, L. M.	448
Ortonville, C. M.	65	Saviour Comfort Me, 7s and 5s	172
Oswald, 8s and 7s	424	Scotland, 12s	479, 628
		Self Surrender, P. M.	61
Palmer, 7s, 6l.	398	Selvin, S. M.	624
Paradise, No. 1. P. M.	615	Serenity, C. M.	245
Paradise, No. 2, P. M.	615	Sessions, L. M.	254
Park Street, L. M.	176, 551	Seymour, 7s	249
Passion Chorale, 7s and 6s, D.	377	Shawmut, S. M.	6
Pax Tecum, 10s, 2l.	186	Sheffield, S. M.	625
Peniel, C. M.	13	Shining Shore, P. M.	592
Perry, 7s, D.	393	Shirland, S. M.	299, 331
Peterboro, C. M.	71	Sicilian Hymn, 8s and 7s, D.	269
Pilot, 7s, 6l.	95	Sienna, S. M.	575
Pleyel's Hymn, 7s	17, 192, 494	Siloam, C. M.	555
Portuguese Hymn, 11s	109, 358	Silver Street, S. M.	44
Potsdam, S. M.	461	Solitude, 7s	516
Priere, 7s, 3l.	315	Spanish Hymn, 7s, 6l.	234, 396
Promise, 8s and 7s, D.	20	Spohr, C. M.	205
Protection, 11s	109	State Street, S. M.	488
		Stella, L. M. 6l.	64, 238
Ratisbon, 7s, 6l.	241	Stephanos, P. M.	185
Rathbun, 8s and 7s	34, 408	Stephens, C. M.	313
Raynolds, 11s and 10s	428	Stockwell, 8s and 7s	460
Regent Square, 8s, 7s and 4s	531	Stuttgart, 8s and 7s	385
Resignation, L. M. 6l.	207	Submission	208
Rest, L. M.	637	Sunset, 6s and 4s	464
Rest for the Weary, 8s and 7s	606	Swanwick, C. M.	312
Resurrection, 7s	390		
Retreat, L. M.	293	Tallis' Evening Hymn, L. M.	244
Rhine, C. M.	602	Tallis' Ordinal, C. M.	326
Rockingham, L. M.	141	Tamworth, 8s, 7s and 4s	563
Rosedale, L. M.	513	Tappan, C. M. 5l.	604
Rosefield, 7s, 6l.	626	Temple Boro, 8s, 7s and 4s	560
Rothwell, L. M.	8	Thatcher, S. M.	330
Ruth, 6s and 5s, D.	163	The Eagle, L. M.	372
Rutherford, P. M.	590	The Lord's Prayer, (Chant)	655

(292)

METRICAL INDEX OF TUNES.

	HYMN.		HYMN.
Theodora, 7s,	90, 468	Vox Dilecti, C. M. D.	84
There Is a Green Hill, C. M.	375	Vox Jesu, 7s and 6s, D.	485
Thermutis, 7s, D.	250	Walton, L. M.	627
Thy Will Be Done, (Chant)	574	Ward, L. M.	609
Tichfield, 7s, D.	11	Ware, L. M.	378
To-day, 6s and 4s	500	Warrington, L. M.	274
Topaz, P. M.	401	Warwick, C. M.	227
Toplady, 7s, 6l.	364	Watchman Tell Us, 7s, D.	539
Troyte's Chant, No. 1	288	Webb, 7s and 6s, D.	146, 549
Troyte's Chant, No. 2	578	Wells, L. M.	321
Uxbridge, L. M.	282	Wesley, 11s and 10s	527
		What a Friend, 8s and 7s, D.	42
		Wilmarth, L. M.	139
Varina, C. M. D.	62	Wilmot, 7s	387
Venite Exultemus, (Chant)	646	With Tearful Eyes, (Chant)	650
Vernon, 8s, D.	191	Woodland, C. M. 5l.	128, 559, 596
Vesper, 8s and 7s	242	Woodworth, L. M.	427
Vesper Hymn, 8s and 7s, D.	301	Woodstock, C. M.	126
Vigil, S. M.	591		
Vigilate, 7s and 3s,	136	Zephyr, L. M.	489, 640
Virgo, L. M.	94	Zerah, C. M.	353
Vox Angelica, P. M.	573	Zion, 8s, 7s and 4s	541

METRICAL INDEX OF TUNES.

	HYMN.		HYMN.
L. M.		Migdol,	285
		Missionary Chant,	533
Amelia,	629	Old Hundred,	1
Angelus,	287	Olive's Brow,	362
Anvern,	553	Park Street,	176, 551
Bera,	30, 333	Rest,	637
Calvary,	444	Retreat,	293
Commandments,	571	Rockingham,	141
Communion,	181, 512, 520	Rosedale,	513
Corina,	290	Rothwell,	8
Duke Street	197	Sanquhar,	284
Ernan,	116	Saviour,	448
Federal Street,	324, 608	Sessions,	254
Gennesaret,	135	St. Crispin,	475
Germany,	125	Tallis' Evening Hymn,	244
Gratitude, L. M.	114	The Eagle,	372
Hamburg,	309, 557	Uxbridge,	282
Happy Day,	448	Virgo,	94
Haydn,	641	Walton,	627
Hebron,	123	Ward,	609
Hesperus,	194	Ware,	378
Hursley,	266, 273	Warrington,	274
Invocation,	281	Wells,	321
Iona,	87	Wilmarth,	139
Louvan,	514	Woodworth,	427
Loving-kindness,	243	Zephyr,	489, 640
Melcombe,	214		
Melita,	221	**L. M. 6l.**	
Mendon,	7	Melita,	221
Mercy Seat,	173	Nazareth,	459

(293)

METRICAL INDEX OF TUNES.

	HYMN.		HYMN.
Resignation,	207	St. Agnes,	119, 154
Stella,	64, 238	St. Johns,	74
St. Matthias,	262, 422	St. Martins,	570
		St. Peter,	224
L. M. D.		Tallis' Ordinal,	326
Creation,	7	There is a green hill,	375
		Warwick,	227
L. P. M.		Woodland,	128, 559, 796
Nashville,	22	Woodstock,	126
		Zerah,	353
C. M.			
Antioch,	355	**C. M. 5l.**	
Arlington,	129, 337	Naumann,	598
Armenia,	349	Tappan,	604
Avon,	152		
Azmon,	117, 304, 603	**C. M. D.**	
Balerma,	310	Athens,	84
Barby,	23	Brattle Street,	120
Belief,	471	Cheltenham,	343
Belmont,	382	Dresden,	376
Bradford,	66	Greenport,	175
Brockway,	100	Salvation,	480
Brown,	226	Varina,	62
Byefield,	179	Vox Dilecti,	84
Chimes,	165		
China,	634	**C. P. M.**	
Choral Song,	195	Ariel,	412
Christmas,	350	Ganges,	567
Cooling,	432	Meribah,	564
Coronation,	420		
Cowper,	504	**P. M.**	
Cross and Crown,	421	Adger,	223
Devizes,	275	Angels of Jesus,	573
Downs,	196	A Safe Stronghold,	4
Dundee,	96, 218	Beyond the Smiling, etc.	594
Elizabethtown,	501	Last Beam,	279
Evan,	435, 450	Lindisfarne,	386
Geer,	436	Nicaea,	24
Geneva,	296	Paradise No. 1,	615
Heber,	456	Paradise No. 2,	615
Henry,	57	Rutherford,	590
Horsley,	430, 455, 595	Self-surrender,	61
Howard,	618	Shining Shore,	592
Lanesboro,	472	Stephanos,	185
Manoah,	356, 403, 481	Topaz,	401
Marlow,	437	Vox Angelica,	573
Mear,	344		
Merton,	182	**S. M.**	
Naomi,	67	Adrian,	105
Northfield,	581	Aileen,	332
Nottingham,	19	Bethlehem,	51
Oaksville,	381	Boylston,	148
Ortonville,	65	Braden,	453
Peniel,	13	Dawn,	643
Peterboro,	71	Dennis,	53, 327
Rhine,	602	Ferguson,	29, 505
Serenity,	245	Gera,	367
Siloam,	555	Green Island,	104
Spohr,	205	Greenwood,	46
Stephens,	313	Horace's Chant,	268
Swanwick,	312	I Hear Thy Welcome Voice,	446

(294)

METRICAL INDEX OF TUNES.

	HYMN.
Laban,	334
Langton,	402
Leighton,	329
Moccas,	632
Mornington,	486
Olmutz,	642
Olney,	106
Potsdam,	461
Selvin,	624
Shawmut,	6
Sheffield,	625
Shirland,	299, 331
Sienna,	575
Silver Street,	44
State Street,	488
St. Thomas,	529
Thatcher,	330
Vigil,	591

S. M. D.

Chalvey,	644
Lebanon,	28
Leominster,	644

S. H. M.

Departure,	631

H. M.

Brooklyn,	216
Claremont,	16
Haddam,	37, 380
Lenox,	25
Lischer,	231

C. H. M.

Hastings,	383

6s.

St. Jude,	40

6s & 4s.

America,	237
Bethany,	132
Dort,	399
Elswick,	465
Italian Hymn,	236
More Love,	465
New Haven,	316
Olivet,	612
Sunset,	464
To-day,	500

6s, 4s & 6s.

Oak,	613

6s, 4s & 7s.

Beulah,	614

6s & 5s.

Entreaty,	92
Merrial,	189

	HYMN.
Ruth,	168

6s, & 5s, D.

St. Albans,	342
St. Gertrude,	341

6s, 8s, 3s.

Gröningen,	190

7s.

Dallas,	78
Hendon,	187, 449
Holley,	517
Horton,	263
Innocents,	454
Kyrie Eleison,	265
Last Hope,	318, 523
Merrill,	110
Nuremburgh,	251
Pleyel's Hymn,	17, 192, 494
Resurrection,	390
Seymour,	249
Solitude	516
St. Bees,	524
Theodora,	90, 468
Vernon,	191
Wilmot,	387

7s, 3l.

Lachrymæ,	298
Priere,	315

7s, 6l.

Eternal Rock,	360
Gethsemane,	363
Havergal,	510
Palmer,	398
Pilot,	95
Ratisbon,	241
Rosefield,	626
Sabbath,	225
Spanish Hymn,	234, 396
Toplady,	364

7s, D.

Amicus,	209
Benevento,	211, 414, 499
Bowditch,	473
Eltham,	540, 588
Everlasting Rest,	85
Hollingside,	85, 431
In Cœlo Quies,	414
Lansdown,	404
Martyn,	400, 431
Mendelssohn,	347
Messiah,	169
Perry,	393
Spanish Hymn,	234, 396
St. George,	219
Tichfield,	11
Thermutis,	250

METRICAL INDEX OF TUNES.

7s & 3s.

	HYMN
Watchman Tell Us,	539

7s & 5s.

Vigilate,	136

7s & 5s.

Capetown,	253
Consolator,	320
Irene,	599
Saviour, Comfort Me,	172
Vesper,	242

7s & 6s.

Evelyn,	317
Litany,	525

7s & 6s, D.

Alford,	585
Amsterdam,	586
Aurelia,	82, 308, 370, 506, 532
Bently,	258
Bona Patria,	620
Ewing,	622
Lux Mundi,	429
Mendebras,	91, 617
Miriam,	619
Missionary Hymn,	537
Munich,	202
Passion Chorale,	877
Vox Jesu,	485
Webb,	146, 549

8s.

Manepy,	134

8s, 6 l.

St. Petersburg,	206

8s, D.

De Fleury,	144, 610
Vernon,	191

8s & 3s.

St. Aëlred,	470

8s & 4s.

Margaret,	426

8s, 5s, 4s & 3s.

Angel Voices,	137

8s & 6s.

Flemming,	174
Just As I Am,	427

8s, 6s, 7s & 6s.

Eden,	558

8s & 7s.

	HYMN
Batty,	425
Dorrnance,	441

	HYMN
Even Me,	180
Evening Prayer,	301
Gentle Shepherd,	286
Oswald,	424
Rathbun,	34, 408
Rest For The Weary,	606
Stockwell,	460
Stuttgart,	385
St. Margaret,	193
St. Sylvester,	138

8s, 7s, D.

Austrian Hymn,	415
Autumn,	215, 482, 497
Bailey,	158
Ellesdie,	440
Galilean Hymn,	442
Greenville,	451
Harwell,	351, 417
Invitation,	161
Land of Holy Light,	142
Middleton,	5, 544
Nettleton,	47
Promise,	20
Sicilian Hymn,	269
Vesper Hymn,	301
What A Friend,	42

8s, 7s & 4s.

Brest,	562
Crown Him,	389
Oliphant,	155
Regent Square,	531
Tamworth,	563
Temple Boro,	560
Zion,	541

9s, 10s & 11s.

I'm A Pilgrim,	584

10s, 2 l.

Pax Tecum,	186

10s, 4 l.

Benediction,	261, 508
Eventide,	288, 630
Langran,	579
Savannah,	526

10s, 6 l.

St. Helen,	36

10s & 4s.

Lux Benigna,	171
Sarum,	578
Submission,	208
Troyte's Chant,	587

10s & 11s.

Hanover,	18
Houghton,	391
Lyons,	204

(296)

INDEX OF FIRST LINES.

11s.

	HYMN.
Come, Let Us Anew	217
Frederick,	600
Goshen,	200, 493
Home Sweet Home,	616
Portuguese Hymn,	109, 358
Protection,	109

11s & 9s.

Comfort,	52

11s & 10s.

Avison,	359

	HYMN.
Come Ye Disconsolate,	484
Folsom,	357
Henley,	260
Raynold's,	428
Wesley,	527

12s.

Scotland,	479, 628

15s.

Alleluia,	393
Gloria,	569

INDEX OF SUBJECTS.

Abide with me, 288.
Activity in Christian life, 330, 333, 334, 335, 336, 338, 339, 340, 586.
Adoption, 150.
Adoration, 11, 78, 80, 85, 96, 97, 98, 137, 143, 289.
Advent, (See Christ.)
Advocate, Divine, 33.
Angel's Song, 137, 351, 352, 573.
Ashamed of Christ, 444.
Aspiration for God, 65, 66, 68, 72, 76, 167, 294.
Assurance, 121, 570.
Atonement, 49, 64, 73, 145, 198, 367, 445, 473, 513.

Backslider returning, 71.
Baptism of Infants, 556, 557.
Bethel, 190.
Blessed County, 142, 620.
Bread of Life, 508.
Brevity of Life, 138, 643, 644.
Brevity of the Conflict, 593, 594, 619, 623, 644.

Calling yet, 122.
Calmness, 69.
Calvary, 375, 393.
Cheer, 17, 111.
Childhood, 555.
Christ, Praise to 5, 27, 48, 49, 378, 421.

Christ, Birth, (See Advent) 347, 350.
Christ, (See Passion.)
Christ, King, 353, 355, 356, 378, 379, 380, 385, 391, 410, 420.
Christ, Light, 241, 266.
Christ, Our All, 166, 176, 426.
Christ, Priest, 33, 381.
Christ, Teacher, 32.

Christ Enthroned, 386, 389, 395, 399, 405, 406, 407, 411.
Christ's Triumph, 389, 399, 415, 417, 419, 531, 535, 536, 540, 553, 554.
Church, The 526, 527, 529, 532, 541, 544, 545.
Come Unto Me, 84, 87, 169, 185, 485.

Comfort, 127, 172, 203.
Coming to Christ, 87, 161, 427, 443, 446.
Communion Hymns, 501–525.
Communion with Christ, 174.
Compassion, Divine, 148, 149, 150.
Confessing Christ, 444, 445, 448.
Confession of Sin, 88.
Confidence, 4, 37, 74, 75, 100, 104, 105, 134, 170, 200, 204, 416, 570.
Consecration, 90, 113, 422.
Consolation in Sickness, 126.
Corner Stone, Laying, 214, 216.
Coronation, 420.
Courage, 20, 576.
Creation, 7.
Cross and Crown, 421.

Cross-Bearing, 210, 374, 421, 440.
Cross, The, 31, 210, 408, 409, 445, 473.
Cross, Worship at the, 424, 425.

Dawn, 543, 545, 547.
Death of a Child, 558, 559.
Death of a Christian, 628, 629, 630, 631, 632, 634, 635, 640, 642.
Death welcome to Believers, 600, 601, 627.
Dangers of Delay, 493.
Dedication of a Church, 215, 216, 218.
Dependence upon Christ, 202.
Devotion, 239, 254, 260, 268, 403.
Divine Government, 6.
Divine Light, 146.
Dominion, God's 25, 26.
Door, Christ at the 83, 489.
Door of Mercy, 443.
Drawing near to God, 192.
Dying in Christ, 580, 583.

Ebenezer, 123.
Election of Grace, 398, 147.
Encouragement to Prayer, 187.
Escape from Sin, 479.
Evening, 191, 242, 249, 250, 252.
Evening Praise, 244, 245, 246, 279, 286, 288, 298, 299, 301.
Exile, 107, 111, 575.
Everlasting Arms, 468.

(298)

INDEX OF SUBJECTS.

Faith, 62, 64, 117, 125, 171, 205, 459, 612.
Father, Heavenly, 78, 80.
Fellowship, 58.
Firm Foundation, 109.
Forgiveness, 285.
Fount of Blessing, 47, 176.
Freedom, 213.
Friend of Sinners, 30, 42, 341.

Gethsemane, 362, 363.
Giving to God, 331, 332.
God's Kingdom, 25, 26, 110, 379, 393, 530.
God's Presence, 255.
Gospel, 32, 282.
Grace, 44, 147, 337, 433.
Gratitude, 12. 60, 114, 296, 382, 626.
Grave, Peaceful, 636.
Growth in Grace, 132.
Guidance, 86, 155, 156, 157.

Harvest Past, 496.
Heaven, Anticipations of, 128, 133, 569, 571, 611, 614.
Heavenly Country, 604, 605, 620, 621.
Heavenly Life, 599.
Hiding Place, 54, 55.
Holy Ghost, Invocation of, 116, 177, 239, 269,313, 314, 315, 316, 320, 322, 326, 329.
Holy Spirit, 313-329.
Home, Sweet Home, 616.
House of God, 234, 235, 265, 275, 284, 297.
House of many Mansions, 571, 577.

Illumination, 139.
Immanuel's Land, 590.
Incarnation, 79.
Indwelling, Divine, 38, 141.
Intercession, 92.
Invitations, 169, 251, 473, 475-500.
Invocation, 173, 237, 264, 274, 272, 295.

Jerusalem, New, 581, 595, 602, 603, 617, 622.
Jesus is Mine, 464.
Jews, Conversion of, 550.
Journeying Heavenward, 217, 613.
Jubilee, Year of, 27.
Judgment, The, 560, 561, 562, 563, 564, 565, 567, 568.

Lead Kindly Light, 171.
Lead Me, 86.
Longing for Christ, 39, 112, 135, 144, 145, 152, 153, 154, 162, 193, 194, 206, 401, 402, 435, 436.
Longing for Heaven, 602, 603, 608, 609, 615, 616, 618.
Love Divine, 158, 193, 268.
Love for Christ, 447, 458, 460, 461, 462, 465, 466, 468, 471, 472, 550.
Loving-Kindness, 243.

Marriage Feast, 475.
Mercy, God's, 43.

Mercy Seat, 103, 173, 247, 248, 257, 293.
Ministering Angels, 134.
Missions, 533-551.
Morning Hymn, 243, 258, 273, 384.
Mysteries of Providence, 99.

Nature and Grace, 13, 198.
Nature's Praise, 7, 282.
Nativity, Hymns of the, 343-459.
Nearer Home, 643.
Nearer to God, 132, 401.
New Year, 211, 217, 220.

Obedience, 50.
Omniscience, 131.

Palestine, 142.
Paradise, 615.
Parting Hymns, 259, 261, 262, 269, 271.
Pasturage Divine, 81, 106, 129, 201, 240.
Passion of Christ, 360-377.
Pastoral Office, 196.
Patience, 36, 51.
Peace in God, 186.
Pilgrimage, 20, 584, 613.
Pilotage, 95, 455, 584.
Pity of the Lord, 148, 149.
Pleading for Mercy, 140, 404.
Praise, 1, 3, 16, 19, 21, 22, 23, 34, 35, 45, 46, 280.
Praise to Christ, 412, 413, 437, 438, 439, 447, 452, 453, 454.
Prayer, 179.
Prayer, Hour of, 290.
Preachers, Prayer for, 281.
Presence of Christ in Sorrow, 164.
Promises, 37.
Protection, 109, 110, 146.
Providence, 99, 101, 102, 120, 123, 124, 197, 204.

Receiving Christ, 83.
Refuge, Divine, 54, 55, 74, 175, 209, 425, 431, 432.
Reflection, Religious, 130.
Rejoicing in Christ, 50, 464.
Religion, Importance of, 165.
Remembrance of Grace, 28, 47. 84, 121.
Renunciation of Self, 199.
Repentance, 70, 71, 73, 77, 82, 88, 115, 140.
Resignation, 67, 92, 93, 118, 119, 207, 208, 292, 574.
Resting in Christ, 89, 182, 185, 429, 430, 625.
Rest in Heaven, 591, 596, 606, 625.
Resurrection of Christ, 259, 383, 384, 387, 388, 390, 394, 397, 400.
Revival, 159.
Rock, The, 170, 364, 619.

Sabbath, 225, 226, 227, 229, 231, 233, 258, 276, 300, 383, 388.

(299)

INDEX OF SUBJECTS.

Sabbath Worship, 8, 10, 23, 45.
Sacred Head, 370, 407.
Saints in Heaven, 578, 585, 689, 597, 598, 610.
Salvation, 57.
Scriptures, 304-312.
Seamen, 221, 222, 223, 224.
Second coming of Christ, 49, 419, 582, 588, 641.
Seed Sowing, 330.
Seeking Jesus, 428.
Shepherding, Divine, 28, 81, 106, 129, 201, 396, 451.
Shining Shore, 592.
Sincerity, 15.
Sinner's Turn, 499.
Sins Repented, 82.
Sleep in Death, 637-640.
Soldiers of Christ, 341, 342.
Soul, Value of, 189.
Sovereignty of God, 104, 105, 110, 113, 197.
Storms, 207, 470, 624.
Submission, 40, 41, 59, 607.

Sun of Righteousness, 139, 241, 266.
Supplication, 180, 263, 298, 371, 426.
Support, Divine, 75, 182.
Surrender, 38, 122, 414.

Thanksgiving, 163, 212, 213, 219.
Thy will be done, 40, 118, 292, 574.
To-day, 500.
Trinity, Invocation of, 236.
Trinity, Praise to 24, 253.
Trinity, Prayer to, 9.
Trust, 29, 61, 63, 91, 107, 434.

Union with People of God, 94.
Unity, 52, 53.
Universal Praise, 16, 21, 24, 34, 280.

Waiting for God, 36, 51.
Watchfulness, 136, 196, 463.
Weariness of Earth, 579.
Welcome to Christ, 270.
Wideness of God's Mercy, 43.
Worship, 6, 228, 291.

INDEX OF FIRST LINES.

	HYMN.
Abide with me, fast falls the eventide	288
A broken heart, my God, my King	283
According to Thy gracious word	503
A charge to keep I have	334
A few more years shall roll	644
A glory gilds the sacred page	304
Alas, and did my Saviour bleed	73
Alleluia, Alleluia, hearts to heaven	395
All hail the power of Jesus' name	420
All people that on earth do dwell	1
All praise to Thee my God this night	244
All that I was, my sin, my guilt	70
Alone with Jesus, O how sweet	173
Along the mountain track of life	401
Amazing grace, how sweet the sound	337
Am I a soldier of the cross	339
And canst thou sinner slight	328
And is it so, a little while	593
And is there, Lord, a rest	591
Angels from the realms of glory	352
Angels rejoiced and sweetly sung	345
Angels roll the rock away	397
Angel voices ever singing	137
Approach, my soul, the mercy seat	247
Arm of the Lord, awake, awake	551
Art thou weary, art thou languid	185
A safe stronghold, our God is still	4
Ascend thy throne, Almighty King	546
Ask ye what great thing I know	449
Asleep in Jesus, blessed sleep	637
As pants the hart for cooling streams	152
As when the weary traveler gains	609
At even, ere the sun was set	287
At the door of mercy sighing	443
Awaked by Sinai's awful sound	567
Awake, ye saints, awake	232
Awake my soul, and with the sun	273
Awake my soul in joyful lays	243
Awake my soul, stretch every nerve	338
Awake, sweet gratitude, and sing	382
Before Jehovah's awful throne	3
Behold a stranger at the door	489
Behold the Man, how glorious He	514
Behold the sin-atoning Lamb	513
Behold what wondrous grace	150

	HYMN.
Be still my soul; the Lord is on thy side	36
Beyond the smiling and the weeping	594
Beyond the smiling and the weeping (chant)	649
Blessed country, home of Jesus	142
Blessed Saviour, Thee I love	510
Bless, O my soul, the living God	254
Bless the Lord, O my soul (chant)	654
Blest are the sons of peace	52
Blest be the tie that binds	53
Blest be Thy love, dear Lord	268
Blest Comforter Divine	327
Blest Jesus, when Thy cross I view	374
Blow ye the trumpet, blow	27
Brethren while we sojourn here	169
Brief life is here our portion	623
Brightest and best of the sons of the morning	357
Brightly gleams our banner	342
By angels in heaven of every degree	392
By cool Siloam's shady rill	555
Calm me, my God, and keep me calm	69
Calm on the listening ear of night	349
Children of the heavenly King	17
Chosen not for good in me	398
Christian, seek not yet repose	136
Christian see the orient morning	531
Christ is coming, let creation	419
Christ the Lord is risen to-day	390
Christ whose glory fills the skies	241
Come christian brethren, ere we part	256
Come dearest Lord, descend and dwell	274
Come every pious heart	380
Come HolyGhost, and through each heart	177
Come Holy Ghost, Creator, come	314
Come Holy Ghost, in love	316
Come Holy Ghost, our hearts inspire	326
Come Holy Spirit, calm my mind	325
Come Holy Spirit come	329
Come Holy Spirit Heavenly Dove	313
Come hither all ye weary souls	477
Come humble sinner, in whose breast	480
Come let us anew	217
Come let us join with one accord	195
Come, my Soul, thy suit prepare	187

(301)

INDEX OF FIRST LINES.

	HYMN.
Come, my Redeemer, come	38
Come, O Creator, Spirit blest	322
Come Sacred Spirit from above	116
Come sound His praise abroad	45
Come Thou Almighty King	236
Come Thou Fount of every blessing	47
Come Thou long expected Jesus	49
Come Thou soul-transforming spirit	269
Come to our poor nature's night	320
Come unto me ye weary	485
Come weary souls, with sin distrest	478
Come ye that love the Lord	46
Come, we disconsolate, where'er ye languish	484
Come, ye sinners, poor and wretched	482
Come, ye thankful people, come	219
*Come, ye weary sinners, come	494
Command Thy blessing from above	295
Crown His head with endless blessing	5
Daughter of Zion, awake from thy sadness	527
Day of judgment, day of wonders	562
Days and moments quickly flying	138
Dear Refuge of my weary soul	175
Dear Saviour bless us ere we go	262
Dear Saviour, if these lambs should stray	557
Dear Saviour we are Thine	505
Deep in our hearts let us record	521
Delay not, delay not, O sinner draw near	493
Depth of mercy, can there be	523
Did Christ o'er sinners weep	149
Disowned of heaven, by man oppressed	552
Do not I love Thee, O my Lord	457
Dread Sovereign, let my evening song	246
Early, my God, without delay	154
Earth with its dark and dreadful ills	583
Eternal Father, strong to save	221
Eternal Spirit, source of light	239
Everlasting arms of love	468
Ever my Lord with Thee	133
Fade, fade each earthly joy	464
Fading, still fading, the last beam is fading	279
Far as Thy name is known	6
Far from my heavenly home	575
Father, how wide Thy glory shines	13
Father, I long, I faint to see	167
Father, in Thy mysterious presence kneeling	260
Father, let Thy smiling face	264
Father of all, whose love profound	9
Father of mercies, bow Thine ear	281
Father of mercies, in Thy word	311
Father, whate'er of earthly bliss	67
Fierce raged the tempest o'er the deep	470
For all the saints who from their labors rest	578

	HYMN.
For Thee, oh, dear, dear Country	620
Forever here my rest shall be	430
Forever with the Lord	577
Fountain of grace, rich, full and free	176
Frequent the day of God returns	226
Friend after friend departs	631
From all that dwell below the skies	280
From every stormy wind that blows	293
From heaven the new Jerusalem comes	595
From the cross uplifted high	473
From Greenland's icy mountains	537
Galilean King and Prophet	442
Gently, Lord, O gently lead us	451
Gently, my Saviour, let me down	638
Give me the wings of faith to rise	598
Give to the Father Praise	108
Give to the winds thy fears	576
Glorious things of Thee are spoken	544
Glory be to God on high	645
Glory be to the Father (chant)	648
Glory to God, the lofty strain	350
God be merciful unto us (chant)	647
God calling yet! shall I not hear	182
God eternal, Lord of all	85
God in the gospel of His Son	309
God moves in a mysterious way	99
God my supporter and my hope	182
God of our salvation, hear us	156
God reveals His presence	190
God with us! O glorious name	79
Go to dark Gethsemane	363
Go to the grave in all thy glorious prime	630
Grace 't is a charming sound	44
Gracious Spirit, Love divine	319
Great God attend while Zion sings	10
Great God how infinite art Thou	96
Great Jehovah we adore Thee	272
Great Ruler of the land and sea	222
Guide me, O Thou great Jehovah	155
Hail, my ever-blessed Jesus	413
Hail, Thou once despised Jesus	410
Hail the day that sees Him rise	388
Hail tranquil hour of closing day	245
Hark, hark my soul! angelic songs are swelling	573
Hark my soul, it is the Lord	517
Hark, ten thousand harps and voices	417
Hark, the glad sound, the Saviour comes	356
Hark, the herald angels say	394
Hark, the herald angels sing	347
Hark, the judgment trumpet sounding	563
Hark, the song of jubilee	393
Hark, the sound of holy voices chanting	569
Hark, the voice of love and mercy	497
Hark, what mean those holy voices	351
Hasten Lord, the glorious time	540
Hasten, O sinner, to be wise	490
Hear my prayer, O Heavenly Father	286
Hearts of stone relent, relent	366

(302)

INDEX OF FIRST LINES.

First Line	HYMN
He dies, the Friend of sinners dies	376
He has come, the Christ of God	348
High in yonder realms of light	589
His are a thousand sparkling rills	372
Holy Father, cheer our way	242
Holy Father, hear our cry	80
Holy Ghost, with light divine	318
Holy, holy, holy Lord! God almighty	24
Holy, holy, holy, Lord, God of Hosts	11
Holy, holy, holy Lord, In the highest	78
Holy Spirit, Lord of light	315
How beauteous on the mountains	538
How blest the righteous when he dies	640
How calm, and beautiful, the morn	383
How can I sink, with such a prop	75
How did my heart rejoice to hear	297
How firm a foundation, ye saints of the	109
How gentle Gods commands	487
How pleasant, how divinely fair	284
How precious is the book divine	310
How oft alas, this wretched heart	71
How shall I follow Him I serve	369
How shall I praise the eternal God	97
How still, and peaceful, is the grave	636
How sweet and awful is the place	501
How sweetly flowed the gospel's sound	32
How sweet the name of Jesus sounds	436
How sweet to be allowed to pray	118
How tedious, and tasteless, the hours	144
I am not worthy, holy Lord	455
I bless the Christ of God	453
I could not do without Thee	202
I do not ask, O Lord, that life may be	208
If human kindness meets return	502
If through unruffled seas	624
I have no hiding place	54
I heard the voice of Jesus say	84
I hear Thy welcome voice	446
I lay my sins on Jesus	429
I left it all with Jesus, long ago	61
I'll praise my Maker with my breath	22
I love Thy Kingdom, Lord	529
I love to steal awhile away	130
I'm a pilgrim, and I'm a stranger	584
I'm but a stranger here	613
I'm not ashamed to own my Lord	439
In all my vast concerns with Thee	131
In every trouble, sharp and strong	153
In evil long, I took delight	438
In the Christians' home in glory	606
Inspirer and Hearer of prayer	134
In the cross of Christ, I glory	408
In the dark and cloudy day	172
In the hour of trial	92
In Thy great name, O Lord, we come	277
Is there a thing beneath the Sun	422
It came upon the midnight clear	343
It is not death, to die	632
I was a wandering sheep	28
I would not live alway, I ask not to stay	600
Jerusalem, my happy home	602
Jerusalem the glorious	617
Jerusalem the golden	622
Jesus, and shall it ever be	444
Jesus full of all compassion	425
Jesus hail, enthroned in glory	411
Jesus is gone above the skies	522
Jesus, I love Thy charming name	456
Jesus, I my cross have taken	440
Jesus, Jesus, visit me	112
Jesus, Lamb of God for me	365
Jesus lives, no longer now	386
Jesus lover of my soul	431
Jesus, Master, hear me now	518
Jesus, Master, whom I serve	511
Jesus, merciful and mild	86
Jesus my Saviour, bind me fast	471
Jesus my Saviour, look on me	426
Jesus name of wondrous love	454
Jesus only, when the morning	460
Jesus, Saviour, pilot me	95
Jesus shall reign where'er the sun	536
Jesus, these eyes have never seen	435
Jesus the very thought of Thee	458
Jesus, Thou art the sinner's Friend	472
Jesus, Thou joy of loving hearts	520
Jesus we are far away	525
Jesus, we look to Thee	461
Jesus, while our hearts are bleeding	607
Jesus, who knows full well	402
Joined in one Spirit, to one Head	58
Joy to the world, the Lord is come	355
Just as I am, without one plea	427
Just as thou art, without one trace	475
Kingdoms and thrones, to God belong	379
Lead kindly light, amid the encircling gloom	171
Lead us, Heavenly Father, lead us	157
Let God the Father, and the Son	230
Let me be with Thee, where thou art	194
Let me but hear my Saviour say	93
Let worldly minds, the world pursue	433
Let Zion's watchman all awake	196
Life is a span, a fleeting hour	559
Life of the world, I hail Thee	371
Lift up to God, The voice of praise	19
Lift up your heads, eternal gates	353
Light of those, whose dreary dwelling	462
Like the eagle upward, onward	409
Lo, God is here, let us adore	255
Lo, He comes, with clouds descending	560
Lo, he cometh, countless trumpets	561
Lo, I behold the scattering shades	582
Lo, Jesus, the Saviour, in mercy draws near	496
Lo, on a narrow neck of land	568
Lo, the stone is rolled away	387
Lo, what a glorious sight appears	581
Look ye saints, the sight is glorious	389

INDEX OF FIRST LINES.

	HYMN.
Lord dismiss us with Thy blessing	271
Lord, I am Thine, entirely Thine	94
Lord, I believe, Thy power I own	62
Lord, I cannot let Thee go	623
Lord, I have made Thy word my choice	307
Lord, I hear of showers of blessing	180
Lord, in the morning Thou shalt hear	227
Lord, in this Thy mercy's day	298
Lord, now lettest Thou Thy servant (Chant)	653
Lord of earth, Thy forming hand	35
Lord of every land and nation	452
Lord of the worlds above	235
Lord, speak to me that I may speak	141
Lord, Thou art my Rock of Strength	170
Lord Thou has been our (chant)	651
Lord, we come before Thee now	192
Lord, when with dying lips my prayer is said	580
Love divine all love excelling	158
Majestic sweetness sits enthroned	405
Make a joyful noise unto the Lord (Chant)	652
Mary to the Saviour's tomb	400
May He by whose kind care we meet	291
May the grace of Christ our Saviour	160
Mid scenes of confusion and creature complaints	616
More love to Thee, O Christ	465
Mortals awake, with angels join	316
Must Jesus bear the cross alone	421
My days are gliding swiftly by	592
My dear Redeemer and my Lord	361
My faith looks up to Thee	612
My God, how endless is Thy Love	114
My God, is any hour so sweet	290
My God, my Father, blissful name	63
My God, my Father, while I stray	292
My God, permit me not to be	294
My God, the Spring of all my joys	228
My gracious Redeemer, I love	145
My hope is built on nothing less	64
My Saviour, as Thou wilt	40
My Saviour, my Almighty Friend	434
My sins, my sins, my Saviour	82
My soul be on thy guard	336
My soul, how lovely is the place	275
My spirit longs for Thee	39
My Spirit on Thy care	29
Nature with open volume stands	198
Nearer, my God, to Thee	132
No more, my God, I boast no more	199
Not all the blood of beasts	367
Not so in haste my heart	50
Not worthy, Lord, to gather up the crumbs	509
Now begin the heavenly theme	416
Now be the gospel banner	550
Now from labor and from care	252

	HYMN.
Now from the altar of our hearts	278
Now is the accepted time	488
Now let our cheerful eyes survey	381
Now let our souls on wings sublime	627
Now let the children of the saints	556
Now lift we hymns of heartfelt praise to Thee	289
Now to the Lord a noble song	378
Now the day is over	189
Now to Thy sacred house	233
O blessed feet of Jesus	506
O Bread to pilgrims given	507
O cease my wandering soul	55
O Christ, with each returning morn	267
O come, let us sing unto the Lord (Chant)	646
O could I find from day to day	72
O day of rest and gladness	258
O eyes that are weary and hearts that are sore	601
Oh, for a closer walk with God	65
O for a glance of heavenly day	181
O for a heart to praise my God	68
O God, our help in ages past	98
O God the rock of ages	619
O happy day that fixed my choice	448
O holy Lord our God	237
O holy Saviour, Friend unseen	174
O how happy are they	50
O how I love Thy holy law	306
O Jesus, let Thy kingdom come	535
O Jesus Saviour, Sweet Desire	135
O Jesus, Thou art standing	83
O Jesus, we adore thee	377
O land of rest, for thee I sigh	605
O Lord of hosts, whose glory fills	214
O Lord, impart Thyself to me	76
O love that will not let me go	193
O mother, dear Jerusalem	603
O Paradise, O Paradise	615
O sacred head, once wounded	370
O that my load of sin were gone	183
O Sun of Righteousness divine	139
O Spirit of the Living God	553
O Thou my light, my life, my joy	60
O Thou that hearest the prayer of faith	565
O Thou, the contrite sinner's friend	30
O Thou to whose all searching sight	88
O Thou who driest the mourner's tear	203
O Thou whose own vast temple stands	218
O Thou whose tender mercy hears	406
O word of God incarnate	308
O'er the gloomy hills of darkness	542
Oft in danger, oft in woe	111
Oh, bless the Lord my soul	403
Oh, come all ye faithful	358
Oh, could I speak the matchless worth	412
Oh, deem not they are blest alone	124
Oh, for a closer walk with God	65
Oh, for a faith that will not shrink	117

(304)

INDEX OF FIRST LINES.

	HYMN.
Oh, for a thousand tongues to sing	439
Oh, for the death of those	635
Oh, gift of gifts, oh, grace of faith	205
Oh, if my soul were formed for woe	77
Oh, speed thee, Christian, on thy way	340
Oh, sweetly breathe the lyres above	447
Oh, that I could forever dwell	89
Oh, that I knew the secret place	66
Oh, that my load of sin were gone	184
Oh that the Lord would guide my ways	14
Oh, the sweet wonders of that Cross	31
Oh, where shall rest be found	625
Oh, worship the King, all glorious above	18
One sweetly solemn thought	643
One there is above all others	441
On Jordan's rugged banks I stand	618
On the mountain top appearing	545
Onward, Christian soldiers	341
Our Father, who art in heaven (chant)	655
Our times are in Thy hand	104
Our yet unfinished story	91
Peace, perfect peace, in this dark world of sin	186
People of the living God	414
Pilgrim, burdened with thy sin	495
Pleasant are Thy courts above	234
Plunged in a gulf of dark despair	450
Praise God from whom all blessings flow	2, 178
Praise the God of all creation (Doxology)	302, 418
Praise the Lord, ye heavens adore Him	34
Praise to God, immortal praise	212
Praise to Thee, Thou great Creator	21
Praise waits in Zion, Lord, for Thee	23
Prayer is the soul's sincere desire	179
Prince of Peace, control my will	524
Religion is the chief concern	165
Rejoice, the Lord is King	26
Return, O wanderer, return	491
Rise, crowned with light, imperial Salem, rise	526
Rise, glorious conqueror, rise	399
Rise, my soul, and stretch thy wings	586
Rock of Ages, cleft for me	364
Safely through another week	225
Saints of God, the dawn is brightening	543
Salvation! O the joyful sound	57
Saviour, again to Thy dear name,we raise	261
Saviour, breathe an evening blessing	301
Saviour, hast Thou fled forever	162
Saviour, I follow on	466
Saviour, sprinkle many nations	548
Saviour visit Thy plantation	159
Saviour, when in dust to Thee	404
Say sinner, hath a voice within	324
See the conqueror mounts in triumph	415
Servant of God, well done	642

	HYMN.
Shepherd, with Thy tenderest love	296
Shout the glad tidings, exultingly sing	359
Show pity Lord, O Lord forgive	115
Sing we to our God above	188
Sinners, will you scorn the message	498
Sinners turn, why will ye die	499
Sion stands with hills surrounded	541
Slowly sinks the setting sun	191
Softly fades the twilight ray	249
Softly now the light of day	250
Soldiers of Christ, arise	335
Sometimes a light surprises	146
Son of God, to Thee I cry	360
Sovereign of worlds, display Thy power	547
Sovereign Ruler of the skies	110
Sow in the morn thy seed	330
Spirit blest, who art adored	317
Stand up my soul, shake off thy fears	333
Star of peace to wanderers weary	223
Stay, Thou insulted Spirit, stay	323
Summer suns are glowing	163
Sun of my soul, Thou Saviour dear	266
Sure the blest Comforter is nigh	321
Swell the anthem, raise the song	213
Sweet is the memory of Thy grace	121
Sweet is the work, my God, my King	8
Sweet is the work, O Lord	332
Sweet the moments rich in blessing	424
Take me, O my Father, take me	161
Take my life and let it be	90
Tarry with me, O my Saviour	164
Ten thousand times ten thousand	585
The Church's one foundation	532
The day is past and gone	299
The day of resurrection	259
The Father and the Son	151
The Head that once was crowned with thorns	407
The heavens declare Thy glory Lord	282
The Lord is my Shepherd, no want	201
The Lord Jehovah reigns	25
The Lord my pasture shall prepare	240
The Lord my Shepherd is	106
The Lord's my Shepherd, I'll not want	129
The morning light is breaking	549
The morning purples all the sky	384
The pity of the Lord	148
The promises I sing	37
The saints of God from death set free	597
The sands of time are sinking	590
The spacious firmament on high	7
The Spirit in our hearts	486
The voice of free grace cries escape	479
There is a calm for those who weep	629
There is a fountain filled with blood	504
There is a God who reigns above	197
There is a green hill far away	375
There is a happy land, far, far away	614
There is a heavenly mercy seat	103
There is a land of pure delight	604

INDEX OF FIRST LINES.

	HYMN.
There is an hour of peaceful rest	596
There is a safe and secret place	74
There's a home for little children	558
There's a wideness in God's mercy	43
Thine earthly Sabbaths, Lord, we love	608
Thine forever, God of love	113
This is the day the Lord hath made	229
Thou art gone to the grave, but we	628
Thou art my hiding place, O Lord	248
Thou art my portion, O my God	15
Thou art the way, to Thee alone	166
Thou boundless source of every good	119
Thou hidden love of God, whose height	206
Thou lovely Source of true delight	312
Thou only Sovereign of my heart	515
Thou who roll'st the year around	220
Though faint yet pursuing	200
Though troubles assail	204
Three in one and one in three	253
Through all the changing scenes of life	100
Through all the downward tracks of time	101
Through the night of doubt, and sorrow	20
Thus far the Lord has led me on	123
Thy Father's house, thine own bright home	571
Thy name, almighty Lord	530
Thy way, not mine, O Lord	41
Thy will be done (chant)	574
Till he come! O, let the words	588
'T is by the faith of joys to come	125
'T is midnight, and an Olives' brow	362
'T is my happiness below	210
"'T is finished," so the Saviour cried	373
'T is not that I did choose Thee	147
To-day the Saviour calls	500
To Father, Son, and Holy Ghost	168
To God the Father, God the Son	423
To God the Father, Son	56
To-morrow, Lord is thine	105
To Thy pastures, fair and large	81
To Thy temple, I repair	265
To us a child of hope is born	354
To whom, my Saviour, shall I go	432
True Bread of Life in pitying mercy given	508
'T was on that dark, that doleful night	512
Unto Thee Triune Jehovah	215
Unveil Thy bosom faithful tomb	639
Walk in the light, and thou shalt know	305
Watchman, tell us of the night	539
We are watching, we are waiting	463
Weary of earth, and laden with my sin	579
We cannot build alone	216
We come, O Lord, before Thy throne	224

	HYMN.
We give Thee but Thine own	331
We journey through a vale of tears	102
We saw Thee not when Thou didst come	459
We shall see Him, in our nature	385
We sing His love, who once was slain	641
We speak of the realms of the blest	611
We would see Jesus, when the shadows lengthen	428
Welcome, delightful morn	231
Welcome, sweet day of rest	300
Welcome, welcome, dear Redeemer	270
What a Friend we have in Jesus	42
What equal honors shall we bring	143
What if our bark, o'er life's rough wave	128
What is the thing of greatest price	183
What shall I render to my God	12
What various hindrances we meet	257
When all Thy mercies, O my God	296
When along life's thorny road	209
When gathering clouds, around I view	207
When I can read my title clear	570
When I survey the wondrous cross	445
When I view my Saviour bleeding	48
When Jesus speaks, so sweet the sound	285
When languor and disease invade	126
When musing sorrow weeps the past	59
When streaming from the eastern skies	238
When the day of toil is done	599
When the worn spirit wants repose	276
When this passing world is done	626
When Thou, my righteous Judge shall come	564
Where high, the heavenly temple stands	33
While life prolongs its precious light	476
While shepherds watched their flocks	344
While the prayers of saints ascend	516
While with ceaseless course the sun	211
Whilst Thee I seek, protecting power	120
With broken heart, and contrite sigh	140
With tearful eyes, I look around	87
With tearful, I look (chant)	650
Why do we mourn departing friends	634
Why should the children of a king	127
Why will ye waste on trifling cares	492
Ye angels round the throne	368
Ye angels, who stand round the throne	610
Ye Christian heralds, go proclaim	533
Ye servants of God, your Master proclaim	391
Ye servants of the Almighty King	534
Ye that in his courts are found	251
Ye tribes of Adam join	16
Ye wretched, hungry, starving poor	481
Yet there is room	474
Your harps, ye trembling saints	107

www.ingramcontent.com/pod-product-compliance
Lightning Source LLC
Chambersburg PA
CBHW031902220426
43663CB00006B/729